Global Christianity

Global Christianity

Current Trends and Developments

VEBJØRN L. HORSFJORD
SVEN THORE KLOSTER
GINA LENDE
OLE JAKOB LØLAND

PICKWICK *Publications* · Eugene, Oregon

GLOBAL CHRISTIANITY
Current Trends and Developments

Pickwick Publications
An Imprint of Wipf and Stock Publishers
199 W. 8th Ave., Suite 3
Eugene, OR 97401

www.wipfandstock.com

PAPERBACK ISBN: 978-1-7252-8111-0
HARDCOVER ISBN: 978-1-7252-8112-7
EBOOK ISBN: 978-1-7252-8113-4

Cataloguing-in-Publication data:

Names: Horsfjord, Vebjørn L. [author]. | Kloster, Sven Thore [author] | Lende, Gina [author] | Løland, Ole Jakob [author]

Title: Global Christianity : current trends and developments / Vebjørn L. Horsfjord, Sven Thore Kloster, Gina Lende, and Ole Jakob Løland.

Description: Eugene, OR: Pickwick Publications, 2022 | Includes bibliographical references and index.

Identifiers: ISBN 978-1-7252-8111-0 (paperback) | ISBN 978-1-7252-8112-7 (hardcover) | ISBN 978-1-7252-8113-4 (ebook)

Subjects: LCSH: Christianity—21st century | Christianity | Christianity—Africa | Christianity—Latin America | Christianity—United States | Christianity—Canada | Christianity—Middle East | Christianity—Asia | Christianity—Oceania | Christianity—Europe

Classification: BR121.3 H67 2022 (paperback) | BR121.3 (ebook)

02/24/22

First publication: *Global kristendom. En samtidshistorie*, Scandinavian University Press, Oslo 2018.

Translated by Brian McNeil. The English translation was made from a revised and updated version supplied by the authors.

Contents

Acknowledgments

This is a revised version of the book *Global kristendom*, published in Norway in 2018 at Scandinavian University Press (Universitetsforlaget). We four authors have written this book together, and the result is a book that none of us could have written alone. It has been written partly by each author alone and partly together. We have discussed the drafts of each chapter several times in the group, and have revised them together before presenting them in the final version. But the main responsibility for each chapter has been individual. Gina Lende wrote about Africa and Western and Central Europe; Ole Jakob Løland wrote about Latin America and North America; Sven Thore Kloster wrote about the Middle East and Oceania; and Vebjørn Horsfjord wrote about Eastern Europe and Asia. We wrote the introductory and concluding chapters together.

We are grateful to many persons who have contributed to this book. These include nuns and monks who have hospitably welcomed us in their communities, pastors and priests who have shared their experiences with us, and laypersons who have generously told us about their daily life of faith and have shown how and why Christianity is important in their lives. This applies also to politicians, academics, human rights activists, and workers in organizations who have given us valuable insights into the role Christianity plays in society—for good and for ill.

We are also grateful for grants we received from the Bequest of Robert and Ella Wenzin at the University of Oslo. We express our thanks not least to the anonymous academic colleagues who evaluated the book manuscript for Scandinavian University Press. And a special word of thanks goes to our translator Brian McNeil for his outstanding work with this text.

Vebjørn L. Horsfjord, Sven Thore Kloster, Gina Lende, and Ole Jakob Løland

I

Introduction

A NUN SILENTLY KISSES an icon under the gilded ceiling of a church in Moscow, while young people break out into songs of praise and dance in a corrugated iron shed in Lagos. Some church organizations work actively to criminalize abortion, while others arrange demonstrations to demand women's rights. The president in the USA swears an oath on the Bible, and the pope in Rome washes the feet of the prisoners in a jail. A young Indian takes monastic vows and gives away all his possessions, while a charismatic pastor in Brazil tours the continent in a private jet and proclaims the recipe for material prosperity and good health. All these are examples of Christianity in the world today. As we shall see in this book, Christianity influences cultures, societies, and individual persons' lives in different ways throughout the world.

After the end of the Cold War, the ideological conflict between capitalism and communism was replaced by other geopolitical antagonisms. The scholar Samuel Huntington claimed that the world faced civilizational conflicts that were largely caused by religious differences.[1] After the terrorist attacks on September 11, 2001, such ideas took on an even greater resonance in the media.

---

1. Huntington, "The Clash of Civilizations?"

Religion has entered more strongly into the global news picture as a political threat to security and as a power factor that is feared, but also as an amusing curiosity and a beloved cultural tradition. Although Islam has received much attention in western media, Christianity remains by far the largest religion in the world.[2] Probably the most rapidly growing religious movement in recent years was not Muslim, but the Christian Pentecostal revival movement.[3]

This growth has consequences for how Christianity develops globally. Although attendance at Christian rituals is declining in Europe, Christianity is growing in many other places both in numbers and in proportion. This has led to the description of Europe as an exception in the world.[4] It is indeed true that the number of Christians is declining in the Middle East too, but that is for other reasons. In North America, there is something of a stagnation,[5] but the numbers of Christians are growing rapidly in Africa, Asia, and Latin America.[6] Taken together, these patterns of development mean that the number of Christians is increasing on the global level, while the Christian power centers are moving from the north to the south. Roughly one-third of the world's population today are Christians, and this is also probably how things will be in a few decades from now.[7] But the global south will constitute Christianity's geographical center of gravity to an even greater degree than today.

"Go, therefore, and make disciples of all nations," says Jesus in the Gospel of Matthew, and biblical exhortations of this kind have often been interpreted in a manner that has made Christianity an expansive and missionary religion. New territories and more people must be reached.[8] The zeal to expand has generated tensions and conflict, both where Christianity grows at the expense of other religions[9] and where evangelism is directed towards other Christians. This occurs in many places today, for example, when Pentecostals gain members from established churches in Latin America, Africa,

---

2. A picture has formed of a Christianity that has lost influence against the background of Islam's increased significance. This has distracted attention from Christianity's growth and revitalization in large parts of the world; see Wilkinson, "Emergence," 93–112.

3. Anderson, *To the Ends of the Earth*, 1.

4. Davie, "Europe"; Davie, *Europe*; Berger et al., *Religiøse USA*.

5. Pew Research Center, "America's Changing Religious Landscape."

6. Pew Research Center, "Global Christianity"

7. Jenkins, *Next Christendom*.

8. Meyer, "Pentecostalism and Globalization," 119.

9. Hunt, "Introduction," 8.

Asia, and Eastern Europe. At the same time, the competition also leads the traditional churches to undergo renewal, in order to keep their members.

Christianity is being changed both from the inside and from the outside. Economic, political, and societal changes in the various countries have consequences for how Christianity is expressed. For example, churches are tightly integrated into various forms of the exercise of power on the local, national, and global levels, and democratization, both on the state level and internally in the churches, has led to changes in the power relationships between state and church, as well as between the laity and the church authorities. Globalization, migration, urbanization, and new technology also help ideas, human beings, and institutions to move quickly, so that new forms of Christianity arise.[10] It was often asserted in the past that the technological modernization of society would lead to less religion throughout the world. But it is precisely new technology, democratization, and globalization that have opened up new possibilities for religious actors and led to a stronger public role for religion in many places.[11] There are fewer scholars today who would claim that modernization and globalization necessarily lead to secularization.[12]

There is, however, a considerable agreement that globalization leads to pluralism.[13] Globalization strengthens networks that cross the boundaries between regions and nation states, and this leads to a greater religious variety within these states and nations. But this variety is made possible by another aspect of globalization, namely, homogenization.[14] As we shall see in this book, while the processes of globalization make the variety of Christianity more visible in many places, there are also tendencies to uniformization on the global level.

Our intention with this book is to show how Christianity is practiced and expressed in many varied ways and in different places in the world at the beginning of the twenty-first century. But in order to do so, we must first ask a question that is both fundamental and difficult: What is Christianity?

10. Globalization is nothing new in the present day. Rather, societal processes have accelerated and become all-pervasive for both nations and churches throughout the world. We do not take a position on the question of when globalization began; we simply note that some claim that globalization is in continuity with the origin and the development in the sixteenth century of a world economy dominated by Europe. See Beyer, *Religion and Globalization*; Hunt, "Introduction," 7.

11. Toft et al., *God's Century*.

12. Casanova, "Public Religions Revisited," 109.

13. Beyer, *Religions in a Global Society*, 99.

14. Hunt, "Introduction," 9.

WHAT IS CHRISTIANITY?

In the past, the study of religion in the West was dominated by studies of texts, and tended to be separated from other academic disciplines. Today, we look at religion as a dynamic and integrated part of society and culture.[15] This also colors our approach to Christianity in this book and leads us to study it in the interplay with cultural processes, the economy, politics, and societal circumstances. We also presuppose that Christianity, like any other religion, is a hybrid phenomenon. In many places in the world, for example, Christianity is marked by the fact that it was disseminated in a colonial context. Where Christianity has taken root, changes have taken place both in Christianity itself and in the contexts that are involved. New realities are created in such encounters. Religion takes on color from the environment in which it occurs and of which it becomes a part; at the same time, it imparts color to this environment. It is not only the colonized who is changed, but also the colonizer. This has made it easier to see that it is not only Christianity outside the West that is hybrid: traditional western Christianity too is, and has always been, hybrid.

In order to operationalize our analysis of how Christianity occurs in the world today, we have chosen to approach Christianity as discourse, as practices, as a fellowship of identity, and as an institution.[16] These are not isolated realities, but overlap and influence each other. For example, the content of the Christian faith gives form to Christian practices, while the content of the faith in turn is affected by the same practices.

Christianity occurs in both organized and unorganized forms. Christianity occurs from below, through what people do, believe, and say, and from above, through what institutions, church leaders, or other public persons declare. In other words, it is not only institutions that regulate the discourses, the practices, and the fellowship; it is just as much the practices and the fellowships that regulate both the institutions and each other. By looking at all these relationships, we bring to light an important concern, namely, power. When we study how Christianity finds expression and occurs in various contexts in the world, we are interested in shifting power perspectives with regard to the question of who regulates whom, how Christianity affects society, and who tries to define what is "correct" Christianity.

---

15. Smith, *Relating Religion*, 193; Bender, *Religion on the Edge*.

16. One who employs such an approach to religion is Lincoln, *Holy Terrors*, 5.

CHRISTIANITY AS PRAXIS AND
IDENTITY ON THE SOCIETAL LEVEL

The variety in how Christianity can be understood can present difficulties when one wishes to select what best or most fully represents Christianity. In this book, we take no position on what is true or correct Christianity. Our starting point is how groups—and sometimes individuals—identify themselves. Those who in one way or another count themselves as Christians are in the focus of this book.

Our principal interest lies in Christianity on the societal level. We are interested in how Christian actors (individuals, groups, or organizations) operate in a large societal context, and in how Christianity thereby finds expression as identity and praxes in public cultural, political, societal, and economic contexts. Where we refer to Christianity as a content of faith and ideas, we will look primarily at how this content comes to expression in culture and society, and how it influences political and social practices.

We emphasize how societal changes leave their mark on Christianity in national and regional contexts, and how the opposite also happens, that it is to say, how Christianity leaves its mark on the societal changes. Since every country has its own specific history, societal processes such as modernization, democratization, secularization, globalization, and economic or politic deregulation will take different forms from one country to other—also in relation to Christianity.[17] Accordingly, a common characteristic of the presentation of Christianity in every chapter is our starting point in how Christianity occurs in the interplay with societal changes and the historical context. This means that our emphasis lies on the situation today, although we must continually draw on history to understand and explain the present day.

We have sought to select examples and stories that concern many people, represent a special characteristic of the region in question, and display important aspects of development. We have also sought to choose examples that show the variety and ambivalence within the major denominations that are presented.

PROBLEMS WITH NUMBERS

Given our broad approach to Christianity, it goes without saying that it is hard to specify how many Christians there are in a specific country or in the

---

17. Eisenstadt, "Multiple Modernities."

world. But the problem of defining Christianity is only one of several factors that make counting and measuring difficult.

For example, in many countries the authorities do not register adherence to a faith or membership of a church. This may be because population surveys are expensive and are therefore not given priority. But it may also be because the state does not wish to have an overview of religious adherence in the population, because such data is also political. In most countries, religious adherence is more than merely a private matter. It can also have consequences when state privileges, resources, and symbols are to be distributed across complex ethnic, religious, linguistic, and regional divisions. In many contexts, numerical superiority would lead to demands for greater privileges in the structures of the state. In multiethnic countries with several religions, therefore, population data about religious adherence can be explosive information.

In those countries where the state itself does not gather such information, one must employ other methods of calculation. In the absence of national statistics, much research literature relies on numbers calculated by various offices of the United Nations, the World Bank, the U.S. State Department, or research organizations such as the Pew Forum or the World Christian Database.

But even in the countries where religious membership is registered, there are many elements of uncertainty. Various actors can be interested in understating the numbers, for example, in order to avoid state sanctions or to reduce social tensions or economic obligations. But actors can just as well be interested in overstating the number of members, in order to strengthen their reputation and increase economic subventions, legitimacy, or political influence.

THE STRUCTURE IN THIS BOOK—A REGIONAL PRESENTATION BY MEANS OF SELECTED COUNTRIES

Many presentations of Christianity have taken their starting point in history and theology as these developed in a western context. Such accounts have had a tendency to say too little about the variety, and not least, to make European or North American Christianity the norm, so that other forms of Christianity appear to be deviations or curiosities.

This book too is written by western scholars, and this naturally influences our analyses. It is risky to study and interpret global Christianity from one particular place in the world. We have immersed ourselves in a great variety of differing practices, traditions, cultures, and rationalities, while attempting to create connection and meaning. This obliges us as scholars to take difficult choices. Our presentation is certainly not free of blind spots, stereotypes, or implicit dogmatic and ideological positions. Nevertheless, we believe that it is both legitimate and meaningful to write a book about global Christianity. We do not believe that we are on a neutral high point from which we look out across world Christianity and regard it objectively. But from our specific vantage point, we describe and interpret the world as we see it. Other researchers describe the world as they see it from where they stand.

The goal of this book is to embrace the great global variety that bears the label "Christianity." This can be done in various ways. One way is to present the different denominations side by side. This can be meaningful, since there are obvious common aspects in how (for example) Catholic church life develops in various parts of the world. Another possibility is to structure the presentation by means of various themes that occur in many parts of the world, such as the relationship between the churches and the state, the churches' relationship to other religions, Christianity and the economy, Christianity, ethnicity, and nationality, or Christianity and gender, sexuality, and family. It is also possible to use the world map as an organizing principle and to give a systematic account of the variety of church life and Christian faith and praxis in country after country or region after region. Presentations of this kind give an overview, but they can become repetitive in what they say about the denominations, and they can also fail to grasp connections with regard to the thematic aspects.

This book combines these modes of presentation. The main division follows continents or regions. Although this division is geographical, the aim is not to give an exhaustive description of Christianity in each region. Our starting point in each chapter is one or a few large countries with a sizable population. This makes it possible for each of the chapters to take up some topics that concern many people and that are typical of the region— though *not* unique to it. After reading a chapter, one ought to be familiar with some central and relevant aspects of development in the region.

One advantage of structuring the book in this way is the possibility of presenting the central aspects of development in various denominations. In the chapter on Africa, we emphasize the strongly growing Pentecostal movements and take as our starting point Nigeria, the country in Africa with the highest population. Here, we want to see what role Christianity has in contexts marked by weak state institutions, rapid urbanization, and great religious pluralism. The chapter on Latin America takes its starting point in Mexico and Brazil, the two most populous countries in the region.

Here, the emphasis lies on the Catholic church, both to see how the center of gravity in Catholicism is moving away from the historical center in Rome, and to see how the church is challenged precisely by growing Pentecostal movements. The emphasis in the chapter on North America lies on Protestant churches in the United States, the country in the world with the greatest number of Christians. In the chapter on the Middle East, we see how Christianity occurs in a context in which Christians are emigrating from their original core areas. Here, the central focus is on the so-called Oriental churches. The chapter on Asia does not center upon one particular denomination; its starting point is the fact that Christianity in most Asian countries is a minority religion. This is exemplified by a presentation of Christianity in the two most populous countries in the world, China and India, with the Catholic Philippines as a contrast. The chapter on Oceania describes the "success" of Protestant, colonial Christian mission by illustrating some of the rich variety of Christian practices and their deep interwovenness in politics and culture in the Pacific islands. The omnipresence of Christianity in the Pacific contrasts not only with the situation in Asia, but also with the secularized white society in Australia—by far the largest country in Oceania. The chapter on Eastern Europe presents Christianity as it occurs in the Eastern Orthodox churches after the fall of communism. The principal emphasis here lies on Russia, the country in the world with the largest Orthodox church membership. In the chapter on Central and Western Europe, we look at how Christianity occurs in a context where fewer and fewer people believe in the priest's or pastor's God, and how the established churches have lost much of the influence they had in the past.

One risk with structuring the book on the basis of regions, with the main emphasis on leading denominations, themes, and individual countries, is that both the regions and the denominations may appear to be homogeneous. Every region is much more varied and complex that we can show in these chapters. In our choice of themes, countries, and perspectives, we have put the emphasis on describing developmental trends and phenomena that concern many persons. The examples we have chosen are concrete illustrations that point to something more general. Another danger is that we risk over-interpreting complex societal phenomena by labeling them as Christianity, thereby favoring religious explanations. Social practices are complex, and are in general generated by a broad spectrum of cultural, political, economic, historical, but also religious factors.

In the final chapter, we bring the threads together and look at some of the themes that make it most urgent to speak about Christianity as a global reality. In addition to being local and national, Christianity is transnational and transregional. This means that we find the same tendencies and developmental trajectories in many different countries and on various continents. Thanks to modern communications technology, networks, the flow of information, and mutual influence between the different parts of the world are stronger than ever before. As a content of ideas, as praxis, and as identity, Christianity too is a global phenomenon to the highest degree.

Another reason why Christianity is global is that there exist transregional and global structures to which many churches and organizations are linked. The Catholic church is itself a global institution with churches, priests, and roughly 1.3 billion members spread across almost every country in the world. Besides this, the Holy See has ambassadors in many lands and observers in many international organizations, such as the UN. The World Council of Churches is a global umbrella organization that states that its 348 member churches have more than five hundred million members in 110 different countries.[18] Another global umbrella organization is the World Evangelical Alliance, which states that it groups together six hundred million Evangelical Christians in 129 different countries.[19] In addition to these structures, there are a number of global so called "world communions" organizations, such as the Anglican Communion, the World Communion of Reformed Churches, the Lutheran World Federation, and specialized ecclesiastical humanitarian organizations such as Caritas, the ACT Alliance, and the International Orthodox Christian Charities. These organizations differ in their mandates and their modes of operation. Some work actively to coordinate churches and policy throughout the world, while others function more as open meeting places. In the closing chapter, we shall look in greater detail at their significance for Christianity in society, and we shall also look back at the presentation of Christianity in various parts of the world, and ask whether it is in fact possible to speak on the global level of Christianity in the singular—must we not rather speak of Christianities? We also discuss briefly whether it is possible to say something about the directions in which Christianity is moving globally.

18. WCC, "Who is the World Council of Churches?"
19. WEA, "Who We Are."

2

Africa

Dramatic Growth

IF YOU SWITCH ON the television in Kinshasa or Johannesburg, the likelihood of encountering Christian messages is high. It may be a Nigerian soap opera about the end times; a miracle campaign broadcast directly from Nairobi; a bishop who urges the need for negotiations between competing political groups in Congo; or a South African politician talking about the importance of having Jesus in one's heart. Christianity comes in many—and new—forms on the African continent. We find it in entertainment, politics, education, in the health sector and in business. Democratization and liberalization of the economy and the media have opened the public arena to new actors. It is the rapidly growing Pentecostal movement that has made the most extensive use of the new possibilities that this public arena gives.

Redemption City lies along the motorway just outside the city of Lagos in Nigeria. The precincts are clearly marked off by surrounding walls. It was built by a Nigerian Pentecostal church, the Redeemed Christian Church of God (RCCG). Inside the walls, we find an elementary school and a university, health clinics, private houses and apartments, the church's own electric power station, cafes, shops, and not least "The Holy Spirit's Arena." The church claims that it brings together roughly one million persons on this arena each month for lively worship, prayer, speaking in tongues, miracles, exorcism, and prophetic speaking. There is also a VIP arena, where presidents and prominent personalities are welcomed, and it is in frequent use.

Building projects are continually underway. About ten thousand people live here on a permanent basis on a campus of over fourteen square kilometers. The church does not lack ambitions: its explicit goal is stated on their webpage: "we will plant churches within five minutes walking distance in every city and town of developing countries and within five minutes driving distance in every city and town of developed countries."[1] In other words, they want to outdo even Starbucks or McDonalds. They claim to have churches in 185 countries as varied as China, Greece, Uganda, Mexico, and Sweden. In the USA, there are plans to build a copy of Redemption City in Dallas, financed with money from Nigeria. When David Cameron, the former British prime minister, was campaigning before the 2015 election, he visited the church's annual festival in London and spoke warmly about Christian values before a congregation of about forty thousand people.[2]

Pastor E. A. Adeboye, or "Daddy G.O." as people call him, is the supreme leader of this church, and he featured in 2008 in the American magazine *Newsweek*'s list of the fifty most powerful persons in the world. But what does his power consist of, and how is it used? What is Pentecostal Christianity in relation to the varied Christian landscape in Africa? How do the different churches respond to poverty, HIV/AIDS, prosperity, and conflict? How do the churches relate to changes in family structure, to migration and to urbanization? And how do they relate to politics? In this chapter, we examine these questions *inter alia* by looking in detail at Nigeria, Africa's most populous country. We direct our attention particularly to sub-Saharan Africa, with an emphasis on the Pentecostal movement.

STRONG GROWTH AND RELIGIOUS PLURALITY

Christianity has had a dramatic growth in Africa. In 1910, about 9 percent of the population of roughly one hundred million on the African continent were Christian. Today, Christians make up about 55 percent of the population of more than one billion.[3] More than 20 percent of all the Christians in the world live in Africa. And this means that, since Africa has a much stronger population growth than other continents, it will in the years ahead

1. See *inter alia* their homepage: RCCG, "Mission and Vision."
2. See "Cameron Attends RCCG's Festival of Life."
3. For statistics of growth in the various Christian traditions and details about regions, see, e.g., Zurlo "A Demographic Profile"; Todd, *Christianity in Sub-Saharan Africa*

become an even more central area in global Christianity. In the space of a century, therefore, sub-Saharan Africa has gone from being an "outpost" in the Christian geography to becoming one of the most important Christian regions. The growth of Christianity has been propelled not only by a strong population growth, but also by colonization and mission. Local leaders embraced the new faith, and millions of everyday missionaries and fulltime missionaries from home and abroad took literally the Bible's words about "making all nations disciples."

The growth started in the second half of the nineteenth century with the European colonization of most of Africa; but Christianity has been present on the continent for nearly two thousand years. It was represented by the great Oriental Orthodox churches in Egypt in North Africa and Ethiopia and Eritrea on the Horn of Africa. The largest is the Ethiopian Orthodox Church (EOC), which with its forty to forty-five million members is the largest Oriental Orthodox church in the world. Christianity was adopted by the Aksumite Empire in the fourth century, and the church and the Ethiopian nation have been closely associated since then.[4]

Islam dominates in the north of Africa, and Christianity in the south. Religious pluralism is strongest in the areas between the two: eastern, western, and central Africa. Countries like Senegal, Mauritania, Mali, Niger, and Somalia are primarily Muslim, with various Christian minorities and many who practice various forms of traditional African religion. The majority of the population in Ethiopia, South Sudan, Ghana, and Cameroon is Christian, but there are large Muslim minorities and a widespread practice of traditional religions. In the countries in central Africa, Christianity is strongest, with the exception of Chad, where the Muslims form the majority. Southern Africa has mainly Christian majorities, but traditional religious faith and practice are widespread. According to some sources, traditional religion is the largest religion on Madagascar and in Botswana and Mozambique, while other sources scarcely register traditional African religions.[5] For many Christians and Muslims, however, traditional African religions is an integrated part of their lives, and the statistics are unable to do justice to this complexity.

4. Eshete, "Ethiopia."

5. See, for example, Pew Research Center, "Table: Religious Composition." For example, Mozambique is said to have 13.2 million Christians and 1.72 million adherents of traditional religion; Botswana is said to have 1.45 million Christians and 120 thousand adherents of traditional religion; in Tanzania, there are 27.54 million Christians and half a million adherents of traditional religion. Others, using the World Christian Database as their source, state that there is no Christian majority in Botswana, Mozambique, and Madagascar; see Kim and Kim, *Christianity*, 3.

There are many reasons to be cautious with regard to statistics about religion. In Africa, as in many other places, religion is not a private matter, and information about religious adherence can have great consequences for the distribution of power and resources. In Tanzania and Nigeria, for example, it is uncertain whether Christians or Muslims form the majority, and many are afraid of the political dynamite that the publication of such statistics can entail. Another problem concerns the favoritism shown to the two large religions, Islam and Christianity, both politically and conceptually. Since traditional African religion does not possess institutions comparable to those of Christianity or Islam, statistic measurements often fail to grasp it.[6] Many Africans do not think of traditional African religion as a unified religion—it is not a religion to which one "belongs" in the same way as Islam or Christianity. The concept of *religion* was first introduced when the European missionaries arrived. They often defined the existing systems of faith and praxis in antagonism to religion, as "uncivilized culture" or "superstition."[7] In most African states today, various forms of traditional religion exist in a sort of legal and cultural limbo—somewhere between culture and religion and without the same legal, political, or cultural recognition that is enjoyed by the newer religions, Islam and Christianity. It is only the small country of Benin in West Africa that recognizes traditional African religions in the country's constitution.[8] Both Christianity and Islam have an ambivalent relationship to traditional African religion. Recent reform movements in these two religions—such as Salafism and charismatic Pentecostal movements—have attacked these traditional practices head-on.

THE POLITICAL BACKDROP

Christianity has grown in periods of huge societal changes on the continent. In today's democratic Africa, there are relatively few restrictions on religious practice, especially in the case of Christianity and Islam. The situation was very different in the 1960s, when many states nationalized Christian schools and gradually imposed severe restrictions on civil society, including the churches. Today, the tendency is rather for the authorities in many countries to facilitate the growth of Christianity, through favorable tax regulations, simple registration systems, and political support.

Many African states lack the capacity to cover the primary needs of their inhabitants, such as education and health services; and in many

6. Haar and Ellis, "The Role of Religion," 354.

7. Marshall, *Political Spiritualities*, 56–59.

8. Hackett, "Traditional," 89–98.

instances, citizens lack basic security in the context of crime or conflict. This
is one reason why the people often have only a weak confidence in political
leaders and state institutions. This gives the state a weak legitimacy.[9] Most
African states south of the Sahara collect relatively small amounts of taxes
from their own people, and this reduces the state's income; but this is also
relevant because it weakens the relationship between the inhabitants and
the state, and between the elected representatives and the people.[10]

Until the 1980s, African states had rather large state administrations,
but these were much reduced as a consequence of the so-called structural
adaptation programs (SAP) that were mandated by the World Bank and the
International Monetary Fund (IMF). The goal was to strengthen the economy in the individual countries and to help African states to enter the global
economic market. The states carried out drastic cuts in welfare measures,
such as schools and the health sector.[11] This development was subsequently
reinforced, and welfare provision remains weak. Christianity, on the other
hand, has grown in influence and in its fields of action.

Liberalization has led to a vigorous religious competition, first and
foremost among various Christian currents, but also with other religions.
The liberalization of the economy and the media, new Christian movements,
new technology, and the emergence of a new global religious activism have
generated a number of challenges.[12] And the issue of how African states
are to tackle the religious plurality that competes about ideas and places
has become an urgent topic, and many questions have arisen: Ought those
Christian churches that earn money to begin to pay tax? Ought it to be
legal to advertise that AIDS patients will be healed? Where is the boundary
between hate speech and aggressive mission? Can a church direct its loudspeakers out onto the street in order to summon an unwilling neighborhood to prayer? And what role should the various churches have in relation
to the state?

THE COLONIAL LEGACY

Jacob Zuma, the then president of South Africa, caused strong reactions in
2011 when national newspapers quoted him as saying:

9. See, e.g., Rotberg, *When States Fail*, for a more thorough discussion.

10. Smith, "Religious Dimensions of Conflict."

11. Freeman, *Pentecostalism and Development*, 4. There are great variations in how
this was done in the individual countries.

12. Hackett, "Traditional."

> As Africans, long before the arrival of religion and [the] gospel,
> we had our own ways of doing things. . . . Those were the times
> that the religious people refer to as dark days but we know that,
> during those times, there were no orphans or old-age homes.
> Christianity has brought along these things.[13]

Many read this statement to mean that the president was blaming
Christianity for the social problems in South Africa. Orphans and the el-
derly were pushed aside into institutions, instead of being cared for by their
relatives. The president's spokesman found it necessary to reassure the many
Christians in the country that President Zuma's words had been misunder-
stood: they were not an attack on Christianity, but an attempt to say that
Africans must not forget their own culture.

The ambivalent relationship between colonial history, western dominance, African culture, and Christianity is a recurrent theme in both African Christianity and African politics. Jomo Kenyatta, the first president in
an independent Kenya, is said to have put it like this:

> When the missionaries came to Africa they had the Bible and we
> had the land. They said, "Let us pray." We closed our eyes. When
> we opened them we had the Bible and they had the land.[14]

During the fight for independence, there were few who predicted that
Christianity would play an important societal role in the new African states
south of the Sahara.[15] With the exception of the Oriental Orthodox churches in what are today's Ethiopia, Eritrea, and Egypt, almost all the churches
on the continent were newcomers, established in the wake of imperialism
and colonization. In the period immediately after most African countries
had achieved their independence, in the 1960s and 1970s, the politicians'
primary concern was about how the new states could get rid of European
cultural and political dominance. For some, this also involved liberation
from the religion of the colonial masters. In Zaire, today's Democratic
Republic of Congo, for example, Christian names and Christian baptism
were forbidden. President Mobutu Sese Soko also introduced a prohibition of neckties in order to counteract the westernization of clothing styles.
However, the opposition to Christianity is only one part of the story. Many
of the new political elites stood shoulder to shoulder with leaders of the
established churches, and argued that national development demanded that

---

13. Henderson, "Jacob Zuma Blames Christianity."
14. Jenkins, *Next Christendom*, 52.
15. Gifford, "Introduction," 2.

the people should lay aside the traditional African lifestyle and faith and embrace Christianity.[16]

Although Christianity has proved to possess a great vitality in African societies, this does not mean that the tension between Christianity as "the white man's religion," on the one hand, and African culture, on the other hand, has disappeared. This remains one of the most central questions for many African theologians today: How can we unite African culture, history, and philosophy of life with a Christianity whose theology and ideology have been shaped primarily by white western men?

There is no one single Christian tradition that is dominant in sub-Saharan Africa. In Namibia, the Lutheran church is the strongest; in Ethiopia, it is the Oriental Orthodox Church, and in the Democratic Republic of Congo, the Catholic church. The Anglican church, which has its origin in England, has far more members today in the former British colonies in Africa than in the land of its origin. The Catholic church is large throughout the entire region, especially in eastern and southern Africa. Among the established Protestant churches, the largest are the Methodists, Presbyterians, and Anglicans.[17] It is these Protestant churches and the Catholic church that are known as the "established churches."

The church map of Africa reflects various European countries and the missionary activity of the churches. But Christianity has also grown strongly in contexts where no western missionaries were directly involved. The so-called "independent African churches" are a central part of African church life. They were particularly strong in the 1950s and 1960s, and are still a vital force in the African church landscape.[18] In southern Africa, they are often known as Apostolic, Ethiopian, or Zionist churches. In South Africa, the independent African churches are the largest Christian confession in the land, and the Zion Christian Church (ZCC) is the largest church in the country. The ZCC has also established churches in the neighboring countries. In western Africa, these churches are called "spiritual" or "Aladura" ("people who pray"), and in eastern Africa, the term "spirit churches" is often used to describe them.

These churches arose as a reaction to western colonization, for it took a long time before western missionaries accepted African leadership in the established churches, and African culture was regarded as unchristian and backward. Paul Makhubu, a South African church leader, has declared:

16. Smith, "Religious Dimensions of Conflict," 6.

17. Asamoah-Gyadu, "Introduction"

18. Asamoah-Gyadu, "Introduction"; Meyer, "Christianity in Africa"; Oduro, "Independent Churches in Africa"

Some white missionaries, instead of teaching Christianity, promoted and taught white civilization. The blacks were stripped of
their customs, and in exchange were forced into a culture they
could never embrace.[19]

The first wave of independent African churches came into being at
the close of the nineteenth century. The churches that were founded were
relatively similar to the established churches, but distinguished themselves
by having African leaders. A few decades later, at the beginning of the twentieth century, a new wave of independent churches laid greater emphasis on
spiritual, prophetic, and healing aspects, often with charismatic leaders who
were called prophets.

These churches typically emphasize the Holy Spirit, dreams and visions, prophecies, healing through the laying on of hands, and exorcism.
In comparison with the established churches, there is a much greater place
in these churches for women leaders, as priests but primarily in the roles of
leaders in prayer, interpreters of dreams, and communicators of prophecies
and visions.[20]

Many scholars today point to the independent African churches as
forerunners of the contemporary Pentecostal movement, which they see as
different expressions of one and the same movement.[21] Both movements
emphasize what are regarded as the gifts of the Holy Spirit, especially the
laying on of hands, exorcisms, prophecies, and speaking in tongues. The
greatest differences lie not in doctrine, but in rituals and form. The independent African churches tend also to use ritual objects, modified from tradition religion, such as holy water, ashes, or (for example) sacred garments.
The church members can often be recognized through their clothes, often
white tunics. It says much that the expression "white garment church" is an
established concept in Nigeria. It is employed by outsiders as a collective
designation of these churches. In the South African Zion Christian Church,
uniforms are also used, but here in different colors—khaki, blue, yellow,
and red.[22] The differences between the Pentecostal movement and the independent African churches can also be seen in their relationship to African
traditional religion and culture. It is the independent African churches who

19. Quotation from Paul Makhubu in Oduro, "Independent Churches in Africa," 432.

20. Lubaale, "Independents"

21. See, e.g., Asamoah-Gyadu, "Introduction"; Kalu, *African Pentecostalism*; Anderson, *Introduction to Pentecostalism*. The different churches will not necessarily have the
same views as the scholars mentioned here; often, they will emphasize the differences
rather than the common aspects.

22. Anderson, *Introduction to Pentecostalism*, 103–22.

have frequently had the strongest links to African traditional religions and culture, *inter alia* through closeness to the rituals and the musical forms. In many places, local political and Christian leaders have worked against these churches, because they have feared their popularity and their practices.

TRADITIONAL, AFRICAN?

Traditional African religions, in all their variety, have neither written sources nor institutions that resemble those of Christians or Muslims; they are practiced and transmitted *inter alia* via oral narratives, social and political structures, rituals, holy places, objects, and art. At the center of their cosmology is the struggle to achieve an equilibrium between the visible world and the invisible spiritual world.[23] Reality is more than what we can see, and through contact with the spiritual world via objects, male and female go-betweens, spirits or ancestors, it is possible to influence the power that the spiritual world has over our life in the visible world. Magic is central, both as a positive and as a negative power.

The very concept of "traditional African religion" is a matter of dispute. Some wish to emphasize the *African* rather than the *traditional*, while others argue that given their long history, both Islam and Christianity are surely just as African as the traditional African religions. Others again hold that the word "traditional" has a negative sound and derives from the Christian missionaries' view of this religion as less valuable and old-fashioned. The relationship to this type of religion has been controversial in the churches in Africa, between elites and laity, between Europeans and Africans, and between different Christian confessions.[24]

Many Africans see no contradiction between being a Muslim or a Christian and at the same time making use of resources in traditional African religions. Examples of this in daily life are the many who consult traditional healers in cases of sickness, or the construction of altars in honor of the ancestors. A survey in 2010 showed that roughly 25 percent believe that sacrifices to ancestors or to specific spirits will give protection against dangers. The same number use *juju*, magic, to achieve goals such as passing an examination, finding a marriage partner, or winning a political election. This can also be a way to ensuring that a contract is life-long: juju can be put on a husband to ensure that he will suffer terribly if he is unfaithful.[25]

---

23. Olupona, *African Religions*; Ellis and Haar, *Worlds of Power*

24. Gifford, *African Christianity*, 329; Patterson, *Church and AIDS*, 17.

25. Pew Research Center, "Traditional African Religious." This 2010 survey covered eleven countries in Sub-Saharan Africa.

However, the skepticism of the established churches means that many prefer to conceal the fact that they consult traditional healers.[26]

There have been some changes in how the established churches relate to traditional African religions. On the one hand, it receives greater recognition as a specific religion; and there is a somewhat greater acceptance of the possibility that traditional African religions can be compatible with established Christian faith. Over the course of several decades, the Catholic church has drawn closer to traditional African religions, through an increased emphasis on cultural sensitivity and the theology of inculturation, and also through interreligious dialogue. In 1986, Pope John Paul II asked traditional African leaders for forgiveness of the church's old sins, and since that time, the church has had formal dialogues with leaders and representatives of traditional African religions. But despite the rapprochements, many of the conflicts endure.[27]

A common explanation of some of the success of the Pentecostal movement in Africa looks to its relationship to traditional African religions and culture. Unlike the established churches, the Pentecostal churches have not doubted the existence of spirits, demons, and witchcraft. Nor have they doubted that spiritual reality has great power—but Jesus is stronger, they say, and one can wage spiritual warfare against the spiritual world. Pentecostals speak explicitly about the need for "spiritual warfare," and say that this is a fight that Christians must take up in order to combat the devil's many demons. The emphasis on spirits and "spiritual warfare" is not unique to the African Pentecostal movement, but is found in numerous variants on all the continents. In Africa, the public demonization of traditional African religions is a central part of the message of the Pentecostal movement, and has generated increased attention in the public sphere to the occult, the demonic, and the spiritual.[28] It is not uncommon for public personalities to be accused of making alliances with dark forces, and Pentecostal pastors often arrange prayer marathons to "cleanse" a building, a street, or a country in order to drive out demonic powers.

This increase in public interest in spiritual warfare is also reflected in popular culture. In Nollywood, the Nigerian film industry, which is very popular in other countries too, it is precisely the spiritual war waged between the new Christians and the old faith that is a well-known theme. The plot is often set in modern urban districts and shows how dark demonic forces work hard to attack good Christians. One example is a popular Nigerian

26. Muketha, "Ameru Women's Spirituality"

27. Gifford, *African Christianity*, 329.

28. Meyer, "Christianity in Africa"; Hackett, "Discourses"

film from the early 1990s, *Living in Bondage*. Its protagonist becomes jealous of his friends who have earned a lot of money. He is tricked into joining a Satanist cult when he is seduced by the alleged possibilities of getting money quickly. He does indeed become rich very quickly, but that is not the end of the story. Things go badly with him in most other areas of life, and the only one who can liberate him from the darkness is . . . (as one might guess) a Pentecostal pastor.[29]

THE PENTECOSTAL MOVEMENT

The classic Pentecostal movement began as a revival movement. The Pentecostals held that the established churches were taking the wrong path, and had departed from the genuine Christian message. Through prayer, Bible studies, and most importantly through the personal experience of the Holy Spirit, people came together in new communities. Their concern was to build up societies of like-minded persons, thereby protecting each other from the dangers in "the world," that is to say, in life outside the church, which was seen as a place full of temptations and dangers. What mattered was that which was not of this world, that which concerned the spiritual dimension, as well as the end times and life after death. This has now changed.

The Pentecostal movement today is so large, varied, and constantly changing that it is difficult to speak of *one* movement. It is especially large in Latin America and Africa, but also in Asian countries like China, South Korea, and the Philippines, and in the USA. The movement has no Rome or Salt Lake City, nor is there a shared formal structure that makes it a group. Anyone who wants can start or operate a Pentecostal church, and there are many discussions within the movement about what falls within this term and what falls outside it. There are great variations from one church to another, and differences in the expressions that dominate in various countries and continents. It is customary to divide the movement on the global level into three great categories: the classical Pentecostal movement, which began in the USA in the first half of the twentieth century; the charismatic movement that grew in numbers in the established churches (above all in the Catholic church) from the 1960s onward; and the neo-Pentecostal movement that emerged especially in the 1980s.[30]

29. Religion finds expression in many ways in African films. There are Christian production companies, but religious themes are also widespread in the non-Christian production branch. See Adogame, *Who Is Afraid*; Merz, "Mediating Transcendence"

30. See Wilkinson, "Emergence," and Anderson "Varieties," for thorough discussions of the origin of the Pentecostal movement. The year 1906 has long been seen

The boundary lines between the various phases are, however, not always so clear, and changes in practice, faith, or structure take place very quickly in this decentralized movement. For example, a huge Nigerian church like the Redeemed Christian Church of God will have both classical and neo-Pentecostal theology and practice inside one and the same structure.[31] We can roughly characterize these churches by saying that the emphasis lies on experience rather than on doctrine. It is a matter of experiencing the Holy Spirit and of a strong faith in a God and spiritual powers that intervene both in society and in the individual's life. The pastors are often highly charismatic, and derive their legitimacy from their vocation more than from their training. Faith demands an individual obligation, which is attained through conversion and an active church life. The structure and practice of Pentecostal churches differ in many ways from those of the established churches, and their enormous growth poses a challenge to how Christianity occurs in Africa.

The most recent phase, the neo-Pentecostals, are at present those who are most powerfully present on the continent. Almost every African south of the Sahara will have an opinion about these churches, across a spectrum from enthusiasm and acceptance to skepticism and fear. Through an active mission via television, advertising, music, outdoor meetings, and door-to-door actions, these churches have made a verbal onslaught on both the established churches and traditional religion. The middle class and the elites too became involved in this phase, and this led to a stronger orientation on the part of the Pentecostal movement to the society outside the church. This has left clear traces on political, economic, societal, and cultural life.[32] Once, they formed a classically withdrawn, apolitical movement that protected itself against the temptations in the world, but now they have taken the step out into society, with the goal of changing it.

Nigeria has become a Pentecostal superpower not only in Africa, but also in other parts of the world. In this way, Nigeria is a good example of the huge changes in global Christianity. It is big on religion, but it is also big in most other ways: with its two hundred million inhabitants, it is decidedly

---

as the origin of the Pentecostal movement, since it was in April of that year, in a little church on Azuza Street in Los Angeles in the USA, that the Holy Spirit is said to have descended upon a small house church. One effect of this was that they started to speak in tongues. This narrative of origins has been challenged in recent years, *inter alia* by West African and South Asian scholars who argue that the Pentecostal movement in their regions was inspired by local revivals with roots going farther back than 1906; see Kollmann, "Classifying African Christianities," 11.

31. Ukah, "African Christianities."

32. Lende, "Rise of Pentecostal Power."

the most populous country in Africa, it has the biggest economy on the continent, it is the seventh largest oil producer in the world, and the local film industry, Nollywood, is the second largest in the world when measured by production. At the same time, the country faces enormous challenges: poverty, corruption, a weak governmental system, and various ethnic, religious, and regional lines of conflict. The religious antagonisms have increased recently. We shall come back to this below; first, let us go to the city.

A RELIGION FOR THOSE WHO WANT CHANGE

Many of those who are born in Africa today will grow up in a city, or else will leave their village at some point in their lives in the hope that their circumstances will change in the city. Forty percent of the population live in cities today.[33] It is precisely in the cities that the new Pentecostal churches have found their form and their largest public. The curious visitor to Lagos, Nigeria's largest city with maybe twenty million inhabitants, will perhaps be most struck by the sound and sight of the churches, once one has got over the traffic and the crowds of people. Posters along the motorway advertise miracle meetings; one hears glossolalia from loudspeakers that are turned out towards the street; songs of praise resound from the radio; and one sees enthusiastic Pentecostals engaging in missionary work on the bus, as well as thousands of small and large churches along the streets. You do not need to search for a church in Lagos—it will find you first.

The churches have names like Deeper Christian Life Ministry, the Synagogue, Church of All Nations, or House on the Rock. Zealous church members have stickers on the rear of their cars with the name of their church: "I attend Mountain of Fire and Miracle," "I love Christ Embassy," or "I am a Winners International." If you buy a local newspaper, it is perfectly possible that you will read in most of its sections (politics, economics, sport, and columns about celebrities) about Pentecostal churches, pastors, or famous Nollywood stars who are "born again." You will also read about the scandals surrounding some of the well-known pastors, such as accusations of sexual or financial infidelity. There is a wide debate about these churches in the country's newspapers.

Many of those who become Pentecostals are women. For a young woman who has left her rural village to seek her happiness in Lagos, membership of a Pentecostal church can become an important compass that gives her orientation in a new life. Newcomers are asked to break radically with their earlier life, with old customs, ways of thinking, and to some extent with

33. Akingbade, "Urbanisation."

their earlier social life too, in order thus to become a "born-again Christian" (the expression many use about themselves). And there are many who need a radical change in a city marked by extensive poverty, high unemployment, and large-scale societal uncertainty. Great emphasis is attached to personal transformation: you have in your own hands the power to change the direction your life is taking, and it is possible to get a new and better life.

However, Nigerian Pentecostal pastors will say that this is possible only if you have enough faith. In order to help you on the path, the bigger Pentecostal churches have an intensive program of large public meetings and conferences, but also small groups who meet regularly so that their members can get to know each other well. In this way, the churches can become a new social network. The churches also want you to acquire the competence that is necessary in the city: formal training, but also courses in entrepreneurship and in building networks, or in drawing up a budget. There are seminars on how one finds a marriage partner, or on how the relationship between the couple is to be kept warm. Women can attend courses on decorating the home, on baking cakes, or on making cosmetics. This competence can be very useful at home—but also if you want to start your own firm in the pulsating Lagos market.

A central idea in the theology of the neo-Pentecostals is that the true believers are to be blessed not only in the spirit, but also materially. The fruits of godliness are to be harvested not only in heaven, but also in life here and now. Change can come in the form of a miracle, and there are many who hope for this. But most of the Pentecostal churches would also underline the importance of investing in action—not only in prayer—so that change may come about.

MATERIAL PROSPERITY

The emphasis on the material dimension is a radical difference from both the classic Pentecostal movement and the established churches. The most popular and best known Pentecostal pastors have large private fortunes that are displayed as a motivation and as proof of their pastoral skills: riches are a gift from God. The preachers declare that poverty is not a virtue, and that Jesus wants all his people to enjoy material abundance. This message is spread daily from the pulpit, but also via the church's Twitter accounts and homepages. Pastor Adeboye, mentioned at the beginning of this chapter, has more than three million followers on Facebook, and frequently updates his status with this kind of affirmation: "No matter how low you're financially, as the Lord lives today the tide will turn for you in the name of Jesus."[34]

But in order to receive, one must give. Although the larger churches have income from private schools, media enterprises, or other business activities, the individual members are important sources of income. Giving money to the church is a central part of the worship service. Although there is a stark discrepancy in the power relationship between rich pastors and poor members, there exists a kind of informal regulation: if a member does not get what she wants, many options are available to her, and she can change to the church down the road. This means that the pastor too is obliged to fulfill his promises.

Scholars have emphasized the Pentecostal pastors as a variant of African "big man" structures. "Big man" analogies refer to the various patron–client relationships that are important power structures in many African societies. In such a relationship, a leader, patron, or "big man" with resources supplies material goods, services, and opportunities in return for loyalty from his adherents. If we wish to understand societal change in Africa, these altered power relationships are a good place to start. Traditional structures are challenged as a result of migration and urbanization, a weaker state, and new values.[35] In this context, the Pentecostal pastors are ready with the promise of a completely new start and a new fellowship, accompanied by an exhortation to leave the old life behind. Some churches in Nigeria have become so powerful that anyone who aspires to political leadership must first seek their alliance and their acceptance.[36] Pentecostal pastors can thus become the president's "big men" too.

The most successful churches earn huge sums of money through a variety of business enterprises, especially in the media and in property. This can be seen in Nigeria and elsewhere on the continent. The wealth of the pastors, the emphasis on material prosperity, and the fact that many of the neo-Pentecostal churches have developed into economic undertakings have encountered considerable skepticism. Religious organizations are exempt from paying tax, and there is little public insight into the Pentecostal congregations. This has led to repeated accusations of corruption and economic malfeasance, and demands that the churches should pay tax, but the Pentecostals argue that the economic activity is an integrated part of what it means to be a church, and that it is one way of doing missionary work.

---

34. Pastor Adeboye's official Facebook profile (https://www.facebook.com/PastorEAAdeboye), March 19, 2017.

35. McCauley, "Africa's New."

36. Obadare, "Pentecostal Presidency?"

They claim that this means that their activities ought not to be taxed.[37] In Uganda, business leaders have argued that Pentecostal churches too should pay tax, because the present situation creates an unjust situation of competition between religious and non-religious enterprises.[38] The authorities in Zimbabwe and South Africa have announced that they wish to tax Pentecostal churches with a high income.[39]

A CONFLICTUAL RELATIONSHIP TO OTHERS

The established churches have often clearly shown their skepticism vis-à-vis the new Pentecostal churches. A publication by the Presbyterians in Ghana declared their "great concern about the use of God's name to trick innocent persons and steal from them," and about "an increasing absence of God's Word from the pulpits in our Christian television and radio programs."[40] The established churches fear, not only new theology and praxis, but also the possibility that they may lose their own members to Pentecostal churches, since it is often Christians from the established churches who are "born again" and convert to Pentecostal Christianity. At the same time, the established churches themselves are influenced by the way in which the Pentecostal movement exercises religion, and it is characteristic of the entire continent that other churches acquire typically Pentecostal traits. This is how a Baptist pastor in Abjua, the capital of Nigeria, puts it:

> All the churches in Nigeria have been influenced by the Pentecostal movement. All of them! Especially the established churches, because of what the charismatic groups have done, prayer revival, faith in miracles, you know. . . . Every church now thinks that we must organize a prayer program, we must fast, we must "wait under the Lord"—that we must pray for it. For if we don't do that, people will go to the Pentecostal churches. So when the established churches asked themselves why people were leaving the church, they look around: We look old-fashioned, we must redesign ourselves, we must make things more beautiful, have flowers, there ought to be coffee. That is what the Pentecostals did, and before you knew what was happening, we

---

37. Lende, "Rise of Pentecostal Power," 121.
38. Briggs, "Taxation."
39. Dube "South Africa to Tax."
40. Gifford, *Ghana's New Christianity*, 192.

were doing it too. None of our established churches is the same
as it used to be![41]

In many ways, the Pentecostal churches present a challenge to the role
religion is to have in the African public sphere. Pentecostals are highly visible, both on the streets and in the media. They have an aggressive missionary style and talk about "waging spiritual warfare," about "capturing cities,"
or "conquering countries." Although this is changing to some degree, the
preaching in the Pentecostal congregations is still marked by an intransigent
attitude to non-Pentecostals. They often say that Catholics, Anglicans, or
Methodists are not genuine Christians, and that only those who have been
born again are entitled to call themselves Christians. Their criticism is often
also directed against traditional religions or against Islam.

Some of the attractiveness in the Pentecostal movement has been its
informality and spontaneity, and an existence in which miracles and incred-
ible testimonies are daily occurrences. No long theological training has been
necessary for pastors (as in the established churches), nor has there been
any need of a comprehensive infrastructure: a garage, a room in a house, an
old cinema, or a discotheque has been easily converted into a church. This
flexibility has contributed to the enormous growth of the Pentecostal movement, but it has also been a disadvantage. A representative of the umbrella
organization of the Pentecostal movement in Nigeria has expressed this as
follows:

> The Pentecostal movement has made itself a laughingstock, es-
> pecially in the established churches such as the Anglican and
> the Catholic churches, that have their structure and that provide
> a theological training before they begin serving the church. But
> Pentecostals can wake up one morning and say: "God has spo-
> ken to me." And thus they do many things with no control.[42]

In the wake of scandals and dubious miracles, the Pentecostal movement has sought internal dialogue and a clearer structure. Theological
studies have become important in most of the larger Pentecostal churches.
National umbrella organizations have been set up, with two particularly
important tasks. First, they have endeavored to bring a large independent
movement together for common projects; and secondly, they have worked
to achieve representation in national forums on the same terms as the other
large churches. In this sense, one can say that the Pentecostal movement too
has become somewhat more similar to the established churches.

41. Lende, "Rise of Pentecostal Power," 163.
42. Lende, "Rise of Pentecostal Power," 100.

POLITICAL CHURCHES

African churches have been active in political life both in the past and in the present, but the form taken by this political involvement is constantly changing. In the 1990s, several countries made the transition from authoritarian rule to the introduction of democracy, and this passage opened up the political sphere to new alliances and new participants. Religious actors were important in this process. But the general story of democratization, and authoritarianism, is not uniform across the continent and appears in different shapes.

In many countries, the established churches played central roles in the transition from authoritarian rule to democracy. Bishops met in national conferences and agreed on pastoral letters and declarations against sitting presidents; they entered into alliances with other organizations of civil society, such as trades unions and student groups. In Kenya, it was the Anglican and Presbyterian bishops who were the clearest in their criticism of the authoritarian president at the time, Daniel arap Moi. In countries such as Benin, Malawi, Madagascar, and Congo, Christian leaders and organizations were central actors in the cause of democratization. In South Africa, the established churches played an important role both in mobilizing national and international opposition to the apartheid regime and in promoting democratization and reconciliation on the local level, and it was the churches that led the Truth and Reconciliation Commission that was South Africa's way of tackling the injustice committed under apartheid. Through national and regional church structures and in collaboration with international churches and aid agencies, the churches mobilized for democratic reform. The established churches remain very central actors in today's Africa, but within the churches there is frustration that they have lost something of the critical voice and the great influence they had in the period of democratization. Scholars offer various explanations of the disappearance of the clear political impact. Some claim that the churches represented elites, whose critique of structures and whose liberal values removed them from what most people were concerned about: work, family, education, and spirituality.[43] Others argue that it was easier for the hierarchical churches to criticize the power in authoritarian regimes than in a decentralized state where the power is diffused.[44]

The Pentecostal movement was not equally unambiguous in its position against authoritarian regimes. It tended rather to be criticized for

43. Gifford, *African Christianity*.

44. Ranger, *Evangelical Christianity*, 15–19.

allying itself with dubious leaders, as in Zambia, Uganda, and Nigeria. In Kenya, the church leaders stood on two different sides: the established churches were critical, while some of the pastors from the charismatic Pentecostal churches claimed that the Christians' task was to support and pray for the political leaders who ruled at that time. An eloquent example is the declaration by a Pentecostal pastor on national television:

> Things in heaven are like the way they have been in Kenya for many years. There is only one party—and God never makes mistakes. . . . President Moi has been appointed by God to lead the country, and Kenyans ought to be glad for the freedom that reigns. We have freedom to worship God, and we can pray and sing in the way we want. What else do we need? That is all we need.[45]

Today, the political involvement of the Pentecostal movement varies greatly across the entire continent, and it is continually changing. Only a few decades ago, Pentecostals regarded the secular sphere, and politics in particular, as areas from which a true Christian ought to hold aloof, but a total shift has occurred today in the neo-Pentecostal movement. Now, Pentecostal pastors everywhere in Africa say that it is precisely they who have the key to a better society. In the words of Paul Adefarasin, pastor in the Lagos-based House on the Rock:

> In our legislative assemblies, the godless have drawn up measures that govern nations. These laws influence persons who have thought that the four walls of the church would give them immunity. The time has come for those who fear God to come out of their hiding places and make use of God's wisdom and power in the various sectors of society, in order to bring about change.[46]

"Those who fear God" are understood in this context as those who are "born again," that is to say, the Pentecostals themselves. This new political theology also contains the idea that the Pentecostal can rule both the spiritual and the physical world. Pentecostals employ the term "spiritual warfare," an established concept in Pentecostal theology, to proclaim that they are to confront and fight against the real powers that lie behind what happens in the physical world. In this theology, poverty, corruption, or the outcome of national political elections can be understood as the effect of spiritual

45. Gifford, *African Christianity*, 4.
46. Adefarasin, *Change Your World*, 162.

powers.[47] When a newly converted Pentecostal, Olusegun Obasanjo, was elected president of Nigeria in 1999, he was accorded almost messianic status by many Pentecostals: he was an answer to prayer, and not an object of criticism.[48] Pentecostals in Nigeria and in many other places are criticized for refusing to look at structural causes of societal problems. In many places, Pentecostals have supported dubious political leaders, in exchange for access to the corridors of power. Today, a number of Pentecostal churches are themselves confronting the one-sided emphasis on spiritual powers and are endeavoring to be more attentive to responsibility—even in "this world."

The political sector is only one of many societal sectors in which the Pentecostal movement is involved. Capturing other societal spheres, such as education, the media and entertainment, business activities, and sports arenas, is just as important as being active in the explicitly political field. Pastor Adeboye from the Redeemed Christian Church of God has intervened several times in the media with prophecies and prayer that Nigeria should win more prizes in international sports. He, like many others in Africa, is guided by an analysis that states that power in society is found in various places: not only in politics, but also in fields such as sport. If the "true Christians" are to have influence in society, they must capture the different arenas of power.

GOD AND HEALTH

It is thought that more than half of all the schools and health services in Africa are run by Christian or Muslim organizations.[49] Many places in Sub-Saharan Africa would have lacked educational opportunities, hospitals, or health clinics, if the churches and religious actors had not been present. The development of welfare went hand in hand with mission in the nineteenth and twentieth centuries, and the churches likewise played central roles in the work in health and in education that was financed by Western aid after the Second World War. Precisely this type of work is a central aspect of how Christianity occurs around the world today, and this is particularly clear in many African countries, where there is large-scale involvement on the part of both local and international actors. For many, the church has a much greater role and influence on their lives than the state: the congregation on Sunday and the social fellowship throughout the week, the message proclaimed on television and radio channels, the school on weekdays or the

47. Heuser, "Encoding Caesar's Realm"; Marshall, *Political Spiritualities*; Lende, "Rise of Pentecostal Power"

48. Obadare, "Pentecostal Presidency?"

49. Ridel, "Transforming Politics," 33.

health clinic when one is sick. In many countries, it is more probable that a person gives tithes to the church than that she pays taxes in the state she lives in. This tells us something important about both the church and the African state.

If, however, we are to understand the role of Christianity, it is not enough to point out that the churches have assumed huge societal tasks. When the churches get involved, they also must make choices, including about the areas in which they wish to work and about how they will do this. Although we have affirmed here in general terms that religion and Christianity have a decisive importance in African societies, this does not mean that the various churches are going in the same direction.

Christian institutions and actors have key roles in matters of health not only because they may provide health services, run clinics and hospitals, but also because they are crucial in providing a narrative and understanding of why sickness occurs, and ideas about how to cure it. It is not unusual for illness, or general misfortune, to be interpreted within a religious framework, as work of the devil or as punishment for collective or individual sin. The COVID-19 pandemic has highlighted this aspect. Across the continent, people have called for divine intervention.

Looking at Ethiopia, a multi-religious country with a relatively strict secular political framework, the pandemic can serve as an example of colliding worldviews—the secular health policies vs. religious beliefs and practices of healing—but also of how these two seemingly opposing worldviews can merge.[50] The religious demography in the country is made up of three major groups, about 34 percent belong to one of the oldest churches in the world, the Ethiopian Orthodox Church (EOC), while about 18 percent are Protestant and about 34 percent are Muslim. Regardless of their background, many Ethiopians interpret the virus as an expression of God's wrath and punishment for sin.[51]

When the first COVID-19 case was recorded in the country Ethiopians flocked to their churches and mosques to pray, confess and ask for forgiveness as a strategy for combatting the virus. The government on its side focused on urging social distancing, in church and in personal relationships. After a short lock-down, the EOC actively defied the restrictions imposed by the government, and kept churches open and urged people to gather for prayer. For Orthodox Christians, more than Muslims and Protestants, the spatial aspect is particularly important—the prayers need to be made in the church, and several of the rituals require communal participation. In the

---

50. Østebø et al., "Religion"

51. Østebø et al., "Religion," 1–2.

first six months of the pandemic, rituals such as fasting and the use of holy water increased among Orthodox Christians, responding to a call from the priests who urged their people to beseech God to protect them from the virus. The poor trust in a weak public health sector encouraged a turn to God.

At first glance, this religious response can be seen as pitted against secular explanations and public health policies. Yet, in everyday life, many Ethiopians see less tension between these two "worlds," the religious and the secular. The religious interpretation of the virus did not prevent people from also recognizing the importance of the public health policies and biomedicine while at the same time maintaining ideas about divine agency.[52] The secular government, recognizing the importance of cooperating with the church and people's sentiments, made unprecedented moves to accommodate religion in the public sphere, such as assigning time for prayers and services on government run television channels.[53]

While the COVID-19 pandemic has hit the continent hard, the present generations are not unfamiliar with outbreaks of serious pandemics. The recent history of how the churches reacted to the HIV/AIDS epidemic is a stark reminder of the problematical aspects of making sin and punishment the dominant framework for interpreting illness and death.

The devastating HIV/AIDS epidemic is a vast societal problem in many African countries, although the extent of the epidemic has been reduced in recent years. Southern and eastern Africa are worst hit, with big differences from one country to another.[54] HIV/AIDS has affected young people with particular severity, with dramatic consequences for families and local societies, and hence also for the churches.

The AIDS epidemic began in the 1980s, at the time when people across the entire continent were moving to the cities and old social structures were undergoing change. It was precisely this change in social structures that was given much of the blame for the epidemic. Young urban women and men were accused of being promiscuous and immoral, and of lacking respect for Christian and cultural tradition.[55] Many churches played a central role in promoting the view that HIV/AIDS occurs solely as a result of sex outside marriage, that is to say, of immorality and sin. In this way, they have contributed to a stigmatization of those who fall sick, and this made it harder to have an open and informed public debate about this topic. Shame and

52. Østebø et al., "Religion"

53. Østebø et al., "Religion," 14.

54. See "HIV and AIDS"; Patterson, *Church and AIDS*, 7.

55. Boyd, *Preaching Prevention*; Van Klinken, "African Christianity"; Patterson, *Church and AIDS*.

ignorance have helped the virus to spread more quickly, and have made it more difficult to live with the sickness.

The churches offer various explanations of how HIV/AIDS occurs and spreads, and thus also of how it can be treated. Some churches have declared it to be God's punishment for immoral sex. Other churches have emphasized that God can heal and that prayer can give protection against the sickness, while other churches again have concentrated on Jesus as the image of the love of neighbor and of care for all.[56] The churches' differing understandings of the sickness have generated a variety of responses.

Some churches have ignored the sickness; others have emphasized talking about sex within marriage; others again have emphasized miracles and healing. Some have developed social services in order to help children or older persons who have lost carers in their family to the sickness.

The church's ambivalent role vis-à-vis the epidemic is clear not only between the churches, but also within the individual church. The Catholic church is especially large in eastern and southern Africa, and spoke at an early date about HIV/AIDS in Africa. In Zambia, for example, the Catholic church in the Ndola region began early in the 1990s to draw up programs to enable volunteers and professionals to help HIV/AIDS patients and their relatives by means of various home care services such as palliative treatment, the treatment of infections, prayer and spiritual support, and financial and social help for the relatives. This model of home-based services was copied by other churches, by secular organizations, and also by the public health services in several African countries.[57] This means that the Church is at the forefront in providing care services. Its controversial position about the use of condoms (which, incidentally, is less strict in practice in many places) can thus be seen as an instance of double standards, given that one primary source of infection with HIV/AIDS is, precisely, unprotected sex.

Like many of the political elites, the churches were for a long time silent about the epidemic. But from early in the 2000s onwards, the established churches in particular, via various church councils and theological institutions, have confronted their own attitude to the HIV/AIDS problematic. Aid agencies and ecumenical councils played a central role in launching the dialogue. In 2001, the World Council of Churches held a large meeting in Nairobi, the capital of Kenya, with representatives from the entire continent. The plan of action after the meeting states:

56. Patterson, *Church and AIDS*, 66.

57. Patterson, *Church and AIDS*, 57. These home-based services are controversial, prompting both enthusiasm and criticism. For a critical approach to how this functions in Malawi, see Pindani et al., "Perception."

For the churches, the strongest contribution we can make to work against infection from HIV is to eradicate stigmatization and discrimination. Churches engaged early with HIV/AIDS, and many have excellent care, information, and counseling programs.

But the challenge to our churches is felt at a deeper level than this. As the pandemic has unfolded, it has exposed fault lines that reach to the heart of our theology, our ethics, our liturgy, and our practice of ministry. Today, churches are being obliged to acknowledge that we have—however unwittingly—contributed both actively and passively to the spread of the virus. Our difficulty in addressing issues of sex and sexuality has often made it painful for us to engage, in any honest and realistic way, with issues of sex education and HIV prevention.[58]

Similar statements have been made by national church councils in many African countries. Clergy infected with HIV have spoken openly about their situation in order to put an end to the stigma. Many churches today work actively in lobbying, in offering treatment, and in spreading information about the sickness. However, the churches' action in connection with HIV/AIDS remains controversial. One side effect of the debates in African churches about HIV/AIDS is that it has opened the door to a wider discussion of gender and sexuality. It is above all women theologians who have pioneered this debate.

CHURCH, GENDER, AND SEX

In Africa, as in most other places, the churches have clear views about how family life ought to be organized, whom the family should consist of, and the roles that women and men have in the church and in the family. Sexuality is likewise a central question.

In recent debates about homosexuality, several value-conservative African church leaders have affirmed that it is they, with their defense of heterosexual marriage, who represent true Christianity. They see western churches' acceptance of LGBTQ clergy and same-sex marriage as proof of the ultimate collapse of morality in the West: it now falls to the African churches to speak on behalf of Christianity.

There are, however, other critical voices who argue that there is nothing particularly African about what are known today as traditional patterns of gender roles and family structures, where the nuclear family is the norm.

58. WCC, "EHAIA Consultation."

They argue that these came with the culture of the European missionaries, who were shocked at what they saw as immoral lifestyles, such as seductive dancing or the revealing clothing of the women. The European culture of sexuality and gender, together with the European family structure, became an integral part of the missionary project. This led to the suppression of the traditional African ways of regulating family life and gender roles, to the benefit of a puritan European culture.[59]

Changed economic conditions, urbanization, migration, and new values are leading to changes in African families, too. At the same time, however, older African views and practices with regard to marriage and family structures remain strong in many places on the continent. Many regard entering into marriage as a pact between families rather than as an agreement between two individuals.[60] Polygamy is legal, or tolerated, in most African states. Many of the independent African churches encourage or tolerate polygamy in their congregations; this has caused problems for their relationship to the established churches. When the Nigerian Celestial Church of God asked to join the World Council of Churches in 1998, its request encountered opposition and was refused because the Council held that the church was insufficiently clear in its condemnation of polygamy.

In the last three decades, African women theologians have influenced the development of a new type of African theology in the established churches, a theology with its starting point in women's experience in African societies.[61] As in Latin America and elsewhere, liberation theology and inculturation theology have been central to the discussion of how Christianity can be relevant in the specifically African context, but many women theologians hold that these perspectives have not taken on board the thoroughgoing discrimination of women on the continent. Liberation theology under apartheid in South Africa concentrated on discrimination on the basis of race and economy, but gender was not specifically thematized. In the same way, inculturation theology has discussed how local contexts and cultures can be used in the communication of the Christian message, but often without articulating questions concerning gender. Many of the most prominent critics have been associated with the Circle of Concerned African Women Theologians.[62] It met for the first time in 1989 in Ghana, and has national sections in many African countries today. The goal of this

---

59. Ojo and Adewale, "Christianity and Sexuality in Africa"; Chitando, "Human Sexuality."

60. González et al., *Frontiers of Globalization*.

61. Van Klinken, *Transforming Masculinities*, 25–28.

62. Phiri, "Circle"; Van Klinken, *Transforming Masculinities*.

network is the elaboration of theology on the basis of the specific African and female context. They maintain that women have been discriminated against and rendered invisible in African patriarchal structures, and that the churches have not taken seriously woman's exposed position in African societies. In concrete terms, the group has undertaken research in order to make visible women's role in the churches; they have identified gender-based violence as a particularly important area that the churches ought to be working against; and they have contributed theological thinking about gender and women's ordination.[63]

The Pentecostal movement attaches great weight to the nuclear family. Much of the teaching and activity in the churches communicates how one can become a better mother, wife, father, or husband. The nuclear family is seen as the most important basic unit in society: if the family is weak or divided, the same will be true of society too. The doctrine states that the woman is to be subordinate to the man—in marriage always, and almost always with regard to leadership in the church. One very important question in research into the Pentecostal movement concerns how this movement influences gender roles. Does the vigorous work to cement gender roles, and especially the subordination of the woman, mean that women are suppressed, while men are idolized as leaders?[64] Or can we speak of a "gender paradox," namely, that despite the churches' doctrine that women and men have different roles, the Pentecostal churches can have a liberating effect for women? While the neo-Pentecostals make no difference between women and men with regard to the material and spiritual development of the individual, they declare that within the family, and as a rule within the church leadership too, the man will be the head.

The question of women's role in the Pentecostal movement was initially discussed by researchers with regard to Latin America, where some have pointed out that the movement is having a successful impact on the macho culture: men stop drinking and prioritize family and work, and this in turn improves life for the women.[65] Research into Africa likewise discusses to what extent the attention given to gender roles in the Pentecostal movement helps to create safer frameworks around the family.[66] Others again underline that the Pentecostal movement provides space for active participation in the churches by laity, both women and men, and point to a growth in the

63. Phiri and Kaunda, "Gender."
64. Soothill, "Gender and Pentecostalism," 192–93.
65. Brusco, "The Reformation."
66. Soothill, "Gender and Pentecostalism."

number of women pastors.[67] But scholars are also cautious in their analyses of changes in the understandings of gender roles, in view of the fact that the theology and ecclesial structure of the Pentecostal movement have clear gender hierarchies, where the subordination of women is the norm.

Homosexuality was almost a non-topic in the African public sphere until the first decade of the present century, when prominent Christians and political leaders began to stand side by side in the fight against LGBTQ rights. They argued that homosexuality is compatible neither with the Bible nor with African culture.[68] The head of the Anglican church in Nigeria, Archbishop Peter Akinola, won international fame in 2003 when he threatened to withdraw the Nigerian church from the international Anglican Communion if the churches in England, and the USA went ahead with the appointments of two gay priests to the episcopate. The British priest withdrew his candidature, but the American refused to do so. Archbishop Akinola became an unambiguous spokesman for an alliance consisting of many who take the same position. They argue that the churches in the West are departing from true doctrine, and that it is up to the churches in the South to defend it. Akinola played a central role in 2008 in arranging the first Global Anglican Future Conference (GAFCON), which subsequently met in 2013 and 2018. It brings together many conservative Anglican church leaders, most of them from Anglican churches in the South. This means that the division in the global Anglican Communion is clear, and has been institutionalized to a large extent.

The strong opposition to homosexuality on the part of many church leaders in Africa may be understood as a warning about future struggles over values between a conservative South and a liberal North. This is the outcome of an analysis that sees the churches in the South becoming stronger, with a numerical superiority and with real power to define church development in the North too; this is exemplified by Archbishop Akinola's activity.[69] This often concerns LGBTQ rights, but also women clergy and abortion.

It is, however, important to differentiate the picture of a sharp division between South and North, since both "the West" and Africa are more complex than this kind of narrative affirms. South Africa legalized same-sex marriage in 2006 with support from some important church leaders, such as the former Anglican archbishop, Desmond Tutu, and this fueled the public debate in Africa. At the same time, not everyone in the West holds liberal

67. Soothill, "Gender and Pentecostalism," 197; Boadi, "Engaging Patriarchy."

68. Van Klinken, "African Christianity"

69. Van Klinken, "African Christianity," 144–46.

values; for example, much of the lobbying for stricter laws against LGBTQ rights in Uganda was the work of North American missionaries, often in league with Ugandan Pentecostal churches. The strong growth of Pentecostal churches with global networks has also helped make LGBTQ rights an African, and Christian, battleground in the public arena.[70]

CONFLICT AND PEACE

Since religion is a very important factor in explaining connections, in motivating to action, and in systematizing social and political life in Africa, it is only natural that it is also important in relation to conflict and peace.[71] We frequently hear of violent conflicts with religious undertones in Africa. In Mozambique, an Islamist terrorist group, believed to have links to ISIS in the Middle East, has launched attacks on civilians, elites and crucial infrastructure since 2017. By 2021, seven hundred thousand people have been displaced due to this instability. In 2015, 149 students were shot and killed in Kenya by a group of men who belonged to the Islamist terrorist movement al-Shabaab. In 2014, the UN warned about a possible genocide in the Central African Republic, carried out by Christian militias against the Muslim minority in the country as part of the repercussions of a failed coup d'état in the previous year. In Uganda, the Lord's Resistance Army, with the Bible in their hands, have massacred and terrorized the local people over several decades. The Nigerian terror group Boko Haram claims to represent the true Islam and threatens all who refuse to submit to their agenda—and they are many. Both Muslims and Christians are attacked by Boko Haram in Nigeria, Chad, Niger, and Cameroun; this has led to a severe refugee crisis in the region.

Where ethnic differences also follow religious boundaries, the conflicts can go deeper still. Christianity is used by both laity and the elites to legitimate power and also to challenge power. All the examples above illustrate that religion is indeed a factor in conflict, but none of the examples can be explained by examining the religious factor alone. Distribution of power, and economic and political conditions are very much factors that must be taken into account when explaining why insurgency and civil unrest occur.

However, some contemporary factors ought to be highlighted in order to explain why religion and religious identity play an important role in some of today's conflicts in African countries. Concurrently with global changes and new local tensions, it is often conflicts involving Islam and Christianity

70. Van Klinken, "African Christianity," 155; Kaoma, *Colonizing*.
71. Titeca, "The Spiritual Side," 140.

that receive the greatest attention. There is a great tension around the development in countries such as Nigeria, where there are large groups of both Muslims and Christians. The conflicts have increased here in recent years, both rhetorically in the public sphere and physically through the use of violence.[72] Some of the explanation lies in the combination of the democratization of the public sphere and the lack of economic, political, and societal development. The growth of reform movements in Islam and Christianity, such as the Salafist groups and the Pentecostal movement, has exploited this sphere and promoted the politicization of religion.[73] Violent Islamist terror groups like Boko Haram and al-Shabaab are one part of this picture. The media are also an important new factor. They can help to shape ideas about community reducing complex conflicts to a question of religious differences and thus fueling conflict further.[74]

Although the relationship between Islam and Christianity is sometimes conflictual in Africa today, sub-Saharan Africa is also characterized by religious tolerance. The every-day religious pluralism characteristic of urban areas across the continent has received much less scholarly attention than violent conflict.[75] Yet, hostilities involving religion have made many religious leaders assume public roles calling for peace and religious tolerance. In the past decades, interreligious dialogue and peace initiatives have become a priority, especially for the Catholic church and the established Protestant churches.[76]

OUTLOOK

"It's the West that needs to be saved now," say many of the African missionaries who walk the streets of Dublin, Kiev, and Amsterdam with the Bible in their hands. A hundred years ago, European missionaries spoke of Africa as the "dark continent" that needed to be rescued—now, Africans have begun to use the same rhetoric about the West. The West has lost faith in God, and now the Africans must give it back.

72. Imo, "Evangelicals."

73. Van Klinken, "African Christianity," 140–42.

74. Smith, "Religious Dimensions of Conflict," 8–10.

75. Lende, "City of Gods."

76. There is an increased interest in many places in including religious leaders in peace processes, but there have been few studies up to now that indicate which strategies are most effective. For a case study from Ethiopia, see Steen-Johnsen, *State and Politics.*

Pentecostals play a central role in this "reverse mission," and African Pentecostal communities have started churches around the world. The use by the African Pentecostal movement of media such as satellite television and live streaming on Facebook makes the message accessible far beyond national boundaries, even without missionaries. But it is not only African Pentecostals who journey out into the world. When African Christians emigrate, independently of their church membership, many of them will find a church in their new home country. This leads to changes in the local churches where they settle. For example, the Catholic church in England has large parishes with people who have immigrated from Africa.[77] And there are other strong meeting points between the continents: given the shortage of clergy in the traditional churches in Europe, Catholic, Anglican, and Lutheran pastors from African countries have been employed in rural parishes in countries such as Germany, England, and France, and many aspiring theologians and pastors from Africa leave the continent to study theology at universities and Bible colleges in other places.

Our primary focus of attention in this chapter has been on the Pentecostal movement, because of its dramatic growth and its strong influence today. We could have covered more of the great variety on the African continent by looking in greater depth at the independent African churches; or we could also have told the story of African Christianity by studying the Orthodox churches, such as the Ethiopian Orthodox Church which since the fourth century has been embedded in the nation and its people, with a historical trajectory that is very different from most other African countries. Or we could have delved into the established churches and examined how different political or cultural contexts shape their roles and engagement. The variations in African Christianity will make themselves felt in the time ahead, far beyond the continent itself.

The center of gravity of the Christian world will lie increasingly in the global South. This means that African churches will have a more important voice in the international churches and in global Christian meeting points such as the Lausanne movement or the World Council of Churches. When a new Catholic pope was to be elected in 2013, there were many who bet that the next pope would be an African. They argued that this would be only natural, given the size and importance of the Catholic church in Africa. When the white smoke rose up from the Sistine Chapel in Rome, it brought the news that while the new pope did indeed come from a country in the southern hemisphere, it was not from Africa this time.

77. Pasura and Erdal, *Migration*.

3

Latin America

Catholicism under Pressure

IN 2013, THE CARDINALS in the Catholic church elected the Argentinian Jorge Bergoglio as the new pope. This meant that for the first time in history, the world's largest religious organization had a Latin American as its chief leader. The new Pope became a living symbol that the center of gravity in Catholicism had shifted over the last hundred years from the global North to the South. With a pope from Latin America, the church had also taken a position vis-à-vis new realities on this continent, where Catholicism has lost adherents and has come under new pressure. It no longer has a religious monopoly in Latin America, but instead faces intense competition on what one can call the religious market.

Latin America is still the most Catholic continent in the world. Nowhere do more Catholic Christians live, and Brazil is still the country in the world with the highest number of Catholics, followed by Mexico as the world's second most populous Catholic land. In this chapter, accordingly, we shall emphasize these two countries in particular. They are representative of Catholicism in the region in two ways: Catholicism is strong in Mexico, but it is losing adherents in Brazil.

Mexico belongs to the group of Latin American countries that have the greatest number of Catholics measured by the percentage of the population. Together with countries like Paraguay, Colombia, and Ecuador, Mexico has the highest percentage of Catholics in Latin America. With regard to religious membership, Brazil belongs to a group of countries that represent a different development for Catholicism than in Mexico. A majority of the Brazilian population is still Catholic, but this majority diminishes daily. South of Mexico, we find Central American countries like El Salvador, Guatemala, and Nicaragua, where the percentage of Catholics has sunk to half the population; many become Pentecostals. The development in Brazil is dramatic: the Catholic church in the country loses more than a hundred thousand members each year, and the Protestant Pentecostal churches gain more and more territory. The number of Pentecostals in Brazil has doubled every ten years since 1970, and the religious mobility is high. So many Christians join new churches and communities in Brazil that it is regarded as one of the core areas of the new dynamic in global Christianity today. Huge groups in the population are breaking away from centuries-old religious traditions.

Nevertheless, Latin America remains overwhelmingly Catholic. From Mexico in the north to Argentina and Chile in the south, the presence of the Catholic church is noticeable almost everywhere. There is a Catholic church in every town or village. In comparison with western Europe, Latin American societies are secularized only to a modest degree. However, some of the countries that have had more active welfare states in recent times have large groups who no longer identify with religion. This applies to Argentina, Chile, and Uruguay, where the Catholic church has not only lost members to Protestant churches. There are many in these three countries who are more secular, either by declaring that they have no religion, or by attending church services seldom. Even in Brazil, the group of those with no religious membership is increasing.

The relationship between state and church is important, if we are to understand the religious influence on society. Mexico has an atypical history in a Latin American context, since the Mexican state introduced strict laws early on in the period of national construction to limit the power of the Catholic church. After changes to the law in 1992, the country has come back to a more normal situation, so that the Catholic church profits from religious freedom and has a considerable influence on politics. In a global context, Mexico is an example of a populous Christian land where secularism has been considerably weakened in recent decades.[1]

In the coming years, a growing percentage of the world's Christians will live in Latin America, both because the population growth is higher here than in Europe and the USA, and because support for the churches is stronger. We also find in Latin America a religious dynamic that is one

1. Fox, *Political Secularism*, 234.

decisive factor for the future of Christianity in a global perspective, especially with regard to the question of how many Catholics there will be in
relation to Protestants. Scholars have increasingly described this dynamic as
a religious market. Individuals can choose freely among a greater number of
religious offers than in the past.

With special emphasis on the regional superpower Brazil, we shall see
how a weakened Catholic church has met this new competition, and we
shall indicate some characteristics of a Brazilian Pentecostal church. Catholicism has been weakened in Argentina too, but the competition from
other Christian groups has not been as intense as in Brazil. In this respect,
the Pope's native land is one of the most secularized Latin American nations. The example of Mexico serves in particular to shed light on a Catholic
church that has lost members to a lesser extent than in other countries in
Latin America, and that has also consolidated its position vis-à-vis the state.
On the continent as a whole, Catholicism is a varied reality with internal
tensions that are sometimes great. This can be seen in strong political antagonisms, but also in economic class divisions that largely follow ethnic
boundary lines. The Catholic plurality can also be traced via the tensions
between the orthodoxy of the priests and the people's own religious practices. Belief in the power of the spirits is strong almost everywhere—a belief
to which charismatic Pentecostal Christianity appeals strongly.

THE CATHOLIC RELIGIOUS MONOPOLY

Latin America has been officially Catholic for almost five hundred years.
Ever since Spanish and Portuguese colonists invaded the land of the indigenous peoples on the continent, conquest and mission went hand in hand.
In 1493, the Pope declared the principal reason for colonization: in order to
convert the Indigenous inhabitants and establish the Catholic religion, the
territories could be conquered by the Spanish and Portuguese kingdoms,
which in return had to contribute to the missionary work. The colonial
power and the Catholic faith were two sides of the same coin, although
Catholic priests like Bartolomé de las Casas (1474–1566) also protested vigorously against the oppression of the indigenous people. In the region that
is today's Paraguay, the Jesuits established mission stations that in practice
were the closest the indigenous population came to a form of independent
state in the colonial period. Here, the Jesuits protected the Guaraní people
against slavery in today's Brazil. Many of these Catholic missionaries were
also driven by the dream of realizing a Christian utopia where all shared the
true Catholic faith. Accordingly, Jews and Muslims, who could pose a threat

to this religious unity, had no access to the New World.[2] After the Reformation, Spain and Portugal also took care to prevent Protestants from getting any share in the conquests.

When several countries in Latin America declared their independence from the European colonial powers on the Iberian peninsula in the nineteenth century, Catholicism remained the dominant religion of the new states. The Catholic church retained a privileged position there, and restrictions were still made on Protestant mission. Until well into the twentieth century, the Catholic church had in practice a monopoly on what was on offer in the religious sphere, although popular religious practices outside the church's control have always been present too.

According to market theory, monopolies will fall if the governing authorities open the door to free competition. Some have described the Catholic church in Latin America as a lazy monopolist that was content to rest on privileges such as power, people's habits, and its close ties to elites; this made it unsuited to develop its religious products or to conduct its operations in a more cost-effective manner as the competition grew.[3] Whereas the Protestant Pentecostal revival simply allows every newly converted person to set up a church and attract new adherents, the Catholic church operates in an unwieldy fashion with strict demands about the conduct of one's life and a lengthy training for its priests. Pentecostal Christianity has offered many in Latin America something that they wanted: a direct experience of God's presence through the individual embracing of charisms such as glossolalia, healings, and exorcism, independently of the Catholic sacraments and Catholicism's intellectual priests. Besides this, the inner division and fragmentation of the Pentecostal movement has led to large-scale innovation and variation in the offers that are made.[4]

Although this intense religious competition has hit Catholicism's monopoly hard, it has at the same time strengthened Christianity's grip on Latin America, because where the Pentecostal movement has put down its

2. Lomnitz, "Secularism and the Mexican Revolution," 101.

3. Levine, "Future of Christianity," 123. Scholars have increasingly compared this competition with an economic market. The current in research into religion that is based on the premise that the social dynamics between religious and Christian groups can be compared and explained with the help of microeconomic models tends to be called "The Religious Economy School." See Bellin, "Faith in Politics," 319. Examples of this current are Gill, *Rendering unto Caesar*; Chesnut, *Competitive Spirits*; Brekke, *Faithonomics*.

4. Not all forms of Christianity fit equally well into the microeconomic model that is presupposed here. For example, this model is suited only to a limited degree to explaining the emergence of the communities with a liberation-theological orientation in Latin America. See Løland, "Om gjenfødelsen."

deepest roots, the level of activity among Catholics has also increased.[5] The Catholics have caught up and intensified the competition via a popular way of practicing religion: a form of charismatic Christianity that Latin Americans can embrace without becoming Protestants—the Catholic charismatic renewal.[6]

BRAZIL AND MEXICO—TWO DISSIMILAR CATHOLIC COUNTRIES

Mexico can be called the Catholic bastion in Latin America. Although the proportion of Catholics is sinking in the continent's most populous nations, Brazil and Mexico, Catholicism remains strong among the Mexican population of 127 million (2019).[7] In Latin America, only Paraguay has a higher proportion of the population who still profess the Catholic faith than in Mexico.[8] With a slightly smaller share than in Paraguay, nearly 80 percent of Mexicans today count themselves as Catholics.[9]

With its 211 million inhabitants (2019), Brazil has a larger population, and for a long time to come, it will have the second-highest number of Christians of any country in the world;[10] only the USA has more inhabitants today who count themselves as Christians. In global terms, Mexico is the fourth-largest Christian nation.[11] Its Catholicism has retained its strong position, despite the fact that secular ideas about a clear separation of church and state found expression early on in the country's constitutions.

The 1917 Mexican constitution deprived priests of voting rights and allowed the imprisonment of priests who criticized the country's laws. It also forbade the establishing of Catholic religious orders. It was only in 1992 that the Catholic church and other churches were given a legal status within Mexico's borders.[12] Only the communist Cuba has a stricter regulation of

---

5. Stark and Buster, "Pluralism," 48.

6. Chesnut, "Conservative Christian Competitors," 102.

7. World Bank, "Mexico."

8. Pew Research Center, "Religion in Latin America."

9. Although the number of Catholics is still sinking, the decline has slowed down. Conversions to confessions outside the Catholic church do not occur with the same frequency as they did twenty or thirty years ago; see Navarro, "Religious Change in Mexico," 80. In 2021, the The National Institute of Statistics and Geography (INEGI) in Mexico reported that 77.6 percent of Mexicans defined themselves as Catholics.

10. World Bank, "Brazil."

11. Pew Research Center, "Global Christianity"

12. Blancarte, "Religion and Constitutional Change," 556–57.

Catholicism in Latin America.[13] In this sense, Mexican secularism has been unique in the Latin American context: while the Mexican state exercised strict control of the Catholic church in an early phase, other states took the opposite path and chose to give the same church active support and a wide freedom down to our own days. In countries such as Argentina, Costa Rica, Peru, and Venezuela, it is still the case that the Catholic church receives large financial contributions and is exempt from paying tax,[14] *inter alia* to allow it to pay the priests' salaries. In Brazil, the Catholic church has fewer privileges than in these countries, but at the same time, the Brazilian Catholic church has had a much freer sphere of action than in Mexico. However, the apostasy of Catholics has been greater in Brazil than in Mexico. One important background to this state of affairs is Catholicism's position during the colonial period.

Catholicism in Spain was a central driving force in the formation of the country's empire in Latin America, where Mexico became a center for both mission and conquest both northwards and southwards after Hernán Cortes's victory over the Aztecs in 1521. Until Mexico ceded territory in 1848, a large part of the southern USA, including Texas and California, was a part of the mission field of the Spanish empire. Portugal's right to colonize today's Brazil was affirmed by the Pope in 1493, but with a small population (1.2 million) and a small fleet of ships (three hundred at most), the country had far fewer resources to exercise control over its empire.[15] The Portuguese royal power was forced to depend on governance by the colonists, but the Spaniards had the economic muscle to build up a much more robust ecclesiastical institution as a part of the new ruling class. There were few bishops in Brazil, and the church's religious freedom was minimal, thanks to the profound dependence on the colonial masters.[16] A large part of the population of Brazil were African slaves, who were taught the faith in the same way as children were taught—they were not given instruction appropriate to adults. Nor did the church have the resources to conduct instruction. It was the slave owners' responsibility to teach their subjects the true Christian faith.[17] It is probably due to this ideology of slavery and to a weak institution that Catholicism has left fewer traces in the population during the colonial

13. In comparison to other Latin American countries, however, Mexican legislation does not regulate religious minorities to a great extent; see Fox, *World Survey*, 293.

14. Fox, *World Survey*, 290–305.

15. Andersen, "Det portugisiske imperiet," 139–40.

16. From 1551 to 1675, there was only one bishop charged with covering the enormous Brazilian territory, and until 1889, the church had only six bishops under the archbishop who was appointed. See Hoornaert et al., *História*, 277.

17. Hoornaert et al., *História*, 338.

period in Brazil than in Mexico, where Catholic practices have permeated people's lives much more strongly.

One symptom of this is the adherence to Catholic praxis that is shown by making a pilgrimage to Catholicism's most important sanctuaries in the two countries. The basilica erected in Mexico over the place where the Virgin of Guadalupe is said to have appeared is the most popular pilgrimage goal of the continent. On a world basis, only Saint Peter's church in Rome is more popular in Catholicism. The legend of this patron saint in Mexico resembles the story of the Virgin of Aparecida in Brazil; both involve the vision of a virgin where mixed ethnicity is an important motif.[18] Many millions of pilgrims travel each year to see the place where the statue of Brazil's patron, Our Lady of Aparecida, is on display, and the numbers have increased since the new basilica was completed in 1999. But although Brazil has far more Catholics than Mexico, the Mexican pilgrimage goal is much more assiduously visited.[19]

According to Catholic tradition, the Virgin Mary first appeared in America in 1531. The narrative tradition relates that it was a poor Indio who saw her and who immediately reported the vision to the Catholic bishop. The Virgin was a mestiza, like the children of Europeans and indigenous people. She is also said to have communicated her message in the language of the indigenous population, the Aztecs.

MEXICO—THE CATHOLIC NATION AGAINST LIBERAL SECULARISM

Mexico has a special form of Catholic nation-building. Unlike other nations in Latin America, where the elites who wanted to secede from Spain tended to be anticlerical, Catholic priests in Mexico were at the head of the fight for independence. The Catholic priests José Maria Morelos and Miguel Hidalgo were nothing less than generals in the army that fought against the Spaniards. This struggle has supplied much nourishment to the idea of Mexico as a Catholic nation.

Hidalgo took up this fight under the banner of the Virgin of Guadalupe.[20] The cult focused on this Marian figure has had an immense importance for the entwining of Catholic and national identity in Mexico, and this

18. In the Brazilian legend, the Virgin appeared to a mulatto, while in the Mexican legend, she appeared to a man from the indigenous population; see González and González, *Christianity in Latin America*, 71.

19. Fraser, "Accommodating Religious Tourism," 329.

20. Ascensio, "La Iglesia ante," 178.

has taken place in an ambivalent and conflictual relationship to the modern Mexican state. The Mexican Virgin has been venerated by a wide spectrum of groups as "the protectress of the nation" and "Mexico's queen."[21] As a national icon, she has often been exploited by political leaders in times of crisis.

The radical leftwing guerillas of the EZLN ("Ejército Zapatista de Liberación National"), which attempted from 1994 onwards to become a legitimate mouthpiece for the poor indigenous population in Mexican society, regarded the Virgin as their protectress, as did the rightwing politician Felipe Calderón from the PAN party ("Partido Acción Nacional"), who was declared the winner of the presidential election in Mexico in 2006. After accusations of electoral fraud in an election won by a narrow margin led to mass protests and a political crisis, Calderón was sworn in as president after first visiting the basilica in Guadalupe to pray to the Virgin.[22] While Calderón was politically conservative the guerilla was leftwing, with a clear inspiration from Catholic liberation theology. This shows how the Catholic faith can function to legitimate politics on both the right and the left wings.

Catholic piety is controversial in Mexican state leaders, because Mexicans strongly approve of the separation between religion and politics.[23] This support for secularism can be attributed largely to the uncommonly conflictual modern history of the country. Liberal political forces that fought to limit the political power of the Catholic church were the victors in the civil wars of the nineteenth and twentieth centuries against conservatives who were allies of the Catholic clergy.

The liberal victors were not content with controlling the Catholic priests. At their most aggressive, they also sought to eradicate popular Catholic religiosity by physically shutting churches and removing statues of the saints.[24] This evoked strong reactions among large sectors of the rural population, and led to several armed uprisings. The Cristero uprising was the most clearly Catholic in character. Its name was derived from the battle cry of the rebels: "Viva Cristo Rey! Viva la Virgen de Guadalupe!" ("Long live Christ the king! Long live the Virgin of Guadalupe!").[25]

21. Napolitano, "The Virgin of Guadalupe," 98.

22. Napolitano, "The Virgin of Guadalupe," 100–101.

23. Blancarte, "The Changing Face," 42.

24. In some places, the state went even further, when police officers set fire to churches and smashed statues of the saints. This has been described as a cultural revolution that was unsuccessful because it met with widespread opposition. See Bantjes, "Burning Saints."

25. Fallaw, *Religion and State Formation*, 13–27.

In 2016, Pope Francis canonized a fourteen-year-old who had been killed on the rebel side.[26] Such religious canonizations by John Paul II and Francis are also political, in the sense that they legitimate this uprising to some extent.[27] The canonizations can be seen as a contribution to the Catholic nation-building: in the eyes of many Catholics, Mexico is not primarily a secular land. It is first and foremost a Catholic nation.

A WEAKENED SECULARISM

The Vatican has long been on the offensive with regard to Mexico. The changes to the law that guaranteed the church a legal status on Mexican territory from 1992 onward can be seen as a diplomatic and political victory for the Vatican, and the same can be said of the attendances at the papal visits to Mexico. The media attention around John Paul II's last visit to Mexico in 2002 was enormous. Millions of Mexicans traveled to Mexico City to be present at the visit, and even more followed it via live broadcasts on television. This was his second visit after the Mexican state had for the first time established diplomatic relations with the Vatican in 1992, but it was the fifth papal visit in all. The fact that the Polish Pope did not visit any other country in the region so frequently indicates Mexico's strategically important role for the church.[28] At the same time, the weakening of secularism in the revised constitution of 1992 shows that it was possible for the church to strengthen its position vis-à-vis the authorities.

In 1992, when John Paul II beatified the poor indigenous man who was said to have had the vision of the Virgin Mary, this was controversial enough—Catholic church leaders in Mexico also protested by affirming that it was not at all certain whether the man being beatified had actually lived, and that the church ought to beatify real persons, not symbols.[29] But the biggest headlines were made when President Vicente Fox kissed the Pope's ring. It was unprecedented for a Mexican head of state to bow his head to

26. Officially, these under-age saints are interpreted as witnesses to Christian fidelity, but to canonize what we today would call child soldiers remains a controversial choice in the eyes of many people. On the fourteen-year-old Mexican José Sánchez del Rio (1913–28), canonized by Pope Francis on October 16, 2016, see the Wikipedia (English) entry "José Sánchez del Rio."

27. According to Catholic canon law, the beatification of an individual deceased person is the first step on the path to canonization. When a person is canonized, he or she is given a place in the calendar of saints of the universal church.

28. See the Wikipedia entry "List of pastoral visits of Pope John Paul II" for an overview of his travels outside Italy.

29. Beatty, "The Pope in Mexico," 326.

Rome in this way, as a choreographed act of submission in the age of the media.[30] The ritual could be interpreted as a direct attack on Mexican secularism, but also as a portent of a stronger political role for the bishops in a country whose inhabitants are suspicious *a priori* of this kind of blending.[31] Besides this, the question of abortion shows that the church's influence in the political sphere is not unlimited.

EVANGELICAL POLITICS IN BRAZIL

Protestant groups were present in Latin America for nearly a century without seeking political power to any great extent. As small religious minorities in lands dominated by Catholicism, they were too few to represent large groups of voters, and their position was far too exposed to allow them to challenge the apparatus of power. Nor had they many adherents in society. In addition, many of them supported a theology that required those who were born again in the Spirit to withdraw from the sinful powers of this world and devote themselves to the fellowship of the saints.[32] But concurrently with their formidable growth towards the end of the twentieth century, Evangelical churches have gradually become political actors in the Latin American democracies. There are now examples in every country in the region of Evangelical churches that promote specific political causes, of pastors who have stood as political candidates, or of other Protestant groups who have attempted to build up their own political parties and blocs. These Evangelical groups are made up of charismatic Christians, many of whom are Pentecostals.

A relatively large group of Protestants, mostly Pentecostals, were elected to the Brazilian Congress already in 1987. They had no very clear agenda, apart from the demand that God should be mentioned in the preamble to the new constitution and that the Bible should have a prominent place in the room where the constitutional assembly met.[33] The fact that they fought for a religious icon rather than for any concrete political issue may indicate that their primary goal was prestige and recognition as a religious minority. A few decades later, this group of politicians had acquired a completely different influence on Brazilian politics. There were far more electors with an Evangelical background, and the campaigning issues of the politicians who

30. Beatty, "The Pope in Mexico," 328.
31. Blancarte, "The Changing Face," 242.
32. Alencar, "Grupos Protestantes," 173.
33. Melo, "Deus."

represented many of them focused on gender and sexuality.[34] Like other Evangelical politicians in Latin America, these Brazilian parliamentarians were involved in political opposition to any relaxation of the restrictive legislation on abortion. They promoted the traditional nuclear family and opposed any extension of LGTBQ rights, which they claimed were nothing else than an expression of so-called "gender ideology." In the 2018 presidential election campaign, several prominent Evangelical pastors and politicians supported Jair Bolsonaro's candidacy, and research indicates that he won the election with almost 70 percent of the votes of Evangelical Christians.[35] In his inaugural address on January 1, 2019, he proclaimed that his mission was to defend the family and fight against "gender ideology."[36]

When the Coronavirus spread to Brazil in March 2020, Bolsonaro's support by Evangelical leaders took on a new dimension. He trivialized the pandemic by claiming that the warnings against the virus were exaggerated and that other types of influenza had taken a far greater number of lives.[37] The reactions among Brazil's Evangelical leaders to the new health threat varied, but many of them took positions close to Bolsonero's. Like the President, the prominent Pentecostal pastor Silas Malafaia warned against panic in face of the virus, while other Pentecostal pastors held that God could intervene to heal believers of the virus. When powerful forces wanted to shut churches and religious buildings in order to limit the spread of the Coronavirus, this belief in miracles and the principle of the freedom of religion were important reasons why Pentecostal leaders and Evangelical politicians mobilized against the closing of churches.[38] Bolsonaro responded to this mobilization by issuing a decree that defined religious groupings as "essential services."[39] The implication was that they must continue to stay open during the pandemic. The decree encountered strong criticism in the courts and had only a limited effect during the pandemic, but the President's attitude was clear: the churches were to remain open at any cost.

Nowhere in Latin America have the Evangelical churches gained greater political power than in Brazil; but there are interesting examples from other Latin American countries of how Evangelical Christianity has abandoned its sectarian and withdrawn social strategy and embraced the possibilities

---

34. Carranza and Cunha, "Conservative Religious Activism"; Smith, *Religion and Brazilian Democracy*.

35. Datafolha, "Intenção de voto."

36. Løland, "Political Conditions," 64.

37. Pfrimer and Barbosa, "Brazil's War on COVID-19," 138.

38. Grossi and Toniol, *Cientistas sociais*, 495–521.

39. Bandeira and Carranza, "Reactions to the Pandemic," 178.

of influence that politics gives. When the Nobel Peace Prize was awarded to
Colombia's President Juan Manuel Santos for negotiating a peace agreement
with the FARC guerilla movement, in order to put an end to Latin America's
longest civil war in recent times, many of the country's Evangelical Christians
took a different view. And there is much to suggest that it was an Evangelical
mobilization that led the majority to say no to the peace agreement when a
referendum was held in 2016.[40] The cause of the Evangelicals' opposition to
the peace agreement was probably the inclusion in the text of the agreement
of formulations about gender and LGBTQ rights.

Many have observed a clearer rightward turn in the role played by the
Evangelical politicians in Brazil,[41] but a new alliance between Evangelicals
and a leftist president has emerged in Mexico. Andrés Manuel López Ob-
rador won the presidential election in 2018 after avoiding taking a position
on questions such as abortion and same-sex marriage. Instead, his election
campaign centered on the moral rebuilding of a Mexico ridden by violence
and corruption. As the candidate of the left, he pulled off the political trick
of getting the rightwing party Encuentro Social to join his coalition; in
Mexico, this is regarded as the party of the Evangelicals.[42]

A CONTINENT AGAINST ABORTION

When abortion up to the twelfth week of pregnancy was decriminalized in
the capital, Mexico City, in 2007, the Catholic church threatened to excom-
municate every politician who voted for this legislative proposal.[43] Under
loud protests from the bishops, the capital was given an abortion law that
was one of the most liberal on the continent—surpassed only by Cuba and
Uruguay. Nor did the church's view prevent the Mexican federal state of
Oaxaca from decriminalizing abortion some years later. In the past, Chilean
women could be punished with imprisonment for up to five years if they
had an abortion, even in the case of severe deformations in the fetus, rape,
or danger to the woman's own life. The law that was promulgated in 1989 by
Pinochet's dictatorship, towards the end of his rule, was abrogated in 2017,
and the abortion legislation was liberalized on these points. The campaign

40. Smith, *Religion and Brazilian Democracy*, 163.

41. Carranza, "Apresentação"

42. Delgado-Molina, "Evangélicos Y Poder Político," 55.

43. Pope Benedict XVI left a mistaken impression that the Mexican politicians had
been excommunicated; but the bishops had only threatened to impose this ecclesiastical sanction; see Thavis, *Vatican Diaries*, 37–38.

to mitigate the law was led by Michelle Bachelet, Chile's president at the time, who is herself a pediatrician.

Across the whole of Latin America, Catholic and Protestant church leaders seek to warn against every relaxation of the abortion laws. They know that most Latin Americans are more liberal on this issue than they themselves, and this is why it is important for them to influence opinion in the direction that they themselves regard as correct with regard to abortion law. However, large sectors of the population support them in their restrictive attitude. Skepticism about abortion is demonstrably higher among people in Latin America than in Western Europe and the USA.[44] And even a strong leftist party like the Brazilian Workers' Party (PT) has made the guarantee at elections that it will not extend the right to abortion in a country where the only valid reasons for having an abortion are rape or danger to the mother's life. In this way, they avoided the otherwise inevitable opposition on the part of Catholic bishops and Evangelical leaders.

In the neighboring country, Argentina, many were surprised at the considerable support given to a proposal to legalize abortion when it was presented for discussion in Congress in 2018. Before the vote was taken, the streets were full of people in green who demonstrated in favor of legalization and people in blue who opposed any relaxation. In response above all to feminist NGOs and social movements, the number of organizations that mobilize against any relaxation of the abortion legislation in Argentina has increased noticeably in recent years. With apparently secular names such as "Eligimos la Vida" (We choose life"), these groups have succeeded in making the abortion issue into something more than a purely religious matter.[45] At the same time, both Pentecostal pastors and Catholic bishops in the country have employed their full moral weight to stop the legalization. This probably contributed to a slender majority against the legalization of abortion in 2018, which meant that the penal legislation from 1921 against women who had abortions still remained in effect. However, after Alfredo Fernandez won the presidential election in 2019 with a promise to legalize abortion, fresh movement came into the issue, and in December 2020, the government's proposal of legal abortion up to the twelfth week in pregnancy passed the two chambers of Congress. This made Argentina the first large country in Latin America to legalize abortion, and this may have a regional ripple effect. No other country in Latin America in the past decade has witnessed a similar political mobilization to elaborate an abortion legislation that breaks with the explicit position of the Catholic church.

44. Htun, "Life," 349.

45. Morán Faúndes et al., "Strategies," 144–62.

There are few countries in the world in which abortion is illegal under all circumstances, and it is not by chance that five of these are in Latin
America. In the Dominican Republic, El Salvador, Haiti, Honduras, and
Nicaragua, the state can prosecute women who have an abortion, even if
their own life is at risk. When Zika fever spread in Latin America in 2015,
some wondered if this might affect the rigid attitudes to abortion in the region, since this fever leads to mothers with the virus giving birth to children
with neurological impairments or functional handicaps. But the church's
doctrine is not changed merely because of situations such as this. According
to Catholic theology, life is to be defended from the moment of conception,
and abortion is to be seen as a murder. This means that abortion is a very
grave sin, so that state laws permitting abortion are immoral. This shows
how Catholicism intervenes in people's lives in a resolute manner.

The abortion question shows how the Catholic church endeavors to
influence politics and legislation. In these attempts to exercise influence,
the church can exploit the politicians' need for legitimacy in the eyes of the
people. The outcome of this power struggle between politicians and bishops
depends largely on credibility: the greater the credibility one has, the less
one will be inclined to yield to pressure from the other group. If the state
loses credibility in people's eyes, it is possible that they will put more trust
in the church. From 2006 onward, Mexico has been hit by a dramatic increase in violence related to drug smuggling. Not only criminal groups, but
also the police and the military have been involved in torture, kidnapping,
and extrajudicial killings. This has thrust the state into a profound crisis of
legitimacy,[46] and this in turn has meant that even the PRI ("Partido Revo-
lucionario Institucional"), the dominant political party, which emerged
from a secularist political tradition, has yielded more and more to political
pressure from religious groups such as the Catholic hierarchy.[47] In many
Latin American countries, the state is associated with corruption, whereas
the Catholic church is one of the societal institutions that enjoys the highest credibility among the people and that therefore possesses considerable
moral capital. There is, however, one country that diverges strongly from
this picture—Chile, whose people have little confidence in the church.[48] In
2010, the accusations against the Catholic priest Fernando Karadima were
made public, and this was followed by a series of abuse scandals that rocked
the country. Several of the most prominent bishops in the country now

46. Carpenter, "Changing Lenses," 139.

47. At the time of writing, Enrique Peña Nieto, President of Mexico since 2012, has
not yet achieved one of his priorities: permitting same-sex marriage on the federal level.

48. Corporación Latinobarómetro, "Informe," 49.

appeared in the public eye as men who had protected pedophile abusers, and many Catholics boycotted their own church in the following years; others left it for good. Pope Francis visited Chile in 2018. In country after country, the first Latin American Pope in history had been welcomed by enthusiastic crowds, but in Chile he was met by huge protests on the streets— the first time that this had happened on a state visit. People demanded that he should put a stop to the abusers, and the Chilean church was in crisis. Three months later, the Pope took a step that none of his predecessors had ever taken: he summoned all the bishops of the country to a crisis meeting in Rome, and all the bishops responded to his intervention by submitting their resignations. This too was a first in church history; never before had an entire episcopal conference resigned. And nowhere in Latin America had the church's reputation been so badly damaged as in Chile.

In addition to abortion, same-sex marriage is a disputed issue where bishops and pastors attempt to influence public opinion and politicians. The outcome of this struggle is uncertain, but neither Catholic bishops nor Pentecostal pastors have succeeded in preventing countries such as Argentina, Brazil, Uruguay, and Colombia from introducing same-sex marriage. The first Latin American land to permit this was Argentina in 2010, despite protests from the then Cardinal Jorge Bergoglio (later elected pope), who called this a project aimed at destroying God's plan for the world.[49] As Pope, however, the Argentinian has spoken in favor of civil partnerships for homosexuals, with a clear reservation that such a partnership is not a real marriage, which exists only between a man and a woman.[50]

ARGENTINA—THE POPE'S SECULARIZED HOME COUNTRY

The then Cardinal Bergoglio's failure to win acceptance for his stance on same-sex marriage was also an expression of the weakened position of the Catholic church in Argentina, as was the vast mobilization for the legalization of abortion in the years leading up to 2020. Argentina is one of the most secularized countries in Latin America, in the sense that the inhabitants take a critical view of the church's attempts to determine what happens in the state and in politics. A poll carried out in 2000 showed that 76 percent of those asked in Argentina held that religious leaders ought not to influence the political choice of voters. The percentage for Argentina was much

49. Larraquy, *Código Francisco*, 352.
50. Wolton, *Future of Faith*.

higher than in Venezuela, Mexico, and Chile.[51] It is only in Uruguay that fewer people regularly attend church services than in Argentina, where the percentage is nearly 25 percent, a relatively low figure in the Latin American context.[52] And after the election of an Argentinian to the papacy in 2013, few signs were seen of a Catholic renaissance among ordinary people, of the kind experienced in Poland in eastern Europe, after their fellow countryman became Pope in 1978. On the contrary, Catholicism in Argentina has been in marked decline during the period in which Francis has been the church's head. Between 2009 and 2018, the proportion of Catholics in the population sank from 76.5 to 62.9 percent, and the proportion who said that they had no religion rose to nearly 20 percent.[53] Statistically, this can be compared with Catholic-dominated European lands; and Argentina has in fact been regarded as one of the most European countries in Latin America. To take one example: the indigenous population constitutes a much smaller part of the population in Argentina than in other lands on the continent.

At the same time, the country has had a relatively high level of prosperity, and a number of welfare structures were introduced under the rule of Juán Perón (1946–55). But Perón's presidency also saw an aggressive secularization, when the popular president reduced the priests' salaries and legalized divorce. Perón's government was the origin of the Peronist political movement. When he abolished Catholic feast days as public holidays and replaced them with Peronist celebrations, powerful forces in the church reacted. The military leaders were waiting for a pretext to overthrow the democratically elected president, and the military took power in a coup in 1955, with the support of Argentinian bishops. The last coup before the transition to democracy took place in 1976 and launched the most brutal political oppression in recent Argentinian history. Members of the leftwing opposition, including Catholic groups with links to liberation theology, were arrested, tortured, and killed under the junta's rule until 1983. The fact that both many victims and many perpetrators were convinced Catholics shows how divided Argentinian Catholicism was.

The military seized power through coups d'état in large areas of Latin America in the 1970s and 1980s, but Argentina was an exceptional case, thanks to the symbolic and explicit support that several Catholic bishops gave to the military regime. While Catholic bishops in other Latin American countries risked their lives in their efforts to defend human rights, most of the Argentinian bishops were strikingly silent about the abuses in their

51. Hagopian, "Introduction," 27.
52. Hagopian, "Introduction," 17.
53. Mallimaci et al., "Religiones y creencias," 15.

native land. This was also the case with Jorge Bergoglio, who was the superior of the Jesuit province in the country during the dictatorship.

In other parts of the world, revelations about sexual abuses in Catholic institutions have given the church an immense credibility problem in the present century; but the Argentinian church already had a huge reputational problem after the dictatorship ceased.[54] Stories of Catholic military chaplains who blessed torture and of bishops who praised the military junta meant that many Argentinians wanted to have as little as possible to do with the church. And while the churches in Brazil, Chile, and Guatemala were important actors in the establishing of truth commissions about the abuses under the dictatorships, the bishops in Argentina worked against the truth commission in their country. While Desmond Tutu became the great symbol of the commission in South Africa, the leader of the work for reconciliation in Argentina was Ernesto Sabato—not a bishop, but a writer and an atheist.[55] This was why the struggle for human rights was carried out in Argentina by groups outside the Catholic church. In the past, ordinary church members were active in the church's own organizations, but now the same members are active primarily in secular NGOs. No other Latin American country has such a low level of participation in voluntary religious associations or organizations as Argentina.[56] In this area too, the country has undergone a secularization.

If the Catholic church wants to have a leader who understands both the religious flourishing that marks many Latin American countries and the secularization that leads people either to distance themselves from the church or to lose interest in it, Bergoglio from Argentina may have been a good choice. As an Argentinian, he has one foot in the European sphere and the other foot in the Latin American sphere. But as an Argentinian who has lived for most of his life in the megalopolis that is Buenos Aires, he has little experience of another important aspect of Latin American Catholicism: the religiosity of the indigenous population.

THE CHRISTIANITY OF THE
INDIGENOUS POPULATION

Latin America has a large indigenous population, roughly one-third of whom live in Mexico. Most are poor; in Mexico, 90 percent of the indigenous

54. Morello, "Transformations," 243.

55. Morello, "Transformations," 246.

56. The survey was carried out in 2000 in Argentina, Brazil, Chile, Mexico, Peru, and Venezuela. See Hagopian, "Social Justice," 279.

population live in poverty.[57] Mexico's national patron, the Virgin of Guadalupe, has been venerated as the benefactress of the poor. At the same time, the dark-skinned Madonna has been regarded as a mestiza, a mingling of indigenous and European. In this way, she incarnates the mestizo identity, which is seen as the primal Mexican reality in a land where "Indio" still bears negative connotations. This means that the 10 percent who count themselves as the indigenous population will present themselves as "mestizo,"[58] *inter alia* in order to avoid discrimination. But precisely the fact that the Mexican mestizo identity of the Virgin has been the example many follow has been one of the signals that the indigenous population never fitted in to the Catholic and national ideals in Mexico.

Even after five hundred years in Mexico, the Catholic church has never become a church of the indigenous population. It has not succeeded in recruiting them to the priesthood, and the distanced relationship that these ethnic groups have had to the church is probably one reason why far more of them have become Pentecostals. In any case, they have never felt themselves to be as Catholic as the mestizo population. Chiapas is one of the federal states with the highest proportion of indigenous persons, and almost half of the indigenous population there no longer regard themselves as Catholics.[59]

In part, this can be interpreted as an expression of a stronger political self-awareness and cultural pride among the indigenous groups in Latin America. Since the five hundred years' jubilee for Columbus' "discovery" of America, in 1992, groups of the indigenous population have organized themselves and mobilized more and more strongly by means of social protests. One of the results of these protests was a president whose profile proclaimed that he came from the indigenous population: the Aymara Bolivian Evo Morales, who was Bolivia's president from 2006 to 2019. He is one of between thirty-five and fifty million inhabitants in Latin America with a provenance in the indigenous population; and these in turn are divided into various ethnic groups with their own languages. Bolivia, Guatemala, Peru, and Ecuador are the countries with the highest percentage of indigenous population. At the same time, no one really knows how many people there are in Latin America who have no European provenance. It is difficult to count; and ethnicity is an important reality that is experienced on the basis of distinct differences in skin color and appearance.

---

57. The figure for the population as a whole is 50 percent. See Lazo de la Vega and Steigenga, "Indigenous Peoples," 559–61.

58. Norget, *Days of Death*, 58.

59. Navarro, "Religious Change in Mexico," 90.

Liberation theology, as a special form of Latin American Christianity, emerged from the 1960s onward. The liberation theologians combined Catholic theology with a radical criticism of society, and were primarily concerned about the dimension of poverty in the oppression in Latin America. Gradually, however, many of them turned their attention to the cultural marginalization under which the indigenous population lived. Already during the Second Vatican Council (1962–65), the Ecuadorian Bishop Leonidas Eduardo Proaño Villalba (1910–88) had argued that one must pay attention to the living conditions of the indigenous population, but this was never mentioned in the conciliar documents.[60] He was one of the more than two thousand Catholic bishops from all over the world who met in the Vatican for what Catholic tradition sees as the only authority that is higher than the pope, namely, a council. An ecclesial meeting of this kind thus enjoys great authority and significance for what the church's teaching and praxis are to be.

For the first time in history, bishops from the global South were in the majority, and this meant that the council agenda included important societal questions such as poverty and underdevelopment. The bishop of Chiapas, Samuel Ruíz García, was one of the council fathers who most prominently urged that the church must spearhead action for the rights of the poor. Originally, the bishop had wanted to make the indigenous population more "western" and "enlightened," but he ended up by himself seeking instruction in the indigenous population's own culture. During his first years as bishop, he wanted the entire indigenous population to learn Spanish, but he then changed his mind: instead, the church's people ought to learn the indigenous languages and elaborate a specific theology of the indigenous population on the basis of the culture that was proper to them. This work was exceptional; otherwise, Catholicism's attempts to become a church for the indigenous population were either lacking or unsuccessful. Under Ruíz García's leadership, deacons from the indigenous population were ordained to serve the church.[61] Endeavors of this kind to give the indigenous population an increased self-determination and to make them owners of Christianity on their own cultural premises are still today an important inheritance from liberation theology in Latin America.[62]

60. Løland, *Lidio*, 79–81.

61. Lazo de la Vega and Steigenga, "Indigenous Peoples," 567.

62. Another important inheritance from liberation theology is the legitimacy and inspiration it gave presidents who represented the political leftwing in Latin America in the 2000s; see Levitsky and Roberts, *Resurgence*. Presidents Luiz Inácio Lula da Silva (2003–11), Fernando Lugo (2008–12), and Hugo Chávez (1999–2013) all came from the political left and had links to the ideas and the groups of liberation theology. On

The central role played by this diocese in creating a greater political awareness among the indigenous population also helps to explain why Mexico's authorities accused Bishop Ruíz of being an accomplice in the flourishing of the guerilla EZLN, which was led by Subcomandante Marcos. But while Mexico's President Ernesto Zedillo accused the bishop of ideologizing the indigenous population, there is little to indicate that the diocese took the step of arming them.[63] Throughout Latin America, however, liberation theology has been an important source of inspiration for social movements, such as the landless movement in Brazil.

On the one hand, the Catholic clergy who were oriented to liberation theology were among the most active in the defense of the culture of groups in the population who were outside the dominant mestizo culture. In Brazil, for example, the liberation theologian Cardinal Paul Evaristo Arns (1921–2016) was a leader in developing a specifically Afro-American theology in close dialogue with the religiosity of the descendants of the slaves from Africa.[64] On the other hand, these liberation theologians were marginalized and were passed over for appointments to influential positions in the church after 1978, under Pope John Paul II, and a part of their work met with direct opposition. Arns was created cardinal by Pope Paul VI in 1973, and it was impossible for later popes to declare this decision invalid. But the Vatican under John Paul II decided that Arns's diocese of São Paulo should be split up into five parts, thus making possible the nomination of more conservative bishops and a reduction in Arns's influence.[65] Together with the censorship of liberation theological literature and the imposition of silence on Leonardo Boff, a central liberation theologian, these church-political moves also meant that some of the most prominent defenders of the indigenous population within the church were pushed aside.[66] Since bishops often remain in positions of leadership for many years, the episcopal appointments of a pope leave their mark for a long time on how the worldwide church is led.

However, the same pope made "inculturation" one of his central concerns. In the Catholic tradition, inculturation is justified by the argument that there are traces of what is Christian in every culture before Christianity's message is proclaimed in it, and this is why parts of these pre-Christian cultures can take their place and be used among the church's symbols and

Chávez's embrace of liberation theology, see Løland, "Hugo Chávez's Appropriation."

63. Stålsett, "Liberation Theology," 150.

64. Arns, "Palavras De Dom Paulo."

65. Cleary, "Brazilian Catholic Church," 261; Hewitt, "Popular Movements."

66. Lazo de la Vega and Steigenga, "Indigenous Peoples," 567–78.

practices. Since a culturally oriented theme like "inculturation" has been more acceptable in the Catholic church than the more politically oriented motif of "liberation," some of the radical theologians have also continued their work among the indigenous population while claiming that they are following the official line on "inculturation." The underlying disagreements with Rome can emerge in this work too, however: while Pope John Paul II held that the Christian gospel had an immutable core that had to be translated into the various cultures,[67] Catholic theologians from the indigenous groups claimed that the content of the gospel took on a different meaning on the basis of the lifestyle, mythology, and rituals of the poor indigenous population. In their eyes, it was European interpretations of the gospel—such as those the Pope proclaimed in his travels across the globe—that had to be wrested from their eurocentrism in order to become a true way of talking about the gospel in the life sphere of the indigenous population.[68]

In addition to a violent conflict about the rights of the indigenous population, the federal state of Chiapas in southern Mexico has also been the scene of some of the most violent reactions on the Latin American continent against Catholics who join Protestant congregations. When Pope Francis visited the federal state in 2016, his silence on this topic attracted a certain amount of attention.[69] Of all the Latin American countries, Mexico has seen the greatest outbreak of religious persecution of those who change to a new Christian denomination. When Mexicans abandon Catholicism, they can encounter strong reactions on the part of family, friends, and their social milieu; this also partly explains why some of them return to Catholicism.[70] In response to door-to-door evangelization by Protestant Christians in the 1990s, one could see signs on people's doors that read: "This is a Catholic home. We do not accept propaganda from Protestants or any other sects."[71]

The Mexican Protestants also part company with another central aspect of Mexican social life, especially in the villages: every place in Mexico has a patron saint and often a huge patronal feast for everyone who lives there. The responsibility for paying for the feast often goes around from one person to another, year by year. The consumption of alcohol is an integral

67. Bevans, *Models of Contextual Theology*, 49–53.

68. Orta, "Inculturation Theology," 598.

69. This was pointed out (for example) in the North American magazine *Christianity Today*, which is part of a Protestant Christianity in the USA that sends a large number of missionaries from the USA to southern Mexico. See Zylstra, "Pope Francis Quiet."

70. Gross, "Changing Faith."

71. Hartch, *Rebirth of Latin American Christianity*, 19.

element at this feast. Whereas Catholics often have a liberal relationship to alcohol, the Pentecostals are restrictive. When a newly converted Pentecostal refuses to fulfill this obligation, which is both symbolic and highly material, the reactions can be strong. Together with pilgrimage journeys, the cult of the saints and religious festivals are basic ingredients in the phenomenon known as "popular Catholicism," the Catholicism of the people.

POPULAR CATHOLICISM AFTER OSCAR ROMERO

As we have mentioned, the Catholic church in Latin America as a whole never became a church of the indigenous population. But nor did it ever become an orthodox church in the sense that the roughly four hundred million Catholics on the continent today are believers in the way that large sections of clergy wish. "Yo soy católico, pero a mi manera" ("I am a Catholic, but in my own way") is a common expression used by Catholics to indicate a certain distance vis-à-vis official Catholicism.

Catholicism worldwide is not only official Catholic doctrines that are taught and practiced among loyal believers. In Latin America, "Catholicism" can be understood as a set of practices, ideas about the faith, and customs that are realized and shaped by various forms of socialization in daily living.[72] When these religious practices are carried out outside the control of the clergy, for example, outside the liturgical and theological frameworks of the Catholic Mass, this can be called popular Catholicism.

In some instances, however, people can try to get the priests' recognition for the practices that they invent or maintain in fellowship, and they can also find inspiration in the church's leadership and its official preaching. In 1980, Archbishop Óscar Romeo was shot by a marksman sent by the regime, after he had criticized the government's death squadrons and their massacres of civilians. It was obvious to the church in El Salvador that Romero was a martyr; indeed, he was shot while he was celebrating Mass. But the Pope was unwilling to canonize him, since he thought that would worsen the political conflict that had hurled the country into a civil war. Nevertheless, people in El Salvador venerated the archbishop as a saint for many years before Pope Francis decided to complete the beatification process in 2015 and to canonize him in 2018. The archbishop was "San Romero" among ordinary Salvadorians long before he received this title officially,[73] although it was primarily the Salvadorian state that sought to

---

72. Norget, *Days of Death*, 65.

73. Hughes, "Contemporary Popular Catholicism," 487–88.

crush his veneration as a saint. During the civil war in the 1980s, a picture of the martyr on people's walls could lead to harassment by the military.[74]

In other instances, the church can attempt more aggressively to abolish popular customs. The cult of the female figure *La Santa Muerte* ("The holy death") became publicly known when a Catholic woman moved her domestic altar out onto the street in 2001. By this time, a stable group of adherents had consolidated the worship of the figure of death as a cult, and since then, many street altars have been dedicated to her, especially in those districts in Mexico City where death loomed as a threat to the inhabitants above all in the form of violence and organized crime. Besides this, many prison guards and police officers are adherents of this cult, where the icon of death is venerated by asking for help in concrete situations, in the same way as Catholics pray to other Catholic saints. Only four years passed before the celebrated cult was banned by the church, which declared it to be heretical.[75] This does not appear to have affected its popularity. Many want to be Catholics in their own way.

WHEN THE DEAD COME BACK

Over the course of history, both the state and the church in Mexico have made sporadic attempts to crush the people's celebration of death, the day of the dead.[76] Today, however, the clergy make cautious arrangements for the celebration of this exceedingly popular feast, and the state regards the whole thing as folklore that can be sold to tourists.[77]

Imagine that you arrive as a tourist in a Mexican town at the end of October. When you alight from the bus and look at the shop windows, you will see loaves shaped like skeletons and colorful skulls made of sugar and chocolate. If you listen to the Mexicans chatting with each other, you can hear them say cheerfully to each other: "Ya vienen los muertos" ("Soon the dead will come").

Then a parade of people pass by—dressed up like death, with skeletons in every conceivable shape and colorful motifs. The faces of the living are covered with paint and masks, and you see death's grimaces everywhere. But death is not first and foremost a serious threat: the dressing up and the playfulness turn it into a carnival. People drink and celebrate at bars and cafés. The city is in a festival mood.

74. Vasquez and Peterson, "Oscar Romero," 271.
75. Kristensen, "La Santa Muerte."
76. Norget, *Days of Death*, 192.
77. Norget, *Days of Death*, 220.

Perhaps you have read in government tourist brochures that the feast is originally pagan and pre-Columbian,[78] but you may be surprised when the Mexicans explain the content of the feast to you with the aid of recognizably Christian terms about heaven and hell, and not least purgatory. According to the Catholic faith, most people must assume that they will have to atone for sin in purgatory before the souls can be admitted to heaven. While Protestantism abolished requiem Masses, the cult of the saints, and the idea of a purgatory, thereby eliminating the possibility of having contact with the dead, Catholicism (and especially the popular Catholicism in Latin America) does not maintain such an absolute division between the living and the dead. The relationship is more mobile and elastic, and this is what the masks on the street parade express: the dead are not completely dead. Unlike a funeral, this is not purely a time of mourning; the dead are able for a short time to see the living and to be with them again, and this is what is celebrated. The souls of the dead come back to their relatives' homes in order to enjoy the fruits of the earth with their loved ones. It is therefore not by chance that this celebration is so popular precisely in Mexico, where harvesting takes place at this time of year.

The feast is celebrated throughout Latin America on All Saints Day (November 1) and All Souls Day (November 2). The manner of its celebration varies from place to place. The anthropologist Kristin Norget relates from her fieldwork in the Mexican federal state Oaxaca that many people go to Mass around these days. They visit the cemeteries, and the graves are decorated with flowers. People take a glass of schnapps and eat a meal with their loved ones who have come back. An orchestra is often hired for the occasion, and in some cemeteries the priests celebrate an open-air Mass for those who are strongly practicing Catholics. This is the public celebration. But if you go into a private home, especially in Mexico, you will find big private altars built in remembrance of the dead relatives. Here, it is not male priests who are the exclusive masters of ceremonies: the women often direct everything, both the practical and the ritual aspects. Pictures of the deceased are placed on the altar together with *ofrendas*, an abundance of food and drink, with lamps and often with incense. In the evening, the family come together before the altar.

As a tourist, you are involved in the further development of this tradition. You are helping the state and industry to commercialize a popular Catholicism that has been practiced by the less well-off sector of the population. The liberal elites have often looked down on this popular Catholicism

---

78. Norget, *Days of Death.*

as something primitive and culturally backward.[79] Today, various interests are at play: for many, the celebration exists in order to honor the dead, while others are mostly concerned about how the tradition can help Mexico remain one of the most popular tourist destinations in the world.[80]

In any case, the day of the dead illustrates a fundamental characteristic of Christianity in Latin America. The assumption that the souls of the dead can come back reflects the belief that spirits or spiritual beings can enter into your life. The prominent role played by supernatural powers in life here and now also leads to a widespread belief in healings among both Catholics and Protestants.

THE SUPPOSITION THAT THE SPIRITS HAVE POWER

Protestantism in Latin America can be divided into two categories. On the one hand, we find the more traditional Protestant churches with a long history in the region: Lutherans, Methodists, and Anglicans, who have an appeal in parts of the middle classes. Belief in spirits plays a lesser role here. On the other hand, we have the Pentecostal revival with a far larger number of adherents, a greater appeal among the poor, and a stronger belief in the power of the spirits. This characteristic, which is shared with popular Catholicism, means that Protestant growth in the form of the Pentecostal revival results in something very different from the Protestantism we know from northern Europe.[81]

Belief in spirits has always been strong in the religions of the indigenous population. On the one hand, the attempts of Catholic theologians to include more of these religions inside the frameworks of Catholicism are one way of making amends to the oppressed faith of the indigenous peoples and of Afro-Americans, and giving this faith dignity. These priests hope that this in turn will generate a greater tolerance in society, especially with regard to the cultures of the poor.

On the other hand, there are churches and sects that zealously carry out missionary work to make the indigenous peoples and the descendants of the African slaves abandon completely the religious inheritance from their

79. This class dimension in popular Catholicism means (for example) that one seldom sees people from the upper economic segments in society eating in the cemeteries. See Norget, *Days of Death*, 68.

80. Morales Cano and Mysyk, "Cultural Tourism," 882.

81. An argument for similarities between the new Pentecostal revival and popular Catholicism can be found in Løland, "Position of the Biblical Canon."

ancestors. One of these churches is the Universal Church of the Kingdom of God ("Igreja Universal do Reino de Deus," IURD), the largest Pentecostal church in Brazil within what is regarded as the Neo-Pentecostal revival.[82] These churches make use of the new media, while at the same time proclaiming the necessity of exorcisms in order to be saved and participate in God's blessings. Unlike classic Pentecostals, the Neo-Pentecostals hold that these blessings find expression through mental good health and material abundance in the here and now. One part of this is imported televangelism from the USA, but this is fused with a number of elements from Brazilian religion. Although classic forms are dominant in Pentecostal Christianity in Brazil, the IURD is a genuinely Brazilian Pentecostal church that illustrates how Pentecostal Christianity is shaped by the specific Brazilian context.

This church has experienced an astronomic growth since it was founded in 1977 by Edir Macedo as a completely new church. Today, it owns the country's second-largest television company and has attracted roughly two million adherents. This Pentecostal church became well and truly known when one of its pastors kicked and crushed a clay statue of Brazil's patroness, the Virgin of Aparecida, on live TV. Since then, the church has also shocked people by exorcising the spirits that are venerated in Afro-American religion: it claims that they are demons. Macedo launched these exorcistic rituals in the church as part of a "holy war" against the demons in the Afro-American faith of the descendants of the African slaves in Brazil. Whether Catholic saints or African spiritual beings, they must be expelled, because (according to Macedo) they have entered into a pact with the devil. In modern eyes, this aggressive preaching is a prime example of religious intolerance, but for many who have grown up with Afro-American rituals such as Candomblé and Umbanda, the Neo-Pentecostals' spiritual warfare is meaningful. They confirm that the pre-modern belief in spirits is worth taking seriously, since life itself is at stake in the encounter with these spirits. The exorcisms are meant to bring healing and to give you hope that you will get well again when neither modern medicine nor the public health sector is adequate.

For these Christians, the devil and the demons are potentially present everywhere. Everything, from financial problems to fear and depressions, can be explained as the work of evil spirits. But since "false religions" are a particularly strong form of demonic possession, it is vital to free oneself from false Catholic and Afro-American religion. In its YouTube videos and mass meetings, the church gives a large place to testimonies from persons who have succeeded in freeing themselves from pagan customs. One of the groups who have testified to their breach with "false" Afro-religion and to

---

82. Scholars tend to employ the term "Neo-Pentecostal" for this type of religion.

their consequent conversion to Jesus is made up of the women known as "ex-mãe-de-santo." Most of these are Afro-Brazilian women who, in accordance with the message of the IURD church, affirm that what they practiced in the past under the wings of Catholicism is a devilish religious practice. The pastors and members of this church regard these women as the best qualified to explain how the demons act in an Afro-Brazilian cult.[83] These testimonies are broadcast via the church's television company, and function both as sensational revelations of "occult witchcraft" and as dramatic accounts of conversions.

MISSION AND CONVERSION

Accounts of personal drama occasioned by Christian conversions flourish in Latin America. Many people can tell about how Jesus has transformed their lives and caused them to abandon their old faith to join a new faith, often in a Pentecostal church. The fact that as many as a quarter of Brazil's adult population have joined another church than the one in which they grew up has caused researchers to be skeptical about the exceptional conversion experience to which the believers bear witness.[84] And the fact that many of them change their religious membership several times in the course of their lives has also contributed to the establishing of "conversion careers" as a research concept. Although many of these religious "careers" revitalize Christianity in Latin America and contribute to its growth, the analyses of them reveals another development: the newly converted tend to be active for some years in the new church, and then leave it. In Brazil, most of the Brazilians who leave a Pentecostal church end up with no religion.[85] This is a rapidly growing group, although they amounted in 2010 only to a modest 8 percent of the population.[86] There are good reasons to ask whether one result of the revivals is that more people part company with organized religion. Of all the Christian groups in Latin America, it is Catholicism that has lost the greatest number of adherents to religious breakaways and conversion. The fact that one was baptized was enough for a person to count as a Catholic. Conversions that have indicated a new direction for life have largely been reserved to the religious elite in Latin America: priests, monks, and nuns.

83. Birman, "Conversion," 120.
84. Frigerio, "Analyzing Conversion," 46.
85. Gooren, "Conversion Careers," 63.
86. See Institutio Brasileiro de Geografia e Estatística, Censo demográfico 2010.

The Second Vatican Council wanted to change the traditional central-
ity of the clergy in Catholicism. The bishops at the Council (1962–65) affirmed that not only the priests were the people of God: the laity, that is to
say, the members who are not priests, were of full value as a part of God's
people, and their mission in the world was just as important as that of the
priests. The conciliar documents state that they too are to be missionary.[87]
Liberation theology in Latin America was one of the ecclesial movements
that were most strongly inspired by the Council to give the laity leading
and important roles, including in the so-called base communities. Although
these never reached the majority of the Catholics in Latin America, they had
a profound influence on ordinary church members, many of whom came
to a new realization of the social and political dimension of faith. In these
communities, it was often the poor who had responsibility for the celebration of worship and the interpretation of scripture, with no priest present.
However, more conservative forces in the church thought that some of this
went too far, and under Pope John Paul II the Vatican issued clear instruc-
tions that the distinction between priests and laity was not to be erased.[88]

Many waited in suspense for the Latin American Pope's first theological writing. It was published as *Evangelii Gaudium* ("The joy of the gospel")
in 2013 and was downloaded very widely. The Argentinian wrote that he
hoped that everyone in the church would "devote the necessary effort to
advancing along the path of a pastoral and missionary conversion."[89] And
a conversion could not simply leave things as they were. The Pope wanted
change, and his wish was that the Catholic church throughout the world
might be "permanently in a state of mission."[90]

Conversion, evangelization, and mission had been keywords for the
Protestant Pentecostal revival in Latin America for several decades. On the
other hand, *inculturation* was a typically Catholic concept, and *mission* has
often been used in a Catholic context for more practical charitable work.
When all the bishops in Latin America met in the Brazilian city of Aparecida in 2007, the concept of inculturation was strikingly absent from the
final documents.[91] Instead, the bishops elaborated a plan for a campaign
that would make all the baptized "disciples and missionaries" through "a

87. Decree about the apostolic activity of the laity, *Apostolicam Actuositatem*, promulgated by Pope Paul VI on November 18, 1965.

88. In 2002, for example, the Vatican Congregation for the Clergy issued the document "The Priest, Pastor and Leader of the Parish Community."

89. Francis, *Evangelii Gaudium* § 25.

90. Francis, *Evangelii Gaudium* § 25.

91. Thorsen, *Charismatic Practice*, 196.

personal encounter with Jesus."[92] The then Cardinal Jorge Bergoglio played a decisive role in the creation of these formulae. In his papal document *Evangelii Gaudium*, this new Catholic agenda for mission from Aparecida is elevated to a global level.[93] The new competition for the Catholics in Latin America has given the world's largest religious organization a leader who is on the offensive.

This is not only a result of the theology of Pope Francis and other Latin American bishops. Zeal for mission was also promoted via Pope Benedict XVI's program for new evangelization.[94] Benedict set up a Pontifical Council for the New Evangelization in 2010, with particular attention to the USA, Europe, and Latin America. As pope, however, Benedict XVI was primarily involved in the Christian Europe, which he saw as threatened by secularization and relativism. In his activity as pope, Benedict continued the work he had carried out over many years in defense of the coexistence between Greek philosophy and Christian theology.

Unlike his predecessor Benedict, Pope Francis was not known first and foremost for his work in theology. He came directly from a more practical work in parishes, with particular attention to urban districts in Argentina's capital, Buenos Aires. This was work carried out in the heart of the new Latin American situation of competition, where a new Catholic self-awareness had emerged, which found expression *inter alia* in what is now the world's largest Catholic lay movement, the Catholic charismatic renewal (CCR). It has obvious similarities to the Pentecostal movement, and embraces glossolalia, songs of praise, and what they believe to be a direct experience of the Holy Spirit. It is difficult to estimate numbers globally, but several scholars in Latin America reckon that the movement has about seventy million adherents.[95] Nowhere else are so many charismatic Catholics to be found.

92. Concluding document of the Latin American Bishops' Conference meeting in Aparecida in 2007, quoted and translated in *Evangelii Gaudium*.

93. Thorsen, *Charismatic Practice*, 217.

94. Under Pope Benedict XVI, the theme of the Synod of Bishops in 2012 was "The New Evangelization for the Transmission of the Christian Faith." In the Catholic church, a synod is a group of bishops from a wide geographical area who meet to function as an advisory organ for the pope on central questions. In 2015, the theme was the family.

95. For example, Chesnut, "Conservative Christian Competitors," 94.

BRAZIL—THE CENTER OF
CHARISMATIC CATHOLICISM

It is an ordinary Sunday, and the Santuário Mãe de Deus church in the Brazilian megalopolis São Paulo is full of people. Masses are broadcast from this church every day, and on Sundays they are extra-well attended: Often, thirty thousand Catholics stand shoulder to shoulder inside the church, while even more stand outside, waiting their turn to get in for the Mass. The church has a capacity of a hundred thousand. It was built after a former factory building became too small for the worshipers—and the factory in its turn had been taken over and adapted after another local church had proved too small. The priest was too popular. His name is Marcelo Rossi.[96]

The faithful do not attend this church because they live in the parish; many come from other parts of São Paulo and Brazil. They may perhaps be members of one of the Catholic charismatic prayer groups that have become so numerous that it is difficult for church leaders or scholars to have a full overview of them. They are mostly made up of young and middle-aged women who have turned to charismatic Catholicism for the same reasons that have led others to join the Pentecostal revival: they are seeking physical or spiritual healing from individual problems such as depressions, drug dependency, and other protracted illnesses. They also want a more wholehearted and pure form of the worship of God. Although these women are looking for one or other kind of healing, they have nothing against the Catholic faith in which they grew up. On the contrary, they desire to cultivate it in a purer form, but without either what they see as a mixture with popular religion or the aid of the aggressive form that is practiced in Neo-Pentecostal churches. In Marcelo Rossi's church, they get a milder form of charismatic religion that is sustained by intimate and soothing songs of praise. They also get a completely distinct form of charismatic Catholicism, with the Virgin Mary at its center. This makes clear the boundary line that separates them from charismatic Protestantism.[97]

Here there is no trace of what many regard as the "syncretistic" popular faith in Brazil that mixes together different religions that allegedly do not belong together. And this is why local saints from the colonial period do not play a central role in worship. Charismatic Catholicism is experienced by many as a purer form of Christianity. And not least: Marcelo's Rossi's clerical attire reassures the faithful that, despite the charismatic form, this is not Protestantism.

96. Cleary, *Rise of Charismatic Catholicism*, 141–42.
97. Alves and Oro, "Renovação Carismática Católica," 124.

Catholics may perhaps recognize some of the songs of praise from Protestant Pentecostal churches; but why should the Protestants have all the best tunes? Marcelo Rossi was ordained as a Catholic priest in 1994, and he decided early on that he would never bore the people who came to church. He was successful in this: Rossi attracted huge numbers by making Catholic Masses music shows where well-known artistes came to appear alongside the priest. In the early years of this century, he became one of the best-selling artistes in Brazil.

Once a bodybuilder, he now became a national symbol of charismatic Catholicism. He called his Masses "Jesus-aerobics,"[98] with songs of praise, dance, modern music, and titles such as: "I am cheerful because I am a Catholic." Rossi told people in his own radio program, with up to seven million listeners every day in Brazil, that Catholicism was meant to make people happy and cheerful.[99] In 2010, he also became the best-selling author in the country when his book of prayer outsold Dan Brown's *Da Vinci Code*. When the priest invited commercial star artistes to a music festival "in the name of Jesus," two and a half million people turned up—the same number that John Paul II succeeded in bringing together on his visits to the country. The traditional hierarchy may find it disturbing that one single priest became so popular in a short time among Brazilian Catholics. Rossi has achieved an authority and a leadership role in the world's most populous Catholic country, a position that was not bestowed on him by the church's traditional structures of authority. Rossi has built himself up on his charismatic authority, and people have thronged to hear him. And although he is the best known, he is not the only such figure.

In Latin America, the Catholic charismatic revival is especially strong in Colombia and Mexico, in addition to Brazil. Precisely because this revival is very largely carried out without the collaboration of the clergy, it is persons without a formal endorsement by the church who become important interpreters of Catholicism. In countries like Guatemala, the number of lay preachers is high, and they get many followers because being "charismatic" has positive associations for more and more Catholics. These preachers acquire a religious power over which the clergy have no control. An investigation in Brazil showed that as many as three Catholics out of ten called themselves "charismatic."[100] This is a drastic change in Catholics' self-understanding. Today's generation of Catholics in Brazil are presumably

98. Abreu, "Fedex Saints," 333.

99. Cleary, *Rise of Charismatic Catholicism*, 146.

100. Freston, "Researching the Heartland," 127. Other investigations have produced even higher figures. A Pew survey in 2006 indicated that as many as 57 percent of Brazilian Catholics were charismatics; ee Thorsen, "Catholic Charismatic Renewal," 466.

also much more self-aware, precisely because the Catholic monopoly in the country no longer exists, and there are so many religious alternatives.

Those who choose to join the Catholic charismatic revival can therefore be said to have taken up a new offer on the religious market. This product is a result of innovation, since some founders of religious start-ups in the Catholic church have created new frameworks in which one's faith can be lived out. But this is also an offer directed towards a market where there is an intense competition to gain Christians. This is an offer for the millions of Latin Americans who want to be charismatic Christians without breaking with Catholicism. In this way, the Catholics too have taken over something of what was the Pentecostals' highly popular niche product, and the music of the songs of praise and glossolalia are now Catholic too.

Many bishops in Latin America were initially skeptical to the revival, and this is not so hard to understand: Why should one open the door to speaking in tongues and baptism in the Spirit, which can make it even easier to go over to the Protestant Pentecostal revival? Of all the bishops in Latin America, the Brazilian bishops had the strongest orientation to liberation theology, and they were especially critical of the revival. Several of them held that it would weaken the fight for social and political justice. The Vatican gave its support to the movement long before the Brazilian bishops did so,[101] but it was nevertheless skeptical about Marcelo Rossi. He became the object of an ecclesiastical investigation, but the Vatican never raised any formal charges against him, as it had done with other controversial theologians. But it kept its eyes on him for a long time, probably also because he was earning so much money.[102]

While the Brazilian liberation theologian Frei Betto has criticized Rossi for creating more attention around his own person than around the Jesus of the Gospels, other liberation theologians have been more positive. The liberation theologian Clodovis Boff has emphasized that the diversity in Catholicism benefits from the presence, side by side, of charismatic spirituality and politically oriented activism. Although Boff believes that the bishops' skepticism was healthy, and although it is easy for charismatic spirituality to

101. The Brazilian episcopal conference was the last in the entire continent to give its official support to the movement; this did not occur until 1994. Cleary, "Catholic Charismatic Renewal." The revival came to Brazil already in 1969; see Abreu, "Fedex Saints," 327.

102. "Then, as journalists of various stripes have pointed out, Rossi was an empresario in the sense that family members managed what seemed to be a lucrative business at his Santuario of selling religious goods." Cleary, *Rise of Charismatic Catholicism*, 144.

cultivate individual feelings at the cost of love and consideration for others, he appreciates the ability of this movement to face up to the competition.[103]

Researchers have wondered whether the charismatic renewal of Catholicism in Brazil can succeed in preventing so many people from abandoning the Catholic church in that country.[104] Although the movement is able to activate many Catholics who formerly were passive, it nevertheless does not seem able to halt the continuing decline in the proportion of Catholics in Latin America.[105] It creates a growth in activity, but this on its own does not mean that a greater proportion of Latin Americans are becoming Catholic Christians.

CATHOLIC RECRUITMENT

From the colonial period onwards, the Catholic church in Latin America has lacked priests, and has been dependent on immigrants from European churches who work on the continent. Foreign priests have made up a large proportion of the Catholic clergy. In the twentieth century, however, the number of students of theology, nuns, monks, and priests grew colossally in the entire region, and for the first time the Vatican requested Latin American churches to send missionaries to other parts of the globe. Mexico was the country in this region that succeeded in recruiting the largest number of its own countrymen for the priestly ministry (women have no access to this activity in the Catholic church), and they also sent out the highest numbers of missionaries, many of whom followed the millions of Mexicans who had emigrated to the USA over the last decades. Unlike the Brazilian bishops, the Mexican bishops mostly took the initiative in spreading the charismatic revival: in the USA, Mexican missionaries and migrants have made Catholic parishes more charismatic.[106]

After 2000, however, the growth in the numbers of Latin American men who wanted to become Catholic priests stopped. With the exceptions of the Dominican Republic and El Salvador, the number of Catholic priests per Catholic declined between 1950 and 2000,[107] and has continued to fall to the present day. Catholic laypersons have become more active on various levels in their church, while an ever decreasing proportion of them have

103. Boff, "Carismáticos."

104. This question is posed, for example, in Clarke, "'Pop-Star' Priests"

105. This is the conclusion about Catholicism in Brazil in Souza, "Igreja Católica e mercados," 57.

106. Cleary, The Rise of Charismatic Catholicism, 152–60.

107. See Table 1.1 in Hagopian, "Introduction," 7.

wished to cross over to the priesthood and live in celibacy. It may be that many find that they can make a valuable contribution to the spread and the practice of Catholicism without renouncing the prospects of founding a family of their own.

In any case, this is surely bad news for a church that wants to arm for the combat in the competition with the Pentecostals, who have far more pastors per inhabitant than the Catholics have priests, monks, or nuns. Some believe that this is a crisis for the Catholic church in Latin America, but the Argentinian Pope has made it clear that he does not wish to compete at any price. On the contrary, he has castigated some bishops who have accepted for the priestly ministry young men who are bad models for the parishes, merely because the church lacks priests.[108]

The Pentecostal movement is in many ways more market-oriented and hence also more open to change than the Catholic church, but they do not have the Catholics' problem of a shortage of workers. Since they do not demand that pastors should live in celibacy and that they should have a lengthy training, they have a surplus of pastors whom they can send to a newly opened church or to other lands as missionaries.

OUTLOOK

A more detailed description of Latin American Christianity could have said more about the specifically Latin American liberation theology, which is undoubtedly one of Latin America's most important contributions to the global renewal of Christianity, especially with regard to new theological thinking in a modern society. But liberation theology and its base communities have had only a limited impact on Latin Americans' religious practice in daily life. Unlike the Pentecostal movement and the Catholic charismatic renewal, liberation theology never became the mass movement many had expected. We could also have written a great deal more about the classic Pentecostal movement, for example, about the thousands of congregations in Latin America that belong to the Assemblies of God churches, with their origin and their headquarters in the USA. This is the largest union of Pentecostal churches in the world, and the Brazilian branch has grown to be much larger than in the country of its origin.

Although this Pentecostal Christianity embraces the largest numbers, we have chosen to highlight the Neo-Pentecostal IURD church, because this is an independent Brazilian Pentecostal church that has expanded to other parts of the world. In the 1990s, the church made a huge investment in

108. Mickens, "The Vocations Shortage."

mission work in southern Africa, and it has been particularly successful in the Portuguese-speaking countries of Angola and Mozambique. However, the Neo-Pentecostals have been controversial in Africa too, which is characterized by a large degree of religious freedom. An important aspect of the Brazilian missionaries' self-image is that they come from a liberated colony without an imperialistic past, and this can also lead them to underestimate the cultural barriers that arise within the churches in the South. In Zambia, the church was banned for a time after other Protestant churches accused it of Satanism. The prohibition was gradually relaxed, and the IURD was able to establish itself here too.[109]

A demonstrable growth abroad can also create a new momentum at home. Church growth in other countries can function as a powerful testimony to the Spirit's movement from Brazil to the ends of the earth. Brazilians can thus experience their church as the center in a global mission.

109. Freston, "The Universal Church."

4

North America

With the Hand on the Bible

AT HIS INAUGURATION AS president of the USA in 2021, Joe Biden took the presidential oath with his hand on the Bible. Donald Trump had done the same four years earlier, in keeping with a long line of presidents before him, although the state has not commanded anyone to do this. The USA has never had an official religion. The president himself chooses which book he will lay his hand on as a sign of his oath to the nation. But it is the Bible that is used. This is an expression of the dominant position of Protestantism in the USA.

The USA has long been the world's undisputed superpower. Every supreme commander of the superpower has declared himself to be a Christian, and there is little to indicate that this will change any time soon. In the choice of the superpower's chief leader, the Christian faith has been given an even heavier symbolic weight in the three last decades. In the same period, Christianity has been the battleground for a public conflict that has gone under the name of "culture wars." By appealing to Christianity's true values, various groups have mobilized around causes about which they feel passionately, such as abortion and homosexuality, in ways that have led to an ever more polarized and divided public opinion. The present chapter will look primarily at this public and political significance of Christianity in the USA.

Although there is a trend in America for fewer to identify with a religion, especially among the white sector of the population, Christianity is strong. With around 70 percent Christians in a population of 328 million (2019), the USA is still the country in the world with the largest number of Christian inhabitants.[1] But in the context of the western and most prosperous part of the world, the USA occupies a special position, along with lands like Italy and Poland,[2] three western countries in which church attendance remains high. But it is only the USA that is dominated by Protestantism. In the West, the USA is the land in which Protestant Christianity has the highest support in the form of people's declared religious adherence. And if we look at what people say in questionnaires about faith in God, religiosity in the form of subjective ideas about faith has up until recently been as high as it was fifty years ago.[3] In most other western countries, it has shrunk. In other words, the USA has been significantly less secularized, and this may explain why the president still lays his hand on the Bible. In Canada, the less populous part of North America, Christians are less active religiously than in the USA,[4] but this chapter will discuss the USA, with particular emphasis on the political importance of the majority religion in the country: Christian Protestantism. At the same time, Catholicism also has a significant presence in North American social life.

Christianity in the USA differs essentially from that in Europe for several reasons. The population in both North America and Europe have long enjoyed a high level of prosperity in comparison with people in the rest of the world. Researchers have therefore asked why it is that the USA has such a high level of religious activity.[5] Here, we attach particular weight to two differences between the importance Christianity has in the USA and its importance in Europe: first, no one church has ever been dominant in the USA, and secondly, the USA has had an influx of migrants throughout its entire history.

A SOCIETY WITH RELIGIOUS COMPETITION

When the American constitution came into force in 1789, it affirmed that the American state is not empowered either to hinder the free practice of religion or to establish an official religion for the nation: "Congress shall make no law respecting an establishment of religion, or prohibiting the

---

1. Total number of inhabitants from the World Bank, and numbers of those who say that they belong to Christianity from Pew Research Center, "America's Changing Religious Landscape."

2. Norris and Inglehart, *Sacred and Secular*, 122.

3. Norris and Inglehart, *Sacred and Secular*, 90–91.

4. Norris and Inglehart, *Sacred and Secular*, 74.

5. Berger et al, *Religiøse USA*, 8.

free exercise thereof."[6] As the third president of the USA, Thomas Jefferson (1743–1826), said, "a wall of separation" was to be erected between state and church. Already in the colonial period, it was in practice difficult to choose one current within Christianity to become the official religion of the new nation. There were simply too many churches, congregations, and sects.

The principles of the constitution have also made it unconstitutional to give the kind of preferential treatment to one church that the state-churches have received in Europe. This is why the state has not given any one version of Christianity privileges that would make it dominant vis-à-vis other forms of religion in the USA.[7] In this way, the various currents of faith that were brought across the Atlantic by the European conquerors were allowed to compete freely to win believers. A plurality of different churches has led to an acute competition in pursuit of adherents, and it is thus characteristic that "religious preference"—an expression that comes from marketing—is a part of Americans' everyday language.[8] There are few places in the world where so many individuals have been able to pick and choose among Christian denominations and traditions as in the USA. One of the consequences is a high level of religious activity and a great internal mobility in American Christianity. At the same time, the freedom to choose one's church in the USA was for lengthy periods strictly limited in the case of Afro-Americans. Two of the oldest Afro-American churches were founded because the whites refused to allow the blacks to attend their church.[9] Even more than one hundred and fifty years after the formal abolition of slavery in the USA, this history continues to impact North American church life: groups of black persons still have their own churches.

In legal terms, there are few restrictions on the competition and the mobility between the churches. The state gives this competition a free hand by refraining from intervening in churches. But the federal authorities can also be said to subsidize religion, especially Christianity: the state promotes religious activity by giving religious institutions tax exemptions and by making financial payments to voluntary "faith-based organizations" that carry out social work.[10] George W. Bush made a considerable commitment

---

6. U.S. Const. amend. I.

7. This applies on the federal level. Before 1789, some federal states had given formal privileges to individual churches; see McConnell, "Establishment and Disesablishment."

8. Berger et al, *Religiøse USA*, 23.

9. The African Methodist Episcopal Church was founded in 1794 and the Africa Methodist Episcopal Zion Church in 1821. See Battle, *Black Church in America*, 62.

10. From an economic perspective, it is difficult to make a clear distinction between this type of tax exemption and the subsidizing of religion; see Brekke, *Faithonomics*, 56–61.

to this policy in 2001, and it was continued by Barack Obama from 2009 and by Donald Trump from 2017 onwards.

Despite fierce competition, no church has emerged as the clear victor. The Catholic church remains the religious institution with the largest number of members in the USA, with roughly 20 percent of the population. It is nevertheless Protestant Christianity that dominates, admittedly as a conglomerate of various Protestant religious currents in which no individual church has more than 10 percent of the population.

Protestantism tends to be divided into two parts. One consists of the so-called "mainline" churches that the earlier immigrants brought with them, such as Methodist, Lutheran, Presbyterian (Calvinist), and Anglican Christianity (the last of these is called "Episcopalian" in the USA). These churches have a lengthy history as organized institutions, and they have liberal attitudes that often aim more at collaboration with the governing authorities, rather than at competition with other churches. But these established churches have long been in decline, and amount in total to about 15 percent of the population. These traditional churches were completely unprepared for the vast exodus from organized religion in the USA from the 1960s onward, in the wake of that decade's countercultures and social struggles. Many of these churches supported Martin Luther King and the civil rights movement, but they lost the struggle to find an answer to the intense searching by the large post-War generation in religious revivals. For example, the membership of the United Methodist Church declined between 1960 and 2000, at the same time as the population of the USA grew by more than a hundred million.[11] The organizations of these well-established churches had no answer to the demand for ever more individualistic forms of religion that claimed to swim against the current of the dominant culture. "Mainline" was simply too established. It was too "mainstream."

It was the other part, the so-called Evangelical churches, that found an answer to the demand for a more individualistic and countercultural Christianity that grew in the 1970s. These churches have grown and have retained their size until the present day. The Evangelical churches have succeeded in convincing religious seekers in the USA that the conservative values they champion are Christian values that are under constant pressure from the larger secular society. Their conservative congregations took members from the more liberal mainstream churches and offered a distinctly religious and countercultural affiliation.[12] The fight against abortion, homosexual partnerships, and the religious-free school has given substantial contents to the

11. Harvey and Goff, *Columbia Documentary*, 7.

12. Harvey and Goff, *Columbia Documentary*, 374.

believers' new life and represents a contrast to what many see as the larger liberal society (often typified by the political elite in Washington, DC).

THE DEMANDING CHRISTIAN VOLUNTARINESS

Many Evangelical Christians define themselves as "born-again Christians," often because they claim to have had a strong spiritual experience that changed their lives. In other words, these are also Christians who attach strong importance to the experiential aspect of faith, while there is an experience of departing and making a fresh start that many persons have been looking for. This too has been typical of the USA, which has been a country for new religious movements and the foundation of new sects.[13]

From well-off neighborhoods in Utah to villages in the Amazonas or slums in Johannesburg, we find small congregational fellowships that have taken their place outside the big Christian churches. Although they have roots in Protestant churches, historically speaking, these are churches with names and theologies that distinguish them from the established Protestant churches: the Seventh Day Adventists, the Jehovah's Witnesses, and the Church of Jesus Christ of Latter-day Saints. These religious groups originated in North America. The last-named is often called the Mormon church, because they regard the Book of Mormon as sacred alongside the Bible. According to this church, the Book of Mormon was revealed to Joseph Smith in the USA in the early nineteenth century.[14] These three churches all came into existence in the USA in the nineteenth century and spread thereafter to every corner of the world. Each in its own way lays down strict rules of life for its members, which mean that the believers tend to stand out from society at large. The expectations that one will visit people at home or in public places are particularly great among the Jehovah's Witnesses and the Mormons, and this strong missionary imperative is also an important reason why these religious minorities from the USA have established themselves in very many countries. At the same time, the groups around the world remain linked to institutional centers in the USA, which send out missionaries, produce the special religious literature for these groups, and to a large extent channel financial resources to newly-founded congregations at "the ends of the earth." The Adventists have their headquarters in Silver Spring in Maryland, while the Jehovah's Witness are centrally directed by a Governing Body in Brooklyn in New York. The Mormons are in a different situation,

13. Roof, *Spiritual Marketplace*, 77.

14. The Book of Mormon is one of the four sacred collections of texts for this church. The Bible is another.

since a large number of the Mormons in the USA live near the church's institutional center in Salt Lake City, Utah. Many of the movement's first adherents arrived here and settled in order to escape religious persecution. No federal state in the USA has a larger concentration of any one Christian denomination than Utah, where more than 60 percent are Mormons.

In general, these three churches demand a high commitment and dedication on the part of the believers; but this was also true of the Protestant churches from which these three emerged. Since the Puritans' early colonization, church life in the USA has made relatively high demands of its adherents. In this typical North American model, the church is not a parish covering a geographical territory, but the "congregation" or assembly of believers. The close bonds between the members of a congregation are well suited to running a church in a society where the entire responsibility rests on the shoulders of the members themselves. In a European state-church, less activity is required of the members in order for the religious life to function and go on. In a North American church, which has no bonds to the state, the members themselves must make contributions in the form of financial donations, maintenance, economic management, and whatever else is needed to run the church. The religious leaders too must work hard to motivate the members to get involved. The pastor and the church will disappear if the members fail to give money. The congregations must be self-supporting.[15] This is a general trait in the USA: in the absence of a strong welfare state, much depends on private benevolence and voluntary work. And Christianity is in many ways the primal, typical American voluntariness: one comes to the aid of a sister or a brother in the congregation who is experiencing difficulties. It is still the case that religion is the form of voluntary organization in which the greatest numbers of North Americans are actively involved.[16]

With its fifteen million members, the Southern Baptist Convention is the largest union among the Evangelical churches, and they have grown steadily. In the present century, however, support for the Southern Baptists and other Evangelical churches has for the first time begun to decline. Every year, the proportion of Evangelical Christians among white Americans is sinking, and this is something new. It is especially the young people, often the children of the converted, who are leaving the churches. It has proved highly demanding to cultivate the intense and countercultural religious identity of their parents' generation. And after that generation in these churches waged war on LGBTQ practices, their descendants have become more open to the

15. Hadaway, "2008 Presidential Address," 123.
16. Putnam and Campbell, *American Grace*, 30.

position that homosexuality should be accepted in the USA.[17] At the same time, the opposition to abortion is just as strong among the young people as among the two preceding generations of Evangelicals.[18]

THE FUNDAMENTALIST REACTION AGAINST SCIENCE

The struggle against abortion has been a particularly defining factor in the intense culture war in the USA between liberals and value-conservatives; many in the latter group have been called "fundamentalists." But fundamentalism arose in the USA long before abortion became a matter of dispute, as a reaction against ideas from modern science. The first wave of modern ideas of this kind penetrated Christianity in the USA at the beginning of the twentieth century and generated a conflict that focused above all on two topics: biblical criticism and Darwinism.

The word "fundamentalism" comes from what a number of Protestant Christian leaders in the USA saw as "fundamental" for the faith in the encounter with modern ideas. The ideas that were particularly threatening were the so-called "biblical criticism," where scholars at the universities read the Bible in the same way as any other historical document; and secondly, Darwinism's idea that the earth had not been created in six days (as the creation narrative describes it), was intolerable. These leaders regarded this scientific view of the development of the earth and of the human being as immoral and an expression of modern decadence. A collection of essays entitled *The Fundamentals: A Testimony to Truth* has since then been an important basic text for Christian fundamentalists. This book sees Darwin's ideas as mendacious propaganda.[19]

More than 160 years after Charles Darwin's book *On the Origin of Species* was published in 1859, some Christian groups in the USA are still waging a war against the diffusion of ideas about evolution. The federal state of Tennessee lies in the upper part of the so-called "Bible belt." It was here that the celebrated "monkey trial" was held in 1925, when a teacher was found guilty of having taught Darwin's theory of development. It was only in 1967 that the law prohibiting the teaching of the theory of evolution was abrogated. As late as in 1999, the majority on the State Board of Education in Kansas wanted to remove the theory of evolution from all school syllabuses. Since then, fundamentalist groups and groups with a secular

17. Smidt, *American Evangelicals Today*, 206.
18. Pelz and Smidt, "Generational Conversion?," 386.
19. Brekke, *Fundamentalism*, 182.

orientation have mobilized in order to win the majority in the State Board. In 2016, the American Supreme Court rejected a request from the pressure group Citizens for Objective Public Education to examine a petition that complained that the new syllabus in the federal state opened the door to the theory of evolution.[20]

Over the years, the alternative to Darwin's theory has acquired the scientific-sounding name of "Intelligent Design," and there is an increasing tendency among the Evangelical groups to argue on the basis of secular science rather than of literal biblical interpretation. Today, these Christian groups argue against same-sex marriage by affirming that the basis of marriage is the ability of a man and a woman to reproduce biologically.[21] The young Americans who choose to abandon religion or who identify with more secular groups are also those who see the greatest conflicts between Christian faith and secular science. For many, being a Christian means that one is obliged to contradict a scientific worldview. This is undoubtedly connected with the culture wars that have been waged by fundamentalist Christians.[22]

THE CULTURE WAR—A BATTLE FOR AMERICA'S SOUL

The expression "culture war" entered the public arena in the USA in earnest with Patrick J. Buchanan's address at the Republican Party's national convention in 1992. As a Catholic, he was an example of how Catholic forces joined arms with Evangelicals in what he called a cultural war against the godless liberalism that had taken root in the USA since the 1960s. In his speech to the Party, he highlighted the fight against abortion, pornography, and "the amoral idea" of same-sex marriage. This was all part of a war that was just as serious as the Cold War against the Soviet Union's communism had been. Buchanan affirmed: "There is a religious war going on in this country. It is a cultural war, as critical to the kind of nation we shall be as was the Cold War itself, for this war is for the soul of America."[23] Since that time, the term "culture war" has been part of the religious and political vocabulary, as a designation of the discrepancy between modern and anti-modern ideas, especially among Christians in the last hundred years century.

---

20. Casci, "Kansas Revives Evolution."
21. Runions, "Biblical Provocations."
22. Longest and Smith, "Conflicting or Compatible."
23. Harvey and Goff, *Columbia Documentary*, 298–99.

Another phenomenon that is somewhat specific to Christianity in the USA is an extremist anti-abortion activism that takes the form of attacks on abortion clinics and does not draw the line at murdering doctors who perform abortions.[24] However, the opposition to abortion has primarily taken peaceful and democratic forms. Ever since 1973, when the Supreme Court made abortion up to the twelfth week of pregnancy a right protected by the constitution, the "pro-life" standpoint has been one of the Republican Party's big mobilizing causes. Together with same-sex partnership, the issue of abortion shows how Christian groups have mobilized against the second wave of liberal ideas that penetrated societal life in the USA in the 1960s: the liberal youth protest that led the way in the sexual revolution.[25] The protest against authorities found confirmation of its validity in the USA's futile war in Vietnam and in the Watergate scandal, but the radical solutions of the young people did not win the day on a higher political level. The radicality erupted in a political violence that shocked the USA, and utopian future hopes were crushed. The North Americans were a politically disillusioned people who now turned in on themselves and found the answers *inter alia*, and to a surprising extent, in forms of Evangelical Christianity that championed "traditional values."[26]

The protest music turned into commercialism, and when Bob Dylan joined the neo-charismatic Vineyard community, John Lennon was not the only one to be both disappointed and surprised. But for many, individual conversions of this kind were also a break with what the Republican Buchanan in his historical speech in 1992 called "failed liberalism," with its origin in all the social, political, and religious protests and experiments in the 1960s. America's soul was at stake, and the value-conservative Christians were fighting in a culture war that was every bit as serious as the struggle against "the evil empire" (to borrow Ronald Reagan's term for the Soviet Union). When the Tea Party movement arose in 2009 as a protest against Obama's politics and the moderate line taken by the Republican political elite, this further polarized the public exchange of words about the core issues of the culture war. A large proportion of the Tea Party activists came from Evangelical Christian milieus.[27] Shortly after Trump was inaugurated as president, he nominated the value-conservative Neil Gorsuch as a new

24. In November 2015, three persons were killed and nine injured in a shooting outside an abortion clinic in Colorado Springs.

25. At the crest of the hippy wave, almost half a million young North Americans gathered at the Woodstock Festival in 1969. The mass protests against the Vietnam war ended in the biggest student strike in the USA's history. See Zinn, *USA*, 515.

26. Flint and Porter, "Jimmy Carter," 30.

27. Pew Research Center, "The Tea Party."

Supreme Court judge. And when Trump seized the opportunities during his presidency to nominate both Brett Cavanaugh and Amy Coney Barrett to the same office, Evangelical Christians could congratulate themselves on new political victories. They had gained even more powerful supporters of their opposition to abortion, strategically placed in the highest legal body of the land.

It is in this way that Christianity plays a decisive role in polarizing opinion in the USA, so that the division between two groups is deepening at the present day: there are ever fewer religious Democrats on the one side, and ever fewer secular Republicans on the other side. The strong links between the Christian right and the Republicans have led many Americans whose political sympathies are with the Democrats to distance themselves from religion.[28] This pattern was also clear in the presidential election in 2020. Most of the Evangelical Christians who voted gave their votes to the Republican Donald Trump, and most of those who state that they have no religion supported the Democrat Joe Biden.[29]

THE NEW THREAT

The culture war acquired an extra dimension after the terrorist attack on the USA on September 11, 2001. In the aftermath of the attack, North American Muslims increasingly encountered prejudice and skepticism: they became the new "others." Evangelical Christians in the USA were distinguished both because they opposed Islam more strongly and because they tended to a greater extent to regard Christianity and Islam as incompatible.[30] Many Evangelicals held that Islam had replaced Communism in the role of Christianity's global number one enemy. Religious tolerance, which had long been a core value in North America, thus came under new pressure. The increased mistrust of Islam meant that the USA had become somewhat more like Europe.

The Evangelical Christians' polemic against Islam as a religion spread in America, and apologias *for* Christianity *against* Islam increasingly featured in the syllabus of Bible colleges and theological seminaries. President George W. Bush's description of Islam as a "religion of peace" after 9/11 was praised by Catholic and mainline church leaders, but he was sharply criticized by Evangelicals. A leading Evangelical like Pat Robertson compared the Muslims' intentions with regard to the Jews to the Nazis' actions during

28. Djupe et al., "Are the Politics?"

29. See "Exit Poll Results."

30. Cimino, "'No God in Common,'" 167.

the Second World War, and Franklin Graham, the son of the great preacher Billy Graham, called Islam a "very evil and wicked religion."[31] In parallel with the increasingly aggressive tone against Islam, it also took its place in apocalyptic countdown scenarios and prophecies among Evangelical Christians: Muslim hostility was now given a central role in the ideas about the end-time. The exceedingly popular apocalyptic and preacher Hal Lindsey held that Islam was now the greatest threat to the continued existence of the world.[32] Researchers believed that they could trace here a special form of Evangelical Islamophobia.[33]

During the 2016 electoral campaign, Franklin Graham was the Evangelical leader who expressed most unambiguously his support for the candidacy of Donald Trump, and when Trump took his oath of office, Pastor Graham was one of the Christian leaders who prayed for him. When Trump in January 2017 launched what was to be the first of many attempts to prohibit the entry into the USA of persons coming from selected countries with a majority Muslim population, Graham publicly supported this prohibition.

MEGACHURCHES WITH SUCCESS

A new strong trend in Evangelical Christianity is the so-called "megachurches," Evangelical congregations that bring together thousands of people in a place of worship, while also making it possible for Christians to lead a large part of their life inside the congregation. In Dallas, for example, the Southern Baptists have established the megachurch First Baptist Church, which owns sports centers with their ownskating rink, fitness studio, and swimming pool. The Baptists can follow the church's own news programs; they can spend their holidays at the church's own campsites; and the children's free time after school can be filled with Bible studies in the church's First Baptist Academy. In this way, the Baptists can experience something of the long American tradition of constructing Christian parallel societies.[34] Robert Jeffress has been the pastor in this megachurch since 2007. He was one of the clearest Evangelical supporters of Donald Trump in the electoral campaign in 2016.

Other American megachurches have completely abandoned the tradition of defining themselves by means of traditional labels such as "Baptists" or "Methodists." The megachurch Lakewood Church assembles up to fifty

---

31. Johnston, "American Evangelical Islamophobia," 228.

32. Cimino, "'No God in Common,'" 167.

33. Johnston, "American Evangelical Islamophobia."

34. Knutsen and Bailey, "Protestantismens," 326.

thousand persons each week for services in a hall in Houston that was used in the past for baseball and ice hockey games. Here, one gets Christian songs of praise and pop music interspersed with charismatic worship and sermons that proclaim the "prosperity gospel" (the *theologia gloriae*) in a way that often leads scholars to categorize it as a Neo-Pentecostal church. It is thus a central heir to the "prosperity gospel" that emerged in the USA in the 1950s and taught that God would reward with material success the one who believed and paid tithes. The prosperity gospel is one of the distinguishing marks of Neo-Pentecostal Christianity. With its message that financial security and the health of the soul are two sides of the same coin, the Neo-Pentecostal Lakewood Church proclaims that the American dream can be realized by entrusting oneself to Jesus. Even when the market collapsed and banks went bust during the financial crisis in 2008, the Lakewood Pastor Joel Osteen preached optimistically:

> I'm going to declare it over you that 2008 is going to be your best year so far. . . . It doesn't mean anything unless you take it into your heart. This is a seed God's trying to deposit on the inside! Why don't you let God birth some new dreams tonight? Why don't you enlarge your vision? . . . It's going to be a year of promotion, a year of increase, a year of favor, a year of supernatural opportunities![35]

In addition to breaking with the traditional divisions between (for example) Baptists, Methodists, and Pentecostals, the Lakewood Church has also succeeded in building up a large interethnic ecclesial fellowship for whites, Latin Americans, and blacks. This means that not all Afro-Americans in the USA belong to a church with a black majority. This hybrid of neo-charismatic Christianity is in many ways the new mainstream Christianity that absorbs therapeutic elements from self-help literature, incorporates popular music, and puts the emphasis on life here and now. It is these megachurches that have a particular appeal to young Christians. And some scholars have also claimed that Joel Osteen, the Lakewood Church's successful pastor, is the most powerful Evangelical leader in the USA today.[36]

While the number of secular North Americans is on the increase, more and more huge megachurch arenas are being built. Researchers have asked whether we are witnessing a "Walmartization" in Evangelical Christianity à la Wal-Mart, the store chain that has won a resounding victory over small local stores. The megachurches succeed only to a small extent in winning new individuals to Evangelical Christianity: those whom they

---

35. Quoted in Bowler, *Blessed*, 218.
36. Sinitiere, *Salvation with a Smile*, 8.

attract have belonged to smaller Evangelical congregations. With their size and their location outside the big cities, they ruin the local activities, so that local congregations must either enter an alliance with them or else resign themselves to losing out in the competition.[37] According to the *Wall Street Journal*, the number of churches on sale in the USA almost doubled between 2010 and 2015.[38]

A NATION OF IMMIGRANTS

The modern USA is largely a result of mass movements by millions of Africans, Asians, and Latin Americans. Nevertheless, the national self-understanding in the USA is influenced by the stories of the Puritan immigrants who arrived on the east coast after fleeing from religious persecution in seventeenth-century England. In the "new world," they could practice their religion freely. The strict protection of the freedom of religion in the constitution is therefore built on historical experiences of the oppression of deviant forms of religion in Europe. North America as the free port for Christian minorities is a strong cultural memory that is kindled anew when politicians like Donald Trump assert that the Evangelicals have been silenced by the authorities in America, and that he wants to give them back their religious freedom.[39] The historical memory of how some minorities were persecuted in their turn by early Protestant colonists, who tolerated no faith other than their own, is not equally strong.[40]

At the same time, it is a fact that throughout history, the churches have been a cultural and societal free port. For Africans who were brought to North America with violence and forced into slavery, the Christian fellowship became an arena of cultural survival.[41] And many of the Europeans who emigrated voluntarily to the same territory attended the churches when they arrived in the new world. For Scandinavians, the Lutheran churches both strengthened their identity on foreign soil and functioned as a springboard for networks, making it possible to solve practical problems such as finding work. This was true of Scandinavian Lutherans just as

37. Wollschleger and Porter, "'Walmartization' of Religion?"

38. Grant, "Now for Sale in Chicago."

39. Nesbit, "Donald Trump."

40. The Mormons, as a religious minority, were persecuted with military means in the nineteenth century. Besides this, the New England colonies on the east coast attempted during the early colonial phase to maintain religious homogeneity by expelling or punishing those who held different beliefs. See McConnell, "Establishment and Disestablishment," 2123.

41. Battle, *Black Church in America*, 57–58.

much as of Irish and Italian Catholics. It was not only the case that Christian congregations were planted afresh on North American soil; these religious institutions also became a part of the construction of society in the colonies that were conquered. The churches could function as community centers, and it remains true that the church building is the central assembly building in many local societies (or "communities," as they are called in the USA).

Unlike the situation in many European countries, in the USA the majority of the refugees who arrived after 2000 were Christians.[42] If we add the immigrants who entered the USA illegally from Latin America, the picture becomes even clearer: most of the migrants who come to the USA are Christians.[43]

The largest ethnic minority in the USA today comes from the continent that has the highest proportion of Christians, Latin America. Latin Americans are to be found on all the branches of the Christian tree, and they fill both Protestant and Catholic churches. A white priest celebrating Mass in broken Spanish for Latin Americans is no unusual sight in Catholic churches. And when newly arrived Latin Americans change their religious membership, it is above all one particular form of Christianity that they choose: Pentecostal Christianity. Many have already been exposed to Pentecostalism in Latin America, but the statistical chance that (for example) Mexicans become Pentecostals increases if they emigrate to the USA. And while white Americans often abandon Christianity, large groups of Latin Americans come in and change the appearance of the parishes: the imprint of the white middle class on Christianity is reduced.

The largest demographic growth that is expected in the American population is among Latin Americans. This group has already helped to turn upside down the religious mix in Los Angeles, which was the whitest and most Protestant big city in the USA at the start of the twentieth century. The west coast has become a multi-religious melting pot where Latin Americans will become dominant.[44] The east coast has taken the opposite direction in denominational terms: while Catholic parishes shrink and then close down in Boston, new Protestant churches are springing up. It is especially Asian Christians, who have emigrated from countries like South Korea and Vietnam, who are revitalizing Protestantism in a region that was formerly dominated by Catholics. The number of Protestant churches in

42. Krogstad and Radford, "Key Facts."

43. According to the Pew Research Center, 52 percent of all the immigrants who resided illegally in the USA in 2014 were Mexicans. In addition, there were Latin Americans from other countries on the continent. Pew Research Center, "America's Changing Religious Landscape."

44. Harvey and Goff, Columbia Documentary, 62.

Boston doubled between 1980 and 2000, and most of these were migrant parishes.[45] The development in these regions illustrates how history repeats itself: migration ensures the consolidation of the position of Christianity in the USA.

THE MIGRANTS' PROTECTOR

In the USA, Catholics have been the Christian branch best known for their extensive social work. The Catholic church has important institutions such as hospitals and schools in many local communities, and no church is more heavily involved in faith-based charitable work for America's poor.[46] A considerable proportion of those who live in relative poverty in the USA are Latin American migrants, for whom the Catholic religious fellowships frequently function as safe harbors. Catholic priests, religious, and ordinary church members get involved in far-reaching ways to improve their situation. Latin Americans not only find invaluable networks and contacts in these parishes: they often also get English teaching, babysitters, and legal aid from Catholics at the grassroots level, and this makes integration into the USA easier for them. Migrants who live illegally in the USA are a particularly exposed group, and in some instances they are the object of police actions. A police raid on a factory of agricultural products in Iowa made huge headlines when they arrested almost four hundred migrants without documents, most of them from Guatemala and Mexico. The workers' wives and children fled to the Catholic St. Bridget parish, where church members gave them food and shelter and stood guard at the church doors. The immigration authority ultimately deported many of the workers, while some of them were allowed to be reunited with their children. The local Catholic priest made one of the clearest media protests against the raid: "The raid ripped the heart out of the community and out of the parish. Probably every child I baptized has been affected. To see them stunned is beyond belief."[47]

The bishops have highlighted societal problems such as economic inequality and the death penalty, but from 2000 onwards, migrants' rights have taken on a more central place for the church's leaders. The pastoral letter "Strangers No Longer: Together on the Journey of Hope" (2002) was particularly important in this respect. This was a joint appeal by Mexican and North American bishops to the authorities in their countries to develop a more humane immigration policy.

45. Johnson, "The Quiet Revival," 250.
46. Wood, "The Catholic Bishops," 10.
47. Quoted in Matovina, *Latino Catholicism*, 204–5.

The prominent position of migration on the Catholic bishops' agenda helps to explain their unison criticism of Donald Trump's entry prohibition in 2017. Blase Cupich, the archbishop of Chicago, whom Pope Francis had created a cardinal some months earlier, called this prohibition a dark chapter in the history of the USA. In comparison with Protestants, most Catholics were somewhat more critical of the entry prohibition than were other Christians.[48]

CATHOLIC WOMEN'S STRUGGLE

Few churches have had so many activists linked to the political leftwing as the Catholic church. Dorothy Day was a self-declared anarchist who founded the *Catholic Worker* movement in 1933, a group that became controversial as a result of its pacifism and its extensive use of civil disobedience. Catholic activist groups of this kind have also been prominent protesters against American foreign policy. Both Catholic religious and laity have been active in the Witness for Peace movement, which has been particularly clear in its opposition to the USA's training of Latin American soldiers in torture, and to the superpower's support of death squads on the continent during the Cold War. Catholic nuns have been particularly active in these groups. Their presence was even more noticeable in the past,[49] but from the 1960s onward, the number of nuns in the USA has declined steeply, and recruitment to the religious life remains a demanding challenge for the church.[50]

In the USA, around thirty thousand nuns are organized under the Leadership Conference of Women Religious (LCWR), which has put up a powerful opposition to conservative Catholic forces both in the USA and in the Vatican. In particular, North American sisters' demand to be ordained to the priesthood in the same way as men has created controversies within the church. Besides this, the sisters' liberal position on abortion and LGBTQ rights led the Congregation for the Doctrine of the Faith, which is responsible in the Vatican for the prevention of the emergence and the spreading of "dangerous" and "unhealthy" theology in the church, to take action against

48. Bailey, "Most Important Catholic Leaders."

49. North American Catholics have become involved, through Witness for Peace and the Leadership Conference of Women Religious, in the effort to put an end to what they maintain has been instruction in how to torture at the military academy that was formerly called the "School of Americas," and is now called the Western Hemisphere Institute for Security Cooperation (WHISC). See Gill, *School of the Americas*, 198–232.

50. Matovina, *Latino Catholicism*, 143.

them. At the request of one of the bishops, it opened an investigation of the sisters' organization.

In 2012, the Congregation for the Doctrine of the Faith concluded that the North American sisters were spreading theological ideas that were directly false; another problem was that their conferences were allegedly dominated by feminist ideas that were incompatible with the Catholic faith.[51] In the previous year, the US episcopal conference had condemned one of the theological writings of a member in the sisters' organization as a heretical breach with Catholic teaching. The nun in question was Elizabeth A. Johnson, who belonged to the congregation of Sisters of St. Joseph. Many were surprised when Pope Francis decided, one month into his pontificate, that the investigation should continue. Three years later, however, he declared that there was no basis for continuing the controversial investigation of the nuns.

THE ABUSE SCANDAL IN THE CATHOLIC CHURCH

North American Catholicism in the twenty-first century has been ridden by a scandal without parallel in modern North American church history: the revelations of the sexual abuse of children by Catholic priests. In 2002, the *Boston Globe* newspaper began uncovering the story of the former Catholic priest John Geoghan, who is said to have abused more than 130 children over a period of thirty years. Documents proved that the head of the archdiocese of Boston, Cardinal Bernard Law, had known about this abuse, and about that by other priests, already in the 1980s and had merely moved them to new parishes. The pressure on Law, who was perhaps the most powerful Catholic leader in the USA, became immense. The media presented case after case, with new stories from the victims of the abuse. Very many of the most active churchgoers demanded the cardinal's resignation, and he resigned in December 2002, something that is rare in a church in which cardinals usually remain in their positions until high old age or death. The pressure only intensified when similar cases of abuse were brought to light in countries like Australia, Canada, and Ireland.

The abuse scandal was like the bursting of a dam. A victim of abuse sued a Catholic priest already in the 1980s, and this first legal action made many other victims reflect on whether they should make their stories public. In the course of the 1990s, more and more spoke openly on American talk shows led by celebrated moderators such as Larry King and Oprah Winfrey,

51. See "Timeline."

and millions saw these television programs. Public opinion in the USA also became familiar with the pattern of reaction from the Catholic bishops. The official view was that it was utterly unlikely that the priests had had sexual contact with members of the church. Church leaders gradually came to want to display understanding—but often with the individual priests who suffered from pedophilia, rather than with their victims. The bishops behaved as if their highest moral duty was to protect their own reputation as a morally spotless institution.[52]

It did not help that although John Paul II did indeed acknowledge the problem in his first official letter to the US bishops in 1993, he spoke of it as a specific problem for a North American society that was sexualized in an immoral manner. Many victims were provoked by the generalized phrases in which the Pope discussed the problem and by his demand for spiritual renewal rather than for investigation and prison sentences. When the abuse scandals spread a few years later to other Catholic-dominated countries, the Pope's assertion lost even more credibility.[53] In the public debate that ensued in the USA, the bishops were criticized for covering things up and for insensitivity towards the victims. The bad culture in the church, along with the requirement for priestly celibacy, was blamed for the high occurrence of sexual abuse in Catholic institutions and milieus. At the same time, the number of legal cases against the church, and claims for restitution, were increasing. In 2008, the demands had crossed the billion-dollar boundary line.[54]

Although the stories of sexual abuse received the most attention in the USA, it gradually became clearer that these acts of abuse were the expression of a global crisis in the Catholic church. As more and more victims came forward, it became more obvious that this was not a local bad culture in the USA. In 2010, it became publicly known that the Chilean priest Fernando Karadima (1930–) and the Mexican founder of the congregation of the Legionaries of Christ, Marcial Maciel (1920–2008), had sexually abused minors. This meant that two highly trusted Catholic authority figures in Latin America had been revealed to be abusers; and this in turn meant that even more cases came to light, so that a dam broke in country after country. The demands for complete openness and investigation grew louder, and shocking reports were published from Australia (2017) France (2021) and Germany (2018). The extent of the abuses committed by Catholic priests, the horrifying character of the crimes, and the fact that the accusations also involved bishops and cardinals caused a massive pressure on a church

52. Flam, "Sexual Abuse of Children," 396–98.

53. Formicola, "The Vatican," 485.

54. Flam, "Sexual Abuse of Children," 403.

that was going through a reputational crisis probably without parallel in modern times. Pope Francis responded by summoning all the presidents of the national bishops' conferences in the world to a meeting about the abuse crisis in Rome in February 2019. The tone from the highest quarters in the church was completely different from in the past, but there was also the enormous media attention everywhere in the world to Catholic priests' abuse of children and young people within what ought to have been the safe context of the church. Pope Francis promised action to deal with the problem. Three months later, he issued rules for how abuse cases were to be dealt with in the church, in a Motu Proprio ("on his own initiative") decree. By then, the Pope had already laicized the former archbishop of Newark and Washington, Theodore McCarrick (1930–), after the Vatican had found him guilty of sexual abuse; he had been forced to resign as cardinal in 2018. The sanctioning of a Catholic priest who had climbed in the church's hierarchy right up to the college of cardinals was historic—the Vatican had never taken such a step before. This attracted attention, and many saw it as a sign that the Vatican was capable of acting and of displaying a new intention to do justice to the victims. In 2020, the Vatican followed this up with yet another historic maneuver. With Pope Francis's blessing, the Holy See published a report about what the church knew and about the decisions it took in the course of McCarrick's ecclesiastical career. It was hard for the Vatican to explain how, despite the accusations of abuse, the church had placed such great trust in a man like McCarrick. This is why the exceptional decision was taken to publish internal matters that could also risk damaging the posthumous reputation of Pope John Paul II—who had by this time been canonized as a saint.

Catholic bishops in the USA have long been on a collision course with many Catholics with regard to central questions of values. In 1968, Pope Paul VI declared that contraception was an offense against Christian morality. And after abortion was legalized by the USA Supreme Court in 1973, the bishops' hostility to politicians who support the abortion laws, especially Democrats, has become ever clearer.[55] When the Democrat John Kerry was presidential candidate in 2004, he was refused Communion in several dioceses because he supported the legislation.[56] However, Catholics in the USA are in general more liberal than Protestants on the questions of abortion and LGBTQ rights. Many disagree openly with the church's official position that priests ought to live in celibacy and that divorce is a sin.[57] Not even the

---

55. Formicola, "Catholic Moral Demands," 9.
56. Formicola, "Catholic Moral Demands," 15.
57. Lipka, "Key Findings."

most actively practicing Catholics are loyal to ecclesiastical orthodoxy in these areas.[58]

The number of young men who want to become priests has sunk drastically since the 1960s. More than half of those who have been brought up in Catholicism in the USA have decided to leave the church, and there is in fact no church in the country that has had such a huge loss of members as the Catholic church. Several hundred thousands have left the church every year in the new century. If it had not been for the large influx of Latin American migrants, the percentage of Catholics in the USA would have declined even more strongly.

In recent years, the opposition to abortion and same-sex marriage has been so strongly highlighted by many bishops that others in the episcopal conference have criticized this as a source of conflict and polarization of the public debate in the USA.[59] One of these bishops is Joseph Tobin,[60] who has also criticized the Vatican for a lack of dialogue with the Leadership Conference of Women Religions (LCWR). In the fall of 2016, he clearly sided with Syrian refugees against the then governor of Indiana, Mike Pence, who had stopped allowing refugees from countries with a Muslim majority to settle in his state (a step that Trump had championed in his presidential campaign). Shortly after this, Pope Francis created Tobin one of the three new American cardinals. This could be interpreted as a strong signal that the Pope wanted the Catholic church in the USA to take a new course.[61]

Irrespective of the direction the church's leaders choose, the church has a serious reputational problem after the abuse scandals. The lawsuits and the guilty verdicts are also a huge financial burden on the Catholic institutions. Several dioceses have gone bankrupt, with the result that Catholic parishes are closed and church buildings are sold. Several Catholic churches are posted for sale on the internet, especially in the north-east of the USA. In New York, a record number of Catholic parishes have been shut down, especially in areas where Irish and Italian Catholics filled the churches in the past.[62] The bankruptcy petitions have given insights into an ecclesiasti-

---

58. Dillon, "Trends in Catholic Commitment."

59. "Whereas the bishops' most prominent interventions in public discourse in the 1980s involved criticism of nuclear weapons policy, economic inequality, and American intervention in Central America, in recent years they have involved criticism of abortion rights, embryonic stem cell research, gay marriage and other forms of domestic partnership legislation. This represents an important shift of public profile." Wood, "Catholic Bishops," 7–8.

60. McElwee, "Archbishop Warns of 'Balkanization.'"

61. McElwee, "Francis Appoints Indianapolis' Tobin."

62. Sweeney, "Catholic Church's Financial Woes."

cal economy which had mostly been kept secret. This information indicates that the Catholic church in the USA, taken as a whole, is certainly not bankrupt; prestigious hospitals and universities make it one of the USA's largest employers, and the church probably employs around one million persons (in comparison, Wal-Mart has two million employees). The *Economist* magazine has claimed that the diocese of New York is Manhattan's biggest landowner, and has called the church a huge firm.[63] However, the church is not one single concern. Juridically speaking, each diocese is one single organization, and this means that while one Catholic diocese can go bankrupt, another can have an enormous surplus.

In any case, however, the closing of many parishes in the north-eastern USA means that the center of gravity of Catholicism moves to the southwest, where mostly Latin Americans live.

POLITICIANS' PUBLIC FAITH

Although some Americans leave the churches in which they grew up and come under the category of "no religion" in the statistics, church attendance in the USA remains high. Roughly 40 percent of Americans tend to respond to questionnaires that they go to church once a week or more frequently.[64] One interesting discovery by researchers is that much suggests that they exaggerate when they reply.[65] When, for example, almost 60 percent of all Southern Baptists state that they go to church at least once a week,[66] we should take this with a pinch of salt. The fact that Americans exaggerate their private religious behavior indicates that religion is important in the USA as a public reality. At any rate, it indicates that church attendance and Christian activity are presented by ordinary Americans as something positive, and perhaps even as an ideal. Religion is not something to be hidden away, but something to be displayed, for example, in politics. It is a public good that ought to be shared, not because the state compels anyone to do so, but because the individual ought voluntarily to embrace it. Former President Barack Obama is one of those who did precisely that: He decided to become a Christian, and he shared the story of his faith at the same time as he was building up his political career.[67]

63. See "The Catholic Church in America."
64. Putnam and Campbell, *American Grace*, 7.
65. Berger et al., *Religiøse USA*, 61.
66. Pew Research Center, "America's Changing Religious Landscape."
67. Elements of this part of the chapter are taken from Løland "Obamas effektive bibel."

Obama relates in his autobiography *The Dreams of my Father* how he wanted to work in Chicago in 1985, immediately after graduating in law from the prestigious Harvard University, to organize poor Afro-Americans to fight for their rights. He was told in clear terms that he should go straight to the Afro-American churches: "With the unions in the shape they're in, the churches are the only game in town," said Obama's mentor at work.[68] Since the trades unions were out of the running, the churches were the places people went to, the places where they found the right values for the creation of societal change.

This episode illustrates the churches' frontline position as bearers of social consciousness and of close contact with the poor in American society. One of the churches Obama came in touch with through his work was the Reformed Trinity United Church of Christ, led by Jeremiah Wright, a pastor inspired by liberation theology. Black liberation theology was based on the presupposition that Christian faith had a political meaning that had to be made clear for the public sphere as a whole. At the beginning of the 1970s, it was a small congregation with fewer than a hundred in attendance at worship, but under Wright's leadership it had grown to a membership of six thousand. Racial consciousness and social questions were at the center of the preaching and of parish life. It was an example of the dynamic American church life that was able to bring many persons together in a new community fellowship thanks to strong leaders and new strategies. And in addition, it had the ability to jolt people into converting to Christianity.

With both Muslims and Christians in his family, Obama had been brought up to be tolerant of others' faith. But in the book that bears the title of Jeremiah Wright's sermon, *The Audacity of Faith*, Obama writes about an experience of conversion that he had when precisely this sermon was preached. Obama describes himself as an enlightened skeptic who was so strongly attracted by the holistic liberation-theological vision that he accepted baptism. In his time as a Democratic senator (2005-9), he gave an account of the free choice to be baptized: "It came about as a choice and not an epiphany; the questions I had did not magically disappear. But kneeling beneath that cross on the South Side of Chicago I felt God's spirit beckoning me. I submitted myself to his will, and dedicated myself to discovering his truth."[69]

The fact that such a successful American politician as Obama appears to have gained all the more credibility by making public this kind of individual religious experiences from a Christian parish in Chicago

---

68. Obama, *Dreams from My Father*, 141.

69. Quoted in Siker, "President Obama," 592-93.

confirms the picture presented by the investigation of church attendance:
many Americans regard religion as something positive. This also explains
why the Democratic Party took care to give enough time for speeches that
highlighted Joe Biden's Christian faith when he was nominated in 2020,
after many years in political life, as the party's presidential candidate. "Joe
believes we were made in the image of God. Joe learned that from his parents and the nuns and priests right here in Delaware, who taught him and
inspired in him a passion for justice," said the Democratic Senator Chris
Coons to the electors at the party's digital national convention, while images
of Biden at prayer moved across the screen.[70] They were to feel sure that he
was "a man of faith," well brought up by Catholic parents, nuns, and priests
in Delaware. If we are to believe the Democratic Party's message, Christian
faith can make politicians better leaders. But there are also boundaries to
the political use that is made of Christianity in the USA.

THE SPLIT ABOUT RACE

This boundary became clear while Obama's struggle to be nominated as the
Democratic Party's presidential candidate was in full swing. ABC News and
other leading media began to send clips from some of Jeremiah Wright's
sermons. One that received wide coverage was the sermon in which Wright
turned the motto "God Bless America" upside down through a critique of
society that ended in the motif "God Damn America":

> And the United States of America government, when it came to
> treating her citizens of Indian descent fairly, she failed. She put
> them on reservations. When it came to treating her citizens of
> Japanese descent fairly, she failed. She put them in internment
> prison camps. When it came to treating her citizens of African
> descent fairly, America failed. She put them in chains. The gov-
> ernment put them in slave quarters, put them on auction blocks,
> put them in cotton fields, put them in inferior schools, put them
> in substandard housing, put them in scientific experiments,
> put them in the lowest paying jobs, put them outside the equal
> protection of the law . . . and then wants us to sing "God Bless
> America." No, no, no. Not "God Bless America"; God Damn
> America! That's in the Bible, for killing innocent people. God
> Damn America for treating her citizens as less than human.

70. See "Chris Coons."

God Damn America as long as she keeps trying to act like she is God and she is supreme![71]

An excerpt from this address was combined with quotations from Wright, detached from their original context, claiming that the USA shared responsibility for the terror attack on September 11, 2001 in view of the superpower's oppression of people in other parts of the world. When ABC News made Obama's spiritual mentor the main news in its bulletin on March 13, 2008, the headline ran: "Obama's Pastor: God Damn America, U.S. to Blame for 9/11." Obama's pastor appeared unpatriotic in the way he spoke of the 9/11 terror, and racist in the way he spoke of white Americans. On the one hand, the radicality in Jeremiah Wright's critique of society prompted recognition in many who belonged to Afro-American churches. On the other hand, the most radical statements were taken out of context in a way that made it harder to understand the rebuke of society in this sermon. As "God Damn America" and other statements by Wright were aired again and again in various news media, Wright increasingly took on the appearance of an angry black man. Indeed, in the media's portrait of him, he could remind people of a vile racist.[72]

Obama's ambition as a politician was to reach the White House, and now he was in the biggest crisis of the electoral campaign: he had to distance himself from Wright, and his response was the address "A More Perfect Union," where he appeared to be a balanced and cool counterpart to Wright, a man who elegantly showed the USA what "the good black American" looked like. He held that racism was not as strong in the USA as Wright claimed, and he proclaimed a message of reconciliation and unity between white and blacks—in a way that did not refute the media portrait of Pastor Wright.

Unlike most blacks, Obama is not a descendant of the slaves in the USA. His mother was a white North American, and his father a Kenyan. The young politician had no direct links to the Afro-Americans who waged the struggle against racial segregation in the USA in the 1960s under the leadership of Pastor Martin Luther King (1929–68). At the same time, he was the bearer of a part of the inheritance from this struggle, since he had the chance to become history's first black president in the USA. The year before the "God Damn America" sermon, he had spoken on the thirty-second anniversary of the human rights march from Selma. Survivors of the human rights struggle and the "Bloody Sunday" (March 7, 1965) were present in the church where Obama spoke. Here, the presidential candidate made clear his indebtedness to the black fighters for freedom: "I am here because

71. Feagin, *White Racial Frame*, 182.
72. Gunn and McPhail, "Coming Home to Roost," 11.

some marched. I am here because you all sacrificed yourselves for me."[73] His frequent references of Abraham Lincoln, president of the USA from 1861 to 1865, linked his electoral campaign to the struggle for liberation that Lincoln had led against slavery.

Racism as a societal problem has not diminished in recent years. The political scientist Thomas Wood has claimed that it is a long time since questions about race played such a large role in a presidential campaign as they did in the election of Donald Trump in 2016.[74] Wood's analysis proved justified. During his presidency, Trump regularly supplied fuel to racial conflicts and white nostalgia, made openly racist statements, flirted with white-power groups, and thereby actively contributed to the mobilization and radicalization of racial-political tensions in American society. However, this also meant wind in the sails for the voices that were raised against Trump's public racism. The mobilization of anti-racist voices had, of course, been going on long before Trump became president, but it took on a new impetus under Trump. Some of this mobilization also has religious aspects that reveal how divided the USA is as a nation; but unlike "the Christian right," this new mobilization often includes several religions, not only Christianity. The Christianity that emerges here is characterized by a greater openness to other religions, and it is also this openness that allows it to form alliances that go beyond the churches. This is why parts of the movement are often called "the religious left" in contrast to the Christian right.[75] This new political force in the multi-religious USA has found its strongest expression in what has been called the twenty-first century's civil rights movement: the Black Lives Matter movement.[76] This movement has organized marches and demonstrations since 2013, with a special focus on police violence against black people. Under Trump, the movement grew and mobilized on a wider front against structural racism and against Trump's immigration policy. After the death of George Floyd in May 2020, the Black Lives Matter protests against racism and police violence spread across the globe.

73. Obama, "Remarks."

74. Wood holds that we must go back to 1988 to find a presidential election where race was higher on the voters' agenda. Wood, "Racism."

75. Olson, "Religious Left."

76. Livingston et al., "Feeling No Ways Tired."

A RELIGIOUS PRESIDENTIAL
ELECTION CAMPAIGN

In 1960, Democratic voters in general were more religious than Republican voters, and it was a great disadvantage to be a Catholic Christian, if one wanted to get elected. Many were critical of John F. Kennedy as the Democratic candidate precisely because he was a Catholic, and Kennedy took the step of assuring the voters that he would not be taking orders from the pope in Rome: the Vatican would not be governing the USA. When John Kerry stood as the same party's presidential candidate in 2004, Catholicism was no longer a hindrance for him.[77] The problem was rather that Kerry was insufficiently loyal to Rome's doctrine on the abortion question. In January 2021, Joe Biden made history when he was inaugurated as the second Catholic president in the USA, which had been dominated historically by Protestantism. While Pope Francis sent his congratulations and many celebrated the inauguration, the president of the episcopal conference of the USA, Archbishop José Gomez, took the occasion to warn against Biden's policies in favor of free abortion, same-sex marriage, and contraception.[78]

Christianity in the USA was less visible in politics between roughly 1930 and 1980, and the American Supreme Court maintained a clear separation between state and church.[79] In 1976, the Democrat Jimmy Carter brought Christianity into politics in a serious way. It had been a long time since a politician had used his personal Christian faith as an argument in favor of electing him, but Carter said straightforwardly: "I'll be a better president because of my deep religious convictions."[80] This strategy was rewarded with electoral victory in 1976. George W. Bush started his attempt to win the Republican nomination in 1999 by declaring in a televised debate that Jesus was his "favorite philosopher." When the moderator asked why this was the case, Bush replied by presenting himself as a "born-again Christian": "Because he changed my life."[81] Al Gore, the Democrat candidate, lost to the Evangelical Bush, and John Kerry lost to the same Republican candidate four years later. Bush won each time with support from Evangelical Christians. When Barack Obama held his historic speech at the Democratic national convention in 2004, there were several in the Democratic camp who had begun to be worried about what they called "the

77. Putnam and Campbell, *American Grace*, 5.

78. Boorstein, "As Biden Is Sworn In."

79. Harding, "American Protestant Moralism," 1279; Berlinerblau, *Thumpin' It*, 9.

80. Quoted in Flint and Porter, "Jimmy Carter," 31.

81. Hogan, "Bush Political Philospher."

God gap."[82] "Republican" had become synonymous with "religious"—and most people in the USA were religious.

In his startlingly rapid path to the top as the Democrats' presidential candidate, and in the two victories in the elections that followed, Barack Obama can be said to have been the answer to the Democrats' "God gap." He succeeded in bringing enough American Christians over to the Democratic side to ensure final victory for the party. This applied especially to Latin Americans, who had played a decisive role in George W. Bush's victory in the 2004 election.[83] But the presidential election in 2009 was also an ethnic question. Not only were almost all the presidents in the USA Protestant Christian men—absolutely all of them before Obama were white.

OBAMA'S GAY-FRIENDLY BIBLE

In the fall of 2015, Donald Trump, newly active in politics and a candidate for nomination, was confronted with questions about his faith. As was customary, the journalists wanted to know what was his favorite verse in the Bible. For a long time, Trump refused to answer, since he found the question too personal. At the same time, he took care to emphasize that the Bible meant a great deal to him, and was "the most special thing."[84] Hillary Clinton, who was to be the opposing presidential candidate from the Democratic party, had declared in an interview with the *New York Times* that the Bible was the book that had had the greatest influence in shaping her both as a human being and as a politician.[85] This meant that, once again, two white candidates were running for president in 2016 with the Bible as a political icon.

The Bible is a source of moral capital for North American politicians who attempt to build up their own credibility. Obama's visionary use of biblical references shows the mobilizing effect this can have. At the same time, his use of the Bible during the 2008 electoral campaign showed how biblical interpretation could be used to create a religious legitimacy in one of the most sensitive topics in North American politics: LGBTQ issues. How could Obama, as a Democratic candidate, defend a liberal view on this issue in the encounter with Christian voters?

This has been an important symbolic question not only for white Christians in the USA, but also for Afro-American Christians. While white

82. DiSalvo and Copulsky, "Faith in the Primaries," 100.

83. Gastón, "Today We Act," 153.

84. Johnson, "Donald Trump."

85. See "Hillary Rodham Clinton."

Christianity is on the retreat, Afro-American churches receive stable support, and the Christians in these churches have become more conservative on the questions of abortion and sexual minorities as the twenty-first century went on.[86] Although the great majority have long voted Democrat,[87] it remains a challenge for a liberal Democratic politician to convince value-conservative black Christians, and not least to mobilize them to vote.[88]

At a campaign meeting in the swing state Ohio in March 2008, Obama declared that he did not "believe in" same-sex marriage, but that he held that homosexuals and lesbians should have the same civil rights as others to contract a partnership. In defense of his position, the presidential candidate only mentioned two biblical texts, without even alluding to anything of their content.

> I will tell you that I don't believe in gay marriage, but I do think that people who are gay and lesbian should be treated with dignity and respect and that the state should not discriminate against them. So, I believe in civil unions that allow a same-sex couple to visit each other in a hospital or transfer property to each other. I don't think it should be called marriage, but I think that it is a legal right that they should have that is recognized by the state. If people find that controversial then I would just refer them to the Sermon on the Mount, which I think is, in my mind, for my faith, more central than an obscure passage in Romans.[89]

The "obscure passage in Romans" to which Obama referred was probably Romans 1:27, which describes how "men committed shameless acts with men and received in their own persons the due penalty for their error." But it is difficult to say what Obama was referring to when he used the Sermon on the Mount as an argument, other than a vague idea about the radicality of this text. Once again, the idea of the Bible as the basis of American social life was confirmed, this time with the Sermon on the Mount as the fundament that showed that the state should not discriminate. And once again, this very vague reference to the biblical texts and their authority could appear to be a political strength rather than a weakness. Obama also made this controversial topic one of the main points in 2013, in the inaugural

---

86. Smidt, *American Evangelical*, 206.

87. Robinson, "From Every Tribe," 599.

88. Hillary Clinton mobilized eight million fewer persons to vote Democrat in 2016 than Barack Obama had done in 2012. Many of those who stayed at home were Afro-Americans and Latin Americans.

89. Obama quoted in Jeffrey, "Obama."

address for his second period as president.[90] In 2015, the Supreme Court, with a slender margin (five against four), made it a constitutional right for homosexuals and lesbians to enter into a civil marriage. This meant that none of the federal states in the USA could any longer forbid them to do so.

The liberals had won a battle in the cultural war. But for the value-conservative Christians, it is not only at home that America's soul is at stake; they also won a great victory only four days after the start of Donald Trump's presidency, when he reversed Obama's aid policy. Under Trump, there was no longer to be any economic support for aid organizations that recommended abortion (this was something that had also been forbidden under the presidencies of Reagan and Bush). If hospitals or health organizations that fight against the Zika virus, the Ebola epidemic, or AIDS in developing countries so much as mentioned abortion as a possibility in their educational work, they could lose economic support from the USA.[91]

ISRAEL AS MIRROR IMAGE

Although the American constitution envisages a separation between state and church, its authors suggested the biblical motif of Moses, with his hand lifted up over the Red Sea, as the national coat of arms; however, they finally decided to use the motif of a bald eagle. The Moses motif was a possibility because the Old Testament exodus from Egypt was an influential model: the departure from Egypt under divine guidance and the liberation from slavery under Pharaoh were seen as a precursor of the American fight for independence. The British colonial rule was seen as a Pharaonic tyranny, and it was their duty to rise up against it.[92] The European emigrants had set out from the old world in Europe and made their way to the Promised Land. These biblical ideas have been an undercurrent in a kind of

90. It should, however, be emphasized that the Bible had a more prominent place in Barack Obama's rhetoric in his first presidential campaign than in his second campaign. In the latter, Obama's personal religious stance was already known, and his religious legitimacy was established. Besides the Republicans' candidate was not an Evangelical born-again Christian; indeed, Mitt Romney was not even a Protestant. This meant that the Republicans had to be extremely cautious about raising the religious flag, according to Jacques Berlinerblau in "Why So Little Religious Politicking in This Presidential Election?" This in turn meant that the Bible was largely left in peace during the presidential election campaign, after having been extensively used in the Republicans' nomination campaign; see DiSalvo and Copulsky, "Faith in the Primaries." If the Bible had been adduced, it could in any case seem that it would work in Obama's favor, despite Romney's endeavors to smooth over the controversial doctrines of his own religious minority.

91. Singh and Karim, "Trump's Global Gag Rule," 387.

92. Langston, *Exodus through the Centuries*, 142.

non-denominational civil religion.[93] In this context, motifs such as the Promised Land, the chosen people, or rebirth have been important factors in defining the USA's national identity.

Motifs of this kind have also been important for the understanding of the USA as unique among all the nations in the world, both because many suppose that the USA is *de facto* superior and because many believe that the USA has a unique task in history. This view of the USA as a nation is often called "exceptionalism." And there are many Christians who believe that this national task has a divine origin, in particular because the USA is the country in the modern world with the largest number of Christians. North American exceptionalism is also nourished by the fear that the USA may not live up to its own greatness and its religious obligation to display leadership. Among Evangelical Christians, there are also been a greater willingness than in the rest of the population to use military force in exercising responsibility as the world's leader.[94]

In combination with apocalyptic ideas from Evangelical theology, this exceptionalism promotes identification with another nation that is unique in the world, namely Israel. On the one hand, the so-called dispensationalist theology, which is particularly strong among Southern Baptists and Pentecostals, ascribes to the modern state of Israel a unique place in God's saving plan for the world. Dispensationalist end-of-days theology assumes that the earthly plan of salvation goes through specific phases in which modern events such as the establishing of the state of Israel are interpreted as signs that humanity is drawing near to the last days. For these Christians, the modern state of Israel is a fulfillment of Old Testament promises and an event that must take place before Christ can return to the earth and salvation is fully accomplished. Best-selling dispensationalist authors like Hal Lindsay have also helped to make concrete this apocalyptic countdown schema, which many Evangelical Christians in the USA have employed to interpret modern political events in the Middle East. In this apocalyptic schema, catastrophic occurrences throughout the world will soon take place, with Israel as the great fulcrum. The Antichrist will reign in Jerusalem, reestablishing the Temple and its sacrificial cult. And the final battle of history will be fought on the plain of Armageddon in northern Israel.[95] One of the most influential dispensationalists among the USA Evangelicals is the Baptist Pastor Robert Jeffress, who was entrusted in 2018 with the task of leading the prayer with which the opening ceremony of the USA embassy in

93. Bellah, "Civil Religion in America," 18.

94. Gluth, "Religion and American Public Opinion," 252.

95. Ariel, "Israel," 459.

Jerusalem began, after Donald Trump had taken the controversial decision to move the embassy from Tel Aviv. One week before that, Jeffress declared that Trump's decision was a historic moment, because the Bible had already revealed, three thousand years earlier, that Jerusalem was Israel's legitimate capital.[96] It is certainly not the case that all the Christians in the USA accept this kind of schema of salvation in a completely literal sense, but this apocalyptic has been so widespread that even American presidents have avowed their faith in elements in it. The fortieth president, Ronald Reagan, said in a speech that he wondered whether his generation would come to see the fulfillment of Old Testament prophecies when Armageddon took place.[97]

On the other hand, the USA's strong military and political support of Israel has been explained by saying that Israel is its mirror image, as the only democracy in the Middle East. And this is a mirror image that can resonate in secular history too. Many North Americans see the Israelis as a mirror image of themselves—a settler society built on ideas of freedom and flight from persecution. As George W. Bush said: "We're both founded by immigrants escaping religious persecution in other lands."[98] The USA is utterly exceptional in the modern world—and so is Israel. While many Christians would defend this state because they regard it as a biblical reality in the plan of salvation realized by God, those with a more secular orientation can see the purely historical parallels between the two nations.

OUTLOOK

The motif of a nation founded by migrants fleeing from religious persecution also establishes in another way the premises for the USA's foreign policy. Both this national self-image and the missionary zeal of North American religious minorities help to put religious freedom on the foreign policy agenda. Church pressure groups have fought since the Second World War to have religious freedom recognized as the fundamental human right on which the USA's foreign policy should be based.[99] In the 1990s, the impact of these Christian groups increased, and legal guarantees of religious freedom were increasingly tied as a condition to American trade agreements,

---

96. Spector, "This Year in Jerusalem," 566.

97. "You know, I turn back to your ancient prophets in the Old Testament and the signs foretelling Armageddon, and find myself wondering if—if we're the generation that is going to see that come about." Reagan, quoted in Boer, *Political Myth*, 146.

98. Bush, quoted in Boer, *Political Myth*, 150.

99. Moyn, "Religious Freedom," 31.

development aid, and humanitarian projects.[100] As religious minorities, Mormons, Adventists, and Jehovah's Witnesses depend on religious freedom outside the USA, if they are to grow globally. It helps them when presidents burnish the picture of the exceptional nation that was founded by those who were persecuted for their religion. And the presidents profit from painting this picture when they address voters who regard themselves as descendants of the persecuted. Through their religious faith, these groups of voters live out the typical American freedom that their ancestors were denied in the old world. Through faith, they show what is genuinely and exceptionally North American: namely, to be the leading Christian nation in the world.

The question for many Christians in the world is nevertheless how far these groups of voters are right—how far this North American exceptionalism is or is not the expression of a leadership that is in accordance with the Christian faith. Besides this, the huge increase in the number of North Americans who declare in recent years that they have no religion can be a warning that the various types of Christianity are going to be weakened in the USA. In that case, the imprint made by North American Christianity in other parts of the world may become noticeably smaller.

100. Hurd, "Religious Freedom."

5

The Middle East
When Cracks Appear in the Mosaic

"YOU CANNOT PRESERVE A culture when the people are being systematically exterminated." This was the response by a Chaldean Christian after
the Chaldean Patriarch in Baghdad had exhorted the Christians not to
flee, but rather to remain in the land of their ancestors.[1] The situation in
Iraq is dramatic. The country lost more than three-quarters of its Christian population after the collapse that followed the American invasion in
2003. Many wonder whether there will be any Christians left in Iraq in
the future.

The debate among Christian Iraqis demonstrates some characteristic traits
of Christianity in today's Middle East. Many Christians leave their homelands. With the exception of the Gulf states, the proportion of Christians
in the region is sinking. At the same time, there are many who do not want
to go, and are in search of alternative strategies for survival and belonging. This is because the countries in the Middle East are not just any lands.
They are biblical lands in which Christians have lived and belonged for two
thousand years.

Unlike some other regions that are described in this book, Christianity
in the Middle East is not characterized by a situation of competition between

1. Zaimov, "Iraqi Christians."

new communities and traditional churches.[2] Mission and evangelization are strictly prohibited in Muslim countries in this region, and in Israel too, such activities are highly undesirable both socially and politically. This means that today, unlike the situation in the past, there is little competition for potential members among the churches in the Middle East. Although some churches are larger and play a more leading role than others, none has a monopoly. All are minorities. This, however, does not mean that there is no rivalry between the churches or between different Christian groups; all it means is that their rivalry draws its nourishment from other sources.

The Middle East has often been called a mosaic, an allusion to the fact that it has been characterized by a great religious and ethnical plurality.[3] In the case of Christians, this is an ethnic, linguistic, and denominational plurality. Distinctions are usually drawn between Assyrian/Syrian, Arabic, Armenian, and Coptic ethnicity among the Christians in the Middle East.[4]

The terms *Assyrian* and *Syrian Christians* are a matter of dispute.[5] "Assyrian" is often employed in European languages as a collective noun for both groups—provoking protests especially by the latter group. While Syrian Christians understand themselves as descendants of the Aramaic civilization with its center of gravity in the western parts of Syria, the Lebanese

2. The "Middle East" refers in this context primarily to Egypt, Israel, Palestine, Jordan, Syria, Lebanon, and Iraq. Sometimes, Turkey too is included, and we shall speak at the close of the chapter about the Gulf States on the Arabian peninsula. We bear in mind the great differences between the various countries.

3. Ethnicity is a much-discussed concept. In this context, we understand ethnicity as both social and cultural: an ethnic group is a group that, within a larger society, regards itself as one group in relation to others, and that is also identified by others as a specific ethnic group. Religious, ethnic, and linguistic identity are often highly interwoven in the Middle East, so that concepts such as "ethnolinguistic" or "ethnoreligious" are sometimes employed.

4. There are also small numbers of Christians in other ethnic groups in the region—for example, Kurds, Turks, or Jews.

5. In European languages, "Assyrian" is often used as a common designation for groups who sometimes call themselves "Syrians," "Assyrians," or "Chaldeans." The differences between these groups can sometimes be confessional; at other times, they can have an ethnic significance. For example, "Assyrians" can have an ethnic meaning and refer to persons who understand themselves as descendants of the ancient civilization in Nineveh. But it can also have a confessional meaning, and refer to members of the Assyrian church (formerly called the Nestorian church). Correspondingly, "Chaldeans" can refer to persons who understand themselves as descendants of the ancient civilization in Babylon, but also to Assyrian Christians who have accepted the Catholic pope as their head. It was only in the course of the twentieth century that it became common to draw a distinction between Syrian and Assyrian as ethnic categories. The Maronites in Lebanon also have West Syriac as their ecclesiastical language, but they understand themselves as descendants of the Phoenician civilization. See Joseph, *The Modern Assyrians*; Brendemoen, "Kristne i Tyrkia," 89.

mountains, and parts of south-eastern Turkey, the Assyrians understand themselves as the descendants of the ancient Assyrian civilization in Mesopotamia. Their core areas have been today's south-eastern Turkey, eastern Syria, Iraq, and north-western Iran. While the Assyrians, to varying degrees, speak different dialects of East Syriac (also called East Aramaic), we find West Syriac (also called West Aramaic) dialects among the Syrians. In most cases, however, the majority of Assyrian and Syrian Christians have Arabic, Turkish, Farsi, or other languages as their mother tongue, depending on which state they live in. East and West Syriac have however been preserved as liturgical languages in the Syrian and Assyrian churches.[6] The Assyrian Christians who belong to a Catholic church are known as Chaldeans.

The Copts form another group. The word *Copt* comes from the Greek word for "Egyptian." They are the largest group of Christians in the Middle East today; they are an ethnic group found principally in Egypt, but also in parts of Libya and Sudan. Their original language was Coptic. Although this retains its place as a liturgical language in church, today's Copts have Arabic as their mother tongue. The Copts claim to be descendants of the ancient civilizations in Egypt.

Another group, the Armenians, are a people with their origin in the Armenian highlands; their mother tongue is Armenian. Although their core areas are today's Armenia, Eastern Anatolia in Turkey, and north-western Iran, they are spread across much of the Middle East (and the rest of the world) as a consequence of a turbulent history.

The largest ethnic group in the Middle East are the Arabs. Most are Muslims, but there are also a number of Christians, who live primarily in Lebanon, Israel, Palestine, Jordan, Syria, and Iraq. They belong to various different Christian confessions. In Lebanon, many Maronites would affirm that they are not Arabs, but a specific ethnic-religious group: they claim to be descendants of the ancient Phoenician civilization. Before the Muslim conquest in the seventh century, people in the Lebanon mountains spoke a West Syriac dialect that the Maronite church has preserved as its liturgical language. But the typical Maronite in today's Lebanon has Arabic as his or her mother tongue.

In addition to these ethnic categories, there are also religious and denominational boundary lines both between and within the ethnic groups. One way of drawing denominational distinctions among Christians in the Middle East is to categorize them according to the rites (that is to say, the liturgical traditions) of the early church: we have the Byzantine (Greek), Antiochene (West Syrian), Chaldean (East Syrian), Alexandrian (Coptic),

6. Mordechai, *Minorities in the Middle East*, 180.

Armenian, and Latin (Roman Catholic) rites. There are also combinations of denominational membership and confessional rites, such as Greek Catholic or Coptic Catholic churches, or Protestant churches that do not use the rites of the early church. We return to this jigsaw puzzle later in the present chapter.

Taken together with struggles driven by political interests, western missionary work, and a variety of alliance partners, these ethnic and denominational divisions have left their mark on the relationships between the churches. However, the situation in recent years with regard to security and emigration has been experienced as so dramatic that it has compelled the churches to stand shoulder to shoulder, to a greater extent than in the past. As we shall see in this chapter, the different churches and Christians do not all evaluate the situation in the same way, and they adopt differing strategies for survival, belonging, and a continued presence in the Middle East. The situation is dramatic, and cracks are appearing in the mosaic.

THE CHRISTIAN EXODUS—
ESPECIALLY IN IRAQ AND TURKEY

Many scholars hold that the pluralism that has been characteristic of this region is under greater threat today than ever before. This is due especially to the escalating conflict between Shia and Sunni Muslims, but also to the fact that many Christians are leaving the region. We hear talk of an *exodus* ("departure" in Greek) of Christians from this area. Will the difficult situation lead the Christians pack their bags today and leave the Middle East for good?

There has been a large decline in the percentage of Christians in the Middle East over the last hundred years.[7] If we look at Egypt, Israel, Palestine, Jordan, Syria, and Lebanon, we see that the percentage of Christians declined from 10 percent of the population in 1900 to 5 percent in 2010.[8] While the percentage was declining, however, the real numbers of Christians in these countries increased from 1.6 million in 1900 to 7.5 million in 2010.[9] The reason for the percentual decline is that other groups in the population have had a greater growth than the Christians: for example, the Muslim population in these countries expanded tenfold in the same period.

---

7. Hazran, "Emigration of Christians."

8. Pew Research Center, "Middle East's Christian Population." It is extremely difficult to estimate the numbers of Christians in many Middle Eastern countries. Where nothing else is stated, the figures in this chapter are based on Pew. See Pew Research Center, "Table: Christian Population."

9. Pew Research Center, "Middle East's Christian Population."

The causes for the lower population growth among the Christians than among other groups include a lower number of births, conversions, and a larger number of emigrations than in other groups. One of the explanations of emigration goes back to the close of the nineteenth century. In parallel to the emigration of many Europeans to America, many Christian Arabs emigrated from the Ottoman province of Syria (today's Syria, Lebanon, Israel, and Palestine) to North and South America. Some went primarily in search of work, freedom, and land in the New World, while others left in order to get away from the conflicts and turbulence that raged at times in the province. In parallel to the emergence of modern nationalism and the collapse of the Ottoman Empire at the end of the nineteenth century and the beginning of the twentieth, the Arab reform movement *al-nahda* emerged, especially in Egyptian, Palestinian, Lebanese, and Syrian regions. Many Christian Arabs took on central positions in cultural, political, and economic life, especially in the British and French spheres of influence.[10] It was now western colonial powers that dominated in the Middle East, and the region was integrated into the new global economy. A new middle class of Christian families with economic capital and a good education gradually came into existence in many of these countries, and they had good contacts in the West, partly as a consequence of the earliest emigration. The second great wave of Arabs who emigrated to the USA (1948–65) consisted mostly of highly educated Christians.[11]

The growth of the middle class had demographic consequences. First of all, many Christian women could afford, or could choose, to have fewer children than many Muslim women. Secondly, it was easier for Christians than for Muslims to emigrate to the West in turbulent periods, because of their resources and their contacts in the West. Muslims have largely emigrated to other Arab countries.

Emigration contains both push and pull factors. Christians have emigrated both because they had to get away (push), for example, as a consequence of war, persecution, or discrimination, and because other places were more attractive (pull) and beckoned to emigrants who hoped for a better standard of living.

Dramatic historical events such as wars, civil wars, or revolutions have also contributed to the decline; this has affected above all Christians in Turkey and Iraq, where the *de facto* number of Christians has decreased dramatically in the course of the last hundred years. During the First World War, between 150 thousand and 300 thousand Assyrian and Syrian

10. Guth, "Kristnes bidrag," 68–72.

11. Cumoletti and Batalova, "Middle Eastern."

Christians were murdered by Ottoman troops and Kurdish tribes in Upper Mesopotamia, in the south-east area of modern Turkey. At the same period, what remained of the Ottoman Empire began mass deportations of Armenians. The question whether or not this should be called genocide has been an inflammatory political issue ever since. It is thought that somewhere between seven hundred thousand and 1.5 million Armenians were murdered or driven out into the desert on what have been called death marches.[12] The Turkish War of Independence and the 1923 Treaty of Lausanne led to an exchange agreement between Turkey and Greece whereby 1.5 million Greek Orthodox were sent from Turkey to Greece, while six hundred thousand Muslim Turks were sent in the opposite direction.[13] Taken as a whole, these events meant that the Christian presence in Turkey, which had once been a core area in the Christian Byzantine Empire, almost ceased to exist. Today, only somewhere between one and four per thousand of Turkey's population are Christians.[14]

While Turkey lost most of its Christians at the beginning of the twentieth century, Iraq lost its Christians at the beginning of the twenty-first century. There are more Assyrian Christians in Södertälje in Sweden today than there are in Iraq.[15] Before the American invasion in 2003, there were about one million Christians in Iraq; today, it is thought that less than 250 thousand remain.[16] Although most of the Christians fled before the terrorist group ISIS had its breakthrough, it was above all after the ISIS devastations (in particular against the Yezidis, but also against Christian minorities) that the world realized what had happened to the religious minorities in Iraq. In 2016, the US Secretary of State, John Kerry, used the word "genocide" when speaking about ISIS' massacres of Yezidis and of groups of Assyrian Christians. This was the first time the USA had officially employed this term since the crisis in Darfur in 2004.

But although Christians emigrate from the Middle East, they do not abandon the native land of their ancestors. There are usually close contacts between the diaspora and its churches in the lands of origin. The mother churches establish new dioceses in the diaspora and send bishops and

12. Brendemoen, "Kristne i Tyrkia," 83.

13. Brendemoen, "Kristne i Tyrkia," 86.

14. Pew says three hundred thousand Christians in Turkey, amounting to about 0.4 percent, while others estimate the figure at under 0.1 percent. See Brendemoen, "Kristne i Tyrkia," 75.

15. Thorbjørnsrud, "De kristne i Midtøsten," 15.

16. Norwegian Church Aid, and World Council of Churches, "The Protection Needs," 11, 15.

priests to them, while the diaspora churches send back money and western political capital.

If you visit the Syrian Orthodox monastery of Mar Gabriel, in the south-eastern part of today's Turkey, you will encounter only a small number of native Syrian Christians—but you may also chance upon busloads of Syrian Orthodox teenagers from Sweden on a summer camp. The monastery is said to have been founded in 397, and is the oldest Syrian Orthodox monastery in the world. The boys in the summer camp have to learn parts of the Syrian Orthodox liturgy in Church Syriac. The young Swedes may not necessarily understand the language, but they are to learn to read and pronounce the words and to chant them to the correct melody. The liturgy and the words are sacred, and they are perceived to create the divine presence. The most important thing is not to understand what is said; the most important thing is that the words are spoken.

Of all the countries in the Middle East, it is Iraq and Turkey that have experienced the most dramatic decline in the percentage of Christians over the past hundred years. But they are far from being the only countries that have experienced war, conflicts, and emigration by Christians.

SYRIA—CIVIL WAR AND CHANGED CHRISTIAN–MUSLIM RELATIONS

High up in the Qalamoun mountains in Syria, just over ninety kilometers north of Damascus, lies the little Christian town of Saidnaya, where (according to local legends) Noah is said to have planted the first vine after the flood. Abel, the first murder victim in the Bible, is said to have been buried in this region. The name "Saidnaya" is Aramaic, the language Jesus spoke, and may mean "Our Lady." The little town with its twenty-one monasteries and more than forty churches is known, not only for being one of the few places in the world where a West Aramaic dialect is still spoken, but also for the *Shaghura*, an icon of Mary and the child Jesus that tradition says was painted by the evangelist Luke. The icon is said to have healing and protective power, and it is therefore a popular pilgrimage goal.

There are many icons in the Middle East. Icons play an important role above all in eastern Christianity, both in the liturgical life in the church buildings and monasteries and in private life, as a picture on the wall, in one's purse, or in a car window.[17] In Orthodox theology, an icon is not mere-

17. It is the Eastern Orthodox churches that have the most comprehensive tradition of using icons. The theology of icons was shaped particularly at the seventh ecumenical Council at Nicaea in 787 (Nicaea II). The breach following the Council of Chalcedon

ly a picture of Christ, Mary, saints, or angels. It is also a sacred object that mediates divine grace in the world.[18] But although this means that all icons represent something divine, there are special icons, such as the *Shaghura* in Saidnaya, to which miraculous powers are ascribed. We should note that it is not the material picture in itself that possesses such powers. According to the theology, it is God who performs miracles through the icon in response to the intercessory prayer of the saint who is depicted on it.

Saidnaya has attracted pilgrims from the entire Middle East for many centuries, after the Byzantine emperor Justinian I, according to tradition, had a church dedicated to Mary built there in 547. The pilgrims come in order to light candles and pray for blessing, protection, and healing. Some bring special objects, such as a newly purchased engagement ring or baby clothes, in the hope that something of the icon's protection power may have a contagious effect.

But the pilgrims are not only Christians. Syrian Muslims too have gone to Saidnaya for centuries, to pray and receive blessings from the icon of Mary.[19] On September 8, Mary's nativity is celebrated by both Catholic and Orthodox churches throughout the world; but in Saidnaya, it has been celebrated for years both by Christian and by Muslim Syrians. Saidnaya thus demonstrates not only a central element of Christian praxis and the life of faith in the Middle East, but also one aspect of the close relationships that have existed at times between Christians and Muslims.

The bloody civil war has changed much in Syria. Saidnaya was attacked several times by Muslim rebels, and the bombardment inflicted considerable damage on Mary's church.[20] Thanks to support from the government troops and Lebanese Hezbollah soldiers—and according to the town's Christians, also thanks to support from the Virgin Mary—the town was never captured by the rebels. It got off more lightly than Maaloula, the other well-known Aramaic-speaking town in Syria, where nuns were kidnapped and several inhabitants were killed.

Although Syria has been hit by a particularly brutal civil war in recent years, statistics show that Christian emigration has not been as dramatic as in Iraq. In Syria, it is reckoned that there were between 1 and 1.7 million

---

in 451 meant that the Oriental Orthodox churches were not represented at Nicaea II. But thanks to ecumenical dialogues under the aegis of the World Council of Churches, these churches accepted in 1990 the Eastern Orthodox theology of icons as this is expressed at Nicaea II. The different Oriental Orthodox churches have varying praxes linked to icons. See Chaillot, "Role of Pictures."

18. Pelikan, *Spirit of Eastern Christendom.*
19. Waddy, *Women in Muslim History*, 223.
20. Jokhadar, "Residents."

Christians in 2011, before the outbreak of the civil war.[21] In November 2016, it was reckoned that more than three hundred thousand Christians had left the country.[22] But these numbers do not tell the full story. One of the Christian groups worst affected by the wars in Iraq and Syria is the Assyrian church (also known as the Church of the East), which spread over vast areas in Asia in the middle ages, from Persia as far as China. After ISIS' assault on the Assyrian core area in the Khabor region in Syria in 2014, reports estimate that only a few hundred Christian Assyrians are left in this area, in contrast to more than fifteen thousand before the war.[23]

One typical trait of the civil war in Syria is that both Christians and the civilian population in general have been subjected to brutal attacks by the regime of Bashar al-Assad and by rebel groups. They have often been used in the propaganda war of these actors. In the attempt to demonize the other side, both parties have committed terrible acts of violence against civilians, and have then blamed their opponents—in the hope of getting international support.

Christians in Syria have reacted in different ways to the civil war. Some have formed militias to protect Christian areas or villages. Some of these groups are allied with the regime, which supplies them with weapons, while others are opposition groups that fight *inter alia* against the regime. One of the largest military Christian opposition groups is the Syriac Military Council (MFS), which consists of about two thousand Christians, mostly Assyrian and Armenian, who have fought alongside Kurdish guerillas against the Syrian regime, against ISIS, and against the Turkish offensive in northern Syria.[24]

Others, like the Christians in Saidnaya, have supported the regime both before and after the civil war broke out. Although more Christians took part in the earliest non-violent protests against Assad, several of the churches in Syria have more or less tacitly chosen to support the regime, after the civil war unfolded and became increasingly sectarian. In this way, they have also to some extent become political parties in the war. Although the churches by and large have sought to avoid taking a political role, this has often been interpreted as fidelity to the regime. Saidnaya, for example,

21. Pew estimates the number at a little over one million in 2010, while the U.S. State Department estimates it at nearly 1.7 million. See also Norwegian Church Aid, and World Council of Churches, "The Protection Needs," 17.

22. Norwegian Church Aid and World Council of Churches, "The Protection Needs," 18.

23. Norwegian Church Aid and World Council of Churches, "The Protection Needs," 21.

24. Khalel and Vickery, "Syria's Christians Fight Back." See also Hellestveit, *Syria*.

is also the location of one of Assad's most notorious prisons for political opponents. This prison has long been known for its cruel treatment and torture, especially of Sunni Muslim Islamist opposition figures, and people speak of it as the "slaughterhouse." In 2017, a report by Amnesty concluded that under the civil war alone, this prison had been the scene of between five thousand and thirteen thousand extrajudicial executions.[25] This makes it difficult to say how far Saidnaya was a religious, a political, or a military goal for the rebels.

MINORITIES, MIGRATION, AND COMPLEXITY

It is not only the minorities who are affected in a war. In a situation of lawlessness, however, minorities are often particularly at risk, and the relative emigration is often greater among minorities than among the majority—provided that they have the resources to flee. This was what happened in Iraq after the country collapsed. There, the relative emigration of Christians has been higher than among both Sunni and Shia Muslims, although it is the Shia majority that has suffered the highest number of losses as a consequence of the civil war—both in relative and *de facto* numbers.[26]

The discourse related to Christian emigration from the Middle East is complex and contentious. It is complex because the causes are composite, and vary from land to land. And it can sometimes be difficult to know whether the emigration should be explained by religious, political, or economic causes. This makes the various accounts of Christian emigration contentious, because they also involve the question of how the history of Christian and Muslim coexistence is written.[27] For example, the blossoming of Islamist movements in the past decades, as well as stronger global tensions between Muslims and Christians related to identity politics (especially after 9/11), have prompted Christians to leave. Although there are differences in scale, Christians in the Middle East have a centuries-old experience of being second-class citizens with fewer rights than the majority groups. In Turkey and the Arab countries, there is a much lower degree of religious freedom than in western states, and a general problem in many of these countries is the low level of security under the law, in states where the authorities are not truly able to protect people. To take one example: Christians in Egypt have experienced a relatively large increase in violence since the beginning of the

25. Amnesty International, "Massehenging i syrisk fengsel." See also Khatib, *Islamic Revivalism in Syria*, 141.

26. Thorbjørnsrud, "De kristne i Midtøsten," 45.

27. See Kloster, "Om forfulgte kristne"; Kloster, "Norske persepsjoner."

present century, although the country is not at war or in a civil war. There is documentary evidence that crimes committed against Copts are, by and large, overlooked by the courts in Egypt.[28]

For historical reasons, Christians in the Middle East have not been willing to speak of themselves as a minority. This concept has been understood as subjection to, or acceptance of, rule by Sunni Muslims (as in Lebanon), or else it has been regarded as a western colonial strategy to fragment national communities.[29] And many of the churches long opposed what they saw as a western rhetoric about the Christians' need for protection. They held that this could reinforce local ideas about inequality and lend support to claims that Christians did not belong to the national community in the same way as the majority population. The fact that more Christians in the Middle East have gradually begun to speak of themselves as a minority is an eloquent sign of the gravity in today's situation.[30]

The Christian minority in Jordan has a relatively strong position, although it does not amount to more than somewhat over 2 percent of the population. Many Christian refugees from Iraq and Syria live there; but otherwise, many of the Jordanian Christians are well-off and highly educated, with good jobs in the state administration, the military, and industry. They have a much larger share in the country's economy than their size would indicate. Nine out of 110 seats in the parliament are reserved for Christians—this too is a number that exceeds their share of the population.[31] The churches have good relations with the royal family, and Christians in both the private and the public sectors get time off on Sundays so that they can go to church.

The explanations of Christian emigration in Palestine have been especially politicized. Representatives of the Israeli authorities often argue that it is Muslim extremists who are driving Christians out of the West Bank, and that Israel is the last place of refuge left to Christians in the Middle East.[32] The Palestinian authorities and the established Palestinian churches have argued that it is primarily economic stagnation and a lack of freedom of movement, as a consequence of the Israeli occupation of the West Bank, that makes Christians choose to leave.[33] For example, in the region around Bethlehem,

28. Kloster, "Om forfulgte kristne," 16.

29. Thorbjørnsrud, "De kristne i Midtøsten," 50–52.

30. Mahmood, "Religious Freedom," 437–40.

31. Minority Rights Group International, "World Directory."

32. One example is Israel's ambassador to the USA, Michael Oren, in "Israel and the Plight of Mideast Christians."

33. Palestinian Center for Policy and Survey Research, "Migration of Palestinian Christians." For more on this topic, see Kloster, "Norske persepsjoner"; Kårtveit,

where most of the Christian Palestinians live, the Israeli West Bank Wall has cut off many Christian families from their fields and olive groves, in addition to making it more difficult for them to work in Jerusalem or visit the city.

For a long time, Palestinian nationalism and the liberation struggle had a secular and socialist basis, but Palestinian churches and church leaders have increasingly become involved politically in the opposition to the Israeli occupation of the West Bank and the annexation of East Jerusalem. Since western churches had largely ignored or even supported Israel's policies vis-à-vis the Palestinians, a group of Palestinian Christians published in 2009 the document "A Moment of Truth: A Word of Faith, Hope, and Love from the Heart of Palestinian Suffering." The church leaders in Jerusalem gave their support to the Kairos document, which spoke of the Israeli occupation as a sin and urged western churches to break with their one-sided support of Israel.[34]

Ten thousands of Christians emigrated from Israel, East Jerusalem, and the West Bank during the Israeli–Arab War in 1948. Today, it is thought that somewhere between fifty thousand and a hundred thousand Christians live in Palestine.[35] About 150 thousand Christians live in Israel, about 1.9 percent of the population; roughly fifty thousand of these are migrant workers from countries such as India and the Philippines, while about twenty five thousand are Russian Orthodox Christians from the former Soviet Union who came to Israel as immigrants in the 1990s.[36]

LEBANON—VARIOUS STRATEGIES FOR BELONGING

It is not only in Israel and Palestine that the churches have been politically active. In Iraq, Syria, Palestine, Jordan, and Egypt, Christians were inspired by leftwing nationalism in the twentieth century. This was a nation-building ideology that was not based on Islam, and some of the ideological founding fathers were individual Christians.[37] In Lebanon, on the other hand, the

"Tilhørighet"; Kårtveit. In Fifteen Years; Sabella, "Palestinian Christians."

34. WCC, "Kairos Palestine Document."

35. Pew gives the figure of one hundred thousand, while other more cautious estimates speak of fifty thousand. For example, see Kårtveit, "Tilhørighet," 96.

36. Thorbjørnsrud, "De kristne i Midtøsten."

37. For example, the Syrian Michel 'Aflaq, who founded the Baath Party in the 1940s, and who held leading positions both in Iraq under Saddam Hussein and in Syria under the Assad dynasty, or the Palestinian George Habash, who founded the Popular Front for the Liberation of Palestine (PFLP) in 1967. Nasser's socialist revolution in Egypt in 1953 was also attractive for many Christian intellectuals, but not for the Coptic

only country in the Middle East in which Christians have genuine political power and influence, there emerged a wholly Christian rightwing nationalism, spearheaded above all by the Maronite church. This took place, not only because the Christians were sufficiently numerous to place their hopes in nationalism with a religious basis, but also because the opposition to Islam and to "Arabization" has been central to the Maronites' self-understanding.

The Maronite narrative of origins begins six thousand years ago, in the Phoenician civilization that was born in what is today's Lebanon. When the Arab conquest of the coastal regions began in the mid-seventh century, some Christians sought refuge in the mountains, where they could fight against the Muslims. There they met the successors of the Christian hermit Maron, for whom the mountain region was a place of refuge from the Orthodox Byzantine imperial church. While other churches in the Middle East explain their continuity and survival under Muslim dominance as the result of strong faith or Muslim tolerance, it is precisely this dual resistance struggle that is a central aspect of Maronite identity.[38] They see Lebanon as a holy land where Jesus and the prophets walked and martyrs died, and as a place of refuge for Christians that is worth fighting for.

The Maronite Eastern Catholic church is the largest church in Lebanon, with somewhere between five hundred thousand and nine hundred thousand members.[39] It played a central role in the achievement of Lebanon's independence from the Ottomans and later from the French, and it has played a dominant role in Lebanese politics since then, either directly as an actor or as a mediator between Christian politicians or Christian parties. This church was a vitally important purveyor of ideology during the civil war from 1975 to 1990. The Patriarch, the church's highest leader, also took on the role of leader of the national opposition against the Syrian presence in the land, which was *de facto* an occupation of Lebanon from 1990 to 2005.[40] Lebanon's national treaty specifies that the country's president and supreme military commander must be Maronites, while the prime minister's

---

Orthodox church, which lost much of its property.

38. Khoury, *Imams and Emirs*, 154. See also Kverme, "Patriarken," 174.

39. There has been no population census in Lebanon since 1932, so all demographic figures are highly uncertain. Besides this, the fact that the formal power in the country is distributed among the religions and confessions is a further factor that politicizes the estimates of numbers. The U.S. Department of State operates with 22 percent Maronites. In a population of slightly more than four million, this amounts to about nine hundred thousand persons. Others operate with lower figures, as low as five hundred thousand, for example, Grung, "De kristne i Libanon," 162.

40. Kverme, "Patriarken," 178–84.

office is reserved to a Sunni Muslim, and the leader of parliament must be a Shia Muslim.

Lebanon's Christians have organized themselves in a variety of political parties, and there are acute political divisions—also among the Maronites. For example, the country was without a president between 2014 and 2016, because the Christian parliamentarians could not agree on a candidate. Gradually, with the escalation of the Sunni–Shia conflict in the region, a new political fragmentation among Lebanon's Christians has arisen. The question is: After the Arab Spring, who is now the greatest threat to a Christian Lebanon? One of today's two leading Maronite politicians in the country, Michel Aoun, formerly chief of the military and now president, fought against Syria in the Lebanese civil war in the 1980s; now, he has allied himself with the Shia Muslim Hezbollah and supported Assad in the civil war in Syria. The other man, Samir Geagea, is the leader of the Lebanese Forces—in the past, a common Christian army during the civil war, but now a political party. Unlike Aoun, Geagea has retained his anti-Syrian politics, and has supported the Sunni Muslim uprising in Syria.[41]

This illustrates why some still see the Syrian state and its ally, the Shia Muslim Hezbollah that is supported by Iran, as the greatest threat to Lebanon, while others see the greatest threat in Sunni Muslim Islamism, as this finds expression in the civil war in Syria. Others again would claim that the Lebanese system itself, with a sectarian division of power, economic mismanagement, and political paralysis, is the greatest threat to a viable Lebanese state. The land has been plunged in recent years into an unparalleled political and economic chaos. The World Bank and other global financial institutions have refused to help, as long as the religious and political elites in the country resist demands for reforms. Statistics show that Lebanon's net migration in 2020 was minus twelve persons per a thousand inhabitants, a negative increase of no less than 46 percent from 2019.[42] One can get the impression that many Lebanese, irrespective of whether they are Christians or Muslims, have lost faith in a future in their country.

41. Kverme, "Patriarken," 184–86.
42. See "Lebanon Net Migration Rate."

EGYPT—THE COPTIC SUNDAY
SCHOOL AS A STRATEGY FOR
MOBILIZATION AND RESISTANCE

In Egypt too, Christians have disagreed about how to relate to the rebellion against the dictators during and after the Arab Spring. While the Coptic Pope, Shenouda III, urged support for the regime during the 2011 revolution, young Copts tweeted and demonstrated against President Mubarak on Tahrir Square in Cairo.[43] In this way, the Arab Spring illustrates an interesting aspect of the Coptic church in Egypt: the generation conflict. This is particularly significant in Egypt, because the church invests its resources above all in young people.

According to tradition, the Coptic Orthodox church in Egypt was founded by the evangelist Mark. It is not only the largest of the Oriental Orthodox churches in the Middle East, but also the largest church of all in the region, with somewhere between four and nine million members.[44] Hundreds of thousands of Coptic children and young people come together every Friday in the church's Sunday schools.[45] They meet on Friday because it is the official day off work in Egypt, but the term "Sunday school" is employed.

The Sunday schools began as a small movement initiated by laypersons about a hundred years ago in opposition to a clerical leadership, but in the past forty years, the church leaders themselves have been former Sunday schoolchildren, and now they give this work highest priority, since it has been shown that the Sunday schools have led to a vast mobilization of the church's members in a way that builds up their identity. All Coptic children are encouraged to take part, and the Sunday schools actively seek out those who do not come of their own accord. The Sunday schools have become so central today that some scholars have said that the church does not *have* Sunday school activities: rather, the Sunday schools *are* the very embodiment of the contemporary Coptic Orthodox church.[46]

43. Vogt, "Den arabiske våren," 10.

44. It is often said that 10 percent of Egypt's population are Christians; this corresponds to roughly nine million persons. The CIA's World Factbook operates with this figure; see CIA, "The World Factbook." This figure is probably too high. Pew estimates that it is a question of about 5 percent of the population, 4.5 million persons; see Pew Research Center, "How Many Christians?"

45. The presentation of the Coptic Sunday school is based largely on Stene, "Mobilisering og motstand."

46. Reiss, *Erneuerung in der Koptisch-Orthodoxen Kirche*, 26, quoted in Stene, "Mobilisering og motstand," 149.

As part of the religious instruction, the children are taught about the liturgy, the stories of saints and martyrs, and biblical stories. Education in correct religious practice also plays a central role. For example, there are many complicated fasting practices that one must learn. Before receiving communion (which Coptic children and young people are encouraged to do), one must not only take off one's shoes (and cover one's head, if one is a woman). One must also have abstained from eating food for up to nine hours (although this time can be shorted somewhat in the case of children). To fast before communion is customary in Orthodox Christianity. But fasting is so important for the Copts that they have more than two hundred and ten fast days in the year. Most of these involve abstaining from animal products and some other products, but the fasting rules in the monasteries are even stricter.

The Sunday schools also constitute a social structure for children and young people. Camps, excursions, and social activities are organized, in addition to the religious instruction. Young people spend much of their time outside school here, and in this way, the Sunday school becomes an important arena of socialization. It is, however, not just an arena where one can meet relatives and friends, or a future Coptic marriage partner, for that matter. It is also a place where the young generation learn to be Copts in Egyptian society. The intention is to equip the Copts not only to be practicing church members, but also to be Coptic citizens.

This is why it is important that children learn how to behave. They are to be obedient to their parents and aim to improve themselves, for example by doing their homework and doing well at school. Investing in education and competence in order to make oneself relevant to the larger society is a well-known strategy for many minorities. The children know that they get nothing gratis from the larger society, and they learn useful maneuvering strategies. At the same time, the church's many stories of the martyrs are related to the daily life of the Copts. Children learn that suffering is part of a Christian life. They must be prepared to suffer for their faith in today's Egypt.

The historian of religion Nora Stene has argued that the Coptic Sunday school can be understood politically as a strategy for resistance to the marginalization and societal exclusion that Copts experience in Egyptian society. Although it can be interpreted as a retreat mechanism and a self-isolation from society, it can also be seen as a mobilization that is relevant to society. When the larger society presses the church to keep a low profile, its response is an intensified construction of organizations and of competences, and it mobilizes from below in order to consolidate the church's continued presence in society.[47]

It may have been this kind of strategy for belonging that led the young Copts to the barricades on Tahrir Square in 2011, where they stood alongside young Muslims in a common cause. One of the slogans was: "We are all Egyptians." But revolutions often follow their own brutal logic. Only a few hours after General Sisi's coup d'état in July 2013 against Mohammed Morsi, the first popularly elected president in recent Egyptian history, the newly elected Coptic Pope, Tawadros II, appeared on television together with the country's foremost Muslim leader, the Grand Mufti of Al-Azhar, and urged the need for unity and support of the general. Once again, the generals had won the power struggle in Egypt, and this time, unlike the uprising two years earlier against Mubarak, the young people stayed at home.

Sectarian tensions have increased in recent years in Egypt, and the church's support of General Sisi has not helped to calm them down. Several church buildings have been hit by bloody terrorist attacks. ISIS and other terrorist groups have claimed the authorship of several of these attacks, claiming that the Coptic Christians had overreached themselves and broken the "contract" with the country's Muslims that gives them a right to protection.[48] After several deliberate attacks on Christians on the Sinai peninsula, and especially in the town of El Arish, large numbers of Copts began to flee from this region in 2016–17. It was no longer safe for Christians to live there.[49]

DIVISIONS AND COOPERATION

If you switch on a television set in the Middle East and find a channel called Sat-7, you can see everything from talk shows and soap operas to explicitly Christian programs. Phone-in programs are particularly popular. One can ring a priest and ask about everything, from whether it is all right to go on a date while one is of school age to what kind of professional training one ought to take.

Many people in the Middle East (or their neighbors) have satellite television. Sat-7 is a Christian channel with its headquarters on Cyprus. It broadcasts satellite TV to countries throughout the Middle East and North Africa. The programs are in Arabic, Persian, Turkish, and other languages, and the channel claims to have up to fifteen million viewers every day.[50]

47. Stene, "Mobilisering og motstand," 154.
48. Tadros, "Copts of Egypt."
49. See "Egypt's Coptic Christians Flee."
50. Sat-7, "We Are Sat-7."

The Middle East Council of Churches is represented on the channel's governing body, which is an example of successful ecumenical cooperation in the region. But such cooperation is the exception rather than the rule. One typical trait of Christianity in the Middle East is the fact that several of the first great ecclesiastical divisions in Christian history continue to influence the relationship between the churches today. Conflicts that are centuries or millennia old are not dead. Even where they have in common the situation of being minorities, they are not necessarily good friends.

The church divisions were caused by both theological and political conflicts. The Assyrian church, also known as the Church of the East, represents the first great schism. This church had its core areas in the Persian empire, and broke with the official church in the Eastern Roman empire some years before the third ecumenical council met at Ephesus in 431.[51] This church has often been called "Nestorian," after Nestorius, the Patriarch of Constantinople, was condemned as a heretic at the council of Ephesus. The next great parting of the ways came with the Oriental Orthodox churches.[52] This is a collective term for relatively different churches, all of which broke with the official church in the Empire at a church council in Chalcedon in 451; this is why they are also called "Pre-Chalcedonian." After these schisms, none of these churches has been in communion with the other Orthodox churches in the region, which are often designated by the collective term "Eastern Orthodox," nor with the Catholic church.

In addition, there are the Oriental Catholic and the Greek Catholic churches, a group of so-called "churches *sui iuris*" within the Catholic church family. The Oriental Catholics were originally Oriental Orthodox or Assyrian, but various reasons led them to join the Catholic church; the Greek Catholics were originally Eastern Orthodox before they did the same. The Oriental and Greek Catholic churches recognize the pope in Rome as their head, but they have preserved their eastern canon law, their rites, and their patriarchal titles.[53]

51. It was at this Council that the church leader Nestorius was condemned as a heretic, and the Assyrian church—against its own will—has had to live with the polemical label "Nestorian" since that time. After this breach, the Assyrian church has not been in communion with any other churches. It is a small church today, mostly present in Iraq, Iran, and the USA. In the middle ages, on the other hand, it spread wide across large parts of Asia, as far east as China.

52. The autocephalous Oriental Orthodox churches are the Coptic Orthodox church, the Ethiopian Orthodox church, the Eritrean Orthodox church, the Armenian Orthodox church, the Syrian Orthodox church, and the Malankara Orthodox Syrian church (in India).

53. The Chaldean, the Coptic Catholic, the Syrian Catholic, and the Maronite churches are examples of Oriental Catholic churches in the Middle East today, while

Many of the Oriental Catholic and Greek Catholic churches came into existence as a result of Catholic missionary activity between the sixteenth and the nineteenth centuries. This, together with the memory of the Catholic "Franks" from the Crusader period, has created a deep distrust of Catholics in many Eastern and Oriental Orthodox churches. Catholics, especially priests and members of male religious orders, can still experience problems when they wish to visit Orthodox monasteries in the Middle East.

This complicates the climate of cooperation between many of the churches, although various Christians have found it perfectly possible on the individual level to live together. Many of the churches succeeded in establishing the Middle East Council of Churches in 1974, an umbrella organization that brings together the Oriental and Eastern Orthodox churches, several Protestant churches, and, from 1991, the Catholic churches (including the Oriental and Greek Catholics). The Council has played an important role in coordinating and intensifying church humanitarian work in the region, whether for Palestinian refugees in Jordan, Syria, and Lebanon, for Lebanese during the civil war, or in connection with the contemporary situation of refugees in Syria and Iraq.

The Pentecostals are not members of the Council, but several of the established Protestant churches belong to it. This is in itself a sign of a new ecumenical orientation, since these churches are almost exclusively the results of the western colonial presence and missionary activity, which was directed, not primarily against Muslims or Jews, but against the local Orthodox Christians. It is unclear whether the ecumenical initiatives in the region (which remain relatively lukewarm) are due to the international ecumenical awakening in the twentieth century or to the more pragmatic needs of minorities for Christians to stick together. It is, however, certain that the churches have cooperated well in the cause of preserving the religious family law, thereby maintaining an important instrument of power over people's daily lives.

THE CONFESSION AS A WAY OF LIFE—RELIGIOUS FAMILY LAW

Most countries in the Middle East have a family law that is regulated in religious terms. In a legal system of this kind, the various religious groups recognized by the state have both legislative and judicative power over their members in the regulation of marriage and divorce, inheritance law, and

---

the Melchite church is Greek Catholic. Unlike the other Oriental Catholic churches, the Maronite church was never Oriental Orthodox, but has always had an Antiochene West Syrian rite.

questions about child custody. This applies not only to Muslims (in Sharia courts), but also to Jews, Christians, and other religions recognized by the state (for example, the Druze in Lebanon and Israel).

This means that there is not one common family law for all the citizens in a country, but different laws and legal systems depending on the religious and denominational affiliation. Accordingly, religious and confessional belonging involve much more for the Christians in the Middle East than faith and attendance at church. Religious belonging has consequences for how one can organize one's life. The submission of the country's citizens to religious institutions in these important legal areas has been criticized for breaking with the idea of a shared citizenship, and also for leading to negative consequences for women in all the religions. The question of religious family law is therefore the object of considerable debate among Christians in all the Middle Eastern lands. As we shall see, this concerns not only the relationship to the state, but also the relations between the sexes, the relationship to the larger Muslim society (or to the larger Jewish society in Israel), and the relations between the Christian denominations.

In Lebanon, there is no secular marriage law, but a total of fifteen religious family laws across the spectrum of the various Christian denominations, Muslims, Druze, and Jews. The family law courts operate in complete freedom from the state, and the public system of law and courts in Lebanon exercises little or no supervision of them.[54]

When Lebanon took over the arrangement with regard to religious and family law from the Ottoman Empire and the French colonial period, freedom of religion was given a constitutional guarantee. It was decreed that it should not be obligatory to be registered according to one's religion. In principle, one ought to be able to choose to get married under a civil marriage law. Down to the present day, however, no such civil law has been passed.

The only possibility for a couple who want a civil wedding—for example, because they belong to different religions or confessions, or simply because they do not want to be subject to a religious family law—is to get married abroad. In such cases, the marriage law of the land in which they marry will be the legal basis that a Lebanese court takes into account, if a conflict should arise. For example, many Lebanese have contracted a civil marriage in Cyprus, and these marriages are then recognized in Lebanon. But if one contracts a civil marriage abroad, one cannot also have a religious ceremony in Lebanon, for in that case, the latter then takes precedence, and the marriage is subject to a religious family law.

54. Human Rights Watch, "Unequal and Unprotected."

It is thus possible to contract a civil marriage if one has the money to travel abroad. In 2013, however, the first civil marriage in Lebanon took place, appealing to the law that establishes both religious freedom and the possibility of not belonging to any religion. The couple were required to renounce their formal religious memberships, and this is a critical matter in a country where (for example) many political positions are assigned to one or other confession. Since there was no Lebanese civil family law, the civil court decided to use the French marriage law.

Lebanese secular activists and NGOs have tried several times to get the system of family law abolished, but every attempt has stranded in parliament,[55] where the religious organizations have considerable power, since the seats in parliament are assigned according to religious and confessional membership. The churches, especially the Maronite church, play an important role in assuring support for candidates for parliament.[56] Neither the churches nor the Muslim institutions have any desire to get rid of the family law system. In this way, the family law system in Lebanon both unites and divides: it unites the reform forces across religious and denominational boundaries in their opposition to it, and it unites both religious leaders and others with a traditional view of marriage in their support of it.

DISCRIMINATION OF WOMEN, DIVORCE, AND REVENGE KILLING

A report by the Human Rights Watch in 2015 documents the discrimination that all the women in Lebanon, independently of their faith, suffer through the country's religious family law system.[57] The various religious family laws all make it more difficult for women than for men to get a divorce. They make women's financial rights in a divorce settlement weaker than men's; women's inheritance rights are poorer than men's; and women are legally in a worse position than men in matters concerning child custody. On one point, however, Christian women in Lebanon have a more equal position than their Muslim and Druze sisters, for whereas Druze and Muslim family law give the man a full right to divorce and the wife only a conditional right, neither

55. Human Rights Watch, "Unequal and Unprotected."

56. According to the Taif Accord (1990), which marks the end of the civil war, the seats in parliament are distributed equally among Christians and Muslims and are then distributed among the various confessions. Of sixty-four Christian seats, thirty-four are allocated to the Maronites, fourteen to the Greek Orthodox, eight to the Greek Catholics, one to the Armenian Catholics, one to the Protestants, one to the Syrian Orthodox, etc. See Kverme, "Patriarken," 178.

57. Human Rights Watch, "Unequal and Unprotected."

Christian women nor Christian men have an unconditional right to divorce. A Christian in the Middle East has very few possibilities of getting a divorce.

Some of the Christian family laws in Lebanon give conditional possibilities of divorce. For example, rape or other forms of violence in intimate relationships form a basis for separation in Protestant and Greek Orthodox family law, and possibly for divorce if the parties have not been reconciled after the separation.

The situation in Egypt is stricter. For Christians there, the only valid grounds for divorce are infidelity or conversion. This is also the case for Greek Orthodox and Protestants, although these churches admit several grounds for divorce in countries outside Egypt. This is because the Coptic Orthodox church, and especially its previous Pope, Shenouda III, got the churches to cooperate in narrowing down the family law on this point.[58]

Islamic family law forbids a Muslim woman to marry a Christian man, but Muslim men are allowed to marry Christian women. This, however, is strictly forbidden—and intensely feared—in all the Christian family laws, because the Muslim Sharia states that the children of Muslim fathers must be Muslims. As long as Christian mission and conversion from Islam are forbidden in Muslim countries, reproduction among their own members remains the only possibility of Christian recruitment and survival.

Among Christians, especially in Egypt, it not seldom happens that one of the partners converts to Islam in order to get a divorce. The prohibition against abandoning Islam makes it almost impossible to convert back to Christianity after the divorce has gone through.[59] This means that the Christian prohibition against divorce (and remarriage) leads both to the loss of church members and to tensions between Christians and Muslims.

The tensions intensified when two Coptic priests' wives, Wafa Constantine and Camelia Shehata, allegedly wanted to get a divorce from their husbands in 2004 and 2010. Muslim versions relate that after the women fled from their homes and converted to Islam, they were kidnapped by Copts and brought back and kept hidden away. The Copts, on the other hand, have claimed that the women were kidnapped by Muslims, who tried to force them to convert. These cases, and the many rumors that spread in their wake, attracted considerable attention and fed the flames of tensions between Christians and Muslims with regard to their respective identities, not only in Egypt but also throughout the entire region. Extremist groups exploited the stories to the full. One Al Qaida group in Iraq claimed

58. Vogt, "Lederskap," 129.

59. Legal processes are under way in Egypt that are meant in theory to make it possible to return to Christianity, provided that a court accepts this in each individual case. In practice, however, it is almost impossible to achieve this.

responsibility for the bloody bombing of the Chaldean cathedral in Bagdad in 2010 and declared that this was revenge for the kidnapping of the two women in Egypt.[60] And in 2011, ISIS captured twenty-one Coptic migrant workers in Libya and executed them brutally on a beach. The propaganda film that spread this crime across the world had the following moving text: "This filthy blood is just some of what awaits you, in revenge for Camelia and her sisters."[61]

The Coptic Pope, Tawadros II, is more open to reform than his predecessor, Pope Shenouda, and he has initiated a work of reform to adapt Coptic canon law better to a new age and new societal circumstances. One change is the liberalization of divorce legislation in certain areas.[62] It remains to be seen how successful this work of reform will be, given that there are such great tensions linked to questions of family law, tensions between women and men, between Copts and the larger society, and between conservative Copts and those who are open to reform, both within the ecclesiastical hierarchy and among the laity.

In 2016, a new family law for Protestants was adopted by the Lutheran and Anglican churches in Palestine and Jordan. This is said to be the most liberal Christian family law in the Middle East. It gives women an equal position in inheritance law and gives unrestricted permission for both women and men to get a divorce.[63] At present, we do not know whether other churches in the Middle East will let themselves be influenced by this development, or whether it will be rejected as Protestant and western decadence.

THE HOLY LANDS

At the beginning of this chapter, we quoted the Patriarch's words about "the land of our ancestors." This not only applies to the Chaldeans in Iraq: it is important for all the Christians in the Middle East, because "the land of the ancestors" in this context means the biblical land. Most of the stories in the Bible are linked to concrete geographical places, and these places are located in the Middle East. This is why the biblical geography has been one factor in the formation of the religious identity of the Christians in the region. Historical places and lands have acquired very special meanings thanks to the insistence that "This is where it happened!" This is where the shepherds were sitting in the fields when Jesus was born, this is where Abraham is

60. See "Deadly Blast Outside Egypt Church."
61. Lia, "Korsfarernes medløpere," 209.
62. Elsässer, "Coptic Divorce Struggle," 333–51.
63. ELCJHL, *COCOP Report 2016*, 10–11, 32–33.

buried, and this is where Moses was allowed a glimpse of the Promised Land.

The biblical texts coalesce with the history of human beings and the history of geography. The places become witnesses to the material of the narratives and create continuity between the universe of the texts and the people who live today. There are also special narratives of how signs and wonders have continued to occur at the place, or of how martyrs have fought and died for their faith. In other words, the history of the place becomes a continuation of the text.

Although the biblical geography is a specific characteristic of Christianity in the Middle East, we should not forget that the phenomenon of "sacred geography" is common elsewhere too. This is because the church's history is a continuation of the biblical narrative. Holy places linked (for example) to martyrs, saints, or stories of miracles are found everywhere in the world, not only in Catholic and Orthodox traditions, but also in Protestant Christianity, which has often distanced itself from specifically holy places.

Although the entire region is generally influenced by biblical geography, the Holy Land has a special position. This is a relatively undefined arena between the river Jordan (including the East Bank) and the Mediterranean, and stretching from the Sinai desert northwards as far as Lebanon and southwest Syria. This is a holy area in Jewish, Muslim, and Christian tradition, largely because of Jerusalem, which all three religions see as a holy city.

For many Christians in this region, the land is holy first and foremost because it was here that Jesus lived, died, and according to Christian tradition rose from the dead. After new nation states took their places on the map, "the Holy Land" has also become *several* holy lands, since Jesus did not set his feet only on today's Israel and Palestine. The Gospel of John relates that he changed water into wine in the town of Cana, which someone claims to be the village of Qana in today's Lebanon. This makes Lebanon too a holy land for many Lebanese Christians. Jordanians are proud that Jesus walked on the East Bank of the river Jordan (in today's kingdom of Jordan), and in Damascus, the capital of Syria, one can visit the house in which Paul is said to have waited to regain his sight after he had been blinded by the encounter with the risen Jesus. And some Copts regard Egypt as a holy land, both because of the saints and holy martyrs in the church's history and because it was to Egypt that the Holy Family was forced to flee when King Herod (according to the Gospel of Matthew) wanted to kill all the male children in Bethlehem.

Holy lands attract pilgrims. Israel has for many years welcomed millions of Christian pilgrim tourists from the whole world, and has a well-developed infrastructure for receiving and caring for the needs of these visitors. In recent years, Palestinian churches have endeavored to attract pilgrims to visit Bethlehem and other holy places on the West Bank.

One of the places that Israel has well equipped to welcome pilgrims is the site at the river Jordan where Jesus (according to the New Testament) is said to have been baptized. But the river Jordan is also the boundary river between Israel and Jordan, and the Bible says nothing about which side of the river Jesus was baptized on. The 1994 peace accord between Jordan and Israel made it possible to clear the East Bank of landmines, and this allowed archaeological excavations of what many claim is the real site of Jesus' baptism. These excavations brought to light ruins of ancient churches and monasteries, hermits' grottoes, and baptismal pools. When UNESCO gave the site official recognition and included it in its World Heritage List in 2015, Jordan gained more stock in the brand called "the Holy Land."[64] Since 2000, the Jordanian King has given the various historical churches building sites close to the newly discovered site of the baptism. Instead of collaborating on one shared church, each is now constructing its own characteristic church building, thereby demonstrating both the plurality and the rivalry among the churches in the Middle East.

JERUSALEM—RIVALRY FOR THE HOLY PLACE

"We should remove every stone of the Holy Sites and transport them to Scandinavia for a hundred years and not return them until everyone has learned to live together in Jerusalem," sighed the Israeli author Amos Oz.[65] He was talking about Jerusalem and the Holy Land, for holy places are also political and economic places, and the control of such places, access to them, and the question of who owns them are important matters.

Jerusalem has experienced painfully how much the struggle for sovereignty has meant in the course of history. Among Christians, the Church of the Holy Sepulcher in Jerusalem's Old City is a good example of how complicated the question of sovereignty over holy places can be. The picture includes various legal accords from a variety of historical regimes, various religious divisions, and economic interests—and all this in a city full to the brim of geopolitical tensions.

The church, which was built over the place where, according to tradition, Jesus was crucified and buried, has been the object of rivalry among Christians almost from the time of its construction in the fourth century. This is why, when Saladin took back the city from the Crusaders in 1187,

64. UNESCO, "Baptism Site."
65. Montefiore, Jerusalem, 538.

he gave a Muslim family the job of keeping the keys to the church and of ensuring that it was opened each morning, since the Christians themselves could not agree about who should do this. This task is still entrusted to a Muslim family in Jerusalem.

Under the Ottoman Empire, sovereignty over the Church of the Holy Sepulcher was shared among several churches. This policy was enforced by a decree about the *status quo* issued by the Sultan in 1853, forbidding changes in the shared area in the church unless there was an agreement among all those churches whose claims to sovereignty had been accepted.[66]

If you visit the church today, you will see an ancient ladder standing on one of the windowsills on the external wall. The ladder has stood there since before 1853, when the windowsills were defined as common property in the Sultan's decree, and this means that it cannot be removed. The *status quo* decree has not lessened the tensions between the churches; nor has it reduced the number of fist fights among the clergy inside the church. One warm summer day in 2002, eleven Coptic and Ethiopic monks had to be taken to hospital after a fist fight that started because a Coptic monk had moved a chair into the shade. The Ethiopians interpreted this as a breach of the *status quo* decree and hence as a dangerous show of force.

The upkeep of the church has also suffered as a consequence of the *status quo* policy. It was only in 1958 that the Orthodox, the Catholic, and the Armenian Orthodox churches came to an agreement about a project of restoration of the Church of the Holy Sepulcher; but disagreements about how to implement the project meant that it did not start until 2016, after King Abdullah II had donated a large sum of money to the Orthodox patriarchate in Jerusalem as a contribution both to the repairs to the church and to the consolidation of his own role in the city. The King of Jordan is the protector of the Christian and Muslim holy places in Jerusalem's Old City, and it has become more difficult for him to carry out this function after Israel's annexation of this district in the city in 1967. Although the King's role as protector is still affirmed in the peace accord between Israel and Jordan, the interpretation of what this means in practice today is a political question that kindles intense debates.

---

66. The sovereignty over the various parts of the church is divided among the Orthodox, the Catholic, and the Armenian Orthodox churches. Later, the Coptic Orthodox, Ethiopian Orthodox, and Syrian Orthodox churches also received their own spaces within the church complex. See Cohen, *Saving the Holy Sepulchre*.

ISRAEL AND PALESTINE—THE
BIG GREEK LANDOWNER

As we have seen, owning land and buildings is important for the churches in the Middle East. Many of them are big landowners, but the Orthodox patriarchate in Jerusalem (that is to say, the Orthodox church in Israel, Palestine, and Jordan) is in a class of its own. Under the Ottoman regime, this church was recognized as one of several millets, that is to say, as a religious group with a relatively large measure of autonomy and control over its own resources. Unlike other churches, the Orthodox church had fewer restrictions with regard to the acquisition and administration of land. For example, it could both buy and possess land, and define this as *waqf* (religious property), thereby gaining exemption from property taxes.[67] This is why this church is by far the biggest ecclesiastical landowner in the Middle East today—something that is not an unmixed blessing.

The Orthodox patriarchate in Jerusalem is in fact one of the largest private landowners in Israel, East Jerusalem, and the West Bank.[68] It owns (*inter alia*) the plots on which Israel's Supreme Court, Parliament (Knesset), and prime minister's residence (Beit HaNassi) stand. Naturally, this property makes the church a political actor in the Israeli–Palestinian conflict. From an Israeli perspective, there is fear that Palestinians may get influence over the church's leadership, so that important properties in Israel could be controlled by Palestinian interests. The Palestinians too are aware of this potential power, and the PLO protested loudly in 2011 when the patriarchate extended to 2150 the land leases on plots in West Jerusalem, including the ground on which the Knesset stands.

The PLO's protest reflects centuries-old tensions between the church's Greek leadership and the Arabs who amount to almost the totality of its membership. Whereas, for example, the patriarchate in Antioch (that is, the Orthodox church in countries such as Syria, Lebanon, Iraq, and Iran) officially changed its language at the start of the twentieth century from Greek to Arabic, and implemented other reforms in order to draw closer to its Arab members, nothing like this has happened in the Jerusalem patriarchate.[69] Although the church's local members do not speak Greek, the leaders and most of the senior priests and bishops are Greek, and Greek is the church's official language.

---

67. Kårtveit, "Tilhørighet," 106.

68. Katz and Kark, "Church and Landed Property," 392–93.

69. McDermott, "Shaping the Church," 49.

When the former Patriarch Diodorus I was interviewed about the Arab displeasure with the church's Greek hierarchy, he replied:

> When did the Arabs come here? . . . The Greeks have been here for over 2,000 years. They came with Alexander of Macedonia in the year 322 BC, and since then we are still here. The Arabs arrived only during the 7th century. This is our Church, the church of the Greeks, if they do not accept our laws, they have one alternative—choose another Church, or establish one of their own.[70]

Another reason for the conflict between the Greek ecclesiastical leadership and Arab church members is that very little of the church's enormous income from its property has benefited the local people.[71] On this point, it differs from many other churches in this region, which have invested heavily in running schools, health services, and social programs for the Arab population. To take one example: the Latin patriarchate in Jerusalem (the Roman Catholic church), which got its first Palestinian patriarch in 1987, runs many schools, health clinics, and other welfare services, including housing subsidies for newly married Catholic couples, in order to hold onto the Christian population. By comparison, a report by a lay Orthodox committee concluded that:

> [T]he Patriarchate has not built one single church, a school, an educational or a social institution in Israel as far back as we know. . . . Almost all the upper hierarchy within the Patriarchate are Greek nationals, totally unconcerned and completely cut off from the affairs of the community where Arabs constitute more than 99 percent [of the population].[72]

This means that the church, with its vast property folio, lives in a delicate tension between its local members, who push for greater influence, and Israeli authorities who are afraid precisely of increased Palestinian control of the church. When Irenaios I was elected patriarch by the church's synod in 2001, Israeli authorities accused him of being a personal friend of the Palestinian leader, Yasser Arafat, and thus of being a threat to Israel's security. Unlike the Palestinian self-governing authority and Jordan, Israel refused to recognize the new Patriarch. This was the first time in the church's long

70. Interview in *Haaretz*, September 25, 1992; see McDermott, "Shaping the Church," 50.

71. See Katz and Kark, "Church and Landed Property."

72. Executive Committee of the Orthodox Congress ECOC board (1994), Annual Report, Nazareth, 4; see McDermott, "Shaping the Church," 52.

history that the authorities who controlled Jerusalem did not recognize the church's election of a new patriarch.[73] But the course of events was to show that this would not be the last time.

In 2004, Israel suddenly changed course and recognized Irenaios. But only one short year later, it was revealed that he had accepted the sale of some of the church's properties in Jerusalem's Old City to American Jewish investors. A storm of accusations of a barter with Israel—land in exchange for recognition—followed. Nor did his situation improve when it also emerged that Irenaios had received help four years earlier, in the patriarchal election, by a man condemned for drug smuggling, a man who had circulated homoerotic pictures of the rival candidate to Irenaios.[74]

The church's synod deposed Irenaios as Patriarch, but this time, Israel refused to recognize his dismissal and his successor. It provided military personnel for Irenaios's protection in the monastery in the Old City. The new Patriarch, Theophilos III, was quickly recognized by the Palestinian and Jordanian authorities.[75] The sale of property in the Holy Land is no trifling matter—especially in Jerusalem's Old City. Some have argued that the logical consequence of this sale may be to make it harder for the Palestinians to secure East Jerusalem as their future capital.[76]

When Theophilos was recognized by the Israeli authorities in 2007, this generated rumors that he too had entered into agreements with Israel, and the PLO's displeasure at the church's renewal of the land leases in 2011 can be understood in the light of this. But in 2017, both Palestinians and Israelis were enraged to learn that Theophilos had sold land in Jerusalem, Jaffa, Caesarea, and Tiberias to unknown holding companies registered in tax havens.[77] Israeli parliamentarians threatened to confiscate the church's land, in order to ensure Israel's control over strategically important territory, while the Palestinians once again accused the Greek Patriarch of selling off their land. The Patriarch personally visited Jordan, Greece, Great Britain, and the Vatican in order to get support for the church's right to administer its own property resources. In this way, he continues to steer the difficult path between Palestinian and Israeli pressure. The church is dependent on its Arab members, if it is to have someone to be the church for; and it is dependent on a good relationship to Israel, if it is to get visas for its Greek

73. McDermott, "Shaping the Church," 50.
74. Smith, "Greece in Revolt."
75. McDermott, "Shaping the Church," 51; Kårtveit, "Tilhørighet," 106.
76. McDermott, "Shaping the Church," 46.
77. Hatuqa, "Holy Land for Sale"; Hasson, "New Details Emerge."

church leaders and to prevent the state from expropriating parts of the church's landed properties.

THE JOYS AND THE CURSES OF ALCOHOL

If you are granted an audience and visit Patriarch Theophilos in Jerusalem, it is highly likely that you will be offered a glass of cognac and some sweets. For many Christians in the Middle East, alcohol is not just a stimulant: it is also an important identity marker and a source of income, since it is mostly Christians who have produced and sold alcohol in Muslim countries in the Middle East (to the extent that production and sale have been lawful). Christian Chaldeans have sold alcohol in Iraq, and Armenians have produced wine and brandy in Iran. And in Lebanon, the production of wine and the sale of alcohol are important sources of income for both churches and individual Christians.

The little Palestinian town of Taybeh lies just outside Jerusalem. It is said to be the last Palestinian village on the West Bank with an almost exclusively Christian population. The principal industry is beer brewing, and these are prosperous times: while five hundred liters of beer were produced per year in 1995, this increased in 2009 to more than six hundred thousand liters per year. Interestingly enough, 50 percent of the beer is sold on the Muslim West Bank.[78] Indeed, alcohol sales increased by 70 percent in the Middle East between 2001 and 2011,[79] and this growth in consumption cannot be attributed to tourists or non-Muslims alone. Even in Iran, which practices a strict prohibition of the sale and consumption of alcohol, the authorities were forced to face up to reality in 2013, when they asked the Shia Muslim clergy for permission to open the country's first rehab center for alcoholics, albeit on the grounds that alcohol dependency was an illness, not a sin.[80]

While there has in general been a positive relationship to alcohol in Jewish and Christian traditions in the Middle East, this is forbidden in the Muslim Sharia. As the above statistics show, this does not, of course, mean that Muslims do not drink alcohol; it means that there is an ambivalent relationship to alcohol in Muslim contexts. Although restrictive Muslim governments have strictly applied the prohibition of alcohol at regular intervals down through the centuries, Arab and Muslim history is full of examples of

---

78. Kalman, "Palestinian Brewery."
79. See "Islam and Alcohol."
80. Matthee, "Alcohol in the Islamic Middle East," 125.

a praxis that involves alcoholic drinks—and thereby also interaction with Christians.

The Christian monasteries that were scattered in the past around today's Iraq, Syria, Lebanon, Israel, Palestine, and Egypt often had their own taverns and inns ("caravanserai," from which the word "caravans" is derived), where they could offer passers-by a bed for the night and food and wine. This was an important source of income for the monasteries and made them the largest producers of wine in the Middle East. But it was not only passing caravans that stopped at the inns to drink wine. They were so popular among many male Arab elites and intellectuals that a specific Arabic literary genre, the *dayriyyāt*, developed in the early Middle Ages: songs in praise of wine (*khamriyya* poems) and stories about festivities in the taverns.[81]

The monasteries, with their inns, were also places where men could meet unveiled women. The stories often speak about beautiful young women who were waitresses in the inns. The word "alcohol" itself comes from the Arabic *al-kohl*. This refers to the coloring agent antimony, which was used as mascara. In these ways, the Christian monasteries were given a place in Muslim literature.

Alcohol as an identity marker can have a double significance for Christians in the Middle East. First, it can be an identity marker vis-à-vis the majority Muslim society. Secondly, alcohol can function in the identity of Orthodox and Catholic Christians vis-à-vis the newer Protestant revivalist Christianity, which is more critical of alcohol than they are. Alcohol plays an important role for Orthodox and Catholics not only culturally, socially, and economically, but also theologically, for example, in connection with the celebration of the eucharist. But an investigation in 2011 showed that 78 percent of Evangelical church leaders in the Middle East held that alcohol was not compatible with a Christian way of life.[82]

But alcohol, or the opposition to alcohol, can also be an important identity marker for Muslims, and hence can also have consequences for both Christian minorities and Muslims with a secular orientation. The way in which a majority Muslim society deals with practices linked to alcohol is thus an interesting starting point for studying the living conditions of both minorities and majorities.

Abu Ahmed, formerly an Iraqi intelligence officer and now a taxi driver in Bagdad, told the British newspaper *The Independent* in 2008: "I drink seven or eight cans of beer a day and a bottle of whiskey on Thursday

---

81. Kilpatrick, "Monasteries through Muslim Eyes," 22–23.
82. Pew Research Center, "Global Survey," 21.

evenings."[83] The journalist emphasized that the security situation in Bagdad had improved so much by this time that Muslims like Ahmed had begun to drink alcohol again in parks and other public places. They had sometimes been able to do this under the secular Baath government of Saddam Hussein, but under the increased sectarian tensions and the chaos that followed in the wake of the American invasion in 2003, Al Qaida groups and Shia militias seized the opportunity to attack many of the places where alcohol was sold. It was only in 2008, when the security situation was sufficiently stable, that people in Bagdad dared to drink alcohol in public again—putting a smile on the faces of the city's Chaldean merchants.

Unfortunately, the security situation in Bagdad has deteriorated gravely since 2008, and the alcohol policy has gradually become more restrictive, in tandem with the increase in unrest and with the new governments. This reached its peak in the fall of 2016, when the Iraqi authorities proclaimed a total prohibition of the sale of alcohol in the country. Extremists took the matter into their own hands and killed a Christian alcohol seller in Basra only a few days after this prohibition came into force. Two months later, three persons were killed in a Christian shop in Bagdad that sold wine and brandy.[84] This means that alcohol is not only a stimulant and a source of income for Christians in the Middle East. It is also a matter of life and death.

THE ARABIAN PENINSULA—A FLOWERING OF CHRISTIANITY AFTER TWELVE HUNDRED YEARS?

Irrespective of what kinds of political strategies the churches in the Middle East have chosen in order to survive and to demonstrate that they belong to the national fellowships, there can be no doubt that we are living in a critical time for the religious plurality in the region. But unlike the countries we have written about up to this point in the present chapter, where the number of Christians is sinking, it is increasing abruptly on the Arabian Peninsula.[85] Christianity disappeared here twelve hundred years ago, but between three and four million Christians live here today.[86] This number surpasses almost the sum total of all Christians in all the other Middle Eastern countries, with the exception of Egypt. The Christians in the Gulf states are not citizens,

83. See "Alcohol Returns to Baghdad."

84. Casper, "They Will Know We Are Christians."

85. The presentation of the flowering of Christianity in the Arabian peninsula builds largely on Thornbjønsrud, "Den arabiske halvøy."

86. Thornbjønsrud, "Den arabiske halvøy," 215.

but migrant workers, mostly from Asiatic countries such as India, the Philippines, and Sri Lanka, but also from countries such as Syria, Egypt, and Ethiopia.

The inflow of migrant workers has led to the construction of churches in the Gulf states, but not in Saudi Arabia, where this is forbidden. But the legal rights of the migrants are very poor, and there are few or no state welfare structures for them. This means that the churches have, not only a spiritual function, but also a social function as a meeting place and a supplier of welfare services for the workers. The churches offer everything from cultural evenings and contact with one's native land to youth work, language teaching, and links to the national authorities. In this way, the churches also contribute to integration and societal development in these states.[87]

The Catholic church appears to have (re)discovered the Arabian Peninsula. Restructurings in 2010 divided the former vicariate of Arabia into two, a northern and a southern vicariate, in order to cope better with the increase in the number of Catholic migrant workers in the various countries on the Peninsula.[88] In the Catholic tradition, a vicariate is an ecclesiastical territory in mission lands that has not yet achieved the status of a diocese. At the same time as the reorganization, the Catholic church officially declared Mary to be "Our Lady of Arabia, protectress of the two vicariates on the Arabian Peninsula."[89] Berit Thorbjønsrud, a historian of religion, has shown how the Arabian Peninsula is integrated in this way into the Catholic worldview and the religious geography. And since diaspora parishes of every confession are dependent on contact, personnel, and support from the churches in their homelands, the Gulf states are also being integrated into the global church's worldview.[90]

One example of the new Catholic interest in the Arabian Peninsula was Pope Francis's visit to Abu Dhabi in the United Arab Emirates in 2019. He was the first Pope to visit a Gulf state, but this is not the only reason why the visit was historic. The Sheikh of Al-Azhar, Ahmed el-Tayeb, also came to Abu Dhabi to meet the Pope. He is one of the greatest symbolic leaders for the world's Sunni Muslims. Pope Francis and the Sheikh took the opportunity to launch a common document on "Human fraternity for world peace and living together." Pope Francis had not only re-established the contact with Al-Azhar, which had been broken under the previous Pope Benedict,

87. Thornbjønsrud, "Den arabiske halvøy," 218; Thorbjønsrud, "Mellom by og ørken"

88. The former Apostolic Vicariate of Kuwait became part of the new Apostolic Vicariate of Northern Arabia; see "Reorganisation."

89. Thornbjønsrud, "Den arabiske halvøy," 220.

90. Thornbjønsrud, "Den arabiske halvøy," 224.

but also launched a common document in which the two symbolic world religious leaders acknowledge each other's religion and present religious pluralism as an integral part of God's work of creation.[91] Both the Sheikh and the Pope wanted to build a bridge between Christians and Muslims, and to counteract geopolitical tensions between Christianity and Islam.

It remains to be seen whether Christianity continues to be a phenomenon restricted to migrant workers in the Gulf states, or whether it puts down lasting roots on the Peninsula. It is well known that missionary activity by Christians in these countries is strictly forbidden, and the churches' permission to be there is entirely dependent on the goodwill of the heads of state. At the same time, several of these states, such as the United Arab Emirates and Oman, are attempting to present a profile as modern and tolerant states, with an eye to integration into the international community even after the oil runs out. In this project, the papal visit is important, just as much as the building of churches and the Christian workers.

OUTLOOK

We have chosen in this chapter to write mostly about Christian emigration, about the various strategies adopted by the churches in order to belong to the national fellowships, and about the importance of the Holy Land. A more exhaustive description of Christianity in the Middle East would have included more about all the Christian schools that have both Christian and Muslim pupils. Running schools is a very important part of many churches' activity in the Middle East. We could also have written more about mission and evangelism—either about new Baptist or Pentecostal congregations that are trying to get established but attract the opposition of the established churches, about Evangelical mission among Jews and the emerging groups of Messianic Jews, or about the Evangelical mission among Muslims, who in many cases become Christians in secret.[92]

We close this chapter in the center of the Holy Land, not only because, as King Abdullah II of Jordan said in 2010, "all roads in our part of the world, all the conflicts, lead to Jerusalem,"[93] but also because most Christians in the world have a relationship to the city without ever having been there. Jerusalem is the world city—sacred for Jews, Christians, and Muslims, a trophy

---

91. Francis and Al-Tayyeb, "A Document on Human Fraternity." See also Thorbjønsrud, "Pave Frans i Emiratene."

92. See Miller and Johnstone, "Believers in Christ."

93. Montefiore, *Jerusalem*, 535.

for conquerors, the location of the Day of Judgment, and a battleground for the contemporary clashes between civilizations.

In his history of the city, Simon Sebag Montefiore has pointed to a paradox: while the idea of Jerusalem promises heavenly, eternal calm, the city has largely been marked by war and rivalry. The contrast between the earthly and the heavenly city is extreme. In this way, Jerusalem tells a story about expectation and disillusionment, where heavenly expectation gives birth to earthly disappointment. By unmasking the contrast between utopia and reality, Jerusalem embodies contrasts and experiences that are contained within many Christian worldviews.

The relationship between Jews, Muslims, and Christians in the Middle East influences an entire world. The conflict between Israel and Palestine kindles interest and commitment everywhere in the world, among both Christians and non-Christians. The attention paid to Christian emigration—or the lack of attention it receives—influences global political and religious discourses about the relationship between Muslims and Christians in particular, but also the relationship to Jews.

But perhaps the reverse is also true. It is not only Christianity from the Middle East that influences an entire world: the entire world also influences Christianity in the Middle East. It is well known that this region is inundated by political, economic, and religious agendas from the outside: geopolitics, oil, foreign fighters, and religion. Everything from Russian Orthodox traditionalists to American Christian Zionists, Nigerian pilgrims, and European peace activists want to leave their mark on the Christian map.

One final important point: enormous sums of money are transferred from the world's Christians to Christians in the Middle East: from the diaspora churches in the West to their mother churches; from Evangelical Christian Zionists to Evangelical Christians in Israel (or to Jewish settlers, for that matter); from organizations dedicated to mission or to safeguarding the human rights of persecuted Christians; or from established churches around the globe to their sister churches in the region. Many want a finger in the pie in the Holy Land, and most all, they want to have a foothold in Jerusalem.

6

Asia

Christianity as a Newcomer
and a Foreign Element

IF WE TAKE OUR starting point in a dream of converting the great masses
of people, Asia is the continent where Christian mission from Europe did
not succeed. Around half the world's population live in Asia, but only a
small proportion belong to the churches. Nevertheless, there are large
churches that influence and are influenced by the cultural contexts to
which they belong. One main question for the churches in Asia is how
Christian praxis and faith are to relate to other religions. What does it
mean to be a Christian while at the same time belonging to a culture in
which Christianity, historically speaking, is a newcomer?

Although the *proportion* of Christians in Asia, taken as a whole, is small, the
numbers of those who belong to the churches are nevertheless large. Three of
the countries in the world with the largest Christian populations are located
in Asia: the Philippines, China, and India. The great majority of the population of the Philippines (just over one hundred million) are Christians, and
more than 80 percent belong to the Catholic church. When Pope Francis
visited the country in January 2015, he brought together six million Filipinos
for the Mass he celebrated in Manila, the largest gathering that has ever come
together to see and hear a pope.[1] In the small country of East Timor, more

---

1. See "Pope Francis in Manila."

than 80 percent of the population are Catholics. In 2010, it was estimated that about 30 percent of the population of South Korea were Christians, and the world's biggest Pentecostal church is located in the capital, Seoul.[2]

The reality for Christians in the rest of Asia is different: in most Asian countries, they are small minorities. In this respect, the situation of the Christians in Asia is like that in the Middle East, but the differences are more striking. There have been churches in the Middle East since the very earliest Christian period. But in the rest of Asia, Christianity—with some significant exceptions—arrived with missionaries from the west, first from Europe and later also from North America. The missionary activity took place in parallel with the governments of the colonial period: Christianity was the religion of the colonial masters. The link between Christianity and the west was strong, and it has remained strong in much of Asia. This confronts Christians with fundamental questions about identity—how can one be fully Christian and at the same time fully Indian, Chinese, Thai, or Japanese?

Not only are the Christians small minorities in most Asian lands. In many places, they also belong to marginalized groups, and the proportion of Christians is often biggest in ethnic minorities. In country after country, Christianity has proved to have the largest appeal to such groups. We must suppose that those who are already on the outside of the societal mainstream have the least to lose, and the most to gain, by joining a new fellowship.

An urgent task for the churches in Asia has been the inculturation or contextualization of the Christianity that the missionaries brought from Europe or the USA. This prompts a number of difficult questions. Many missionaries endeavored to understand Asian culture and religion, but it was often the elites' culture that they were interested in, and that they came to know and tried to unite to the Christian tradition. One of the problems that the churches gradually had to tackle is that the culture of the elites in Asia, as elsewhere in the world, frequently contains elements that oppress other groups of persons. Christians who belong to these societal groups that are often oppressed and marginalized, such as the indigenous population or ethnic minorities, can face a hard dilemma: on the one hand, there is the need to accept the dominant culture in order not to exclude oneself from the national fellowship, and on the other, the need to work against oppressive aspects of the dominant culture in order to avoid being marginalized to an even greater extent. The churches' relationship to the caste system in India is one concrete example. We shall look at this in greater detail later in the present chapter.

2. Connor, "6 Facts."

The remainder of the chapter will focus primarily on India and China, before we close with a look at the Philippines. This is a radical delimitation, not least since we lose sight of all the churches that live in countries with Muslim majorities, such as Pakistan, Bangladesh, Indonesia, and Malaysia. But although we mostly look at India and China, we shall encounter very varied expressions of Christianity that relate to many different cultures. One-third of the global population live in India and China, which are the native lands of some of the world's most important religious traditions: Hinduism, Buddhism, Sikhism, Confucianism, and Taoism. The common thread in the presentation of Christianity in these two vast countries is the question that is equally urgent everywhere in Asia: For historical reasons, many persons associate Christianity with the west. What are the churches doing to prevent Christianity from being a foreign element in Asia?

We shall see that the concrete challenges entailed by making Christianity an Indian and a Chinese religion are very different, thanks to some fundamental differences between the two countries. India is often called the biggest democracy in the world. Throughout most of the period since independence from British colonial rule in 1947, the state's politics can be described as secularist, but with the intention of making religious plurality easier to cope with. In recent years, this policy has come under pressure from a growing Hindu nationalism, and religious minorities—Muslims, even more than Christians—have been exposed to an ever greater pressure especially since 2014, when Prime Minister Narendra Modi and the Bharatiya Janata Party (BJP) came to power. In the same period, China has been governed exclusively by a Communist Party that has sometimes seen all religion as a threat to the state, and that has created very specific ecclesiastical structures by means of a strict regulation. At the close of this chapter, we shall look at the Philippines, which forms a contrast to India and China and is decidedly an exception to the circumstances under which Christianity exists in Asia. Here, Catholicism was woven at an early date into dominant cultural currents in such a way that the church and Christianity have played a central role in nation-building, and the Philippines have become one of the largest Catholic countries in the world.

INDIA—"AD 52 CHRISTIANS"

Banners and placards carried on a quiet procession along the main streets in the megalopolis of Chennai in southern India at the end of January 1999 had the message: "All Christians are AD 52 Christians." Hundreds of Indian Christians were protesting against the violence and the attacks on

Christians that had increased in the preceding months. A crackling loud-speaker transmitted the words of a bishop, telling the story of the Australian Baptist missionary Graham Staines, who had been murdered with his two small sons a few days before this. A mob had set fire to the car in which they were sleeping, and the three were burnt alive.[3] People in India and the rest of the world reacted with horror to this killing. The bishop called out that Christians were every bit as much Indian as all the others in the country. And that is how it looked: those who carried the placards were not visibly different in any way from the onlookers who stood on the sidewalk, nor from the policemen who ensured peace and order.[4]

When they referred to year 52 of the Common Era, the demonstrators wanted to recall the churches' long history in India. There is a widespread belief that the apostle Thomas came to India in 52 and founded a church there. The Thomas Christians form an important part of Indian Christian life, but the majority of India's Christians belong to churches that were founded by European missionaries more than fifteen hundred years later. The missionaries' endeavors were unsuccessful, if we measure them against the goal of "Christianizing India." But Christianity gained a foothold among some groups in the population. Staines worked as a missionary among the group whom the Constitution calls "tribals," but who now are often called "Adivasies." The great majority of Indian Christians are Advisasies, or belong to the "Dalit," who are the lowest in the Indian caste system.

The murder of Staines and his sons was a symbol and a warning of what was to come. From the last years of the twentieth century onwards, Christians have experienced waves of violence and killings. The demonstrations in Chennai and the murders that occasioned them bring together some of the central themes in any description of Christianity in India: the churches' long and fractured history, the role of the missionaries, the demanding and sometimes fruitful encounter across religious borders, and the political position of Christians, both as an influential group and as a goal for Hindu nationalist violence. A common thread that runs through all these topics is a question: "What does it mean to be both Indian and Christian?"[5]

The official numbers from the 2011 census say that 2.3 percent of the population of India are Christians, amounting to just under Thirty million persons. However, many scholars suggest that the number is higher, and

---

3. Karlsson, "Entering into the Christian Charma," 134.

4. One of the authors, Vebjørn Horsfjord, was present at this protest; these are his observations.

5. Daughrity, "The Indianness of Christianity."

solidly based estimates vary between 2.5 and 4.9 percent.[6] The highest estimate corresponds to almost sixty-five million persons, which would mean that there are more Christians in India than in any west European country. The numbers are uncertain, but no matter how we look at them, the fact remains that while the *proportion* is small, we are nevertheless talking about very many persons. Christianity is India's third-largest religion—smaller than the Hinduism of the majority, and also much smaller than Islam, but larger than Sikhism, Buddhism, and Jainism.[7] In geographical terms, the centers of gravity of Indian Christianity lie in the north-east and the south-west. In the federal states to the north and east of Bangladesh, the churches are experiencing a growth in the number of members, and it is also in these federal states that the proportion of Christians is highest. But it is in the much more populous federal states in the south, and particularly in the south-west, that we find the largest number of Christians.

Most of the large churches have left their traces on Indian history, and live side by side in India today. But India was also one of the first places in the world to see the development of post-denominational churches, that is to say, churches that were not bound by the historical divisions between various denominations. As early as 1947, most of the Protestant churches in southern India, including Anglicans, Methodists, and Reformed, came together to establish the Church of South India. In 1970, the Church of North India was established. A traditional theological understanding would find this an even more demanding union, since this church structure also included Baptist churches. This church thus includes both members who baptize infants and members who believe that baptism presupposes an active choice. Indian Protestants made it clear in this way that what divided Christians from each other in the Europe from which the missionaries came did not constitute decisive questions for Indian theology. The Lutherans have remained outside both of these churches, and there are at least twelve different Lutheran churches in India today.

THE THOMAS CHRISTIANS—CHRISTIANS WHERE THE PEPPER GROWS

St. Thomas Mount lies slightly to the south of the megalopolis of Chennai, where Christians of various denominations presented themselves as "AD 52

---

6. Pew Research says 2.5 percent, while the World Christian Database estimates the percentage of Christians at 4.9; see Daughrity and Athyal, *Understanding World Christianity*, 61.

7. Daughrity and Athyal, *Understanding World Christianity*, 168.

Christians." According to legend, the apostle Thomas was killed and buried here in 73 CE. Although it is scarcely possible to verify the details of the legend, there are reliable accounts that Christians regarded the mountain with Thomas's grave as a holy place, and that it was visited by people seeking healing almost a thousand years before the Portuguese came to India, as the first European colonial masters, in the sixteenth century.[8]

However, the stories about Thomas, and not least the churches that link their history to him, do not belong primarily in the region around Chennai, but on the south-west coast. When the Portuguese came, there were probably around two hundred thousand Christians in the area that is today the federal state of Kerala.[9] Like all the other inhabitants, they had Malayalam as their mother tongue, but their liturgies were celebrated in various forms of ecclesiastical Syriac. Although they lived far from the original core regions of Christianity in the Middle East, they belonged to an Oriental Orthodox church.

Today's Thomas Christians regard the foundation of the church in 52 CE by the apostle Thomas almost as an article of faith.[10] The more critical eye of the historians is unable to confirm this idea, but some scholars point out that it is completely possible that an apostle *could* have traveled from Jerusalem to India in the first century. There was already a Jewish population there, and there was a continuous coming and going of merchants between India and the Middle East.[11] In the sixth century, a merchant (or possibly a monk) from Alexandria, Cosmas Indicopleustes, related that he had encountered a living church "where the pepper grows," that is to say, in southern India.[12] There are several similar accounts from the same period.

It was precisely pepper and other spices that later drew the first European colonial power, Portugal, to India. Catholic missionaries accompanied the Portuguese. Although they rejoiced to find Christians in India, they soon realized that Indian Christianity was not in exact accordance with the doctrine of the Catholic church, and they saw it as their responsibility to do something about this. The encounter between Indian Thomas Christians and various other ecclesial traditions, first and foremost via the missionaries, has profoundly marked today's Christianity in the Thomas tradition: between ten and fifteen different churches trace their roots back to the apostle. There are churches with East Syriac and West Syriac liturgy, depending on

8. Frykenberg, *Christianity in India*, 101; Moffett, *History of Christianity in Asia*, 35.

9. Daughrity and Athyal, *Understanding World Christianity*, 17.

10. Frykenberg, *Christianity in India*, 115.

11. Moffett, *History of Christianity in Asia*, 29–35.

12. Frykenberg, *Christianity in India*, 110.

which church leaders in the Middle East the various ecclesiastical fractions have adhered to in the course of history. Two churches with a Syriac liturgy recognize the Catholic pope and thus belong to the structure of the Catholic church as Eastern Catholic churches. But other churches do not recognize him, and are counted among the Oriental Orthodox churches. Protestant mission too has left its traces among the Thomas Christians, with the result that one of the larger churches, the Mar Thoma Syrian Church with around one million members, belongs to the Anglican Communion. There is also an independent Thomas church with a more Evangelical orientation.[13] All these churches are at home first and foremost in Kerala, but many of them also have established daughter churches in other parts of the world, not least in North America, over the course of time.

In general, the Thomas churches have attached little importance to carrying out missionary work. They tend to experience themselves as a demographic group that became distinct from Indian society at an early date, but is nevertheless fully integrated into this society. They have had central roles throughout history in the spice trade and in the military.[14] They have often been counted among the higher social classes: in times past, they had the right to ride on elephants, a sign of high dignity.[15] This distinguishes them from much of the rest of India's Christians.

THE CATHOLIC CHURCH—EDUCATION AND POPULAR PRACTICE

Roughly half of India's Christians belong to the Catholic church. Most of them come from the lowest castes, which have traditionally been marginalized. But Catholics are not without influence in society. The most influential of all is Sonia Gandhi, as leader of the powerful Congress Party. Mother Teresa (1910–97), winner of the Nobel Peace Prize and well known for her work among the poor and the dying in Kolkata, is the only person without a political post who has been honored with a state funeral in India.[16] But it is through its educational institutions that the Catholic church exercises the greatest influence on society as a whole. There are more than fifteen thousand Catholic schools spread over the subcontinent. More than half of the

13. Frykenberg, *Christianity in India*, 141; Daughrity and Athyal, *Understanding World Christianity*, 81.

14. Koepping, "India," 15.

15. Daughrity and Athyal, *Understanding World Christianity*, 13.

16. Daughrity and Athyal, *Understanding World Christianity*, 73.

pupils are Hindus, and a further 10 percent are Muslims.[17] As in many other countries, a Catholic education gives advantages on the job market, because Catholic schools generally have a high standard. Many of the Catholic universities and colleges are counted among the best in the land.

Some educational institutions offer formation for service in the Catholic church itself. The church has about 150 bishops, twenty-one thousand priests, and sixty thousand nuns.[18] The growing number of parishes means that there is a great need for priests, but many priests leave for other countries, so that India is now one of the world's biggest exporters of Catholic priests.[19]

There are about ten thousand Catholic parishes, which exhibit a very varied Christian praxis. Although the basic structure in Catholic spirituality, with the great annual feasts and the weekly celebration of Mass at its center, is largely identical everywhere in the world, Catholic life in India has an unmistakably Indian character. For example, one study describes street processions in southern India in which religious statues are borne on colorfully decorated carts through the church's neighborhood. This is an old custom that has been taken up again in many places in recent decades, and it has a clear parallel in Hindu customs that are practiced in the same neighborhoods. Hindus carry the statues of their gods in processions, and when it the Catholics' turn, they go in procession with a statue of the Virgin Mary. The celebration of which the procession forms a part has a strongly popular character, and is not linked to any of the great feasts that are usually considered to be the most important in the church year. The priests often take part in the rituals, and it is said that the archbishop takes part in the celebration in Chennai. In this way, the hierarchy sets the stamp of its approval on a celebration that came into being from below.[20]

There are small but important differences between the Hindu and the Catholic processions with their statues, but this custom nevertheless underlines the similarities between persons who belong to differing religious traditions, and emphasizes how Indian Christianity is permeated by Indian culture. It is not uncommon for Hindus to take part in the rituals around the Christian statues. In this way, the festivals are examples of Christianity's encounter with other religious traditions, especially with the Hinduism of the majority.

---

17. Daughrity and Athyal, *Understanding World Christianity*, 71.

18. Conference of Catholic Bishops in India, "As an Organization."

19. Daughrity and Athyal, *Understanding World Christianity*, 70.

20. The description is based on Waghorne, "Chariots of the God/s."

THE ENCOUNTER BETWEEN
CHRISTIANITY AND OTHER RELIGIONS

Throughout their entire history, the churches in India have lived side by side with other religious traditions. India's Constitution is secular, and the state institutions have displayed a certain distance vis-à-vis religious practices during most of the period since independence. But Indian secularism does not mean that religion plays a negligible role in society. On the contrary, this secularism is a way of regulating the religious plurality. Emperor Akbar the Great, who reigned over the Indian Mogul Empire in the second half of the sixteenth century, is often cited as an example of an Indian attitude to religious plurality that is a contrast to the typical western attitude. Akbar was interested in theology and religion. When he received a visit from Jesuit missionaries, he delighted them by assuring them that he was a Christian. They were all the more perturbed when they learned that he also regarded himself as both a Muslim and a Hindu.[21] Although this picture is pretty much of a cliché, it contains a truth: in many Indian traditions, there has been less concern with the religious boundaries than has been typical in the Europe from which the missionaries came.

Like missionaries and young churches everywhere in Asia, many missionaries to India encountered Hinduism and other religious traditions with a total rejection. But this is far from the whole picture. Bartolomäus Ziegenbalg is regarded as the first Protestant missionary in India. He arrived in the Danish–Norwegian colony of Trankebar in 1706. He was very much interested in the doctrine of the gods that he found in India, and wrote the book *Genealogie der malabarischen Götter* ("Genealogy of the Malabar gods"). He was rebuked for this by the Pietistic leader of the mission, August Francke, at home in Halle in Germany. Francke declared that the missionary's job was "to extirpate heathenism, not spread heathenish nonsense in Europe."[22]

From the mid-twentieth century onwards, many churches gradually became more open to seeing something valuable in other religious traditions. A decisive shift took place in the Catholic church in the 1960s with the Second Vatican Council, and the Protestant churches collaborated in the World Council of Churches on theological development work. This made the encounter with other religions more than just a question of converting as many persons as possible. Like other churches, the Indian churches were influenced by these processes, but the movement went just as much in the

21. Doniger, "Foreword," xi.
22. Koepping, "India," 20.

opposite directions: these changes, which affected churches everywhere in the world, were in many cases inspired by experiences in India.[23] Some leading Catholic theologians went far in incorporating elements from Hinduism into their Christian thinking. This met with strong resistance in the Vatican, but at the same time, it opened a sphere in many places in the world for theological thinking about the meeting between religions.

Both ordinary Catholics' processions with statues and the theologians' dialogue with Hindu tradition are examples of how Christianity is formed by the culture in which it puts down roots. These are expressions of an inculturation or contextualization that appreciates positively the context in which the Christians live. But tensions also arise in such processes: What aspects of a context or a culture can the churches embrace, and what will they reject?

THE CHURCHES AND CASTE

A bishop in a Protestant church in southern India told the story of a group of new converts who were to be baptized and thus become members of the church. They had read narratives about baptism in the Bible and had persuaded the bishop to carry out the ceremony in a river not far from the church building. On their way to the river, the candidates for baptism said that they were glad that they would be baptized in the river rather than in the church building, because after all, they came from a higher caste than most of the others who attended that church. The bishop recalled that he immediately stopped, and declared that there would be no outdoor baptism: they must either be baptized in the same way as those from the lower castes, or give up the idea of being baptized.[24]

When Indian Christians attempt through their daily life to say what it means to be a Christian and an Indian, caste is often part of the story. With its intricate rules connected to religious purity and impurity, the caste system is an aspect of much social intercourse in India. In many instances, the higher castes have looked down on those who belong to the lower castes, and have regarded them as "unclean." The various groups have led separate lives. Persons in the unclean castes have often lived in villages of their

23. Indian theologians who have contributed to fundamental new thinking about the relationship between Christianity and other religions include the Catholics Raimundo Panikkar and Jacques Dupuis. The Protestants M. M. Thomas and Stanley Samartha were key persons in the development of the World Council of Churches' thinking and strategy for the meeting between religions. See also Behera, "Introduction."

24. The present-day bishop told the story of this event at a conference in Kodaikanal in April 1999 at which one of the authors, Vebjørn Horsfjord, was present.

own, or in specific parts of the common village. In some places, the unclean castes are still not allowed to fetch water from the village's common spring. Another symbolically important sign of the caste distinctions can be seen when tea sellers on the streets operate with a double set of cups: some for high castes, others for low castes.

The caste system is complex and in continuous development. Western criticism of caste oppression has sometimes linked the caste system much too strongly to Hinduism. In its most oppressive form, however, it was not primarily an expression of a vaguely understood "Hinduism"; rather, it represented the ideal of the elites and took care of their interests.[25] And combating the oppressive aspects of the caste system has been an extremely important issue in India. Justice for the lowest castes was a vital concern of Mahatma (Mohandas) Gandhi, but it was another liberation leader, Bhimrao Ambedkar, who played the most central role in the struggle against caste oppression in the independent India in the 1940s and 50s. Ambedkar himself came from the lowest castes. He was a lawyer and is regarded as the father of the Indian Constitution, in which he and other leaders in the newly independent India included a prohibition of discrimination on the grounds of caste, as well as detailed regulations for a positive discrimination with regard to access to education, public posts, and political positions for persons from the lowest castes ("reservation"). In order to give dignity to those who were lowest in the caste hierarchy, Gandhi called them "harijan," "God's children." This expression was never embraced by the persons themselves, and the customary term today is *Dalit*, which means "oppressed" or "downtrodden."

Ambedkar himself converted to Buddhism together with many of his adherents, with the explicit goal of escaping from the caste oppression that he associated with Hinduism. Others converted to Islam and to Christianity for the same reason, often in large groups. But the Constitution's positive discrimination of the Dalits has not benefited the Christians. The regulations presuppose that caste oppression has its root in Hinduism. Accordingly, the rules about positive discrimination do not apply to Christians and Muslims, because they are regarded as standing outside the caste system. The Christians see this as a fundamental misunderstanding: the ideas about purity and impurity, and the notion that some groups are destined from birth to carry out the least respected tasks in society, affect low-caste Christians just as much as Hindus. Many church leaders therefore see low-caste Christians as "twice alienated."

25. Frykenberg, *Christianity in India*, 49.

How Christians relate to the caste system is important in answering the question of how one is both Christian and Indian. To put it in extreme terms, this question can be formulated as follows: If Christianity is not to be a foreign element in India, but must embrace Indian culture and tradition, must it not then also accept the caste system as a part of Indian-ness? This question has preoccupied the churches since the sixteenth century, sometimes in this explicit manner, other times in the form of inarticulate tensions in the churches where Dalits have been under-represented among the leaders.

Francis Xavier, one of the founders of the Jesuit order, who traveled across large parts of Asia in the sixteenth century, directed his missionary work in India to the lower castes. Another prominent Jesuit, Roberto de No- bili (1577–1656), has remained the symbol of another approach. He believed it was important to reach the highest social classes, the Brahmins, and to try to live as they did. This involved observing their rules about purity and impurity, and therefore also avoiding contact with persons from the lowest castes.[26] De Nobili doubtless understood his activity as an attempt to make Catholicism more Indian, and in one way, he was centuries ahead of his time in the endeavor to free Christianity from its specifically European cultural baggage and allow it to unfold and grow inside other cultural frameworks.

Although few in the churches went as far as de Nobili in an active embrace of the caste system, a tacit acceptance has been dominant in the churches. There was a tendency both among Catholics and among Prot- estants for the missionaries to divide various ethnic groups or communi- ties between themselves, so that the churches that were established were homogeneous with regard to caste membership. Where this did not hap- pen, it was customary for a long time for Christians of differing castes to sit separately in the church building. Separate celebrations of the eucharist, so that those from higher castes could maintain the traditional prohibition of eating together with those from low castes, was a particularly controversial custom. There are still Catholic cemeteries where low-castes and high-castes are buried on the opposite sides of a wall, although the church leadership is trying to resist this practice.[27]

DALIT THEOLOGY

The struggle for the rights of the Dalits is led by people who belong to dif- ferent religious traditions, as well as by secular activists. In parallel to this struggle, there has emerged a "Dalit theology" inspired by Latin American

26. Daughrity and Athyal, *Understanding World Christianity*, 27.

27. Natarajan, "Indian Dalits."

liberation theology and the churches' struggle against apartheid in South Africa. This movement has made an impact on both Catholic and Protestant church life, and has been described as a paradigm shift in Indian theological thinking.[28] Dalit theology has been strongest in the established Protestant churches, and it has been an important element in theological education since the 1990s.

Dalit theology is a method, more than a completely elaborated theological system of thought. Like the liberation theologies that inspired it, Dalit theology has asked what it means to be church (ecclesiology), and how one is to interpret the Bible and the church's tradition (hermeneutics) in a situation where persons are exposed to systematic oppression. The method is explicitly contextual—in other words, a thorough analysis of societal circumstances is an important part of the theological work. The question of what it means to be Indian and Christian is answered by pointing to the experience of social exclusion and economic marginalization that many Christians share with other Dalits or Adivasies. The Dalit theologians emphasize that this aspect of Indian culture must be fought against, not respected or embraced.

Dalit theology has criticized both the overarching structures in society and the way in which caste affects life in the churches. The latter issue concerns not only who gets leading positions, but also what cultural expressions are esteemed.[29] The goal of many of the missionaries who were the first to interpret Christianity in the Indian context was to come near to "the people," but in practice, it was the language and the culture of the higher social classes that came to dominate in the churches. Those from the lower social classes found it just as attractive to acquire the western cultural expressions as to embrace the cultural expressions of the Indian elites.[30]

The Dalit theologians maintain that neither the culture of Indian high-castes nor that of western colonists has the answer to what Indian Christianity ought to be. Some have turned to the traditional popular culture that was disparaged both by western missionaries and by local elites. One example is the Protestant theologian Theophilus Appavoo, who has worked to make it possible for Christian Dalits to gain self-respect through using their own language and traditional music in church buildings.[31] Another example is Sathianathan Clarke's interpretation of the traditional drum used by one

---

28. Daughrity and Athyal, *Understanding World Christianity*, 269.

29. For example, Nelavala, "Visibility of Her Sins"; Melanchthon, "The Servant in the Book of Judith."

30. Sherinian, "Dalit Theology," 238.

31. Sherinian, "Dalit Theology," 236.

particular Dalit caste in Tamil Nadu as an expression of a Christian revelation of God.[32]

CHRISTIANITY AMONG INDIGENOUS PEOPLES IN INDIA

Almost every country in Asia includes a large number of different ethnic and linguistic groups. In some places, one or a few of these groups dominate life in society, while other, smaller groups live outside the societal mainstream socially, economically, and often geographically. Some of these are indigenous peoples, many of whom continue to lead a more traditional life than what came to dominate in most Asian countries in the course of the twentieth century. Many of these groups are also religiously distinct, either by having completely distinct religious traditions or by practicing versions of the majority religion (Hinduism, Buddhism, or Islam) in ways that differ from the dominant groups and are often regarded as deviant, unorthodox, or impure. In many of the Asian countries where Christians are a small minority, it was among such groups that the missionaries' work to convert people to Christianity met with the greatest success. Today, the proportion of Christians in many ethnic minority groups is larger than in the majority populations both in India and in countries such as Vietnam, Myanmar, and Indonesia.[33]

According to the 2011 Indian census, the category "tribals"—Adivasies—constituted between 8 and 9 percent of the population, a little over a hundred million persons.[34] Like the (Hindu) Dalits, they benefit from the Constitution's prescriptions about positive discrimination, and like the Dalits, they are over-represented among the poorest in the country. Christian mission addressed the Adivasies at an early date. It was among Adivasies that the missionary Graham Staines had worked for more than thirty years when he and his two sons were killed by a mob in 1999 (see above), and it is among Adivasies that conflicts about conversions have been most intense in recent decades.

What happens when Adivasies convert to Christianity, and why do they do so? The answers give a further perspective on what it means to be Asian and Christian. A study of the Rabha people in West Bengal offers some examples. Here, as in many tribal societies, it was a Baptist missionary

32. Clarke, *Dalits and Christianity.*

33. Phan, "Vietnam"; Prior, "Indonesia."

34. The official English term, which is employed in the constitution, is "tribals." In this context it is not regarded as entailing a negative view of these groups.

who brought Christianity. Among the Rabhas, the village is an important social unit, and if some of its central figures convert, others follow. This does not mean that mass conversions on a huge scale take place. On the contrary, it seems that going over to Christianity is something of an individual choice—or at any rate, a choice on the family level. This means that the villages consist of both Christian Rabhas and Rabhas who practice the traditional religion.[35] It is important for the missionaries and for the new converts to erect a church building as soon as possible. Like other houses, it is constructed initially of bamboo, earth, and straw, and if the community grows and money is available, a little wooden church will be built later on. Local leaders are appointed, with responsibility for leading worship and prayer meetings, giving instruction, and otherwise supporting the members of the community.[36]

Christian Rabhas give basically the same explanation of why they converted. This is only to a small degree a question of adherence to Christian dogmas and convictions of faith. It is much more a matter of lifestyle and benefits: traditional religious rituals are expensive. When someone falls ill, the Christian rituals are simpler. All you have to do is to buy medicine, sing some hymns, and give the medicine to the sick person. Christians can also use traditional medicine, but they tend more strongly to use modern medicine, which they often find has a greater effect at a lesser cost. In the case of the Rabhas, conversion to Christianity also means that they stop drinking the rice beer that has an important role in many traditional rituals. When they no longer drink alcohol, their prosperity increases, both because of the effects on their health and because their resources can be employed for other things. In short, Christianity is experienced as "cost-effective."[37] Each group has its own history, of course, and the prohibition of alcohol is not specifically Christian; on the contrary, it is very typical of numerous religious revival movements in India and elsewhere in the world. Studies have identified a similar pattern in many other places in Asia, where the utility value forms a large part of the explanation of conversions.[38] The converts' subjective experience is that they get a higher quality of life.

Do the newly converted Rabhas become less Rabha? There is no unambiguous answer to this question. Those who do not convert will probably think the answer is yes, and some fear that the traditional Rabha culture will disintegrate. But the picture is more complex. Many Christian Rabhas

35. Karlsson, "Entering into the Christian Charma," 149.
36. Karlsson, "Entering into the Christian Charma," 149.
37. Karlsson, "Entering into the Christian Charma," 151.
38. Karlsson, "Entering into the Christian Charma," 150n53.

experience becoming "Rabha in another way," but not thereby less Rabha. They believe that the modernization that goes hand in hand with Christianity, not least in connection with health and education, is a necessary condition if the Rabha culture is to resist the pressure from the larger society towards an ever greater accommodation to the dominant—Sanskrit—Indian culture.[39] Christianity can reinforce pride in being a Rabha.

Even further to the north-east, in the Indian regions to the north and east of Bangladesh, live the Nagas, an ethnic group of about two million persons. They have been described as the ethnic group in Asia that has experienced the largest transition to the Christian faith, second only to the people on the Philippines.[40] Among the Nagas, Christianity has gone hand in hand with a form of political awakening, or what one could call a new construction of the Naga identity in clear opposition to the dominant cultural and religious currents—Hindu or Islamic—in central India. Over the twentieth century, there emerged a strong movement for political autonomy that has also included an armed uprising or a liberation struggle (the definition depends on the eye of the beholder).[41]

If being Indian means being linked to the culture and religion that have the dominant position in central India and among the traditional elites, there can be no doubt that Christianity has made Rabhas, Nagas, and other groups "less Indian." But "less Indian" in these cases does not automatically mean "more western," although this charge is widespread. One Naga leader described his Christianity as follows:

> Europeans do not have a monopoly on Christianity. . . . Christianity came to Europe from Asia and some Indians were Christians 500 years before the Europeans. When Europeans became Christians, they made it a European indigenous religion. They changed their names and founded festivals in relation to their cultures. Now I, like many Nagas, am a Christian, but I am not a European. I have a relationship with my God. Now my God can speak to me in dreams, just as happened to my Angami ancestors. I don't have to be like Anglicans or Catholics and go through all those rituals, I don't need them. What I am talking about is Naga Christianity—an indigenous Naga Christianity.[42]

This, however, is not the full picture. Church leaders in north-east India are worried about westernization and a growing individualism. Some

---

39. Karlsson, "Entering into the Christian Charma," 151.

40. Frykenberg, *Christianity in India*, 443.

41. Frykenberg, *Christianity in India*, 445.

42. Quoted in Frykenberg, *Christianity in India*, 443.

of them speak of secularization and a decline in church attendance.[43] At the same time, the strong ethnic identity that may have been reinforced through the Christian mission is a hindrance to collaboration in the churches across the numerous ethnic boundaries. On top of all this, there is a new wave of missionaries from South Korea who plant Pentecostal churches all over India. They are said to have great resources and to be especially capable evangelists, but they have little interest in collaboration with existing churches. This means that there are many trends among Christian Adivasies that point in different directions.

VIOLENCE AGAINST RELIGIOUS MINORITIES

As we wrote at the beginning of this chapter, the great majority of India's more than 1.3 billion inhabitants are Hindus, but the country's Constitution and political system are, in principle, secular. The tolerant and respectful attitude to religion and religious minorities that Indian secularism presupposes accords well with that form of Hinduism that is associated with many of India's leading figures, such as Swami Vivekananda and Mahatma Gandhi. Throughout much of the postwar period, an open attitude to religious plurality was a structural element in the Congress Party, which was the dominant political party. In parallel, however, another view of Hinduism and Indian-ness was growing, which saw them as two sides of the one coin. *Hindutva* has become the term for an ideology that combines nationalism with the cultivation of Hindu history and identity. In order to be completely Indian, one must be a Hindu. Other religions, especially Islam and Christianity, are regarded as foreign elements in society. The Hindutva ideology strengthened its position in society through a brutal campaign in the early 1990s that culminated in December 1992, when two hundred thousand "volunteers" tore down the Babri mosque in Ayodhya. Several thousand Muslims were killed in the violence that followed.[44]

When the missionary Staines and his two sons were murdered in January 1999, the BJP (the political wing of the Hindutva movement) had been in power for a few months. While other representatives of the official India condemned the killings in the strongest terms, Prime Minister Atal Behari Vajpayee used the occasion to declare that the country needed a "national dialogue about conversion."[45] In the twenty-first century, the BJP and its allied partners have held power for lengthy periods both nationally and in

43. Daughrity and Athyal, *Understanding World Christianity*, 99.
44. Frykenberg, *Christianity in India*, 477.
45. Frykenberg, *Christianity in India*, 477.

many large federal states. It was precisely accusations linked to conversion that have legitimated continual waves of violence against Indian Muslims and Christians, and in many cases, the political leaders have done little to stop or to punish the militant and violent parts of the Hindutva movement.

The dispute about conversion largely concerns the identity of indigenous peoples. It is often alleged that forced conversion takes place. To counteract this, the Hindutva movement started campaigns for "reconversions," in which simple ceremonies mark the transition from Christianity to Hinduism. It is in such contexts that murderous waves of violence directed against Christians have unfolded, for example, in the federal state of Odisha (known as Orissa until 2011) in the fall of 2008, when it has been calculated that more than one hundred persons, most of them Christian Adivasies, were murdered in a wave of violence that started when a Hindu leader was killed in unclear circumstances.[46]

The aggression and violence that regularly target Christians in India can be understood only with reference to the appeal that Christianity has had among groups who traditionally have been marginalized in Indian society. Although only a small proportion of Adivasies and Dalits are Christians, a large proportion of Christians are Adivasies and Dalits. Campaigns to reconvert Christians are also campaigns to bring these groups into the Hindu fold, where many of them have scarcely ever felt at home. This has been described as an attempt to hold fast Adivasies and Dalits in their oppression.[47] But the picture is more complex, since the Hindutva movement has not primarily emphasized the traditional dividing lines that the caste system has drawn up between the various social classes. The Hindutva offer marginalized persons a "pure" Hindu identity, but they have little space for complex identities and hybridity. They demand a choice: either Hindu and Indian, or Christian and not Indian. Christians perceive this as an artificial antithesis. This was why they marched together under the motto "All Christians are AD 52 Christians" when the violence increased just before the turn of the millennium. When we leave India for its even larger neighbor to the north-east, we will also encounter Christians under pressure. However, the state has a completely different role in China than in India, and it is to the state that Christians must prove that they are fully Chinese.

46. Akkara, *Kandhamal.*
47. Frykenberg, *Christianity in India*, 481.

CHINA—CHURCHES UNDER STATE CONTROL

In 2014, the authorities in Wenzhou demolished one of the city's largest churches in a sensational action. Wenzhou, with between three and four million inhabitants, is one of the Chinese cities where Christianity has a strong position. In the course of a few decades, hundreds of new church buildings have been erected, and Christian businesspeople have played an important role in the city's economic life. The authorities knew that the twelve-year-old church had been built illegally: it was much larger than the construction permit allowed. The intention in knocking it down may have been to make an example as a warning to potentially corrupt builders and bureaucrats, just as much as to attack the churches.[48] But over the following years, the authorities turned their eyes on very many other church buildings in Zhejiang (the province to which Wenzhou belongs). Few were torn down, but many were obliged to remove crosses from their roofs and church towers. It appears that the authorities wanted to reduce the churches' visibility in the public sphere, but without intervening in the activities that take place inside the buildings. Some Christian communities accepted the authorities' demands as part of the price they have to pay for practicing their religion in relative freedom, while others have protested. In some communities, this issue has led to strong internal tensions.[49]

This situation illustrates the churches' relation to the state throughout China. In the last couple of decades, the state has given the churches greater freedom, and one can sometimes have the impression that the churches' activity is regarded as valuable and a contribution to society. But the churches also know that this freedom is relative, and that it can flourish only within the narrow parameters set by the state—as is the case for business activity and civil society too. Freedom of religion in China is extremely limited. One of the authorities' concerns is to avoid foreign interference in religious life. This explains both why the churches' contact with churches elsewhere in the world is strictly regulated, and why China has its own state-controlled churches. This strongly marks church life in China.

When Mao Zedong and his Communist party came to power in China in 1949, all the western missionaries were expelled from the country, and the state took over the hospitals and educational institutions that the churches had operated. Under heavy state pressure, the churches were obliged to find completely new ways to organize themselves. One state-controlled Protestant church soon came into being, and one state-controlled Catholic

---

48. Lodwick, *How Christianity Came to India*, 61.
49. Johnson, "Decapitated Churches."

ecclesiastical structure that was in continual conflict with the Vatican's Catholicism. Other churches were forbidden. They either went underground or disappeared completely.

In 1966, during the Cultural Revolution, the Communist party prohibited all religious activity, which remained illegal until the close of the 1970s. The ecclesiastical structures that had existed before the Cultural Revolution were reestablished from the 1980s onward. Today, the state controls the churches (and other religions) through the State Agency for Religious Affairs (SARA). The authorities count Catholicism and Protestantism as two of the five recognized religions, the three others being Islam, Buddhism, and Taoism. It remains impossible to combine membership in a church with membership in the Communist party. This prevents church members from having a formal political career or occupying leading positions in society. The churches received more and more freedom between the 1990s and the 2010s, but the development towards greater freedom has stopped in recent years, as the example from Wenzhou can illustrate.

CHRISTIANITY BETWEEN THE BIG CITY AND THE RURAL VILLAGE

If you visit a church in one of China's many big cities today, it is highly likely that you will encounter a very different community than you would have met if you had visited them a couple of decades ago. The churchgoers are more prosperous now than in the past. Many of the community members may belong to a middle class that is basically well-off. They are teachers, academics, and other highly educated persons with good jobs that pay well. The community may have sufficient financial means to support social work and evangelization among the many streams of new workers who find their way to the city. Twenty-five years ago, China was a much poorer country, and the Christian community members too were also poorer in relative terms.[50]

The church in the big city may be affiliated to the Three-Self movement, or it may be an unregistered church. In the latter case, it is akin to the many so-called "house churches" that are neither registered nor recognized by the authorities. The lack of recognition no longer means that the activity necessarily takes place in private homes or in secret. Whether the church you are visiting is a Three-Self church or a house church, it is probable that the form of worship will be very free, and will remind you of what one finds in Pentecostal churches elsewhere in the world. You will probably hear a sermon from a priest or pastor who takes the Bible's words more or less literally.

50. Bays, *A New History*, 200.

Although the members of a big city community can be relatively well-off, the majority of Christians in China (as in other Asian lands) belong to groups that, historically speaking, have been marginalized: ethnic minorities, women, people in the villages. The members in the big city have also migrated from the villages, like more than a hundred million other Chinese in recent decades.[51] In the same period, however, a new movement has begun: industry is increasingly established in new regions, with the result that people move in the opposite directions, from big city areas on the coast back into the rural districts. The Christians will take back with them the form of Christianity from the big cities to these new districts, and Chinese Christianity will continue to develop new forms in the encounter between cultures and traditions, as it has done ever since the first European missionaries entered the land in the seventeenth century.[52]

In China, as in other places, a calculation of the number of Christians entails a question about precision in counting and a question about who is to be counted. The authorities' total of twenty-three million is probably too low. On the other hand, the estimate of over a hundred million, by Evangelical groups who like to demonstrate vigorous growth, is probably too high. One well-founded estimate, lying roughly in the middle, is sixty-seven million—about 5 percent of the population.[53]

Francis Xavier, who left an imprint on church history over much of Asia, never quite made it to the Chinese mainland, but it was Jesuits who were responsible for much of the early Christian mission in China too. Matteo Ricci arrived in Beijing in 1601 and started Catholic missionary work, but he was far from the first Christian missionary in China. Assyrian missionaries had been in China a thousand years earlier, and Franciscan missionaries worked in the country in the thirteenth century, when Genghis Khan ruled his Mongol empire.[54] None of this led to a permanent Christian presence, and it was only with the European mission from the seventeenth century onwards that Christian churches with continuity down to our own days were established. In other words, China has no "AD 52 Christians." This means that the question of what it means to be a small Christian minority has been at least as urgent in China as in India. The form of government may have been based on Confucian ideology, as in much of Chinese history,

51. Bays, *A New History*, 200.

52. Lodwick, *How Christianity Came to China*, 171.

53. Sixty-seven million, according to an estimate from Pew Research; see Lodwick, *How Christianity Came to China*, xiv–xvi.

54. Ying, "Mainland China," 150.

or on Communism, as in recent times—in either case, the authorities have suspected the Christians of exercising western influence on society.

There can be no doubt that the churches have had a much greater influence in China than their numbers would indicate. Catholic missionaries conducted schools and health work in China from the beginning of the missionary period, and the Protestant missionaries who came in large numbers in the nineteenth and the beginning of the twentieth centuries followed in their footsteps. When Mao took power in 1949, the Protestant churches were operating more than a thousand elementary schools, 247 schools for older children and youth, and thirteen universities.[55]

A leading expert in Chinese church history has described Chinese Christianity as one of the most important and interesting examples in modern times of how Christianity has put down roots and become inculturated in a culture that in the past was scarcely influenced by Christian history.[56] Both Protestant Christianity—often in the form we associate with the Pentecostal churches—and Catholic Christianity have been combined with other religious practices and ideas that are widespread in China. It was easy for Pentecostal Christianity, which acknowledges the importance of a world of spirits and emphasizes miracles and other supernatural experiences, to find an echo in the Chinese rural villages.[57] Christianity is not necessarily regarded by the individual or by a community first and foremost as a confession of faith. It is evaluated in terms of how effective it is—to what extent it is able to influence the world of the spirits.[58] Catholic praxis too, with its saints and its Marian piety, can be accommodated to popular ideas and customs with a great variety of gods and of rituals that put people in contact with them. In the villages, Catholic church life has often been closely integrated into the rest of family and village life. Catholics have woven their own feasts into the already-existing yearly rhythm of celebrations and feast days.[59]

CHINESE PROTESTANTISM— "THREE-SELF" AND "HOUSE CHURCHES"

It is customary to use the term "Three-Self Church" for the only Protestant church recognized by the Chinese authorities. This ecclesiastical structure has been governed since 1980 by two organs that function like "two hands of

55. Ying, "Mainland China," 161.

56. Bays, *A New History*, 205.

57. Ying, "Mainland China," 166.

58. Bays, *A New History*, 194.

59. Bays, *A New History*, 199.

one body" (to use a preferred phrase): the China Christian Council (CCC) and the Three-Self Patriotic Movement of Protestant Churches in China (TSPM).[60] Both have, in principle, a democratic structure in which the leaders—who are largely identical in the two organizations—are elected by national congresses every five years. In both cases, however, the authorities have strict control both of the choice of leaders and of activities in general. The main task of the China Christian Council is to promote the Christian life in the thousands of Protestant communities that belong to the church. They compile liturgies and hymn books, publish Christian literature, and organize the training of pastors and of volunteers. They also supervise co-operation with other churches, and the China Christian Council has been a member of the World Council of Churches since 1991.[61] The TSPM is responsible for patriotic education and for the church's contact with the authorities. The basic regulations of this organization from 1997 say that its task is "to serve as the patriotic and church-loving organization of Chinese Christians . . . to lead Christians to love the nation and the church, to safeguard the independence of the church, to strengthen unity within the church, and to serve the aim of making the Chinese Church well run."[62] The TSPM and the CCC have their headquarters in Shanghai, with regional and local branches in most provinces and larger cities.

The concept of "three-self" refers to an ideology linked to the churches' autonomy—in the first instance, autonomy from the missionary organizations that helped to establish them: *self-supporting, self-governing,* and *self-propagating.* This concept is associated primarily with official Protestantism in China today, but its genesis is much older, and some have called the way in which the Chinese employ the three selves as an "undermining" of the original idea behind the concept.[63] The ideal of the three selves was born among missionaries and churches in the latter half of the nineteenth century as the expression of a wish for a form of equality between the churches in Asia, on the one hand, and in Europe and North America, on the other. The new churches were not to be governed from the west, but were to take responsibility for their own selves. This also entailed that political governments, especially those with an explicitly atheist foundation, were not to seize power over the churches. This was how many Protestants experienced the establishing of the Three-Self Church in the 1950s. Others, however, held that the Three-Self Church was a good arrangement, either for pragmatic

60. Wickeri, "Three-Self Patriotic Movement," 846.
61. Wickeri, "China Christian Council," 146.
62. Wickeri, "Three-Self Patriotic Movement," 846.
63. Kim and Kim, *Christianity.*

reasons or because they sympathized with the antiimperialist ambitions of the Communist regime.

The strict regulation by the state means that none of the traditional Protestant denominations (Lutheran, Methodist, Anglican, or Baptist) exists as a separate church in China. In this sense, the Three-Self Church, and more precisely the China Christian Council, is a post-denominational church, a contextualization of Protestant Christianity in the specifically Chinese circumstances.[64] As a union of various Protestant churches, it resembles somewhat the Church of South India and the Church of North India, but the historical presuppositions are very different. Unlike the situation in India, this post-denominational church is a fruit of the authorities' wish to shape the church.

The state regulation of the church imposes strict limitations on the churches' work *ad extra*. There was for a long time no space in China for any civil society in which the church's involvement in society could develop. But in 1985, the China Christian Council set up the autonomous Amity Foundation, which today is one of the large and relatively free organizations of civil society in China. It is not a part of the church, but cooperation is easy. The goal is to contribute to education, health, and development in the villages, and it works in large sectors of China. The Amity Foundation also has printing works where large quantities of Bibles in various languages are printed.

"House churches" are the other aspect of Protestant church life in China. They emerged during the period in the 1970s when all religious activity was forbidden and the Three-Self Church was shut down. Originally, they were quite literally domestic communities, small groups of Christians who met in secret in private homes. When the China Christian Council was established in 1980 and the Three-Self Church resumed its activity, there were many who could not accept the state control, and the house churches continued to grow. Today, many house communities have grown out of the private homes and moved into other premises, but they still operate outside the law, and hence not in buildings that the authorities recognize as churches. This does not mean that they necessarily conduct their activities in secret; some still do so, while others work fairly openly.[65] The pressure that these churches experience does not usually take the form of active oppression by the authorities; rather, their place in society is not clarified. The official religious politics of the state declares that the activity of the house churches is not lawful, but says at the same time that they are not to be

64. Ying, "Mainland China," 158.
65. Bays, *A New History*, 191.

exposed to interventions by the authorities.[66] This gives the house churches considerable freedom in practice, but thousands of regional and local political leaders also have considerable freedom to deal with these churches in a way that promotes their own interests.

There is considerable variety among house churches. There is, naturally enough, no form of common organization, and they do not constitute a monolithic reality in Chinese society. The relationship to the Three-Self Church also varies. In some instances, house churches are a clear alternative to the Three-Self Church, with strong antipathies among both leaders and members. In other instances, more pragmatic reasons, such as geography or the lack of Three-Self pastors, lead a community to operate outside the Three-Self structure.[67]

Several scholars in recent years have warned against the way in which Chinese church life is sometimes presented by Christians in the west, especially in the USA. The idea of "the persecuted church" is vividly alive among Evangelical groups. This has historical roots in the expulsion of the missionaries in 1949, and not least in the prohibition of religion during the Cultural Revolution. But much has changed in the last decades, and some persons may have political and religious reasons for portraying the situation as worse than it actually is. For example, money is still being collected to smuggle Bibles into China. Those behind this action tend not to mention that tens of millions of Bibles are printed in complete openness by the Amity Foundation in Nanjing. They also ignore the fact that this kind of smuggling can quite unnecessarily cause serious problems for Christians in China, if the authorities' spotlight is turned on them.[68] While it is true that the Bible is not freely on sale in China, it is distributed through the official ecclesiastical structures, and it has also become accessible to everyone recently on the internet.

The churches in China are not free. But they were not free in earlier days, when they were largely governed from the west. The original three-self idea about making the churches autonomous—an idea that lives on both in the Three-Self Church and among the house churches—can be understood as an attempt to make the churches more Chinese, and thus less western. The suspicion that Christians' loyalty belongs somewhere other than China has given nourishment to the Chinese authorities' antipathy to the churches. This created even greater challenges for Catholics than for Protestants.

66. Bays, *A New History*, 190.

67. Ying, "Mainland China," 159; Lodwick, *How Christianity Came to China*, 57.

68. Bays, *A New History*, 204.

TWO CATHOLIC CHURCHES

It is estimated that one-fifth of China's Christians are Catholics.[69] The authorities' attitude to the Catholic church corresponds, in principle, to the line taken with the Protestants. When the authorities embraced the Three-Self ideology, it was applied to the Catholic church too, with the requirement that it must be self-supporting, self-governing, and self-propagating. For Protestants, the question of the form of governance and the appointing of leaders is mostly a practical matter. If it is seen that leaders teach and live in accordance with Christian doctrine, they will be accepted. For the Catholic church, on the other hand, the appointment of leaders, and especially of bishops, is a dogmatic question. To belong to the Catholic church means, in principle, to be in ecclesial fellowship with the pope, and this fellowship is expressed concretely through the appointment and recognition of bishops (and through them, of the priests too) by the pope. It is therefore difficult for the church to drop its link to the Vatican. This link became the church's Achilles heel in the encounter with Chinese authorities, who saw loyalty to the Vatican as undermining the Catholics' loyalty to China.

As a parallel to the Protestant Three-Self structure, the authorities established the Chinese Catholic Patriotic Association (CCPA) in 1957. The CCPA broke with the Vatican and gradually began to appoint its own bishops. This was the genesis of a church that stood in the Catholic tradition, but was not recognized by the Vatican. In parallel, there came into being an illegal underground church that was loyal to the Vatican. During the Cultural Revolution, many of the bishops of the underground church landed in prison. When a thaw set in the 1980s, they were released from prison, but their attitude to the Communist authorities was scarcely any friendlier than in the past, and they continued their activity in the underground church.[70]

There are thus two Catholic ecclesiastical structures in China: the official church, where Chinese authorities have a strong influence, and the unofficial underground church. The numbers of Catholics in each structure are probably roughly equal.[71] The internal Catholic tensions have been great, but just as in the case of the official and the unofficial Protestant churches, one cannot draw an absolute boundary between the official Chinese Catholic church and the underground church. The link between them is sometimes greater than one would guess from the actors themselves.

---

69. Ying, "Mainland China," 152.

70. Ying, "Mainland China," 155.

71. Bays, *A New History*, 192.

The official church has appointed more than 170 bishops without recognition by the Vatican.[72] But the underground church, which is loyal to the Vatican, has also appointed bishops without the prior approval of the Vatican. They have done so by appealing to the extreme pressure on the church, and Pope John Paul II accepted this practice.[73] But the Vatican has never completely given up the official Chinese Catholic church. In the course of the 2010s, the Vatican held negotiations with the Chinese authorities both about diplomatic relations and about who was to control episcopal appointments. An agreement was reached between the parties in 2018, and was renewed in 2020. Both sides keep secret what precisely China and the Vatican agree on, but it is clear that it concerns a procedure for the nomination of bishops that gives both the Chinese authorities and the pope influence over the process. It is possible that future diplomatic links are also part of the negotiations.[74] The accord shows that the Vatican is willing to go very far in order to integrate Catholic Chinese into the worldwide ecclesial fellowship. Pope Francis, who often speaks on behalf of marginalized groups, has displayed extreme restraint about criticizing the Chinese authorities for their behavior in Hong Kong or towards the Uighurs.[75] Paradoxically enough, it is those loyal to the Vatican, in the underground church, who oppose the Vatican by rejecting every form of collaboration with the authorities. In one sense, therefore the conflict that envelops the Catholic church in China concerns what it means to be both Chinese and Christian; but the bonds of loyalty are tied in very complex ways.

CULTURAL CHRISTIANS AMONG THE CHINESE?

Although one can meet rather well-off and highly educated churchgoers in the big Chinese cities today, Christianity in China (as in India and in most of the rest of Asia) has primarily been a religion for the marginalized, who had the least to lose by displaying a lack of loyalty to the Chinese state, whether Confucian or Communist. This means that something very new is happening, when members of China's intellectual elite have begun in the present century to cultivate an interest in Christianity.

As China's Communist party has gradually dropped Maoism as its ideological compass—in practice, if not necessarily in theory—it has become acceptable to investigate other potential sources of cohesion and

72. Ying, "Mainland China," 156.

73. Bays, A New History, 192.

74. Allen, "Vatican and China Renew."

75. Allen, "Vatican, China Courtship."

morality in society; indeed, some people were positively encouraged to do so. Religion, and Christianity in particular, is no longer "the opium of the people." It has been investigated in view of its potential aid in building up society. Some Chinese historians and sociologists are interested in the role Christianity can have had in the emergence of a European "civil society," a space independent both of the state and of the business world. Others have been fascinated by Max Weber's analysis of Protestantism as a presupposition of early capitalism.[76] This led to the creation after 2000 of a number of new centers for the study of Christianity at public universities; some speak of a "Christianity fever."[77] This entails a new role for Christianity in China, quite different from the function it has had hitherto, irrespective of whether it was Protestant or Catholic, state-regulated or illegal.

Many of those who are attracted to these new studies of Christianity have little or no contact with the churches, and many have no interest in helping to strengthen the churches' structures. This makes it somewhat unclear how Christianity can have a role in building up society, since such a function is dependent on places that take care of the Christian traditions, narratives, and rites, of everything that nourishes Christian ideas that can perhaps contribute to civil society, economic growth, or ethical consciousness.[78] Sober observers have warned against an exaggerated faith in this kind of cultural-Christian growth and in a further strong growth in the existing churches. They believe that the churches will most probably continue to experience progress to some extent, but certainly not to the extent that their position will be radically altered.[79] There is also a great tension linked to the space for development that the Chinese authorities will give the churches in light of the increasing tension between China and western countries, especially the USA.

THE PHILIPPINES—ASIA'S CATHOLIC NATION

While Christians amount to a few percent of the population in India, China, and most Asian countries, the situation in the Philippines is completely different. When the Black Nazarene, a wooden statue of Jesus carrying the cross, is borne in procession through Manila, the capital, on January 9 each year, up to fifteen million people throng the streets. Half a million take part in the ritual by walking barefoot, and they push and shove to get close to

76. Bays, *A New History*, 200.

77. Ying, "Mainland China," 163.

78. Ying, "Mainland China," 164.

79. Ying, "Mainland China," 168; Bays, *A New History*, 205.

the statute, since many believe it possesses healing power. The authorities mobilize thousands of police to ensure peace and order.[80]

The Philippines has a population of a little over a hundred million, more than 90 percent of whom are Christians. The great majority, over eighty million persons, belong to the Catholic church.[81] This means that the Philippines' Catholic population is larger than that in the USA; only Brazil and Mexico have more Catholics. It was precisely from Mexico that the Black Nazarene made its way across the Pacific to the Philippines at the beginning of the seventeenth century, and as in Mexico, it was Spanish missionaries, often hand in hand with the Spanish colonial government, who introduced Christianity. It thus arrived in the Philippines several centuries later than Islam, but it quickly put down roots and now makes a visible impact on almost the entire country. It is only in the furthest south that Muslims form the majority.[82]

One characteristic trait in Catholic history in the Philippines is that the Filipinos assumed a relatively strong position in the church at an early stage in the history of the mission. As early as 1822, nine hundred of the roughly one thousand parishes in the country were led by Filipino priests.[83] When this proportion diminished considerably in the course of the nineteenth century, this led to the so-called "Filipinization Controversy" about the extent to which the church's leadership should be in Filipino hands. This conflict coalesced with the opposition to the Spanish colonial regime, which grew in strength in the second half of the nineteenth century, with priests and church leaders on both sides of the dispute. Although the Catholic church was the church of the colonial masters, it also had a central role in the development of an independent national identity in a manner completely unparalleled in the rest of Asia.[84]

After Spain ceded the Philippines as a colony to the USA in 1898, Filipino Catholicism came under more varied influences in the twentieth century, not least thanks to missionaries from the English-speaking world, especially the USA and Ireland.[85] At the same time, many popular ideas and practices, such as belief in fate and in spirits and various street processions, continued to exist and were taken into the world of Christian ideas. Some

---

80. The description of the procession is based on Reuters Staff, "Millions of Devotees."

81. Pew Research Center, "Philippines."

82. Sitoy, "Philippines," 654.

83. Sitoy, "Filipinization Controversy," 289.

84. Sitoy, "Filipinization Controversy," 290.

85. Francisco, "Philippines," 112.

scholars hold that Catholic life in the Philippines today can be divided into two categories: "official Catholicism" and "popular Catholicism,"[86] but this is surely too schematic. As is the case wherever Christianity is more than a completely marginal phenomenon, religion has acquired specific local expressions.

It is not only in January that the Black Nazarene is borne in procession on the streets of Manila. On Good Friday too, huge masses of people follow the statue through the city. And at Easter there is another, even more spectacular tradition that attracts greater attention: in order to experience in a completely concrete manner the suffering that the New Testament says Jesus endured, young men let themselves be crucified alive, surrounded by curious Filipinos and tourists. This custom is highly controversial in the Catholic church, and even if there are only a few men who undergo this ritual, photographs are spread across the entire world and shape an impression of Filipino religiosity.[87]

Conscious work to integrate the Filipino culture and language into official Catholicism, under the label of "inculturation," received a formal stamp of approval through the Second Vatican Council (1962–65). This watershed in recent Catholic history also gave legitimacy and encouragement to an increasing commitment by the church to social justice, from the 1960s onward.[88] The Catholic tradition also contributed to a special Filipino identity as "Asia's only Christian nation." This identity also functioned as a bulwark against Communist expansion during the Cold War, when American military bases in the country had a great strategic importance.[89]

Representatives of the dominant religious tradition in the country have been found on both sides in important political disputes in Filipino history. In general, there are close relationships between the church's leaders and the authorities, but one also finds priests among the adherents of the armed communist rebel movement that has fought for several decades against the government forces.[90] In the widespread popular opposition to President Marcos in 1986 and to President Estrada in 2001, the Catholic church's mobilization was a significant factor, although the church did not speak with only one voice in these cases. When the newly elected President Rodrigo Duterte launched a highly aggressive "war on drugs" in 2016, leading bishops took on a kind of opposition role. They harshly criticized the

86. De Mesa, "Filipino Folk Catholicism," 291.
87. Francisco, "Philippines," 97.
88. Francisco, "Philippines," 114.
89. Francisco, "Philippines," 112.
90. Francisco, "Philippines," 115.

wave of many thousands of killings carried out by the police on persons whom the authorities suspected of drug crimes.[91] A large number of those killed were impoverished young men. It is perhaps possible to see here a tendency for the church's moral influence to weaken in recent years, since, despite the bishops' clear words, Duterte still had the support of over 80 percent of the population after his first year in office as president.[92] Given that the great majority of the people are Catholics, one can get the impression that the average Catholic does not simply follow the church's leaders in political questions.

In another type of question about values, it still appears that the church and the people agree. According to a large-scale international questionnaire in 2013, 93 percent of Filipinos hold abortion to be morally unacceptable. This was the highest proportion in any of the forty countries, from every part of the world, that were investigated. The view taken of divorce—another question on which the Catholic church officially takes a strong line—is generally negative: 67 percent replied that it was "morally unacceptable"; 65 percent answered "no" to the question whether homosexuality was morally acceptable.[93] In general, therefore, the Filipino population is socially conservative, and the majority appear to agree with the Catholic church's official line. At the same time, we should note that there is also a considerable number of Catholics among those who—despite the church's official teaching—hold that divorce or homosexuality is morally acceptable.

Protestant missionaries were not allowed to enter the Philippines until after the USA became the new colonial power in 1898. Most of the traditional Protestant churches became established in the country in the course of the twentieth century.[94] But the Philippines has also given birth to churches of its own at the point where Catholicism, Protestantism, and Filipino nationalism intersect. One of the most concrete fruits of the Filipinization Controversy in the nineteenth century was the founding of the Iglesia Filipina Independiente (the independent Filipino church) in 1902, when Filipino priests and laity in the struggle for national autonomy also wanted full freedom for the church. To begin with, as much as a quarter of the population may have belonged to this church, which continued to observe Catholic teaching and praxis, but without the pope and without foreign interference.[95] During the twentieth century, it experienced many

91. Crux Staff, "Church in Philippines."

92. Crux Staff, "Church in Philippines."

93. Pew Research Center, "Global Views on Morality"

94. Francisco, "Philippines," 108–11.

95. Ranche, "Iglesia Filipina Independiente," 359.

schisms and gradual changes. Today, it has a close relationship to the Epis-copalian (Anglican) churches. According to official statistics, it makes up only 1 percent of the population, despite its efforts to revitalize the national-ist inheritance from the early twentieth century.[96]

The Protestant churches make up a total of about 10 percent of the population of the Philippines.[97] As is the case in most of the world, it is the Pentecostal churches that have experienced the greatest growth in recent years, but the religious center of gravity in the Philippines lies in the Catho-lic church. It came to the Philippines in a Spanish Catholic packaging, and it was in the encounter between Catholicism and traditional Filipino culture that the modern Philippines was formed.

OUTLOOK

If we paint with the broadest brushstrokes, Asia is the continent where Eu-ropean Christian mission has not been successful. Of all the countries in the world, it is India and China that have had the greatest number of European missionaries, but even after several hundred years, the Christians are only small minorities, and there will surely be no drastic change to this situation. Nevertheless, many of the examples presented in this chapter allow us to speak of a variety of genuinely Asian forms of Christianity.

A more exhaustive description of Asian Christianity would have to give more space to Pentecostal Christianity. It is equally important to men-tion that the charismatic form of Christianity that is associated with the Pentecostal churches also has a strong influence on other churches. For ex-ample, in the Catholic-dominated Philippines, 4 percent of the population replied in a 2006 questionnaire that they were Pentecostals, while as many as 40 percent identified themselves as "charismatic."[98]

Another topic that could have been discussed in greater detail is Christianity in Muslim-dominated countries. In some Muslim countries, conversion from Islam is forbidden. This means that Christians with a Mus-lim background can encounter special challenges, both in relation to the state authorities and in the matter of adapting Christian faith and life to established cultural frameworks. According to some estimates, Indonesia is the country in the world with by far the largest number of Christians with a Muslim background (it is also the country in the world with the largest

96. Philippine Statistics Authority, *2015 Philippine Statistical Yearbook*, 1–30, 360.
97. Pew Research Center, "Philippines."
98. Pew Research Center, "Spirit and Power."

number of Muslims); but there are also large numbers of Christians with a Muslim background in Bangladesh and Iran.[99]

The examples from India and China show that Asian Christians also influence churches that lie far beyond their own geographical areas. Much of what has been thought and done in the field of reflection on the theology of religion, both in the Catholic church and in the World Council of Churches, has Asia as its most important frame of reference. At the same time, the post-denominational Protestant churches function as an example of how the theological and political conflicts of past centuries in Europe need not define ecclesiastical structures for all time to come.

In recent decades, South Korea has become known as a country where the Pentecostal churches have had a particularly strong growth, and it is one of the countries in the world that sends out the greatest number of missionaries. At the same time, the Catholic church is alive and well in many Asian countries, and it is in fact growing at the expense of Protestant churches in South Korea too.[100] Both the Philippines and India are now big exporters of Catholic priests to other parts of the world. Through missionaries and priests, as well as through the influence that is due to China's strong economic growth, Asian forms of Christianity will certainly leave an even more powerful mark on global Christianity in the decades ahead.

99. Miller, "Believers in Christ," 16.
100. Kim and Kim, *Christianity*.

7

Oceania

Christian Flourishing and Decline

IN 1983, TWO IMMIGRANTS from New Zealand, Brian and Bobbie Houston, founded Hillsong Church in the outer Sydney suburb of Baulkham Hills. Strong growth and success mean that Hillsong today has a hundred thousand church attendees on a world basis, and that more than a hundred million people listen to their programs in roughly sixty different languages. This makes it probably the most powerful example of global influence by Australian Protestantism. But although several Pentecostal churches in Australia have experienced yearly growth rates of between 20 and 30 percent in the last decades,[1] it is secularization that has left the deepest traces on the country. This, however, is in stark contrast to the development on the Pacific islands, where Christianity flourishes.

Oceania is made up of sea and land areas that amount to one-third of the surface of the earth, but it has a total population of only about thirty-five million, corresponding to 0.6 percent of the world population.[2] There are, nevertheless almost one thousand different languages in Oceania, amounting to roughly a quarter of the world's languages. The many languages are an expression of the cultural, social, and historical plurality that characterizes this region.

1. Piggin and Lineham, "Christianity in Australia and Oceania," 585.
2. Thuesen, "Oseania."

Oceania covers three areas with Pacific islands: Micronesia, Melanesia, and Polynesia. Micronesia in the north includes islands such as the Federated States of Micronesia, the Marshall Islands, Kiribati, Nauru, and Guam. Polynesia in the east and south includes islands such as Hawaii, Samoa, Tonga, Tuvalu, French Polynesia, Tokelau, the Cook Islands, and New Zealand. In the west lies Melanesia, with islands such as Papua New Guinea, the Solomon Islands, Vanuatu, and Fiji—to mention only a few. In this book, we also include Australia in Oceania. When we speak of the Pacific, Australia is not included.

Oceania forms a contrast to Asia, for while Asia is the part of the world in which Christian mission meets with little success, the opposite is the case in Oceania. Forty years ago, the missiologist Charles Forman wrote that Oceania was "in all probability, the most solidly Christian part of the world."[3] He meant that the great majority of the island dwellers in the religion not only belonged to Christian churches, but also "were more devoted in Christian belief and gave to the churches a larger place in their life than did the people of any other region." The missiologist's first assertion is still valid: of the fifteen countries in the world with the highest proportion of Christians, six are in the Pacific region. With the exceptions of Fiji and Nauru, the proportion of Christians in all the countries is more than 80 percent of the population, and is well over 90 percent in most of them (if we disregard Australia and New Zealand).[4]

The other assertion, that the island dwellers are more Christian in a qualitative sense than anywhere else in the world, is, of course, problematic. For what does it mean to say that a human being, a culture, or a part of the world is "solidly Christian?" As we have written in the introductory chapter, this is an assertion that can mean many different things. But we can agree with Forman that Christianity is deeply woven into the culture and the societal life in the island communities in Oceania. Although it is not older than two hundred years in this region, it has succeeded in becoming an integral part of the Pacific societies. And although it was introduced with the might of the colonists, Christianity has put down profound roots and has developed on local premises after the colonial masters relinquished power. In Australia and New Zealand, on the other hand, the situation is different. In recent decades, a comprehensive secularization and pluralization have contributed to a change in conditions for Christianity there.

---

3. Forman, *Island Churches*, 227.
4. Tomlinson and McDougall, "Introduction," in *Christian Politics in Oceania*, 1–2.

THE "SUCCESSFUL" MISSION IN THE PACIFIC

In 1796, the *Duff* set sail from England, bound for Tahiti.[5] The ship had been hired by the London Missionary Society, and on board were more than thirty craftsmen and other missionaries. The missionaries ended up on various Pacific islands. Those who reached Tahiti were forced to flee to New South Wales in today's Australia, two years after their arrival, but the Tahiti mission continued. In 1812, Chief Pomare II converted to Christianity, and the entire population of Tahiti followed. Pomare received new western weapons, with which he was able to conquer the Society Islands, and this led to mass conversions of the island dwellers there too.

In the course of the following two centuries, Christianity became dominant in the region, and at the turn of the millennium, about 90 percent of the population on the Pacific islands belonged to various Christian churches.[6] Various explanations have been offered for why Christianity spread so quickly and gained such a solid position in the Pacific.[7] Some scholars have suggested that the material prosperity of the missionaries and their literary skills appealed to the island dwellers and opened the door for them onto a world with new possibilities and a new lifestyle. The access to western weapons was also highly appreciated, and this led many chiefs to welcome the Europeans. Other scholars have suggested that it was the missionaries' power and strength that attracted the islanders, and that they believed that, in order to get a share in this, they would have to accept the missionaries' God.[8] Others again have pointed to the outbreak of sicknesses that often followed in the missionaries' steps. Smallpox, measles, influenza, and other European sicknesses were understood as punishment for not submitting to the white man's God.[9] Often, it sufficed for the chief to be persuaded, as on Tahiti, because then the missionaries won the whole people along with him. The transition in the Pacific from traditional religions to Christianity on this basis has been described as pragmatically, rather than dogmatically, motivated.[10]

Another important reason is also highlighted, namely, a wide-scale use of indigenous missionaries. Spanish Jesuits had carried out missionary work in Micronesia from the mid-seventeenth century onward, without

5. Piggin and Lineham, "Christianity in Australia and Oceania."

6. Ernst, "Changing Christianity in Oceania."

7. Ernst and Anisi, "The Historical Development," 589–90.

8. Garret, *Footsteps in the Sea.*

9. Zocca, "New Caledonia."

10. Crocombe, *The South Pacific.*

great success. The island dwellers were not convinced by the foreign Jesuits' demands for a new lifestyle, rites, morality, and monogamy. It was only with the Protestant missionaries at the beginning of the nineteenth century that the mission began to have results. In particular, the actions taken by the London Missionary Society were effective. They involved convert Christian islanders, and it was only thanks to the missionary work and schooling carried out by island dwellers themselves, especially from Tahiti, Cook Island, and Samoa, that Christianity seriously put down roots on the Pacific islands. The New Zealand historian Raeburn Lange has described how hundreds of indigenous clergy, deacons, evangelists, and teachers helped in the course of the nineteenth century to spread a Christianity that incorporated local customs and cultural practices in the island societies in Oceania.[11] Inculturated and indigenous forms of Christianity of this kind gained a solid foothold in the various island cultures, and have helped Christianity to be an inseparable part of the cultures and of the public and collective life in the island states today.[12]

Against this background, scholars have claimed that the Christianization of the Pacific islands has led to a new political order in the region, where local conflicts and traditional warfare within and between many of the island societies have ceased.[13] On the other hand, the rivalry between Catholics and Protestants, mainline churches and revival movements, traditional expressions of the Christian faith and practicing of the beliefs of indigenous people, as well as intersecting alliances between missionaries, indigenous chiefs, and colonial powers, have also generated new and sometimes serious conflicts.

AUSTRALIA AND ITS CONTESTED PAST

The history of the colonization and Christianization of Australia is completely different. The missionaries achieved little among the Indigenous peoples. Christian evangelization was able only to a very small extent to influence local Indigenous thinking or religious practices—at any rate, in the first one hundred and fifty years. Christianity had, in fact, little impact on

11. Lange, *Island Ministers*. This account has also been criticized for overlooking cultural differences among the various island societies. Critical voices have pointed out that the British could act with greater cultural sensitivity than indigenous native missionaries who came from other islands. See McDougall, "Saving States."

12. Tomlinson and McDougall, *Christian Politics in Oceania*; Ernst, "Changing Christianity in Oceania."

13. Fer, "Religion."

the way in which the Indigenous peoples organized their colonial existence. Robert Tonkinson has claimed that: "to a great extent Christian proselytizing fell on barren ground in Australia, seemingly unable to dislodge an indigenous religious system so pervasive and integrated that it was synonymous with, and inseparable from, the fabric of life itself."[14]

The history of the colonization of Australia and of the Europeans' behavior towards the Indigenous population is a disputed and painful history. When Australia celebrated its national day on January 26, 2021, one word in the national anthem had changed in the course of the previous year. Now, they no longer sang: "For we are young and free," but: "For we are one and free." This change was one link in the process of reconciliation, an attempt to create unity between the peoples in the country. It signaled that Australia, with its First Nations population, is not a young nation, but one of the world's oldest civilizations.

We must go back to January 26, 1788, when the first fleet with British convicts and soldiers sailed into what was to become Port Jackson, and today is the big city of Sydney. In 1938, 150 years later, the Aboriginal Progressive Association declared January 26, Australia Day, a day for grief and protest. The Association wrote to George VI, who was king at that time. They grieved over the deaths of many thousand Indigenous persons who had been brutally murdered, over the loss of the land, and of the rapes of their women by white invaders.[15]

The Britons came to Australia with the idea of a *terra nullius*, a land that belonged to no one. But it proved to be very far from empty of human beings. The continent was inhabited by several hundred Indigenous peoples and Torres Strait Islanders, with their respective languages and cultures. The bond to the soil meant much for these peoples. The collision between the Indigenous hunter and gatherer society and the Europeans' need for large tracts of land for cattle farming and agriculture was brutal. There is considerable disagreement about how many Indigenous Australians were killed by white colonists, but estimates show that, as a consequence of colonial genocidal actions such as state-sanctioned massacres, the First Nations population went from an estimated 1–1.5 million before the arrival of the British to less than a by the hundred thousand early 1900s.[16] For example, almost all the Indigenous persons had been killed or expelled from Tasmania a mere forty years after Europeans settled on the island.

14. Tonkinson, "Spiritual Prescription," 186.
15. Larsen, "Australia."
16. Miller et al., *Discovering Indigenous Lands*, 175.

Australia's history and the relationship between the whites and the original population are highly fraught. Even after the Federation was set up in 1901, nothing short of massacres continued into the 1920s in some federal states. "Civilization programs," enforced removals from one place to another, reservations, and other forms of assimilation-political assaults continued even longer. Many children were separated from their parents and placed in public institutions.

In 1992, the Australian Supreme Court rejected the idea of *terra nullius* in the case *Mabo v. Queensland.* For many Indigenous persons, this meant that the state had finally acknowledged that they existed. After two hundred years, they at last got rights to some of the soil on which they had always lived. But although the country began a public reconciliation process in the 1990s, the traces of the assaults on the Indigenous peoples and Torres Straits Islanders are still highly visible in investigations into living conditions and other social statistics. Australian society continues to be marked by what has been called structural violence and racism.[17] The consequences include poorer health and an exaggerated use of imprisonment in these population groups. In the short time since 1991, more than 474 Indigenous persons have died in police custody in Australia.[18]

What role have the churches and Christianity played here? Noel Loos, Professor of Indigenous history and politics in Australia, has pointed out that the historical churches in his country were largely characterized by the same racial ideology as the rest of the settler society until well into the 1950s. It is true that the Anglican archbishop of Sydney had proclaimed in 1881 "that a great responsibility rested upon those persons whom God had permitted to occupy this land,"[19] but the ecclesial "responsibility" and work targeting the Indigenous population consisted by and large of conducting schools on the reservations and assisting the assimilation policy of the authorities. In this way, the churches played an instrumental role in administering some of the most deleterious parts of the colonization process.

Things began to change in the 1960s. Indigenous and non-Indigenous civil rights activists, including some churches, as well as an increased attention to human rights, led the majority society gradually to grasp how harmful the assimilation policy was, and that political change was needed. In 1967, a referendum on the political status of the Indigenous peoples was held. Many Australian churches gave loud support in public to a change of the policy, and a total of 91 percent of the population finally voted in favor

17. Bond, "Now We Say."
18. See "Death Inside."
19. Loos, "The Australian Board of Missions," 205.

of this. This referendum remains a symbol of the shift in mentality in the 1960s in Australia, where there occurred a gradual alteration from an assimilation policy to a policy based on self-determination.[20]

Over the last decades, many churches have become seriously involved in the fight for the rights of the Indigenous peoples and in reconciliation work. The text of the parliamentary motion of reconciliation that Prime Minister Hawke proposed in 1988 was taken from a pamphlet entitled "Towards Reconciliation in Australia" that had been drawn up by fourteen Australian churches.[21] The Australian Catholic bishops sent their Indigenous affairs adviser to lobby the political parties for support. The churches continued to support the official reconciliation process in the 1990s, and the Council for Aboriginal Reconciliation itself had Christian members who clearly saw connections between their faith and the Council's work. From the mid-1990s, churches everywhere in Australia have made official declarations in which they express their sorrow and apologize for their share in the injustice inflicted on the Indigenous peoples and the Torres Strait Islanders.

Although Australia as a nation has faced up to its colonial past, this confrontation has also kicked off what have been called "Australian history wars," an ongoing public debate about the interpretation of the history of the British colonization and the development of modern Australian society, especially with regard to its First Nation peoples.[22] An ideological struggle has developed between two disparate visions for the Australian nation. The first vision was circulated by the Australian Prime Minister Paul Keating from the Labour Party, who regarded racial injustice and making amends as an important political priority. He set up the Council for Aboriginal Reconciliation in 1991, acknowledged in 1992 that white settlers were responsible for many of the problems affecting the Indigenous communities, and commissioned the *Bringing Them Home* report, which was completed in 1997 and concluded that the mandated removal of Indigenous children from their families and local communities had violated their human rights and caused long-term and systematic harm to the Indigenous society. The second vision for Australia was circulated by Prime Minister John Howard from the Liberal Party, who began to reconstruct a more conservative alternative after he came to power in 1996. Howard claimed that the stories of Indigenous dispossession were undermining confidence in the nation. Accordingly, he attempted to present a narrative about Australia's identity and history based on "Judeo-Christian ethics, the progressive spirit of the enlightenment and

20. Gardiner-Garden, *The 1967 Referendum.*
21. Phillips, "Aboriginal Reconciliation."
22. George and Huynh, *Culture Wars.*

the institutions and values of British culture."[23] He employed his so-called "Sense of Balance" policy to encourage a return to a national narrative that appreciated Australia's history and the achievements of earlier generations. The idea of the white man who has fought his way forward through the bush, laying the foundations of a rich Australia built on wool, cattle, and minerals, has a powerful position in the national self-image, even among Christians.[24] When Australia Day is celebrated on January 26, this remains a highly ambivalent event, despite the change in the national anthem. Some would prefer to grieve, rather than to celebrate this Day.

NATIONAL CHRISTIAN IDENTITY, INDIGENOUS TRADITION, AND NEW RELIGIOUS MOVEMENTS

One special aspect of Christianity in the Pacific region is its strong link to national identity. Although several of the island states gradually acquired national independence from the western colonial powers, they nevertheless retained the religion of the latter, and linked this strongly to their "new" national identities. In this way, Christianity has acquired an official and overarching function of providing identity in many island states that are otherwise marked by great ethnic and linguistic variety. Scholars have claimed that "Christianity is endorsed by the state as a 'key idiom' to unify its citizenry, and especially those who belong to different language and ethnic groups."[25]

In this way, heads of state and politicians in the Pacific islands have used Christianity to create and form political cultures. The governments in this region usually welcome new churches and support them in preaching their version of Christianity to the island dwellers. Nor is it unusual for international "superstar" evangelists like Benny Hinn, Bill Subritzky, or Reinhard Bonnke to be treated like visiting heads of state. Besides this, many governments are regularly active and willing to support, organize, and take part in evangelizing activities, such as prayer meetings and prayer breakfasts.[26]

The anthropologists Matt Tomlinson and Debra McDougall have shown how national and political identity projects find expression *inter alia*

23. Fordham, "Curating a Nation's Past."
24. Fordham, "Curating a Nation's Past."
25. Robbins, "Comments to Part 3," 208.
26. Newland, "Miracle-Workers"; Ernst, "Changing Christianity in Oceania."

in many of the Constitutional texts of the relatively young states.[27] In Samoa, for example, which (after Vatican City) is the country in the world with the highest proportion of Christians, the 1960 Constitution begins as follows:

> IN THE HOLY NAME OF GOD, THE ALMIGHTY, THE EVER LOVING [.] WHEREAS sovereignty over the Universe belongs to the Omnipresent God alone, and the authority to be exercised by the people of Samoa within the limits prescribed by His commandments is a sacred heritage [;]
> WHEREAS the Leaders of Samoa have declared that Samoa should be an Independent State based on Christian principles and Samoan custom and tradition, . . . we the people of Samoa in our Constitutional Convention, this 28th day of October 1960, do hereby adopt, enact and give to ourselves this Constitution.[28]

The 1968 Constitution of Nauru begins in a similar manner:

> WHEREAS we the people of Nauru acknowledge God as the almighty and everlasting Lord and the giver of all good things: And Whereas we humbly place ourselves under the protection of His good providence and seek His blessing upon ourselves and upon our lives.[29]

Kiribati and the Marshall Islands likewise mention "trust in God" in the first sentence of their Constitutions, while Papua New Guinea and the Solomon Islands declare that they are "under the guiding hand of God."[30] Tuvalu apostrophizes "the guidance of God," while Tonga's Constitution begins with a "Declaration of freedom" that employs theological vocabulary to link the freedom of its inhabitants with the will of God.[31]

Many of these Constitutional texts communicate a harmony between Christianity and the traditions of the indigenous peoples, as (for example) the text from Samoa's Constitution shows: Samoa should be based on Christian principles *and* Samoan custom and tradition. Traditional cosmologies and practices are described as positive supplements to Christianity, and in some instances, they are blended together with Christianity. In Tokelau's Constitution, for example, the Christian deity and the traditional deities Maui and Yui Tokelau are woven together in a unified religious narrative of identity:

27. Tomlinson and McDougall, "Introduction," 6–7.

28. Tomlinson and McDougall, "Introduction," 6.

29. Tomlinson and McDougall, "Introduction," 6.

30. Tomlinson and McDougall, "Introduction," 6.

31. Tomlinson and McDougall, "Introduction," 6.

> We, the people of Tokelau, declare, Tokelau is permanently founded on God. This foundation is made manifest in the villages and when the people cooperate and live together peacefully and happily. At the dawn of time the historic islands of Atafu, Nukunonu, Fakaofo, and Olohega were created as our home. Since the days of Maui and Tui Tokelau the land, sea, and air have nurtured our people, and God has watched over us.[32]

However, the relationship between Christianity and the traditions of the indigenous peoples has not always been as harmonious as these texts might lead one to suppose. Although the first missionaries are said to have contributed to inculturated forms of Christianity, Christianity also encountered opposition when it was washed ashore on the Pacific beaches. Scholars have employed the collective terms "nativistic movements" or "new religious movements" to describe extremely varied and different forms of innovative, collective religious responses by islanders in the Pacific to European colonial activity.[33] These have arisen over the last two centuries as a consequence of rapid societal changes caused by new technical and cultural revolutions. Many of these movements have been an alternative to the Christian churches, but also to the traditional religions.

One example are the so-called "cargo cults," a type of revival movement that had its origin primarily in pre-industrial tribal societies in some regions in New Guinea and parts of Melanesia. There were wide variations between the different cults on the numerous islands, but they often focused on material wealth—hence the word "cargo"—via spiritual and religious rituals linked to the veneration of ancestors. Material goods were understood as gifts from the gods and ancestors, and these cults experienced a considerable growth during and immediately after the Second World War, when the people in the region observed the Japanese and the American military importing huge quantities of goods. The cults are centered on various rites to enable access to these gifts. Other types of "new religious movements" have arisen in response and in opposition to the exploitation by western companies of the natural resources in the region; others again have developed as offshoots of Christian mainline churches, and have laid the emphasis on ecstatic and charismatic expressions, on visions, or on cultic practices described in the Hebrew Bible.

A large flourishing of so-called revival movements throughout Oceania has been observed since the 1970s. These have often had their origin in established churches, but they have frequently led to new independent

---

32. Tomlinson and McDougall, "Introduction," 6–7.
33. Trompf, "New Religious Movements in Oceania."

churches, because they have generated new practices, attitudes, and doctrines that have not been accepted by the original churches. The revival movements have usually had Pentecostal characteristics both in form and in content, and they have often distanced themselves strongly from indigenous religion.[34] The movements have tended to condemn indigenous religion, and new converts have been encouraged to destroy objects that were used in traditional rituals. They have sought in this way to cleanse their Christian life by abandoning inherited traditions and practices that they experience as syncretistic. Although the focus for these revival movements lies on the rejection of traditional religion, the similarity to traditional religious practices—for example, ecstatic expressions, prophetical dreaming, healing, and a strongly spiritual and dualistic worldview—has, paradoxically enough, made it easier for people to join the new movements. Accordingly, scholars have discussed to what extent Christian revival movements are in fact movements that build on indigenous forms of religion, or movements that build on the rejection of these forms. For example, Franco Zocca's researches have shown how the millennial, spiritual, and magical elements in many new religious movements and revival movements fit the pattern of traditional Melanesian religion and experience.[35]

Despite extensive local differences, many of the revival churches also display Pentecostal characteristics that are better-known and more universal. Manfred Ernst has written about how globalization influences cultural changes and religion in Oceania too.[36] His conclusion is that the historical churches, which traditionally have had rigid structures, landed property, and political influence to a greater degree than the Pentecostal newcomers, are gradually losing terrain to the latter. According to Ernst, the new Pentecostal churches are marked by a globalized and Americanized charismatic style, attitudes, music, and worship patterns, but also by a greater inclusion of the laity. This makes it possible for them to generate various types of capital, especially among young people and women. The leaders in the historical churches have differing attitudes to the growth of the charismatic churches, but Ernst writes that those historical churches that adapt and open the door to charismatic expressions are more successful in keeping hold of their members than those that oppose this—also in Oceania.[37]

34. Robbins, "Whatever Became of Revival?"
35. Zocca, "'Winds of Change,'" 181.
36. Ernst, "Changing Christianity in Oceania."
37. Ernst, "Changing Christianity in Oceania," 39–42.

SECULARIZATION AND HILLSONG

Pentecostal Christianity is growing in Australia too, but at the same time, the country is marked by powerful processes of secularization. Although the values-conservative Prime Minister from 1996 to 2007, John Howard, frequently referred to God and Christian values in Australian politics,[38] it is hard to believe that Australian politicians today would talk about God and Christianity in the same way as many politicians on the Pacific islands do. Unlike the Pacific region, Australia has undergone large-scale processes of secularization and pluralization on the same lines as a number of western European countries.[39] Immigration from non-Europeans grew after Australia abolished the White Australia Policy in 1966. In particular, incomers from south-east Asia and the Middle East have led to increases in the Hindu, Buddhist, and Muslim population. In 2016, slightly more than 8 percent of the country's population belonged to non-Christian religions.[40] But it is secularization that has made the deepest impact on Australia in recent decades in terms of people's worldview. While 88 percent of the population saw themselves as Christian in 1966, only 52 percent did so in 2016, while one-third of the population (30 percent) said that they had no religion. This group grew noticeably from 19 percent in 2006 to 30 percent in 2016. There has, in other words, been a marked increase of persons in the country's non-indigenous population who have no religious affiliation, and a continuous decline in the number who see themselves as Christians.

This, however, does not mean that Christianity is being wiped out of Australian society. In addition to the historical churches, their institutions such as schools and hospitals, and other parts of the country's Christian cultural heritage, there are two things in particular we wish to highlight when we draw a picture of contemporary Christianity in Australia: Christianity among the indigenous population and Pentecostal Christianity.

Around two-thirds of Australia's Indigenous population identify as Christians.[41] Although this is small in comparison to the rest of Oceania, it is much higher than in Australia's non-Indigenous population. It is also a high number, when we bear in mind that (as we have mentioned) the early European missionary work among the Indigenous population has been described as meeting only a limited success.[42] Some have argued that

38. Maddox, *God under Howard*.

39. Magowan and Schwartz, "Introduction."

40. All statistics are taken from the Australian Bureau of Statistics, "Religion in Australia."

41. Magowan and Schwartz, "Introduction."

42. Tonkinson, "Spiritual Prescription."

the Indigenous peoples became more open to Christianity after the implementation of the state's new self-determination policies in the 1970s.[43] This public shift of policy from assimilation to self-determination marked the close of the mission period, and the administration of missions was handed over to local secular councils. What was later known as "the Aboriginal Revival" began in 1979 in the Uniting Church in Elcho Island. Few islanders were untouched by it, and the revival spread quickly to other parts of Australia. One of its consequences was the indigenization of Christianity in a way that had not taken place in Australia hitherto.[44] Others have pointed out that Christianity became for many Indigenous peoples a means to tackle the societal revolutions that were generated by the encounter with modern Australian society. Faced with social problems such as poverty, violence, outsider status, and substance abuse, Indigenous communities have been attracted both to traditional Christian prescriptive values—everything from "do care" to "don't drink"—and to charismatic prosperity gospels. This has led many First Nation citizens to embrace Christianity.[45]

The second thing we wish to highlight is the increase in Pentecostal movements and megachurches. In the short period from 1997 to 2007, Pentecostal Christianity grew by 26 percent in Australia; in the federal state of New South Wales, there was a growth of 48 percent.[46] By 2011, Pentecostals were the second-largest group of Christians in Australia; only Catholics were more numerous. In other words, they had outstripped both the Anglicans and the other mainline Protestant churches.

Over the last decades, it was especially Evangelical and neo-Pentecostal missionaries from the USA and Korea who have had influence in Australia, while in the same period, missionaries from the Pacific islands have also moved to Australia and started communities there, primarily among Pacific immigrants, but also among other Australians.[47] But Australia has been just as much an exporter as an importer of Pentecostal Christianity. Missionary organizations in Australia have a long history of sending missionaries overseas. The independent research foundation National Church Life Survey (NCLS) has estimated that roughly nineteen thousand Australians went on

43. Schwartz and Dussart, "Christianity in Aboriginal Australia Revisited,"; Tonkinson, "Spiritual Prescription."

44. Piggin and Lineham, "Christianity in Australia and Oceania," 582.

45. Tonkinson, "Spiritual Prescription" 197.

46. Austen and Clifton, "Australian Pentecostalism," 390.

47. McDougall, "Australian Intervention in Solomon Islands."

short-term or long-term mission trips in 2015 and 2016 (seventeen thousand on short-term trips).[48] Roughly 6,500 of these were Pentecostals.

Australia exports Pentecostal Christianity in other ways too. The country's greatest influence on global Christianity has perhaps come through a rebranding and renewing of Pentecostal worship styles. In particular, new types of worship music from churches such as Hillsong and Planetshakers have made Pentecostal-style worship mainstream in Evangelical churches around the world.[49]

Hillsong Church is not only the largest individual congregation in Australian history, but perhaps also the most powerful example of global influence by Australian Protestantism. Soon after it started in 1983, the church became a place "where winners hang out," and this is how the media described it.[50] In 2005, Hillsong programs were broadcast on television in about 120 countries. In 2009, there were Hillsong campuses in twenty-four countries on five continents, with more than 260 different worship services every weekend. Hillsong attracts twelve million followers on social media, ten million television viewers each week, and 140 YouTube visits each year.[51]

Hillsong has been described as "a new, commercial breed of Christianity," with a yearly turnover of several hundred million US dollars.[52] It is a trademark and a style that helps to form a global Christian youth culture. With a hundred thousand attending the church's worship services across the whole world, and a listening public of perhaps a hundred million persons in about sixty different languages, Hillsong is a global phenomenon.[53]

CLIMATE ACTION AND
CHRISTIANITY IN OCEANIA

Like other places in the world, Oceania is hard hit by climate changes, which affect the island states in the Pacific with particular severity. When the sea rises as a consequence of increased global warming, many people in these countries are at risk of losing their homes. The highest point of land on Tuvalu lies only 4.5 meters above sea level. The risk there is that saltwater from the sea may penetrate the groundwater and destroy both drinking water and agriculture. In the worst-case scenario, the climate changes will put large

48. NCLS Research, "Australian Church Attenders."

49. Austen and Lewis, "Concluding Remarks."

50. Austen and Clifton, "Australian Pentecostalism," 388.

51. Austen and Clifton, "Australian Pentecostalism," 388.

52. Ferguson, "'God's Millionaires.'"

53. Austin and Clifton, "Australian Pentecostalism."

parts of the island community under water. The UN estimates that the entire island state of Kiribati, with its roughly a hundred thousand inhabitants, will be uninhabitable in thirty years if the sea continues to rise at the same rate as today.

While the sea is rising in the Pacific, the climate changes take other forms in Australia, which is especially exposed to extreme drought and forest fires. The years 2019 and 2020 had the warmest summers in Australia since measurements began in 1910. One study has concluded that the enormous forest fires and bush fires that raged in recent years have become at least 30 percent more likely thanks to human-caused climate changes.[54] But this is not the only factor that makes the climate question acute in Australia. Although its population is small in the global context, its greenhouse gas emissions per capita are among the highest in the world.[55] As the world's second-largest exporter of coal, Australia is an important actor in international climate politics. And this is also one of the reasons why the climate has been a relatively polarized political arena in the country in the past two decades.[56]

Although climate questions continue to be much debated in Australian politics, the traditional churches in the country have been strongly involved in the climate campaign.[57] This mirrors the climate involvement of the same churches and ecumenical organizations elsewhere in the world. Since early in the present century, many of these churches, such as Catholics, Anglicans, and the United Church, as well as the National Council of Churches in Australia, have made official declarations about climate policy, exhorting their members, the general public, and the governing authorities on various levels to take care of the earth and to be generous towards those societies that are most affected by climate changes.[58] The United Church, which is a union of Methodist, Congregational, and Presbyterian churches, has had the strongest political involvement. Climate change advocacy has been a central part of the church's involvement in society on both national and federal-state levels since the turn of the millennium. This involvement has included submitting proposals for legislation, conducting meetings with parliamentarians, writing resource materials for use in the churches, and

---

54. World Weather Attribution, "Attribution of the Australian Bushfire Risk."
55. World Bank, "World Development Indicators."
56. Beeson and McDonald, "Special Issue."
57. Douglas, "Religious Environmentalism."
58. Pepper and Leonard, "Climate Change."

encouraging church members and others to take part in public events and lobby campaigns targeted at politicians.[59]

Climate engagement and care for the Earth have also proved to be causes that are suited to interreligious collaboration in Australia. Interreligious appeals and cooperation on climate action increased from the beginning of the 2000s, and the largest faith groups formed the Australian Religious Response to Climate Change in 2008, a multi-faith, membership-based organization that carries out advocacy work from a perspective of faith. Its aim is to influence both individual persons and public policy to contribute to climate justice, and it recognizes "the special place that Aboriginal culture and spirituality have in upholding care for the Earth."[60] When the organization helped to organize a big demonstration in front of Parliament House in Canberra in February 2020, an Anglican priest led a large interfaith ritual of grief over the victims of the enormous forest fires that were ravaging the country at that time.

This, however, does not mean that all the churches in Australia have become involved against human-caused climate changes. Marion Maddox has pointed out the existence of contact and cooperation between interested parties in the mining industry and rightwing Christian organizations in Australia.[61] Several of these organizations, together with many Pentecostal congregations, have channeled their political involvement, not into the climate issue, but into opposition to same-sex marriage, abortion, and legislation that regulates the right to discriminate in work on the basis of religious convictions.

The question of political support for a less ambitious climate policy is relevant also to Christian groups outside the Christian right wing, since the political priorities of church leaders do not always coincide with those of churchgoers. Studies show that there has been a consistent positive association between service attendance and voting for conservative Parties in Australia since 2007.[62] Churchgoers thus tend to cast their political votes for conservatives, even though their churches lend support to a more radical climate policy. Accordingly, even if almost 90 percent of churchgoers believe that Australia ought to take steps to solve the climate problem, and almost half believe this even if it involves significant cost,[63] one can get the impression that it is not climate questions that weigh most heavily when

59. Pepper and Jason, "Ecological Engagement."

60. ARRCC, "Who We Are."

61. Maddox, "Right-Wing Christian Intervention."

62. Donovan, "The Irrelevance." See also Pepper and Leonard, "Climate Change."

63. NCLS Research, "Most Churchgoers."

Australian churchgoers decide which Party they will vote for. In this way, the situation in Australia also shows how churches and Christians are often divided on questions of values and political priorities. In Australia, as in many other countries, evaluations of climate policy largely follow the dividing lines between the political Parties, and Christians are to be found on both sides.

OUTLOOK

A more detailed account of Christianity in Oceania could have given a description of the development in the Anglican church in Australia, which once was the largest church in the country and played an important role in this part of the British Empire, but which gradually lost members and has been overtaken by both Catholics and Pentecostals. Parts of the church have also been marked by a renewed flowering of conservative Evangelicalism in the last forty years; this has also been seen in some Presbyterian churches in the country. The Anglican Moore College in Sydney with its "biblical theology movement" has been a powerhouse in this movement, which has set its stamp above all on the diocese of Sydney. This diocese has been called "one of world Anglicanism's evangelical powerhouses."[64] It has a clear countercultural profile, and it was prominent in its opposition to the ordination of women and gay clergy. Peter Jensen, rector at Moore Theological College and archbishop of Sydney from 2001 to 2013, has been one of the leading conservative voices in the Anglican Communion. He came to public notice *inter alia* by building powerful alliances with other Anglican church leaders in the global South, for example, in Nigeria, and through his role in the setting up of GAFCOM, about which we have written in chapter 2. Conservative Evangelicalism in Australia has established a solid alliance with the Catholics, who have a larger tradition of active political involvement. In this way, the movement has been described as the aim "to defend by legislative means, what they have failed to achieve by cultural influence: a conservative moral society, based on Christian values."[65]

This chapter could also have included more about the vast variety of Christian cultural, social, and political practices that characterize the island societies in the Pacific. There could, for example, have been a description of the growing diversification of Christianity on the Pacific islands and about the success of global Christian organizations such as the Church of Jesus Christ of Latter-day Saints, the Seventh Day Adventists, and the Jehovah's

64. Piggin and Lineham, "Christianity in Australia and Oceania," 586.
65. Piggin and Lineham, "Christianity in Australia and Oceania," 586.

Witnesses, all of whom have experienced a solid growth in the island societies in recent decades. The Church of Jesus Christ of Latter-day Saints is especially well established in Polynesia (Tonga, Samoa, American Samoa, and French Polynesia), where it amounts to almost, or more than, 10 percent of the respective population.[66] These three churches have little in common in terms of doctrine and worship, but all have their origin in the USA and have a highly centralized and hierarchical worldwide structure, with the head office in the USA. In this way too, the Christianity that makes its mark on Oceania is both particular and integrated into local culture, while at the same time being tightly interwoven with Christianity elsewhere in the world.

66. Ernst, "Changing Christianity in Oceania."

8

Eastern Europe

Orthodox Defense against Liberal Values

THE COLLAPSE OF THE Soviet Union at the beginning of the 1990s was one of the most important historical events in the second half of the twentieth century. It had vast consequences for the churches in Eastern Europe, especially for the Orthodox churches that had their heartlands there. These churches, formerly oppressed and marginal, now assumed in the space of a short time a central role in society. In Russia, the Orthodox church has become a close ally of President Putin in his endeavors to strengthen a national identity in contrast to the West. The idea of an Orthodox civilization is cultivated by the church's leadership. In other countries in Eastern Europe, political and cultural life is torn between East and West. At the same time, many Christians live out their faith in a way that is largely unaffected by the struggles that politicians and church leaders are waging.

In a grandiose ceremony on Saturday, August 19, 2000, the head of the Russian Orthodox church, Patriarch Alexy II, consecrated the cathedral of Christ the Savior in the heart of Moscow. If you stand on the Kremlin walls a few hundred meters away, the church makes a powerful impression. The gilded cupola towers 103 meters into the sky and makes it Russia's tallest church. The summer sun makes the white marble shine. The impression is equally overwhelming when you enter the building. The faithful say their prayers surrounded by walls and ceilings that gleam like gold. Over the icons hangs the fragrance of incense. There is room for five thousand people here, if they stand close together. The church is constructed in modern materials, with air conditioning, elevators, and an underground garage, but otherwise it is built to look like the church that stood here in the past.

The original cathedral of Christ the Savior was opened in 1883; it had been built to commemorate Russia's victory over Napoleon in 1812, and Tchaikovsky's 1812 Overture was written for the opening. But the church was not allowed to remain standing: in the period of his greatest hostility to religion, Stalin ordered it to be torn down, and it was demolished in 1931. In 1958, the largest open-air swimming pool in the Soviet Union opened here; this was closed in 1994. Six years and more than four hundred million US dollars later, the church was rebuilt and consecrated as a symbol of the radical rebuilding of the Russian Orthodox church after the oppression of the Soviet period, and now it is Russia's most prominent cathedral. It is here that President Putin comes to services on the greatest feast days, and it was here that President Yeltsin was buried. It is claimed that millions of Russians made financial contributions to the project, but the contributions from industry and the governing authorities were much more important.[1]

The cathedral of Christ the Savior brings together in a focal point much of what is important about the church in Eastern Europe in the early 2000s. Orthodox church life is characterized by aesthetic beauty: God's presence in the world is not primarily mediated by means of words, but is experienced with all the senses. But the freedom to worship God in this way is very much a new-found freedom. After the Second World War, the Soviet Union exported its communist form of government to almost the whole of Eastern Europe, and Eastern European Christians lived under atheistic dictatorships until the end of the 1980s. The degree of oppression varied from country to country, but the churches were nowhere free. The political changes around 1990 brought a dramatic alteration. In the course of a few years, the churches went from a clandestine existence to occupying a central place in many Eastern European societies. The Orthodox churches received new privileges and in some cases a significant influence both on individuals' lives and on the politics of the state.

Eastern Europe has no natural geographical boundary. In the decades after the Second World War, the dividing line between West and East crossed through Germany. When the Iron Curtain was drawn aside, the boundary became more unclear. In the present chapter, we let "Eastern Europe" be defined by the influence of the Orthodox church. We discuss the Catholic countries that belonged to the Eastern Europe of the cold war, especially Poland, in the chapter about Central and Western Europe. It is thus Orthodox

---

1. Knox, *Russian Society*, 120.

Christianity that takes the center stage here, and we shall approach this tradition with our starting point in Russia, which with its 144 million inhabitants is clearly the largest country in this region and which has also been a dominant power to which other countries were forced to relate.[2]

Those parts of Europe that were under the Ottoman and the Russian empires in the course of history have had a different cultural and political development from the countries further to the West, and their Christianity shows the traces of this. When the American political scientist Samuel Huntington identified a specifically Orthodox civilization in his controversial 1996 book about the clash of civilizations, he did so against the background of this history.[3] Huntington believed that future conflicts would take place between different civilizations, each of which was defined by its own religious tradition. In today's Russia, this idea of a deep gulf between an Orthodox and a Western Christian civilization is embraced by politicians, the church leadership, and ordinary Russians. Seventy-five percent of all the Russians who took part in a survey in 2015 answered that there is a conflict between Russia's traditional values and Western values.[4]

A presentation of the Orthodox form of Christianity that dominates in Eastern Europe could have begun in Greece, where Christianity arrived before the New Testament was written, or in Istanbul (once called Constantinople), where Emperor Constantine laid the foundation in the fourth century for the strong ties between state power and church power that have marked the church's life from the Roman Empire down to our own days. But when one aims to give a presentation of the Orthodox tradition as a living and significant religion today, it is equally natural to begin in Moscow. In most Orthodox churches, the highest leader has the title "patriarch." The patriarch of Moscow leads the world's second-largest church and is the head of more than half of the world's Orthodox Christians. An even larger number of the world's Orthodox, far more than two-thirds, lived until 1990 in countries under a strong Soviet Russian influence. The Russian Revolution in 1917 and the collapse of communism just over seventy years later have been called the two most central events for the Orthodox church in the modern age.

After a presentation of the Orthodox tradition in Russia, we shall move through borderlands where the perception of a clear Orthodox civilization is put to a serious test, especially in Ukraine. We shall end up in the ancient imperial capital of Istanbul, which is still known in the Orthodox context as

2. World Bank, "Russian Federation."

3. Huntington, *Clash of Civilizations.*

4. Pew Research Center, "Religious Belief."

Constantinople. We shall also glance en route at other forms of Christianity that constitute minorities everywhere in this region.

RUSSIA—"THE MOST BEAUTIFUL OF THE RELIGIONS"

Nine hundred and fifty years passed from the arrival of Christianity in today's Turkey and Greece, until it became the religion in the emerging Russian realm. Towards the close of the tenth century, Prince Vladimir governed a realm that had its center in Kyiv in today's Ukraine. The myth relates that he sent emissaries to the neighboring countries to learn about their religions and to find out which would be the most suitable in his domains. They visited Muslims in the East and Christians in the West, but they found nothing of any value. When they arrived in Constantinople and were welcomed in the great cathedral of Hagia Sophia, everything changed:

> We knew not whether we were in heaven or on earth. For on earth there is no such splendor or such beauty, and we are at a loss how to describe it. We only know that God dwells there among men, and their service is fairer than the ceremonies of other nations. For we cannot forget that beauty. Every man, after tasting something sweet, is afterward unwilling to accept that which is bitter.[5]

If we are to believe this myth, therefore, it was the beauty of the worship that made the Russians Orthodox. The beautiful shining interior of the cathedral of Christ the Savior in Moscow is overwhelming, but not unique. The churches everywhere in the Orthodox world are built to mediate God's greatness to the senses. Gold gleams where the rulers have left their mark on the churches, as in the great cathedrals and for example the church in the winter palace of the Russian imperial family in St. Petersburg. But even in more ordinary churches, the decoration is itself an expression of a theology in which the deity reaches out to human beings in order to divinize earthly life. The incense is meant to lift the people's prayers up to God, but it also reminds them that God blesses those who come into God's house.

Apart from the priest's sermon, there is very little that is spoken in an Orthodox service. Everything is sung. In many churches, the vernacular is now used in the liturgy, but in the Russian Orthodox church and in some other countries with a Slavic language, one still encounters the old Church

---

5. This translation is from Cross and Sherbowitz-Wetzor, *The Russian Primary Chronicle*, 111.

Slavonic language in the service. A solid male voice is one of the most important instruments for a priest. The idea that women could become priests is remote for most Orthodox church leaders, and the movement for women's ordination is very marginal in the Orthodox churches. Recently, however, women have been given more prominent roles in the liturgy when they sing in the choir, conduct the music, and read prayers.

There is most often a choir in the church, but musical instruments are never heard, and the others who are present, the ordinary churchgoers, say very little in the course of a service. The separation between the priest, on the one hand, and the laity on the other, is underlined by the iconostasis, the wall that separates the altar from the main part of the church, with the result that the altar and what happens there are visible only when the gates in the iconostasis are opened at specific points in the liturgy. The priests and deacons move back and fro in the course of the liturgy between the congregational side and the altar side of the iconostasis. Some parts of the liturgy are conducted in front of the iconostasis, on the people's side, while other parts are conducted at the altar. But despite this striking separation, where the laity neither sing nor draw near to the altar, they often participate actively in what is going on, not least by making the sign of the cross at all the correct places in the liturgy.

During the liturgy, the congregation stands and looks towards the altar that marks God's presence, but what they see is the iconostasis with its rows of icons. This brings us to one of the most central and characteristic elements in Orthodox spirituality. The paintings of holy men and women are not perceived as decoration or art (although they can be this too); they are important liturgical objects and are understood as mediators of God's grace. They are not visible only on the iconostasis. Icons can be set up in many places in a church interior, and the believers can stand in a queue to light candles, to utter a prayer, and not least to touch the icons or kiss them.

It is often said that Orthodox spirituality is collective rather than individualistic.[6] There is some truth in this, but the Orthodox practice of faith is also expressed in the individual's adoration, *inter alia* in front of the icons in the church. Besides this, many attach importance to the individual preparation for the liturgy, including fasting and the personal confession in which one confesses one's sins to a priest. Icons are found in people's homes, and it is not unusual to have small traveling icons that one can take on journeys. These can give orientation to the individual's prayers, and popular belief says that the simple fact of taking them with you gives protection against dangers.

6. Binns, *An Introduction*, 142.

MONASTERIES, PILGRIMAGES, AND FASTING

The cathedral of Christ the Savior has been Moscow's most important church since 2000, but another church in the city is surely just as well known to many Western Europeans from TV images and tourist brochures: Saint Basil's cathedral with the colorful onion domes on Red Square, named after Blessed Basil (d. 1552) who is remembered as a holy fool, because he walked naked through the streets of Moscow and spoke out openly against Ivan the Terrible.[7] The latter idea was surely the most foolish of all, because it was so dangerous. But the holy fools were able sometimes to challenge power, and they were often protected by the reverence that surrounded them. Basil is an example of how Russian and Orthodox life has found strength from other sources than the city's church buildings, where the hierarchical ecclesial structure with its bishops and metropolitans (particularly high-ranking bishops; the word comes from "metropolis") have ruled the roost. Today, these fools largely belong to the past, but the more normal monastic life has experienced a tremendous upswing throughout the entire Orthodox world in the last decades. It was the fall of communism that made this possible in the countries of the former Eastern bloc, but an upswing for monasteries had already been visible from the beginning of the 1970s in the most important of the Orthodox monastic centers, Mount Athos in Greece.

Unlike the Catholic tradition, the Orthodox churches do not have orders of monks and nuns with their own structures alongside the rest of the church structure.[8] Monasteries have often grown "from below," but they can also have been established by the official church structure, sometimes as part of attempts to Christianize new regions. Some monasteries have been contemplative and more or less closed to the outer world; this is more often the case with convents of nuns than with monasteries of monks. But the doors have stood wide open in most monasteries, and they have been closely integrated into the daily life of those who live near them. Some had hospitals or schools, and ordinary people would have visited the monastery just as readily as they would have visited the church's priest, when they sought advice or a blessing. Some monks have been particularly appreciated for their wisdom and their skills as spiritual guides. Dostoevsky has given the best known description of such a monk in Father Zosima in his novel *The Brothers Karamazov*. Zosima is the spiritual guide and teacher for the youngest of the brothers, the pious Ilyusha. The people of the town visit the monk in the monastery, since they suppose that he can heal and see

---

7. Binns, *An Introduction*, 121.

8. Daniel, *Orthodox Church and Civil Society*, 48.

into the future. His spiritual descendants are still being visited in Orthodox monasteries today.

Traditionally, many monks and nuns were recruited from the class of poor agricultural workers, and had little education. At the same time, the monasteries have also been places of learning and have been custodians of the theological tradition. In the Orthodox churches, there have been few theological institutions of the kind we find in Western churches, and academic work in theology has not been highly esteemed. A "theologian" in the Orthodox sense has been one who experiences God, just as much as one who reflects on God—one who prays, just as much as one who writes.[9] A large number of new theological faculties or departments have been set up at already existing universities in recent years, especially in Russia. Moving theological work into the established university structure is a completely new development.

During the years of communist rule, monastic life (like the rest of church life) was brutally oppressed, but not wiped out. The revival of the monasteries in the last twenty-five years became possible in Russia not least because the state handed back monastic properties that had been confiscated in the Soviet period. This entailed a number of challenges. In the past, monasteries had been an organic part of local society, but now they were introduced in some places from the outside or from above, because there happened to be buildings that had once been monasteries. There was no corresponding restitution of property to others in society. The church was given possibilities of a strong growth, but at the same time, it was tied more closely to the state.[10]

The great monasteries can be important pilgrimage goals, not least on great feasts such as the patronal day of the saint to whom the monastery is dedicated. In some places, hundreds or thousands of pilgrims come to the monastery, often on the eve of the feast day. They often spend the evening and the night near the monastery church, singing, praying, or listening to spontaneous sermons while liturgical ceremonies are carried out inside the church itself. On the saint's day, the monastery may offer a meal to all who have come, and then the pilgrims go home. The striking element in this practice is that many pilgrims feel no need to go into the church while the ceremonies are going on. It is enough for them to be in the right place (the monastery) at the right time (the saint's day). This does not mean that it is irrelevant to them whether or not a service is happening; on the contrary, this is constitutive for their experience. The bishop performs the liturgy inside

9. Binns, *An Introduction*, 107.

10. Daniel, *Orthodox Church and Civil Society*, 56–57.

the church, and the people sit outside. This is a pattern we find throughout the Orthodox world, and it points to a type of very ancient popular spirituality that is practiced alongside, and in parallel to, the liturgical life in the church.[11]

Another aspect of Orthodox spirituality in which the church's official norms and ordinary people's practices come together is fasting. The Orthodox church year has many periods and days of fasting, which usually means abstaining, not from all food, but from meat and dairy products. When one of Russia's celebrity priests, known through TV and radio talk shows, was suddenly transferred from a leadership position to an ordinary parish church, one of several accusations against him was that he had been photographed in a McDonalds on a fast day. Many found it difficult to believe his claim that the photographs showed a vegetarian burger.[12]

PARISH GROWTH AND
INVOLVEMENT IN SOCIETY

At the beginning of the 1990s, most of the Orthodox churches found themselves in a new and completely unknown situation. Before the 1917 Revolution, there had been roughly eighty thousand churches in Russia. In the mid-1980s, six thousand church buildings were in use.[13] But now, completely new possibilities opened up, not only thanks to the freedom of religion that was introduced throughout the Soviet Union under Gorbachev in 1990, but also thanks to the church buildings that the state handed back. There was also a strong interest and curiosity among ordinary Russians who had long abandoned communism as an ideology, but who had also kept the church at least at arm's length. Between 1991 and 2015, the numbers of Russians who identified as Orthodox Christians rose from 37 to 71 percent.

The 1990s were a very turbulent period for Russian society. The economic system was completely restructured. While a few, the so-called oligarchs, became extremely rich, many became poorer. The social problems grew, and life expectancy dropped dramatically. Many turned to the church in search of a form of stability and security.

Among those who contributed to the Russian church's choice of giving priority to the construction of active congregations in the tens of thousands of local communities in the country were Alexy, at that time the newly elected patriarch, and Metropolitan Kirill, who succeeded him as patriarch

11. The description in this paragraph is based on Binns, *An Introduction*, 136.

12. See Walker, "Russian Orthodox Church."

13. Richters, *Post-Soviet Russian Orthodox Church*, 3.

in 2009. They saw to it that the priests' skills were improved and they developed the church's liturgical life. They believed that the church had to get
involved with the sick and the poor, who soon increased in numbers during
the dramatic changes in the 1990s.[14] There were also some who aimed for
a more fundamental involvement of the church in societal questions, as an
explicit corrective to the policies of the government.[15] But such a role for
the church has never been a dominant tradition in Orthodox church life.
These critical voices in Russia became weaker in the 1990s; the winners
were those who saw that the church could profit from being more closely
tied to the state authorities.

At a meeting of the Russian Orthodox synod of bishops in the days
prior to the consecration of the cathedral of Christ the Savior in 2000, the
bishops adopted the document "The social concept of the Russian Orthodox
church." This affirms the church's views on a number of contemporary questions, such as the relationship between church and state, bioethics, marriage, and abortion. The eighty-page document was something very new in
the Orthodox churches, which have not been accustomed to make declarations on urgent societal questions. It was not, however, very well received by
the newly elected President Putin, who reacted negatively to the statement
that Christians should have recourse to civil disobedience if the state leads
people into grave sin. Putin held that the church ought to have consulted the
state before the document was adopted. The president's protests did not lead
the church to change its position officially, but by means of his explanation
of what kinds of sin could prompt civil disobedience, Kirill showed that, in
practice, this would not happen.[16] In the years that followed, the idea of
civil disobedience became even less relevant in Kirill's eyes, and Putin had
more and more reason to be content with the church.

CHURCH POWER AND REBELLION

Many in the West first heard of the cathedral of Christ the Savior in winter
2012. On February 21, a few days before the election in which Vladimir
Putin was to be elected for a new period as Russia's president, the feminist
punk rock group Pussy Riot performed a stunt in front of the iconostasis in
the most important Russian sanctuary. The young women were put on trial
and given prison sentences. But this scene drew attention to the increasingly
close links between the church's leadership and the state power. The video

14. Daniel, *Orthodox Church and Civil Society*, 32, 42.

15. Daniel, *Orthodox Church and Civil Society*, 42.

16. Richters, *Post-Soviet Russian Orthodox Church*, 27.

from their stunt, which was spread on YouTube and in Western media, is a constructed version in which the group's music and recordings from another church are spliced together with video recordings of the few minutes that the performance in the cathedral lasted before the guards intervened. The video underlines the idea behind the action. The main point was to get across a message. The women sing: "O Virgin Mary, remove Putin from power," while they kneel and make the sign of the cross in front of the icons, and they sing about a church that "praises rotten dictators" and carries the cross "in a procession of black limousines." Patriarch Kirill himself was one of the main targets of the action.

Kirill, who was one of the church leaders most respected by the intelligentsia in the mid-1990s, had been elected as patriarch in 2009, and his ties to Putin had grown ever closer. In connection with the 2012 election, he gave active support to Putin's campaign, in contradiction of the directives in his own document about the social concept, which said that churchmen should keep away from party politics. At the same time, the criticism of the expensive habits of church leaders was growing. There seems to be a gulf between the church that was exposed to active persecution until the mid-1980s and the church that was represented twenty-five years later by bishops who arrive in Rolls Royces at churches in the Kremlin, the stronghold of power. The scandal prompted by the revelation that the church's press department had airbrushed Kirill's expensive wristwatch from an official photograph shows that the church's leaders themselves sensed that this gulf had grown excessively wide.[17]

The church leaders' luxury was only one aspect of the new reality. The greater problem in the critics' eyes was that the church acquired an ever closer relationship, theologically and structurally, to the state power and a growing role as supplier of an ideological superstructure to the Russian state. Feminist punks and bloggers protested loudly and found much sympathy in other parts of Europe when they expressed their wishes for a church that was less intent on gaining power and for rights for women and LGBTQ persons—but they won little support among ordinary Russians. Although the church had endured great sufferings under communism, what was now being reestablished was more of a normal situation in Orthodox state–church relations.

Let us come back to the synod of bishops in Moscow in mid-August 2000. It was not the document about the social concept that attracted attention to the synod, but its declaration that Russia's last Tsar, Nicholas II, and his family were saints. The canonization was celebrated in the cathedral of

17. See "Russia's Patrick Kirill."

Christ the Savior on the day after its official consecration, August 20.[18] The
imperial family were killed by the Bolshevists after the Revolution. Through
the canonization, the church underlined its ties to the past and recalled
indirectly the close ties that had existed between the church and the state
power in the centuries down to 1917. This was the norm, not only in Russia,
but basically in every region where the Orthodox tradition has been important. For example, we read in a ninth-century Byzantine law book: "Unity
and concord in all things among the government and the clergy, therefore,
mean peace and happiness for their subjects in spirit and in body."[19]

The law book describes the ideal relationship between the state power
and the church in the Orthodox tradition. This has often been called *symphonia*, "harmony" or (literally) "that which sounds well together." Both
sides are to aim at this harmony. Priests and princes are to reach out to each
other, so that what they do will be to the greatest benefit of the people.[20] One
seldom sees a church in active opposition to the state power in the Orthodox world. Under communist rule, the relationship to the state made huge
demands of the churches. Some Christians attempted to oppose the state,
but eventually found no alternative to emigration to the West. Others were
punished harshly by the authorities. The Russian Orthodox church today
recognizes a long list of historical persons from the twentieth century as
martyrs, because they died for their faith. There was also a tendency for the
church behind the Iron Curtain to find ways of living in a hard-won quasi-
harmony with the atheistic rulers. This can scarcely be called *symphonia*,
because unlike the empires of the past, both church and state held that they
were *not* working towards the same goal. Nevertheless, one can recognize in
much of the twentieth century the same basic impulse to be loyal to the state
authorities that runs through Orthodox history.

What the church can offer the state today is a kind of ideological-
visionary superstructure as a replacement of the communist vision that
governed Eastern Europe for much of the twentieth century. At the start of
the new century, the newly elected President Putin sent Christmas greetings
to the Orthodox faithful, stating that:

> Orthodoxy has traditionally played a special role in Russian his-
> tory. It has been not only a moral touchstone for every believer
> but also an unbending spiritual core of the entire people and
> state. Based on the idea of love for one's neighbor and on the
> commandments of good, mercy, and justice, Orthodoxy has

18. See "Nicholas II."
19. Daniel, *Orthodox Church and Civil Society*, 12.
20. Daniel, *Orthodox Church and Civil Society*, 12.

largely determined the character of Russian civilization. . . . It
is my firm belief as we are entering the third millennium today
that its ideals will make it possible to strengthen mutual understanding and consensus in our society and will contribute to the
spiritual and moral rebirth of the Fatherland.[21]

The spiritual and moral rebirth that Putin wanted for the country was
not only a renewal after the fall of communism, but also an alternative to the
Russians' partial embrace of what were seen as Western ways of thinking in
the 1990s. At the center was the brutal—and unsuccessful—liberalization of
the economic systems, which not only led to a growth in poverty but also
opened the door to Western popular culture as well as to pornography and increased prostitution. The state authorities and the church joined hands in the
confrontation with the West and in their idea of a specific Russian civilization.

In opposition to what they regard as the decadence of the West, the
Russian Orthodox church offers the idea of "Holy Rus" called after an ancient ethnic group that may have given its name to today's Russia. This is
an old idea in Russia; it is sometimes linked to the idea of Moscow as "the
third Rome," which arose towards the end of the fourteenth century.[22] The
first Rome had long since been abandoned, both politically with the fall
of the Western Empire and ecclesiastically with the division between the
Church in the East and in the West. This idea affirms that when Constantinople—"the new Rome"—was conquered by the Muslim Ottomans in 1453,
Moscow became the center of the Christian world. When the communist
regimes began to suffer their last agonies at the close of the 1980s, the Russian church was given the possibility of holding a grandiose celebration
of the thousand years' jubilee of the Christianization of Kyiv in 1988. This
laid the foundations for breathing new life into the idea of Holy Rus in the
course of the 1990s, which was then ready for use by the state authorities at
the turn of the millennium.

TRADITIONAL RELIGIONS AND
TRADITIONAL VALUES

When the Soviet Union was disintegrating in 1990, a new and radical religious legislation was brought in, which gave almost complete freedom
of religion. Initially, the Russian Orthodox church was very pleased with
this law, but it changed its mind during the 1990s, since it was not only

21. Daniel, *Orthodox Church and Civil Society*, 73.

22. Jardar Østbø has thoroughly examined the idea of "the third Rome" in Østbø,
The New Third Rome.

the Russian Orthodox church that benefited from religious freedom: other churches and religious groups did so too. Many of these came from the West and had a long experience of active missionary work; and they often also had powerful economic muscles. According to one statistic, the number of Catholic parishes in Russia increased tenfold between 1990 and 2004, and there was a corresponding growth among Hare Krishna adherents and Buddhists. Muslim communities roughly quadrupled, while the number of Orthodox parishes increased "only" a little more than threefold.[23]

The church's leaders experienced the huge growth in other groups of believers as a threat. In particular, the growth of the Catholics was regarded as illegitimate proselytism, that is to say, winning over adherents from one church to another. This was a challenge to the Orthodox idea of canonical territories, which states that each church has its own region, where it has in principle a monopoly. The Orthodox leaders saw that Western Christians had huge resources, and that their behavior could display little respect. The accusations of proselytism remain one of the greatest wounds in the relationship between the patriarchate of Moscow and the Vatican. But both the media and the church leadership often exaggerated the size and influence of the new churches, and when we read descriptions of the tremendous growth of the Western churches, it is easy to overlook the fact that the point of departure was very small figures. Even if the Orthodox growth is smaller on a percentage basis, there were still almost fifty times more Orthodox than Catholic parishes in Russia in 2004.[24] In 2015, less than 1 percent of Russians said that they were Catholics, while roughly 2 percent belonged to other churches than the Orthodox church.[25]

A new religious law that was more to the church's taste was promulgated in 1997. This gives the Russian Orthodox church special privileges, while also affirming that Islam, Judaism, and Buddhism are traditional religions in Russia, and that they therefore are entitled to a certain measure of special treatment. Other religions are free to practice, but they have a limited possibility of gaining recognition as autonomous religious denominations.[26]

The idea of the traditional religions is important for the church. The recognition of Islam, Judaism, and Buddhism in the 1997 law is natural and necessary, since some regions in Russia have large ethnic groups that have belonged to these religions for centuries. The essential point was to draw a boundary line against what came from outside, and especially from the

23. Richters, *Post-Soviet Russian Orthodox Church*, 37.
24. Richters, *Post-Soviet Russian Orthodox Church*, 37.
25. Pew Research Center, "Religious Belief."
26. Daniel, *Orthodox Church and Civil Society*, 70.

West. This binds these religions, and in particular the Orthodox church which is far and away the largest of them, closely to Russian tradition, and the idea of a fellowship in values among the various traditional religions is emerging. In the early 2000s, it became clear that the church's leadership saw itself as the custodian of traditional values. In some cases, the fight for traditional values resembled opposition to everything associated with the West, including democracy, capitalism, liberalism, and ecumenism.[27]

For the senior church leaders, traditional values also involved regulations against blasphemy and insulting religious symbols and feelings in public. Pussy Riot is one example, but there have also been controversies about art exhibitions and plays in theaters. Above all, however, the appeal to traditional values has concerned what are often called family values. There is skepticism about equality between women and men, opposition to artificial insemination and other technologies connected to human reproduction, and not least opposition to LGBTQ rights.[28]

The wish to protect the traditional family also constitutes the background to the church's strong opposition to a system of youth courts that could intervene against juvenile delinquency. A declaration by the church's bishops in 2013 claims that the challenges posed by juvenile delinquency are caused by the "moral disorientation" of society, and that the problem must be solved within the family, without any involvement by the state. This means that parents' rights take priority over any rights that children might possess.[29] The same logic also leads the church to get involved *against* laws that prohibit violence against children and women in the family: the aim is to protect the integrity of the family against state interference. In practice, this is a defense of established patriarchal structures.

Through its opposition to interference by the authorities in family life, the church makes the family the most important unit in society. The idea is that the family is under pressure both from individual rights and from the state. Skepticism vis-à-vis the state is also expressed in church opposition to digital identity cards, which the church's representatives have seen as attempts by the state to monitor and control individuals' lives.[30] First and foremost, however, the state has been the church's partner. Some speak of an "orthodoxification" of the Russian state in this period.[31]

27. Daniel, *Orthodox Church and Civil Society*, 38.

28. Agadjanian, "Tradition," 44.

29. Agadjanian, "Tradition," 46.

30. Agadjanian, "Tradition," 47.

31. Curanovic, *Religious Factor*, 79.

The church's agenda for traditional values has prevailed in parliament in a number of issues. There has been a group of members of parliament for what is called the defense of Christian values since 2012. In 2013 the blasphemy legislation was tightened and there were also introduced a prohibition of so-called propaganda for non-traditional sexuality vis-à-vis minors and a prohibition against the adoption of Russian children by same-sex partners in other countries. From 2015 onwards, Russia's official national security strategy includes the protection and development of traditional Russian spirituality and Russian moral values.[32] When parliament amended the constitution in 2020 following a referendum, one of the selling points of the changes (which also extended the president's powers) was the inclusion of a ban on same-sex marriage.

Two arenas where the church interacts with—and therefore has the opportunity to influence—ordinary people are the school system and the armed forces. In the 2000s, the church established a close collaboration with the armed forces, and it supplies them with a large number of military chaplains. Its department for collaboration with the armed forces not only provides worship services and pastoral care among the soldiers, but also contributes actively in the construction of narratives with a nationalistic orientation in which the military victories of the past can be depicted as the direct result of fidelity to the Orthodox faith and as God's blessing on Russia. Sometimes priests also bless weapons before soldiers go into battle.[33]

Attempts to introduce a subject of religion in schools, with confessional instruction, have also stood high on the agenda of the Russian Orthodox church. In 2009, a subject was introduced, permitting parents to choose which religion the pupils were to be taught; a new law in 2012 made this subject obligatory.[34] Many choose instruction in the Orthodox faith, and the church has played a strong role in the creation of the teaching materials. The critics believe that this subject not only gives the pupils an orientation about religion, but also teaches them how to become good Orthodox Russians.[35]

The traditional values for which the church is working are in sharp contrast to the values that Pussy Riot wanted to promote through their stunt in the cathedral of Christ the Savior. In Western Europe, the feminist punkers became heroines for many, but most people in Russia are critical. Does this mean that the church exercises a strong influence on the attitudes of ordinary Russians? The picture is complex. There are a number of organizations

32. Agadjanian, "Tradition," 52.

33. Richters, *Post-Soviet Russian Orthodox Church*, 57–74.

34. Agadjanian, "Tradition," 52.

35. Richters, *Post-Soviet Russian Orthodox Church*, 47–52.

outside the church's own structure that are working for the same causes, such as organizations of Orthodox women or Orthodox physicians. But despite all the talk of a strong growth of the church, there is still only a small percentage of Russians who go to church regularly. In 2015, about 5 percent of all Russians declared that they went to church weekly, and 17 percent answered that they prayed every day.[36] This percentage is on the same level as in many Western European countries. At the same time, more than 70 percent answered that they were Orthodox. Being Orthodox is thus linked more closely to a Russian identity than to religious praxis or adherence to church doctrine.[37] But this picture too can be somewhat oversimplified. Being Orthodox is not necessarily linked to regular churchgoing or to personal faith. Many people hold that the priests and the church hierarchy can safely take care of such things. It is on the great feast days, and perhaps on the fasting days, that many display their adherence to the church.[38]

The traditional values enjoy great support among Russians, but it is not certain that it was the church that created these attitudes in the period after the Soviet Union's collapse. It is more likely that various forms of value conservatism are joining hands here. Homosexuality was a taboo in the Soviet Union too. Eight-five percent of all Russians say that homosexuality is morally wrong, and even among the minority who do not identify with any religion, nearly 80 percent say that society ought not to accept homosexuality.[39] In the case of abortion, the record numbers of abortions in the Soviet Union can seem daunting to many even of those who are not strongly convinced of the Christian faith. About a third of the population supports a liberal abortion law.[40] The authorities and the church have similar positions on this question, but with different starting points: the church shares its skepticism about abortion with almost all other churches, while the state authorities are concerned about the dramatic decrease in the population. It is absolutely necessary that more Russians should be born.[41]

Shared work for traditional values is an expression of the most fundamental interest that brings state and church together: namely, the conviction that the Orthodox or the Russian civilization is a bulwark against Western decadence, and that it must be ready in the long term to take over hegemony in the world, once the West has ensured its own destruction. Although the

36. Pew Research Center, "Religious Belief."
37. Pew Research Center, "Religious Belief."
38. Binns, *An Introduction*, 237.
39. Pew Research Center, "Religious Belief."
40. Pew Research Center, "Religious Belief."
41. Richters, *Post-Soviet Russian Orthodox Church*, 33; Agadjanian, "Tradition," 43.

packaging is new, it is easy to see that there is also a continuity from the communist period, when the authorities consolidated their own position in the people by pointing to a profound gulf in values between the Soviet Union and Western capitalism. But unlike in the Soviet period, it is now Christianity itself that Russia must defend. A speech in 2013 is only one example of how Putin employs this idea, thereby aligning himself completely with the church:

> We see how many Euro-Atlantic countries have de facto chosen the path of cutting ties with their roots, including their Christian values, which are at the foundation of western civilisation. They reject moral foundations and all traditional identities—national, cultural, religious, and even sexual. Their policy places large families and same-sex partnerships, the belief in God and the belief in Satan on the same level. . . . People in many countries of Europe are ashamed to speak about their religious affiliation. . . . And these countries are aggressively trying to impose this model upon everybody, the entire world. I am certain that this is a direct path to degradation and primitivisation, to a deep demographic and moral crisis.[42]

Political and ecclesiastical leaders in Russia thus have a shared interest in cultivating the idea of a clearly demarcated Orthodox civilization. But when we turn to some other countries with strong Orthodox churches, it will become clear that this idea is very problematic.

UKRAINE—BORDERLAND BETWEEN EAST AND WEST

When the Soviet Union collapsed, a number of new independent states were born. The relationship to the patriarchate of Moscow is a hot question in many of the "new" Orthodox countries. From Moscow's perspective, there is a close link between the idea of Holy Rus and the idea of the canonical territory. The patriarchate of Moscow claims that its canonical territory must include the entire "Holy Rus kingdom." This is not a new idea, but it has been emphasized more strongly and (some would say) used politically in the period after the fall of communism.

Armenia and Georgia are different from the other former Soviet states, because both countries have a very ancient Christian tradition, and each has its own Orthodox church that is independent of Moscow. Armenia's church

42. Agadjanian, "Tradition," 53.

is regarded as the first church in history to be linked to the state. It belongs to the Oriental Orthodox tradition, while the autonomous church in Georgia is one of the Eastern Orthodox churches. The Orthodox church in Belarus, which is the majority church, is dependent on Moscow, but unlike in Russia, the constitution also gives certain privileges, for historical reasons, not only to Jews and Muslims, but also to Catholics and Lutherans.[43] This reflects a history of rulers of various religions who have left their mark on the country. Aleksandr Lukashenko, who has been its strong ruler for most of the period since Belarus gained independence, describes himself as an "Orthodox atheist." He means that he is a convinced atheist, but one who belongs to an Orthodox cultural tradition.[44] In one sense, the Orthodox church is the privileged church, but its closeness to the state also means that it has a very restricted room for maneuver in a country with little religious freedom.

Ukraine is home to today's deepest and most complex conflict within the Orthodox tradition. Several Orthodox churches compete for members and recognition, and their conflict has repercussions throughout the Orthodox world. The relationship between the churches was tense long before the outbreak of armed conflict in Ukraine in 2014, and reflects how the country has been tugged for centuries between East and West. Russia's foreign policy interest is to prevent Ukraine from binding itself too closely to the West. This overlaps with the Russian Orthodox church's thinking about Holy Rus and the canonical territory. This appeals to the Russian-friendly part of Ukraine.[45] On the other side, Orthodoxy is mobilized to provide support for Ukrainian nationalism which resents Russian influence. With a population of forty-four million (2019), Ukraine is Eastern Europe's second largest country, after Russia. We must therefore take a closer look at Ukraine's church life.

For Russian Orthodoxy, the conflict in Ukraine touches on central questions of its self-understanding with regard both to its history and to its size. As we have mentioned, the Christianization of what gradually became Russia began in and through today's Ukraine. From the nineteenth century onwards, most of this area was integrated into the Russian Empire, and the country subsequently became the most important republic in the Soviet Union alongside Russia. The dominant church was a part of the Russian church. After the Russian Revolution, a competitor church arose, which called itself the Ukrainian Autocephalous Orthodox Church (UAOC). By using the term "autocephalous" the church claimed independence from other churches. The new church structure was abolished by Stalin some

---

43. Richters, *Post-Soviet Russian Orthodox Church*, 129–30.

44. Richters, *Post-Soviet Russian Orthodox Church*, 140.

45. Curanovic, *Religious Factor*, 138.

years later, but it continued as a church for Ukrainians in the West, especially in North America.[46] When Ukraine became independent in 1991, it
was rapidly re-established in the country, with a clear anti-Moscow profile.[47]

At the same time as UAOC was re-established in Ukraine, the new
president, Leonid Kravchuk, attempted to make the Ukrainian part of the
Russian Orthodox church, which had existed in the country throughout
the Soviet period, national and independent of Moscow.[48] Many saw the
Moscow church as a part of the system of oppression: now, the church was
to be set free. The process resulted in yet another church structure known
as the Independent Ukrainian Orthodox church or the Ukrainian Orthodox church, patriarchate of Kyiv (UOC-KP). Although many parishes and
priests switched to the new church, the patriarchate of Moscow succeeded
in retaining the governance of the larger part of the church. This remained
an integral part of the Russian Orthodox church, but was given a large measure of internal autonomy.[49] It also took the name "Ukrainian Orthodox
church." In order to distinguish it from the patriarchate of Kyiv, its adherence to Moscow is often added: UOC-MP.[50]

One can wonder whether the competition between various patriarchs,
metropolitans, and church structures actually plays any great role for ordinary people. A survey in 2000 indicated how ordinary Ukrainians at that
time thought about the ecclesiastical conflict. While the patriarchate of
Moscow had three times as many Ukrainian parishes as the patriarchate of
Kyiv, the strength ratio was turned upside down when people were asked
which church they belonged to: 22 percent answered: "the patriarchate of
Kyiv," and only 12 percent "the patriarchate of Moscow." The largest group,
25 percent, answered that they were Orthodox, but did not belong to any
church. The survey became really interesting when it asked: "Who is the
head of your church?" Or, "Which patriarch does one pray for especially
in your church?" Here, the answers were reversed, and the largest group
answered that prayers were said in their church for the patriarch of Moscow,
something that usually happens only in those churches that belong to his
patriarchate. In other words, this answer suggests that many of those who
replied that they went to a church linked to the patriarchate of Kyiv in fact
attended a church linked to Moscow.

46. Brüning, "Orthodox Autocephaly in Ukraine," 96.

47. Bremer, "Religion in Ukraine," 17.

48. French, "Orthodoxy in the Ukraine," 608.

49. Krawchuk, "Redefining Orthodox Identity," 185.

50. Richters, *Post-Soviet Russian Orthodox Church*, 96.

The obvious interpretation of these numbers is that ordinary people were not much concerned about the differences between the Orthodox churches. As Ukrainians, they felt a tie to the capital, Kyiv, and answered that they belong to the patriarchate of Kyiv, although they *de facto* regularly attended a church that belonged under Moscow.[51] In other words, there seemed to be a gulf between the politicking of the ecclesial elites and the daily lives of ordinary churchgoers. The tumultuous period of armed conflict since 2014 and the struggle over which churches gain international recognition, which peaked in 2019 and to which we will return below, might have increased ordinary people's attention to church politics. However, even now research shows that the number of those who identify as "just Orthodox" remains high.[52]

From Moscow's perspective the Ukrainian church must remain part of the Russian Orthodox church, and this is non-negotiable. This conviction is supported by the idea of Holy Rus and the canonical territory. The revival of the church in Russia after the communist period began precisely with the celebration of the thousand-year jubilee of the baptism of Rus in Kyiv in 1988. But beneath this, there are also concrete material concerns. Once again, we must look at statistics. In 2010, the Russian Orthodox church declared that it had 12,400 parishes in Russia, and the number it declared for Ukraine was almost as large: 11,800. There are also a little over five thousand parishes in other countries. Without the Ukrainian parishes the Russian Orthodox church would be dramatically reduced in size and possibly lose its unrivalled position as the world's largest Orthodox church.[53] It would not only lose territory that can be called historically or symbolically important: it would also lose an important argument in favor of taking the leadership role in the Orthodox world. The strength ratio between Constantinople and Moscow would shift to the advantage of the former.

In 2018 the intra-Orthodox conflict was stepped up further when the two non-Moscow churches, the UOC-KP and the UAOC, united to form the Orthodox Church of Ukraine.[54] Unlike its predecessors it sought and gained recognition from several other Orthodox churches. Recognition from other churches is of great importance within the Orthodox world. Traditionally, being recognized as independent—"autocephalous"—by the Ecumenical Patriarch in Constantinople has been regarded by many as the sign of full membership of the Orthodox family of churches. However, because of the

51. Richters, *Post-Soviet Russian Orthodox Church*, 98.

52. Denysenko, "Reflections on Resolving Problems," 513.

53. Bremer, "Shoulda," 446.

54. Denysenko, "Explaining Ukrainian Autocephaly," 426.

long-honored principle that churches should not have overlapping "canonical territories," only the Moscow oriented church in Ukraine has enjoyed this status.[55] This changed when the Ecumenical Patriarch, Bartholomew, signaled that he would indeed grant such status to the newly merged church.[56]

The president, Petro Poroshenko, had made both unification and autocephaly important parts of his political project to pull Ukraine away from Russian influence.[57] In early January 2019 he participated in a highly publicized ceremony in Istanbul in which Bartholomew formally declared the new and elevated status of the Orthodox Church of Ukraine.

Bartholomew's move, however, infuriated both political and church leaders in Moscow. Patriarch Kirill declared that the ecclesial bonds between his church and Constantinople were severed.[58] The same would apply to all other Orthodox churches that recognize the new Ukrainian church.[59] It should be underlined that the severing of relationships was unilateral. Constantinople continued to recognize Moscow, but in practice other Orthodox churches now had to choose between following Moscow or Constantinople, causing a deep rift through the entire Orthodox world, at least on leadership level.[60]

It has been customary in the Orthodox tradition to warn against establishing churches based on ethnicity, but this has not prevented new autonomous churches from arising and being recognized when new states have seen the light of day. In ecclesial terms, Ukraine now attempts to follow in the footsteps of other Orthodox countries further to the West: Greece, Bulgaria, Romania, and Serbia received their autocephalous churches in the nineteenth and early twentieth centuries, as the respective states gradually acquired their independence.

CATHOLICS AND PROTESTANTS

If the question of autocephaly in Ukraine is a struggle between the "third Rome" and the second, the real Rome, the center of the Catholic church, also has its interests in the country. The third-largest church in Ukraine, measured by the number of parishes, is the Ukrainian Greek-Catholic

55. Bremer, "Shoulda," 444.

56. Denysenko, "Explaining Ukrainian Autocephaly," 427.

57. Denysenko, "Reflections on Resolving Problems," 513.

58. Bremer, "Shoulda," 446.

59. Krawchuk, "Orthodox Church of Ukraine," 468.

60. Krawchuk, "Orthodox Church of Ukraine," 467.

church. With between four and six million members, it is the largest Greek-Catholic church in the world.[61]

Greek-Catholic (or Byzantine Uniate) is the term for churches that are Orthodox in their liturgy and spirituality, but that recognize the pope of the Catholic church as their head and are therefore a part of the Catholic church. The question of the primacy of the pope was one of the core questions when the Western and the Eastern churches parted company in the Middle Ages. There are about fifteen million Greek-Catholic Christians in the world.[62]

The Greek-Catholic church in Ukraine came into being at the end of the sixteenth century, when much of today's Ukraine was under Polish-Lithuanian rule and it was therefore advantageous, not least for the elites, to belong to the Catholic church. They negotiated an agreement whereby they recognized the pope but continued to celebrate the Orthodox liturgy.[63] In the twentieth century, the Soviet communist regime was very skeptical about the church's ties to the West. In 1946, many Greek-Catholics were forced to convert to the Orthodox church, and the church lived on only as an underground church and abroad.[64] When Ukraine gained its independence, the scene was set for conflicts about rights of ownership to church buildings, since the church was re-established and wanted to get back churches that had in the meantime been taken over by the Orthodox church.[65]

Until recently, patriarchs of Moscow have refused to meet with the pope due not least to Catholic offensives on a traditionally Orthodox territory. When Pope Francis and Patriarch Kirill eventually met in February 2016, for the first ever meeting between a pope and a Russian patriarch, the relationship between the Catholics and Orthodox in Ukraine was one of the most difficult points on the agenda. The pope went to great lengths to accommodate the patriarch, and the Greek-Catholic leaders in Ukraine were subsequently alarmed, since they felt that the pope had sacrificed their cause in order to improve relations with Moscow. "Ukraine" literally means borderland, and centuries-long disputes, experiences from the Soviet period, theology, and today's political situation continually intersect with each other.

The idea of the bond between the country and the church influences how the Christian minorities are seen in many countries with an Orthodox majority. The national boundaries in Eastern Europe have moved again and again in the course of a turbulent history, as empires and rulers succeeded

61. Avvakumov, "Ukrainian Greek Catholics," 25.
62. Avvakumov, "Ukrainian Greek Catholics," 25.
63. French, "Orthodoxy in the Ukraine," 607.
64. Binns, *An Introduction*, 221.
65. Bremer, "Religion in Ukraine," 7.

one another. This is why most countries have minority groups with a long history of living there, and in many cases, they form Christian minorities. For example, both Ukraine and Romania have a German minority, most of whom are Lutheran or Reformed, and a Hungarian minority, most of whom belong to the Catholic church. Other Protestant groups, especially Baptists, Adventists, and Pentecostals, have grown as a consequence of Western missionary work. Direct discrimination is rare, but it is usual for these minority groups to be perceived as less representative of the Christian life in the country, even if their numbers can in fact be very large.[66] During the war in eastern Ukraine, Protestant churches were pressured to leave the region. They were not necessarily seen (unlike the patriarchate of Kyiv) as representatives of the government in Kyiv, but rather as representatives of an undesired Western influence.[67]

We find in the Ukrainian capital one of the foremost examples of how the new Pentecostal movement is also making its mark in Eastern Europe. In 1993, the Embassy of the Blessed Kingdom of God Church for All Nations was founded in Kyiv by the Nigerian student and pastor Sunday Adelaja. The community began as a little Bible study group, and now has more than twenty thousand members, most of them Ukrainian by origin. It also has daughter churches in Russia and other Eastern European countries.[68] Although the church experienced a setback after Adelaja was accused of fraud, it remains a driving force for Pentecostal revivalism in Eastern Europe.[69]

CONSTANTINOPLE—THE OLD MAN AND THE SEAS

One sunny day in early summer 2003, a venerable figure with a black beard and a tall bishop's headdress went on land from the research vessel "Sars" in the harbor in Trondheim, the old church capital of Norway. In this historically Lutheran, but now rather secular, town, Patriarch Bartholomew of Constantinople drew both curious attention and shrugs of indifference. The occasion of his visit was the General Assembly of the Conference of European Churches (CEC). In preparation for the ecumenical meeting the patriarch had convened Europe's most senior church leaders for a voyage along parts of the Norwegian coast in the company of politicians and research scientists. On their way, they had discussed environmental questions,

66. Bremer, "Religion in Ukraine," 14.
67. Kochan, "Shaping Ukrainian Identity," 111.
68. Adogame, *African Christian Diaspora*, 185–88.
69. Bremer, "Religion in Ukraine," 14.

especially those concerning the North Sea. It was not a one-off event for the patriarch. In previous years, he had undertaken similar sailings in other maritime regions of the world, with the aim of drawing media attention and inspiring people to debate the pollution of the seas.

Bartholomew bears the title "Ecumenical Patriarch," and is counted as the first among equals among the patriarchs of the various autocephalous Orthodox churches. In the first centuries of the Common Era, the idea developed that the bishops in the most important Christian cities, Rome, Jerusalem, Alexandria, Antioch, and Constantinople, were the church's most important leaders. The importance of Antioch, Alexandria, and Jerusalem waned when they came under Muslim rule, and from Constantinople's perspective, Rome went its own way from roughly the turn of the first millennium. This meant that Constantinople's leadership position went unchallenged over most of the Orthodox world for many centuries. And as the tensions in Ukraine show, it is still the case that being recognized by Constantinople is the most significant confirmation a church can receive that it is a church in good standing in the Orthodox world.

Constantinople was captured by the Muslim Ottomans in 1453, and the patriarch's prestige declined thereafter. The patriarchal office was marked by conflicts and corruption. The Ottoman sultan, who appointed the patriarch, could demand a high sum from those who desired the office; but many were in fact interested, and in the century from 1595 to 1695, there were sixty-one changes of patriarch, involving thirty-one individuals. Many of them were dismissed from office and reinstated several times.[70] While Constantinople was weakened, Moscow grew in strength. In the twentieth century, the ecumenical patriarchate rediscovered a leading role, but since Moscow too gained considerable strength after 1990, the rivalry between the two patriarchates for leadership in Orthodoxy is perhaps stronger today than at any time in the past.

The difference between the patriarchs in Moscow and Constantinople is great, and cannot be reduced to a question of the type of social questions they take up. Bartholomew's position as leader bears no relation to the little church of which he is the head. In his heartland, today's Turkey, there are no more than two thousand Orthodox Christians, and the Turkish authorities see to it that their numbers do not rise. Although the patriarch is also the leader of some other Orthodox Christians—those in parts of North-Eastern Greece, the monasteries on Athos, the Finnish Orthodox church, and not

70. Binns, *An Introduction*, 175.

least the Western diaspora, a total of perhaps seven million people—his flock is small in comparison to Moscow's more than a hundred million members.[71]

The size of the church in Turkey brings us to another aspect that distinguishes Bartholomew's position not only from that of Moscow today, but from almost all the other Orthodox leaders in Eastern Europe: he has his seat in a city and a country in which he has neither the support of the state authorities nor any influence on them. On the contrary, the Turkish authorities act systematically against the patriarch. In 1971, they closed the theological seminary that trained priests, but Turkish law nevertheless prescribes that the patriarch must be a Turkish citizen. It is an open question whether it will be possible in future to find competent heirs to the patriarch's office.

When Patriarch Bartholomew sets out on his environmental sail, it may look like a media stunt. But we can also describe it in another way: he makes use of his symbolic power to draw attention to a theme he believes to be important. One of the sources that have inspired Bartholomew in his involvement is the creative theological work that took place in the early twentieth century, especially among Orthodox theologians in Paris and New York, many of whom were originally from Russia and came to the West after the Russian Revolution. They joined forces with other Orthodox, and were at the same time challenged by Western theology and philosophy to interpret anew (or to rediscover) the Orthodox theological tradition. It was above all the leading theologians of early church history, the so-called church fathers, who were at the center of the new interpretation. By no means all who belonged to this neo-patristic revival were inspired to get involved in the environment, but this is where Bartholomew found important insights.[72] The neo-patristic movement has also found a great measure of interest and recognition in the international and ecumenical theological debate, and has inspired many Catholic and Protestant theologians, but it is striking how little impact it has had on the mainstream of Orthodox church life in Eastern Europe.[73]

The term "ecumenical patriarch" has nothing to do with modern ecumenical endeavors to bring the various churches closer together, but the Ecumenical Patriarchs in recent decades have taken important initiatives in this work. They have for example been actively involved in the World Council of Churches, and Patriarch Athenagoras I declared in 1965 that the excommunication of the pope in 1054 was no longer valid. This declaration was published simultaneously with the declaration by Pope Paul VI

71. McGuckin, "Patriarchate of Constantinople," 137.

72. Louth, "Patristic Revival," 198.

73. Plekon, "Russian Religious Revival," 215.

that his predecessors' excommunication of the patriarch of Constantinople was no longer in force. The 1965 declarations removed at least one of the hindrances to closer collaboration between the churches. Successive popes and patriarchs in recent years have met regularly, although full reciprocal recognition is not on the horizon.

OUTLOOK

In this presentation of Christianity in Eastern Europe, size has been the decisive criterion of selection. This has made Orthodox Christianity the center of our discussion, exemplified by the situation in the two largest countries in the region. We have also presented the Ecumenical patriarchate, which represents a theological and church-political counterweight to the dominant position of the patriarchate of Moscow. Many in the West may associate Orthodox Christianity with Greece rather than with Russia, but the Greek Orthodox church has not been given a place in this chapter. Christianity in Greece has one foot in the East and one in the West. The Orthodox church dominates numerically, and as in other Orthodox countries, national identity is closely linked to the church. At the same time, however, the people are less socially conservative. On questions of LGBTQ rights and abortion, for example, Greece is more like the Catholic countries in Central Europe, where very large groups take positions that deviate from the churches' official teaching. Adherence to the church is also declining in Greece, as in many Catholic lands.[74]

Nor has the Athos peninsula in North-Eastern Greece received the attention it perhaps deserves. Athos, with its celebrated mountain, is an autonomous theocratic monastic state within the republic of Greece, where more than two thousand Orthodox monks from all over the world live. It is a source of inspiration for the renewal of monastic life and Orthodox spirituality throughout the entire Orthodox ecclesial family.[75]

The Orthodox churches have little tradition of carrying out missionary work in distant lands, nor had they the necessary resources for this during most of the twentieth century, where most churches had more than enough to do, simply to survive as churches under extremely difficult conditions. Orthodox churches outside the Middle East, Eastern Europe, and the former Soviet Union are mostly the result of migration. Many parishes in Western Europe and not least in the USA were set up by Christians who fled to the West from countries under communist rule. This explains why there have

74. Pew Research Center, "Religious Belief."
75. Conomos, "Mount Athos," 403.

been periods of considerable tension in the relations between the churches of the countries of origin—which were obliged to find a way to survive under the dictatorships—and the émigrés, who could be much clearer in their criticism of the atheist state authorities. Western converts too have gradually joined what were originally émigré churches, which have in the course of time taken on an increasingly local character, particularly in the USA.

Orthodox influence on the world outside the traditional heartlands is not, however, due only to Orthodox Christians who live elsewhere. Bartholomew's environmental activity is one such example, and he has also taken an active role on questions about war and human rights. After Pope Francis came to power in 2013, the two church leaders have appeared together on a number of occasions, especially in connection with the conflicts in the Middle East.

Patriarch Kirill too has won influence, not least by making an impact on Russian foreign policy. The church's support of traditional values, which it counterposes to universal human rights, has given guidelines for how Russia acts in international arenas. For example, traditional values have clearly become an area in which Russia is active at the United Nations and the Council of Europe, where it seeks alliances with other countries against what it likes to call aggressive Western secularism.[76]

However, the maneuvers of patriarchs and other church leaders in the political arena must not be allowed to paint the full picture of the Orthodox churches, either in Eastern Europe or in the rest of the world. The work for local church development that Kirill initiated in the 1990s, and that has been carried out in a similar way in many other Orthodox churches, has borne fruit. Orthodox church life unfolds in local churches, in monasteries, and in seminaries. Ordinary people fast, celebrate feasts, kiss the icons, and visit pilgrimage sites in search of intercession and healing, often with minimal interest in what the church leaders think.

76. See, e.g., Stoeckl, *The Russian Orthodox Church*; Stoeckl, "The Russian Orthodox Church as Moral Norm"; Horsfjord, "Negotiating Traditional Values."

9

Western and Central Europe

Between Power and Powerlessness

DURING AN INTERVIEW WITH Vanity Fair in 2003, Tony Blair, the British Prime Minister, was asked about his Christian faith. Alistair Campbell, Blair's communications director, stepped in as soon as the question was put, and said: "We don't do God." He was afraid that the religious side of Blair would cut a bad figure with the voters. The Prime Ministers after Blair have taken a different line. When David Cameron said in 2011 that Great Britain was "a Christian country," reactions varied from indignation to support.[1] For what does it mean to call Great Britain a Christian country? More than 50 percent of Britons declare that they do not belong to any religion, and the proportion of those who have another religion than Christianity is growing. Are Cameron's words a retrospective on history, or a description of the contemporary situation?

Over a short period, the position of Christianity in Europe has changed dramatically. In the 1950s and 1960s, most people got married in church; they had their children baptized, and a priest or pastor held the ceremony when they buried their dead. The Christian *rites de passage* were a part of the societal and cultural norms in the majority culture. This was what was expected. The clergy had considerable authority, not only as ministers of the church's rituals and doctrine, but also as public leaders. Christian

---

1. See "David Cameron."

Democratic parties dominated in countries such as Italy, the Netherlands, Austria, Belgium, and Germany.[2] Belief in God and membership of the church were often taken for granted in the public sphere. This situation has changed.

The majority no longer has the same cultural or social expectations about church membership or participation in church rituals. Expectations have been replaced by free choice, and today's Europeans increasingly opt out of the old established churches and of organized religion in general.

The history of Europe is closely interwoven with Christianity. This is reflected in its geography. In towns and villages, churches occupy a prominent position in the landscape and are central points of reference for those who live there. Christianity structures time: the weeks and the years follow the Christian cycle. Sunday is a public holiday, and the Christian feasts of Christmas, Easter, and Pentecost are holidays. In view of the earlier strong ties between the nation and the church, ties that still exist to varying degrees, there are many Europeans who regard the church as one of many public goods that one can make use of, if one wishes.[3] And many of Christianity's symbols, such as the cross, places of pilgrimage, cathedrals, or hymns, are so deeply anchored in the culture that it becomes artificial to draw a distinction between what is "religion" and what is "culture." The symbols and the rituals have the potential to appeal simultaneously to both religious and secular ideas. In today's Europe, the former British Prime Minister Cameron is far from alone in wishing a renewed public debate about Christianity's role in society.

The emphasis in this chapter lies on Christianity in western Europe, although we shall also speak about central Europe, especially Catholic Poland. When we refer to "Europe" here, eastern Europe is not included. A contemporary look at Christianity in Europe must include the ongoing decline in Christian faith, practice, and membership—a decline that is both historic and dramatic—but it is equally important to see changes in how Christianity occurs. For example, Christian institutions remain central actors in education, health, and other welfare sectors. And Christianity in Europe is not cut off from global changes. We have seen a charismatic revival in the established churches in other parts of the world, and we shall find it in European churches too. Migration, increasing pluralism, individualization, urbanization, and changed political and economic circumstances leave their mark on the development of Christianity here too.

2. Müller, "The End of Christian Democracy." In Germany, the Christian Democratic Union (CDU) retains a dominant position, but this is an exception in Europe.

3. Davie, *Europe*, 23.

The main emphasis in this chapter will lie on the established churches and on how their relationship to state and society plays out. We shall identify some general tendencies and differences in what is happening on the continent by looking at individual countries, including Germany, England, and Poland. But this chapter will also visit regional institutions such as the EU and the European Court of Human Rights. We begin by looking at the religious map. While the southern and central parts of Europe are dominated by Catholicism, Protestantism has a more important position the farther north one comes. Spain, Italy, and Portugal have historically a close relationship to the Catholic church, while the majority of the population in the Scandinavian lands are members of Lutheran churches. Germany, the Netherlands, and Belgium have big Protestant and Catholic churches. In Croatia, Slovakia, and Slovenia, the Catholic church has traditionally been the largest, while Protestant traditions have dominated in Estonia and Latvia. If we look at membership numbers and participation in church rituals, Poland is the country in Europe with the greatest support for the church.

The proportion of those who declare that they do not belong to any religion is growing everywhere. The Czech Republic tops the list, with 72 percent who say that they are either atheists, agnostics, or "nothing special."[4] In England, Estonia, and the Netherlands, the majority say that they have no religion, and in France and Germany (as in the USA), roughly a quarter say the same.[5] The number of those who identify as Christians is declining throughout Europe.

EUROPE—THE EXCEPTIONAL CASE

It was long thought that the secularization in Europe was the first sign of a universal trend: with modernity and democracy, it was natural that the role of religion would be limited to people's private lives. This, in brief, was the theory of secularization that dominated for a time in the study of religion and society, and that still functions as a frame of reference for many scholars. Many today hold that the theory of secularization, as a great universal theory about how religion and society develop in the same way everywhere in the world, has a limited value. In view of the continuing strong position religion has in the USA, and the many religious revivals in the new democracies in Africa, Asia, the Pacific, and Latin America, the case of Europe was

4. Pew Research Center, "Religious Belief."
5. Woodhead, "The Rise of 'No Religion,'" 249–50.

no longer seen as the rule. It was now regarded as the exception, and the question was: What is it about Europe?[6]

Various theories of secularization are alive not only as theoretical models at the universities, but also as a part of many people's understanding of history. The sociologist José Casanova writes about what he calls the "myth of a secular Europe," which he sees as a part of Europe's collective memory. A shortened version of this myth runs as follows: Once, long ago, Europe too mingled religion and politics, and that was a time marked by conflict. With the age of Enlightenment and the secularization of the state, we got rid of the religious warriors. Europe began to appreciate rationality, science, and reason, and learned to separate politics from religion. This has paved the way for a society that appreciates equality, tolerance, and respect.[7]

In other words, the European self-understanding sees religion as something people engaged in in the past. Unlike North Americans, Europeans tend to associate religion with conflict. This emerged in a large-scale European survey in 1998. This was before religion had become a central aspect of the global war on terror, but no less than two-thirds replied that religion is "intolerant," and the majority in almost all western countries replied that "religion creates conflict."[8]

Despite these tendencies, Christianity is still clearly present in Europe. This makes it interesting to ask what Europeans mean when they say that religion is intolerant or a threat. Might it be that the idea of the secular Europe is so strong that many are blind to their own religion, or see their own way of exercising religion as correct, whereas the religion of others creates conflict? In the survey mentioned above, Denmark was the country where the largest proportion (86 percent) answered that "religion creates conflict." At the same time, Denmark is one of the countries in Europe with the highest church membership. This is an interesting paradox.

More than 75 percent of the Danish population are members of the Lutheran church, and Danes are generally willing to pay for the church through the church tax that is administered by the state. The church has responsibility for the population register, and it registers births, deaths, and changes of name for all Danes, including those who are not members of the church. Almost all the members visit the church building in the course of the year, perhaps to go to a concert, to take part in a funeral, or to attend an ordinary service. A majority of Danes have their children baptized in this church (64 percent), are confirmed, and choose a church funeral for their

6. Davie, *Europe.*

7. Casanova, "Religion Challenging the Myth," 21.

8. Casanova, "Problem of Religion," 66.

dear ones (83 percent). But fewer choose a church wedding (34 percent).[9] No other country has such high trust in the church as the Danes. But only 2 percent go regularly to church on Sundays,[10] and in comparison with large parts of the world, only very few Danes believe in the central Christian dogmas.[11]

Denmark illustrates how difficult it is to draw a distinction between the religious and the secular. Should we place the emphasis on what people believe in, or on their practices such as participation in church rituals or regular attendance at worship? Does institutional adherence through membership count more, or is the essential point Christianity's role in the public sphere and the relationship between state and religion? Depending on how the answers to these questions are emphasized, Denmark (for example) can be described as either highly religious or highly secular.

THE ESTABLISHED CHURCHES
UNDER PRESSURE

Some trends are indisputable. Since the 1960s, Europeans have had an ever weaker adherence to organized Christianity. Even those who state that they are believers express this belief in a new way that is less tied to authority. There is, however, a great variation in how the decline occurs in the various countries. The lack of support for the established churches must also be seen in connection with structural societal changes in Europe. Other big popular institutions, such as political parties and trade unions, have lost members and the authority they had in the postwar years.[12]

Throughout Europe, there are few who attend church every week. On average, Catholics attend more frequently than Protestants; this may be connected to the fact that Sunday worship is more important in Catholicism than in Protestantism. Traditionally, the Mass is an obligation for every Catholic, although the majority do not follow this rule in practice.[13] Participation in Sunday worship is lowest in England and Denmark, at less than

9. Woodhead, "The Rise of 'No Religion,'" 254. Figures from 2014. These statistics do not include the number of confirmations.

10. Manchin, "Religion in Europe." In the same survey, only 21 percent of Swedes say that they trust religious institutions. This bears witness to great differences between the Scandinavian neighbors.

11. Zuckerman, "Why Are Danes and Swedes?," 55–57; Woodhead, "The Rise of 'No Religion,'" 254.

12. Davie, *Religion in Modern Europe*, 50.

13. Auweele, "Den romersk-katolske kirke."

2 percent,[14] while the Catholic countries Poland and Italy have the highest attendance.[15] In comparison with England, France, and the Czech Republic, the ecclesiastical rituals such as baptism, confirmation, and weddings enjoy greater support in the Scandinavian countries, despite the fact that less than 5 percent of the population regularly go to church services.[16] Only a small majority choose to be confirmed in England, but confirmation is much more common in Spain, France, and Italy.[17] The ritual that overall has the greatest support is church burial.

The decline takes various shapes in the western and central European countries. The very dramatic change in Spain is exemplified by church weddings. In 2000, 75 percent of the couples got married in church, but this had sunk in 2016 to the historic low of 22.2 percent. There are several reasons for this dramatic decline in the number of church weddings; the story also involves a general decline in the number of couples who get married, including civil weddings. Alternative forms of living together are accepted both legally and societally, and marriage is only one of several choices.[18] Another reason for the decline is that more marriages today take place between persons who are divorced. Since the Catholic church does not accept remarriage, civil marriage or cohabitation replaces church weddings.[19] At the same time, the dramatic fall in support of church weddings indicates a secularization that is late, but speedy by European standards. The Catholic church has suffered many losses in recent decades, as for example in 2005 when Spain became one of the first countries to recognize same-sex marriage despite loud protests by the Catholic church. And in 2021, the Spanish parliament defied the church once again by legalizing euthanasia under certain conditions. The Spaniards were no longer listening to a religious authority that traditionally had been strong. They have become increasingly indifferent to the church. The country has witnessed a profound secularization, especially after 2000.[20]

One tendency that can be seen everywhere in Europe is for young people to have less trust than their parents in institutional Christianity, and for their parents, in turn, to belong to a lesser degree than *their* parents. But

14. Woodhead, "The Rise of 'No Religion,'" 254.

15. Norris and Inglehart, *Sacred and Secular*, 72; Pew Research Center, "Religious Belief."

16. Zuckerman, "Why Are Danes and Swedes?," 55.

17. Pew Research Center, "During Benedict's Papacy." For a case study from Spain, see Pérez-Agote, *Cambio religioso*, 44.

18. Laborde, "'La gente te mira.'"

19. Auweele, "Den romersk-katolske kirke," 229.

20. Andrés, "Los múltiples rostros," 455–526.

there are interesting variations here. The generation gap is much larger in countries like Spain and Ireland than in Finland, Denmark, and Norway.[21]

More than opposition, however, it is indifference that characterizes young people's relationship to Christianity. The French sociologist of religion Danièle Hervieu-Léger describes religious life in its institutionalized form in Europe as "a chain of memories" in which faith is formed and handed on via the legitimacy of tradition. Young people's declining participation in church rituals need not be a matter of opposition or rebellion against the church, against "tradition," as was the case with some in their parents' generation. It is rather a matter of distance and a lack of interest.[22] As contact with church traditions and institutions lessens, there is also a lower level of experience of Christianity, and of religion in general. Hervieu-Léger argues that Christianity today is employed more as a cultural heritage, a resource for memories and symbols that the individual can choose to use. It is the individual, more than the institutions, that has charge of this heritage.[23]

The assumed lack of knowledge of religion in Europe is a topic that some politicians and researches have been increasingly concerned about, at a time when religion has become more visible and varied in the public arena. They express a worry that a lack of knowledge of religion can lead to difficulties in interpersonal relationships and in how to deal with religion in schools, the bureaucracy, the legal system, or in hospitals.[24] It can seem paradoxical that while Europe is becoming more multireligious, competence with regard to Christianity, the traditional religion of society, is sinking.

Another urgent problem for European churches is that a smaller proportion of young Europeans want to become clergy. This applies in particular to Catholics. Between 1950 and the turn of the millennium, the number of priests per Catholic in Europe halved.[25] The role of the clergy has changed in keeping with the changes in the church and in society in general. Today, one priest often has responsibility for many churches at the same time. It is rarer to see the old village priest who knew everybody, who visited people in their homes, and who followed several generations through life's great transitions. Europeans also move more often than in the past, and more people live in towns than in the countryside. This can mean that the clergy have less

---

21. Bruce, *Secularization*, 18; Gundelach, "The Impact of Economic Deprivation," 141.

22. Pérez-Agote, *Cambio religioso*, 134–54.

23. Hervieu-Léger, *Religion as a Chain of Memory*, 168.

24. Dinham and Francis. *Religious Literacy*.

25. Mourão, "Determinants."

interaction with people, and more administrative work.[26] In the Catholic church, there are increasing demands that the law of celibacy for priests should be abolished, in order to attract younger generations of priests.

Another solution for the Catholic church is to look outside Europe, especially to Africa and Asia. For several decades now, the church has fetched personnel from outside national borders. There are more than 1,300 non-French priests in France, many from Africa, and in Germany, almost 10 percent (or about 1,300) of the priests in the Catholic church come from other countries, many from India.[27]

I BELIEVE IN MY OWN WAY

Although fewer persons in Europe declare that they are Christians, this need not mean that religiosity is correspondingly declining. A new vocabulary has emerged for the many who do not recognize themselves in the categories "religious" or "Christian."[28] One can, for example, be "spiritual" or "a seeker" without needing to tie oneself to one particular religion. One characteristic of today's Europeans is that they have a faith that is less strongly linked to authority, a weaker link to one particular religion, and a greater emphasis on religious experiences than on dogmas. Pluralism and individualization are often employed as key words to describe the situation in Europe.

In order to concretize and nuance a picture of an increasingly secularized Europe, we can look at the growing interest in pilgrimages to old and new (especially Catholic) pilgrim goals. In recent decades, the Catholic church has taken several initiatives to strengthen the pilgrimage tradition, with the starting point in Europe's important historical Christian places. But it is not only Catholics who have embraced this revitalization of the pilgrimage tradition.

Popular pilgrim goals exist in several countries, including Spain, Poland (the Black Madonna in Częstochowa), England, and the Netherlands. In the two last-named countries, the pilgrim goals are sites of Marian apparitions (Walsingham in England and the "Lady of All Nations" in Amsterdam). Another site of Marian apparitions is France, where several million people each year visit the little town of Lourdes in the south of the country, where according to a Catholic tradition, Mary appeared several times to Bernadette Soubirous, a fourteen-year-old girl, in 1858. Lourdes is today a

26. Schlamelcher, "Decline of the Parishes."
27. Salden, "Shrinking Catholic Church."
28. Davie, *Religion in Britain*, 8.

center of Catholic spiritual renewal in Europe and also a place where, according to Catholics, medical miracles can take place.

Santiago de Compostela in Spain has been one of Europe's most important pilgrim goals, and each year up to two hundred thousand people walk for parts of the pilgrimage route before they finish in the cathedral in Santiago.[29] This cathedral has the shrine that, according to tradition, contains the relics of the apostle Jacob, the patron saint of pilgrims. But for many, it is the path itself that is the goal. The town has been regarded since the high middle ages as the third most important pilgrim goal for Catholics, after Jerusalem and Rome. In 1979, the paths to Santiago were revived for modern pilgrims after several years of rehabilitation, and there are inexpensive hostels and restaurants along the path, making it possible to walk for both shorter and longer distances. As in most pilgrimages, there is a great variation in the reasons why people choose to walk here. For some, it may be a holiday of a different kind, a break from normal life, quite devoid of religious references. For others, it may be an existential journey: there is something in their life that they have to come to terms with. For still others, it is a highly religious action. But it is the pilgrims themselves who determine what makes the pilgrimage meaningful.

It is typical of some of the most popular pilgrim goals in Europe today that they have an ecumenical character and an openness to non-Christian worldviews.[30] One can find Protestants, non-religious persons, and adherents of other religions along the route. At the end of the journey, in Santiago, the pilgrims can choose whether to receive a Christian pilgrimage diploma or a neutral diploma with no reference to Christianity.[31] In other words, one and the same ritual is open to both Christian and non-Christian interpretations.

The British sociologist of religion Grace Davie has employed the concept of "believing without belonging" to describe the situation of the many who do not take part actively in any specific church. They identify with a faith and a tradition, but they do not take part actively in a religious fellowship. Davie claims that we find a somewhat different situation in the Scandinavian countries, where there are more who say that they belong to the majority church than those who say that they believe.[32] In other words, more "belonging" than "believing." In both these forms of faith/belonging,

29. Mikaelsson, "Gjenfødsel på caminoen."

30. Coleman, "Christianity in Western Europe," 71.

31. Mikaelsson, "Gjenfødsel på caminoen," 94–96. She refers here to the scholar of religion Ingvild Gilhus Sælid.

32. Davie, *Religion in Modern Europe*, 2–3.

there are few who attend church on Sundays, and in both variants, according to Davie, it is accepted that the majority church administers religion on behalf of the majority in the population. She calls this "vicarious religion." For example, many Europeans take it for granted that the church is present in crisis situations and on great public anniversaries. The acceptance of the majority churches depends on whether the ecclesiastical authorities correspond to people's expectations, with regard both to personal morality and to available services.[33]

However, in view of the fact that there is an increasing number of persons in the whole of Europe who say that they have no religion, and a decline in the proportion who identify as Christians,[34] it is worth asking whether Davie's thesis of a silent support of a "vicarious religion" is tenable. If the religious "memory" diminishes with each new generation in Europe, one can ask when it will finally disappear.[35]

Just as Christianity experiences a tension between local belief and established theology in India, Mexico, or Nigeria, so too the churches in Europe experience a tension between local belief and practice, on the one hand, and the ecclesiastical tradition, on the other. The funeral of Princess Diana is an example of precisely this.[36] Her funeral service in 1997 was held in an Anglican church with a clear Christian framework, but including elements that were not so customary at that time, such as the reading of a poem by her sister and a song by her close friend, the popstar Elton John. There were no Christian references in the poem and the song. It has become more customary to arrange rituals in this way. The church increasingly adapts its services to individual needs. New rituals for funerals and weddings often have a place for cultural elements that the mourners or the bridal couple themselves can choose. Family and friends take part in the elaboration of the rituals to a larger extent. There are few places where this is clearer than in England, where only 25 percent say that they want a "usual" Christian funeral.[37] The adaptation often takes place in collaboration with the clergy, but this too increasingly happens outside ecclesiastical frameworks. In the 1990s, the alternative to a church funeral in England was often a secular humanist funeral, which was at that time a clear signal that the deceased was an atheist who did not want any religious element. Today, however, it is not

---

33. Davie, *Religion in Britain*, 6.

34. Woodhead, "Rise of 'No Religion.'"

35. See, for example, Voas and Crockett, "Religion in Britain." They argue that in England there exists neither believing nor belonging.

36. Davie, *Europe*, 80.

37. Woodhead, "Rise of 'No Religion,'" 247–48.

only the traditional Christian funeral that is under pressure in England, but likewise the religion-free funeral. Britons seek personal rituals, and they can easily find inspiration in a variety of religious and secular traditions.[38] This plurality from below is also reflected in political debates about the relationship between church and state.

CHANGED STATE–CHURCH RELATIONSHIPS

The historically close relationship between the majority churches and the state is a European characteristic. Almost all the European states give a privileged status to one or two churches. The ways in which this privilege takes form varies greatly from one country to another, but it is nevertheless possible to draw some general conclusions. The model of the state-church is in retreat, but this does not mean that it is replaced by the kind of strict separation between the state and religion that we see in France.[39] Most European countries lie somewhere between a close linkage and a strict separation between state and church. The choices they make are marked by both pragmatism and principles, informed by historical circumstances and by new realities. One reason for the changes is that an increased pluralism in faiths and worldviews has made it difficult to give preferential treatment to one particular church at the expense of the plurality.[40]

At the turn of the millennium, all the Scandinavian countries, which have been dominated by the Lutheran tradition, had state-churches. Over the next two decades, great changes took place, but the outcome was not an absolute separation between church and state. In Sweden, the state-church model was dismantled in 2000, but the country retained a complex system in which the Lutheran church maintains a privileged role. A privileged role of this kind can also entail restrictions on the church's autonomy, for example in connection with the preservation of historical buildings or geographical priorities. The liberalization of state-church models in Iceland, Norway, and Finland has led to regulations that strengthen the churches' independence. One such change in Finland and Norway was the system whereby the churches' bishops were appointed by the churches themselves, not by the state. The state continues to finance parts of the church's activities, while at the same time providing support to other registered religious groups.

Many countries with a Catholic majority regulate the relationship between the Catholic church and the state by means of a concordat, an

38. Woodhead, "Rise of 'No Religion,'" 248–49.
39. Ferrari, "Law and Religion in Europe."
40. Ferrari, "Law and Religion in Europe," 154.

agreement in international law that is the result of negotiations between the Holy See and the individual state.[41] There is a common praxis in the countries in Europe whereby the state gives economic privileges to the established churches, for example, through tax exemptions, the maintenance of church buildings, or (as in Germany and Denmark) by administering a church tax. In general, the rights of religious minorities and other Christian churches have been strengthened, so that they too have the possibility of state recognition, tax exemption, and in some places access to public funds.

But deeper analyses are needed, if we are to understand Christianity in today's Europe. It is not enough to describe the formal and legal situations on the state level. Historical circumstances, complex systems of financing, tax privileges, access to educational institutions—these are various factors that influence Christianity in Europe.

For example, although Ireland has no state-church, the state has formed close links to the Catholic church, *inter alia* through education. The state pays for primary schooling, but the church owns and runs almost 90 percent of all the primary schools in the country.[42] Baptized church members have priority when the admissions offices prepare new school years; where places are in short supply, baptized Catholic children get priority.[43] Ireland was long regarded as the most religious country in western Europe. It had a high level of participation in church activities, and was the last country in Europe to legalize divorce, through a narrow majority in a referendum in 1995. In the wake of factors such as vast abuse scandals in the church in the 1990s and 2000s, Irish support for the church fell dramatically. In a 2015 referendum, 62 percent voted in favor of the legalization of same-sex marriage, and three years later, even more (66 percent) voted for the legalization of abortion, despite strong Catholic opposition. It is uncertain to what extent declining support for the church will affect its central role in education. Reform has hitherto proved difficult. The church's role in the educational sector has a strong legal and constitutional protection, with roots in historical circumstances all the way back to the nineteenth century.[44]

A completely different example is France's relationship to the church. The French secular policy of *laïcité* regulates a strict separation between state and religion. In the USA, the separation between state and religion is regarded as important, to protect the churches from the state; in France,

41. Davie, *Religion in Modern Europe*, 17–19; Horsfjord, "Religionspolitikk i Europa."

42. O'Mahony, "Religious Education," 56–57.

43. Dalby, "Catholic Church's Hold on Schools"; O'Mahony, "Religious Education," 162.

44. O'Mahony, "Religious Education," 156.

for opposite historical reasons, the state must be protected from a powerful church. The 1905 law about religion declares that the republic is not to recognize any religion, is not to give economic support to any religion, and is at the same time to ensure freedom of religion for all.[45] In practice, it is more difficult to set up clear demarcations. In order to ensure freedom of religion for patients in hospitals, for military personnel, and for prison inmates, the French state finances Christian, Muslim, and Jewish religious pastoral care in such institutions. Religions indirectly receive economic privileges via tax relief. For historical reasons, the French state owns all the churches built before 1905, and this means that it has the responsibility for their maintenance. Roughly 20 percent of the country's schools are private, and 90 percent of these are Catholic. Many of these schools receive support from the public purse. Immigration to France, especially from Muslim countries, has led the French state to take a more active role vis-à-vis the religions. For example, teachers employed in the public sector are given courses in how religion affects society, and the state has taken several initiatives to establish a more formal relationship to representative Muslim institutions.[46]

LIBERAL PROTESTANTISM

There have been relatively close ties to the state in the big Protestant majority churches in the Scandinavian countries and in parts of Germany. These churches have often understood themselves as the "church of the people" (*Volkskirche*), and changes in attitudes in the majority population have also been reflected to a large extent in the churches.[47] This has gradually led to the adoption of liberal standpoints in the churches, for example, in the view they take of women clergy, of homosexual clergy, of unmarried clergy who live in a stable relationship with a partner, and of same-sex marriage. Although a liberal Christian view of gender and cohabitation is not unique to these churches in northern Europe, they nevertheless represent a type of liberal Protestantism that is an important part of the global ecclesiastical map.

In 1989, Denmark was the first country in the world to pass a law about registered civil partnerships, and in the course of the 2000s, it was possible in several Danish dioceses for same-sex couples to have their partnership blessed in church. In 2012, a law that permitted same-sex marriage also included same-sex weddings in the nation's church. Sweden passed a law permitting same-sex marriage in 2006, and the Swedish church opened the

45. Horsfjord, "Religionspolitikk i Europa."
46. Ferrari, "Law and Religon in Europe," 154.
47. Morgan, "Religious Foundations."

door to same-sex church weddings in 2009. In the same year, Eva Brunne
became the bishop of Stockholm, thus giving the Swedes their first lesbian
bishop who lived with her partner. In Norway, the law permitting same-sex
marriage was passed in 2008. The (Lutheran) Church of Norway accepted
cohabiting LGBTQ clergy in 2007, and allowed same-sex church weddings
in 2017. Several Protestant churches in North America and South Africa
have likewise opened the door since 2000 to cohabiting LGBTQ clergy and
to same-sex church weddings.

Denmark had its first Lutheran clergywoman already in 1948, followed by Sweden in 1960 and by Norway in 1961. In 1992, Maria Jepsen
in Germany became the first Lutheran woman bishop, followed in 1993 by
Rosemarie Köhn in Norway. However, it was not the European Lutheran
churches who led the way with regard to women clergy and bishops. Some
Protestant churches in the USA, such as Methodists, Baptists, Mennonites,
Quakers, the Salvation Army, and some Pentecostal communities had
women clergy as early as the nineteenth century.

But although the Protestant majority churches in Scandinavia and
parts of Germany were not the first, and were far from being alone, they
have nevertheless been important promotors of liberal values linked to
equality and LGBTQ rights. The fact that they are North European majority
churches makes them also rich by global standards, and they wield much
influence in international ecumenical organizations and in international
church debates.

Some of the emergence of liberal attitudes with regard to equality and
cohabitation is due to the churches' relationship to the state. For example,
the opening for women clergy in several of the churches was propelled by
changes in the state laws. But much of the explanation lies in the general
change of attitude in the population in these countries. Comprehensive
processes of democratization have taken place in these churches over several decades. Commissions and committees have been set up in order to
ensure a broader representation in the churches, both locally and nationally.
Women have gradually been admitted to leadership of the churches, and
clergy training has also increasingly reflected changed attitudes to family,
gender, and cohabitation.

However, the changes in attitude have not been painless. The churches
are squeezed between those who desire change and those who want to
keep things as they are. The questions of female leadership and same-sex
cohabitation have been two of the most passionately discussed questions in
recent decades in the churches in large parts of Europe. These themes raise
fundamental questions about who has the authority to take decisions in the
church, how the Bible is to be interpreted, how a plurality of views in the

church is to be tackled, and how the churches are to change in tandem with the rest of society.

It has been claimed, both by some scholars and in debates within the church, that it is those forms of religion that demand strong personal commitment, and present themselves as an alternative to the majority culture, that will be successful in a secularized Europe. Some hold that if the church becomes too much like the larger society in its values and attitudes, it will lose its own specific character and gradually make itself irrelevant.[48] The consequence of this reasoning is that close ties between church, state, and population are a disadvantage, and that it is the "free" church without historical, legal, or financial ties to the state that has the greatest chance of surviving. The Scandinavian churches are interesting in this connection, because Scandinavia is supposed to be one of the most secularized areas in Europe. In the European context, however, the churches in Norway, Sweden, and Denmark do surprisingly well in indicators such as their members' trust, the high number of members, participation in rituals, and the willingness to pay church tax.[49] The majority churches in Scandinavia and the northern countries can therefore also be examples of how different types of churches are suited to appeal to people, including the big majority churches that have few requirements linked to membership, and have values that largely coincide with those of the majority population.

GOD IN BRUSSELS

It was at the beginning of the twenty-first century that the question of the Christian identity of the European Union really came onto the agenda for the first time.[50] Communism had fallen in the East, and the EU was about to experience a great expansion. New countries in what many western Europeans had regarded as a peripheral area of Europe were now knocking on the door and enquiring about membership. This gave vital importance to the question: What makes Europe a specific unity? Is it geography, political membership, or a common base in history and in values? Europe sought to create a shared political project out of a collection of strong nation-states,[51] and Christianity became relevant here.

48. Jenkins, "Godless Europe?"; Mickethwait, *God Is Back*.

49. There are variations in the adherence to the individual Nordic Lutheran churches. For example, the Swedish church is experiencing a stronger decline in the number of members than the other counties.

50. Roy, "Beyond Populism," 191.

51. Challand, "From Hammer and Sickle," 60.

One potential new member of the EU was Turkey. The EU had co-operated with Turkey over a long period without Islam being regarded as a problem; the relationship was influenced by the idea of shared European values.[52] The reactions to a possible Turkish membership concerned several issues, including the country's large population and relatively weak economy. But from early in the century onwards, Turkey's cultural and religious identity also acquired importance for both opponents and supporters of Turkish EU membership.[53] The former French President Valéry Giscard d'Estaing declared that if Turkey joined the EU, that would mean the end of the Union, because Turkey's culture was different from that of the European countries. A similar statement came from a former Dutch EU commissioner, who warned that Turkish membership would lead to the "Islamization of Europe."[54] Others, however, argued that Turkish membership was important precisely in order to counteract the idea of Europe as a Christian fortress, and that a big Muslim country in the EU would be a strong symbol of an inclusive Europe—a symbol that could aid the work of integration in the various EU countries.

At the same time as Turkish EU membership was being vigorously discussed, the debate about the EU's "Constitution" became more intense. Both debates put religion on the agenda in the EU, though in different ways. Several Christian organizations, first and foremost the Catholic church, strove to have God and Christianity mentioned in the preamble to the "Constitution."

All the big European churches and organizations have offices that represent them in Brussels and lobby for them, in the same way as other large organizations in civic society. These include umbrella organizations, Christian humanitarian organizations, and also a number of big churches, such as the Catholic church, the Russian Orthodox church, the Protestant church in Germany, and the Anglican church.[55] Christian lobbying with regard to European integration has been carried out ever since the Second World War, but the number of religious actors has increased greatly in the last decades, and their relationship to the EU has become more professionalized.[56] The

52. Challand, "From Hammer and Sickle," 64–68.

53. Tank, "Er Tyrkia USAs nye modell."

54. Tank, "Er Tyrkia USAs nye modell," 54.

55. Horsfjord, "Religionspolitikk i Europa," 349–50.

56. It is the Catholic church that has been most strongly involved in Brussels since the 1950s. After the Second Vatican Council, there was a great increase in the number of Catholic organizations working on global themes such as education, poverty, and health. Since 1980, the Catholic church has had formal representation via the Commission of Bishops' Conferences of The European Community (COMECE).

organizations cover a wide spectrum of interests, such as education, bioethics, climate, development aid, religious dialogue, and religious freedom.[57] It is nonetheless hard to know whether this increased presence influences the elaboration of policy in the EU. In the course of the work on the EU's "Constitution," the Christian lobby was not sufficiently powerful. The wish, especially on the part of the Catholic church, that "God" should be mentioned explicitly in the preamble, was not granted, and the final formulation ran as follows:

> DRAWING INSPIRATION from the cultural, religious, and humanist inheritance of Europe, from which have developed the universal values of the inviolable and inalienable rights of the human person, freedom, democracy, equality and the rule of law.[58]

The EU did not, in the end, get a "Constitution," but this formulation was integrated into the treaty basis of the EU via the Treaty of Lisbon, which was signed in 2007. In parallel with the negotiations aiming at ensuring the place of God in the "Constitution," the churches had worked to establish a mechanism that would allow their voices to be heard in Brussels. This too was specified in the Treaty of Lisbon, with an explicit mention of the churches:

1. The Union respects and does not prejudice the status under national law of churches and religious associations or communities in the Member States.

2. The Union equally respects the status under national law of philosophical and non-confessional organizations.

3. Recognizing their identity and their specific contribution, the Union shall maintain an open, transparent, and regular dialogue with these churches and organizations.[59]

Although the EU does not have a policy about the relationship of the member states to religion, this text nevertheless lays down several guidelines for what we can call the EU's *de facto* religious policy. Point 1 gives the states the freedom to regulate their own relationship to religion, Point 2

57. Leustean and Madeley, *Religion*.

58. Horsfjord, "Religionspolitikk i Europa," 349–50. The so-called EU Constitution was rejected after referendums in the Netherlands and France. The words quoted can now be found in the Treaty on European Union.

59. This text is often referred to as "article 17" in the Treaty of Lisbon, but this is imprecise. The Treaty of Lisbon stipulates how the text in the older treaties is to be altered. The Treaty of Lisbon is a technical legal document that is not meant to be read separately.

specifies that organizations with a non-religious worldview are to be given equal treatment with religious organizations, and Point 3 formalizes the cooperation between these organizations and the EU.

The EU largely allows the various member states to practice their own religious policy. It is, however, possible to glimpse a certain homogenization of the policy by means of the EU's praxis. For example, greater weight is attached to the equal treatment of religions.[60]

But there are other European institutions that are also important for Christianity's symbols and institutions. One central actor on this level is the European Court of Human Rights (ECHR). Recent decades have seen an increase in the number of cases concerning disputes about religion.

BRINGING THE CRUCIFIX TO THE COURTROOM

The so-called Lautsi case is one of the most discussed ECHR cases related to religion. Soile Lautsi's two teenaged sons attended a public school in Italy, and Lautsi held that the crucifixes that hung in their classrooms violated both their and her own religious freedom. Such crucifixes hang in public schools everywhere in the country. She first took contact with the school's rector, but when her request was not accepted, she took the case to the legal system.

It took five years through national and European courtrooms before the Grand Chamber of the ECHR rejected Lautsi's demand in 2011. This decision came two years after a lower chamber in the ECHR had reached the opposite conclusion, namely, that the crucifixes in Italian classrooms violated freedom of religion. The first ECHR verdict in 2009 prompted many people to get involved, both supporters of Lautsi and those who held that the crucifixes must be accepted. One side saw the case as a test of minorities' rights and of equal treatment in a modern democracy. The actors on the other side held that the Court's initial verdict had confused neutrality with secularism, and they saw the case as a battle between an aggressive secularism and a cultural tradition with Christian roots. Although the crucifix was a religious symbol, they saw it also as part of Italian tradition, far transcending the matter of individual beliefs and convictions. A number of central and eastern European countries got involved on Italy's side, as did the Holy See and the Catholic church, and the Russian Orthodox church. They were supported by American Evangelical groups, who had experience from the American legal system of lawsuits concerning religious freedom.[61]

60. Horsfjord, "Religionspolitikk i Europa."
61. Annicchino, "Winning the Battle."

In the final verdict, which went in favor of Italy, the Grand Chamber did not take a position on the question of the symbolic significance of the crucifix. Instead, the verdict emphasized that European countries must have a large "margin of appreciation" to decide in cases like this, against the background of national circumstances. Europe has a large variety of arrangements regulating the relationship between religion and the state, as well as different degrees of secularism. The verdict agreed with Italy that, in view of the country's long Christian history, it is allowable to give Christian symbols a prominent place in the public sphere, provided that symbols of other religions are not excluded.[62]

This verdict has been much discussed, and it is not clear what consequences it has for other countries. As with other ECHR verdicts about religion, it is hard to draw direct conclusions about how similar cases ought to be resolved. The central point, instead, is that the Court gives the member states of the Council of Europe a large measure of freedom to solve such cases, with a starting point in national circumstances. This is very similar to the EU's attitude to religious policy, which has the same fundamental principle, namely, the acceptance of a great variety among the member states.

Other aspects of the Lautsi case are just as interesting as its legal consequences. Like the discussion about the EU's "Constitution," it is an example of how increased attention has been paid to religion in the public debate in Europe. It is not only the traditional Christian institutions that speak prominently of Christianity in European countries. In keeping with an increase in pluralism, questions of identity have become stronger, and Christianity has increasingly been a part of the discussion.

WHO OWNS CHRISTIANITY?

In September 2015, during the refugee crisis that came in the wake of the war in Syria, Pope Francis appealed to Europe's Catholics: "I appeal to the parishes, the religious communities, the monasteries and sanctuaries of all Europe to . . . take in one family of refugees."[63] This was not the first time that the Pope had spoken on behalf of refugees. His first journey outside Rome after his election in 2013 was to the little Mediterranean island of Lampedusa, which has welcomed thousands of refugees in recent years, many of them arriving in boats from Libya. Here he criticized the rich world for neither seeing the suffering nor caring about it. He prayed for forgiveness

62. The verdict can be found under http://hudoc.echr.coe.int/eng.
63. Reuters, "Pope Calls on Every European Parish."

"for those whose decisions on a global level have created situations that lead to tragedies like this."[64]

Active work for refugees and integration is a typical trait of many European churches today. Various churches and Christian humanitarian organizations are active in everything from handing out blankets to newly arrived refugees, to language teaching in local communities, and to political lobbying. One of the Christian actors that work on migration in Europe is the ecumenical organization *Churches' Commission for Migrants in Europe* (CCME), which was set up in 1964 and brings together mainly Protestant and Orthodox churches and organizations in Europe. They are active in political lobbying to promote the rights of refugees, counteract xenophobia, and promote inclusion.[65] Caritas, the Catholic church's worldwide humanitarian organization, lobbies actively in countries such as Italy, France, and Great Britain to strengthen refugees' rights.[66]

The churches' involvement on behalf of refugees and their work for integration in Europe are not uncontroversial in the churches nor among their members. When a Catholic priest spoke at an event in support of the anti-Muslim Pegida movement in Germany, there was an uproar. The bishop told the priest not to preach nor to act as a representative of the church, because, in the bishop's words, the priest's message "was incompatible with the Christian message about love, kindness, and inclusion."[67]

But it is not only the churches and the Christian organizations that employ Christianity's message in reacting to the situation of the refugees in Europe. A number of politicians, independently of their political situation, make use of Christian rhetoric and references to the Christian tradition. This is true also of several of the European rightwing populist parties.

The Austrian Freedom Party references Christian language in its slogans: "The West in Christian hands" and "Love your neighbor," with the subtitle: "For me, these [neighbors] are our Austrians."[68] Over the past twenty years, this rightwing populist party has gradually identified more strongly with Christianity, and it actively uses a Christian vocabulary in its campaigns. The Freedom Party is in open conflict with the Catholic archbishop of Vienna,[69] who holds that they are misusing Christianity to

64. Hooper, "Pope Attacks 'Globalisation of Indifference.'"

65. CCME, "Areas of Work."

66. Erasmus, "Diverse, Desperate Migrants."

67. Erasmus, "Diverse, Desperate Migrants."

68. Hadj-Abdou, "The 'Religious Conversion,'" 42.

69. The Church's reaction has been ambivalent with regard to these movements. In the anthology by Marzouki et al., *Saving the People*, the established churches' reaction to populist parties in various countries is discussed: Italy: 23–27; Austria: 40–44;

promote their own interests and to sow the seeds of religious conflict. The church in his diocese has stood on the front line, offering blankets, a roof over their heads, and a meal to the many new arrivals in the country. The Freedom Party holds that the church is naïve and dangerous in its openness to dialogue with Islam and its liberal attitude to migration. They claim that it is the rightwing populists who must rescue Europe's Christian heritage and identity.

Austria is not the only land where rightwing populists are making gains. In recent decades, several European countries have seen the emergence of rightwing populist parties. There is a great deal of variation among the parties, such as Law and Justice in Poland, the Lega in Italy, the Alternative für Deutschland in Germany, the National Front in France, Vox in Spain, and the Freedom Party in Austria. While these parties largely agree that Islam is a threat to Europe, there is a greater variation in the way they see Christianity. Many of them embrace references to Europe's Christian identity, as one of several defining characteristics of Europe.[70] This is often a secularized Christianity in which the central point is cultural identity rather than dogmas or institutions. Christianity is defended as an integral part of the liberal, secular European tradition.[71] The Law and Justice Party in Poland differs from the western European rightwing populist parties by identifying with the Catholic church and maintaining a social conservative line on questions such as women's rights, abortion, and LGBTQ rights. Unlike Poland, and unlike Austria for that matter, a number of rightwing populist parties wish to anchor their opposition to Islam and to Muslim immigration in a more secular rhetoric. In that case, secularism, freedom of expression, and criticism of religion are highlighted as central European values that are in contrast to Islam.

Increased pluralism, migration, and the public debate about Islam in Europe have made Christianity more important as a marker in the politics

---

Switzerland: 55; the Netherlands: 70–72; France: 88–89; Great Britain: 106–7.

70. Brubaker, "Between Nationalism and Civilizationism," 8; Marzouki et al., *Saving the People*. Originally, the churches and Christianity were also defined as a part of the social elite, and several of these movements made no bones about their opposition to the churches in the 1980s and 1990s. For example, the Lega Nord in Italy had clear preferences for paganism, and the Austrian Freedom Party was explicitly anticlerical. At the turn of the millennium, several of the rightwing populist parties changed their rhetoric to embrace Christian values and culture more clearly, as a part of a larger "we." From 2013 onwards, the National Front in France has dimmed its rhetoric about Christian values in favor of the French model of *laïcité*, whereas in Switzerland, Austria, Italy, and Scandinavian, populist parties have in various ways defended Christianity as a defining factor for the nation's identity and cultural heritage.

71. Brubaker, "Between Nationalism and Civilizationism," 3–4.

of identity in many countries and in various political camps. The Christian identity can be used to defend a stricter immigration policy and the preferential treatment that is given to Christian institutions rather than to other religions. In Germany, Angela Merkel, who was federal chancellor from 2005 to 2021, replied to those who were afraid of Islam in Germany by saying that the problem was not "too much Islam," but rather "too little Christianity." She exhorted Germans to reflect on the Christian values and anthropology in the encounter with new cultures.[72]

THE CHURCHES AS WELFARE ACTORS—GERMANY AS EXAMPLE

European states have a variety of welfare systems, from the Scandinavian model, in which the state has a strong presence, to countries like Italy, where there is relatively little public welfare. But all the countries are involved today in the discussion about the pressure on the systems.[73] Until the beginning of the twentieth century, it was Christian actors who were largely responsible for care of the sick, education, and help for those in need. The European states overtook welfare to varying degrees and at varying times.[74] This happened partly in collaboration with the churches, as in England and the Scandinavian lands, but also in conflict, as in France.[75]

From the 1990s onward, many western European states have increasingly begun to look to the private and voluntary sector to complement or replace the state's welfare tasks; this also includes Christian organizations.[76] Increased needs mean that in many fields, the churches' social work today is more comprehensive than it was in postwar Europe.[77] This brings both challenges and possibilities for the churches and the Christian organizations. On the one hand, involvement of this kind creates new arenas in which the churches can be relevant. On the other hand, there is the question of capacity and priorities, especially given that the churches face a decline in support and are under financial pressure. Besides this, ethical questions too are a part of the picture—while some churches are willing to accept support from the public purse and to follow the guidelines that this entails, others fear the compromises that would have to be made. Another question is how a

72. Heneghan, "Merkel Urges Germans."
73. Davie, "Welfare and Religion in Europe."
74. Davie, "Welfare and Religion in Europe."
75. Göçmen, "Role of Faith-Based Organizations," 500.
76. Hien, "Return of Religion?," 23; Davie, "Welfare and Religion in Europe," 11.
77. Davie, "Welfare and Religion in Europe."

population that is increasingly secular sees the churches' presence and work in what are perceived as vitally important public welfare tasks.[78]

Christian institutions operate kindergartens, old people's homes, schools, universities, and hospitals. In many countries, Christian organizations are very active in social work in areas such as care for substance abusers, support for undocumented immigrants, or among the poor. Church work has a broad spectrum. At one end is the purely local voluntary work, for example selling tickets at the church bazaar with the aim of financing new playground equipment in the town, collecting clothes for needy persons in Madrid, or volunteers visiting lonely old people in Rotterdam. At the other end are many Christian institutions that are large-scale national welfare actors in close collaboration with the state. The states often give indirect or direct financial support to this work.

Germany differs from other European countries through the close collaboration on welfare tasks between the big churches and the state. The churches' considerable role as suppliers of welfare has long historical roots.[79] With the expansion of the welfare state in the 1960s and 1970s, Catholic and Protestant organizations were systematically integrated into the West German state as independent suppliers of services.[80] Taken together, the christian suppliers of welfare, the Catholic Caritas and the Protestant Diakonie, are the second-largest employer in Germany, with roughly a million employees in various church organizations.[81] Besides this, both churches have a large number of voluntary workers.

In the 1950s, almost all Germans were members of the Catholic church or one of the Protestant churches in the federal states. Nowadays, only two-thirds are members. Less than 4 percent of Protestants and around 12 percent of Catholics attend church regularly.[82] Increasing religious pluralism in Germany has led to a reorganization in which other faith-based organizations and private actors can compete for money from public funds. However, an increased pluralism in religions and worldviews has not weakened the position of Diakonie and Caritas as Germany's most important welfare actors.[83] Such a close collaboration is not always unproblematic for the churches or for the state. The close relation of Diakonie and Caritas to the churches means that the organizations are seen as religious undertakings,

78. Davie, "Welfare and Religion in Europe."
79. Leis-Peters, "German Dilemma," 97–99.
80. Göçmen, "Role of Faith-Based Organizations," 505.
81. Bäckström et al., *Welfare and Religion*, 188.
82. Hien, "Return of Religion?," 14.
83. Hien, "Return of Religion?"; Göçmen, "Role of Faith-Based Organizations"

and this gives them exemptions from parts of the employment laws, including those concerning discrimination and equality.[84] This makes it possible for the church's doctrine to function as a governing principle in the welfare organizations too.

One example is the 2012 case when a victim of rape was denied emergency contraception ("morning-after pill") in two Catholic hospitals. That same year, there had already been huge controversies about employment cases in Catholic institutions, where people were discriminated on the grounds of cohabitation, sexual orientation, or having the "wrong" religion. There have also been lawsuits and media controversies in connection with the Protestant Diakonie with regard to the wearing of the hijab and to marital infidelity.[85] The court cases and the huge debates in the media have led to some changes. For example, Caritas has relaxed some of the requirements it used to impose on its employees.[86]

POLAND—A STRONG CHURCH, OPPOSITION AND SUPPORT

Mass demonstrations took place in October 2020 in Warsaw, the capital of Poland, in other big cities, and even in many small towns across the country. A good many of the demonstrators were young women, but there were also many others, from trade unionists to football fans. The background was a decision in the Constitutional Tribunal to tighten the already strict abortion laws in the country.[87] Since 1993, abortion has been allowed only in cases where the pregnancy is due to rape or incest, or in cases of grave damage to the fetus. The new resolution meant that the last of these criteria was in conflict with the constitution, and must be eliminated. There have been many demonstrations in recent years in connection with abortion legislation. The new feature this time was that the protests were addressed, not only against the ruling Law and Justice Party (PiS), but also directly against the Catholic church. People gathered outside the bishops' residences, and some sat on the church benches with placards declaring: "Let us pray for the right to abortion."[88] The protests tell the story of a Catholic church that has

---

84. Hien, "From Private to Religious Patriarchy," 3.

85. Hien, "From Private to Religious Patriarchy," 1–2.

86. Hien, "From Private to Religious Patriarchy," 24.

87. Grzymała-Busse, "Poland Is a Catholic Country."

88. Grzymała-Busse, "Poland Is a Catholic Country."

acquired considerable power to influence political developments, but also of a growing criticism of the church's active political role.[89]

No fewer than 87 percent of Poland's roughly forty million inhabitants identify as Catholics.[90] In comparison with other European countries, the statistics in Poland for participation in church rituals and acts of worship, and for religious faith, are high.[91] In 2016, 61 percent said that they attended church at least once a month. This is by far the highest number in Europe, even if we include Orthodox countries such as Russia, Romania, and Armenia.[92]

Two great events have dramatically changed Poland in the last decades: first, the process of democratization after the transition from the Communist regime in the 1990s, and secondly membership in the European Union in the 2000s. The ties between the Polish nation and the Catholic church go back a long way, but it is above all the church's opposition to the Communist regime during the Cold War that gave the church a position as the nation's protector.[93] This role became even more prominent when the Pole Karol Wojtyła was elected Pope in 1978 and took the name John Paul II. He was a stubborn opponent of Communism, and contributed to the failure of the Communist regime's attempts to neutralize the church by integrating it into the state. The Catholic church gradually became synonymous with the people's opposition to the Communist state, and the church was regarded as the primary defender of the Polish nation.

This has given the Catholic church great moral authority. At the change of regime in 1989, both the democratic opposition and the sitting Communist regime held that the Catholic church's moral authority was decisive for societal stability.[94] The church was welcomed to the negotiating table at which the premises for the new Poland were established. Even before the Communist regime departed, the church had negotiated good conditions that ensured its autonomy and various financial privileges, such as tax exemption for income and property, exemptions from customs dues, and the restoration of church property.[95] At the transition to democracy, the church enjoyed popular support to take on a strong public role, and the democratically elected leaders gave the church the institutional space

89. Grzymała-Busse, *Nations under God.*

90. Pew Research Center, "Eastern and Western Europeans Differ," 18.

91. Mandes and Rogaczewska, "I Don't Reject the Catholic Church."

92. Pew Research Center, "Eastern and Western Europeans Differ."

93. Grzymała-Busse, *Nations under God,* 152.

94. Grzymała-Busse, *Nations under God,* 11.

95. Grzymała-Busse, *Nations under God,* 158.

it asked for, in order to ensure legitimacy for the new democratic political project. The church's most important concerns were the abortion laws and the introduction of Catholic religious education in the schools, and this was introduced in various ways early in the 1990s, with the active involvement of the church. The church gained full control of Catholic teaching in public schools; only five months after the law was changed, religious instruction had been introduced for more than 95 percent of all school pupils. But despite strong support, the church was criticized for its use of power when it succeeded in getting this new legislation passed thanks to its close ties to the state and to politicians.[96]

When the question of EU membership came onto the political agenda in Poland, the sitting government party regarded the church's moral and political authority as very important in ensuring the people's support for Polish EU membership. The church's bishops were ambivalent, but they gave their support some months before the referendum in 2003—in exchange for guarantees that Poland's existing laws about abortion and about marriage as exclusively between a man and a woman would remain in effect, and that the church's legal and economic position would not be altered. In 2015, the rightwing populist party Law and Justice (PiS) won a clear majority in the election.

The close ties between the ruling party and the church have contributed to the church's political victories, especially in the issue of abortion. It has, however, also become ever clearer that there are strong political tensions within the church. While a powerful fraction with a nationalist orientation supports most of the government's policies, the Polish episcopal conference has warned against nationalism and has criticized the government's restrictive refugee policy, as well as political reforms that have taken an undemocratic direction. On these points, the Catholic church in Poland is realizing both some of Pope Francis's important priorities and something of the inheritance from the only Polish Pope, John Paul II.[97]

While most Poles have a high level of trust in the church, they are more skeptical than in the past to the bishops and their political role. This ambivalence is especially visible among young people. Almost as many (96 percent) say that they were raised as Christians as those who say that they regard themselves as "currently Christians" (92 percent).[98] But although a majority still feel that they belong to the church, there is a general decline

96. Grzymała-Busse, *Nations under God*, 168–69.

97. Resende and Hennig, "Polish Catholic Bishops," 13.

98. Pew Research Center, "Eastern and Western Europeans Differ."

in participation in rituals and Catholic practice.[99] There has been increased attendance at Catholic events that are outside the control of the traditional ecclesiastical hierarchy. Various types of festivals, pilgrimages, and lay preachers are popular. Many young people find answers by visiting new Catholic arenas of this kind, rather than by listening to the priest's sermon.

MIGRANT CHURCHES

For centuries, Europe has set the terms for various Christian expressions across the world through mission, colonization, and western hegemony. But a look at contemporary Christianity in Europe would be incomplete without an acknowledgment that European Christianity too is influenced by global trends. Christian migrants are some of the most active churchgoers in today's Europe. On an ordinary Sunday in London, perhaps half of those attending services will have an African or Afro-Caribbean provenance.[100] In Copenhagen, migrant churches account for approximately a third of all church attendance in any given week.[101] Christian migrants have a strong presence in the established churches, especially in the Catholic church, but they have also started their own churches, so-called "migrant churches." Many of these are independent or Pentecostal churches. Others are Baptists, Methodists, Presbyterians, Orthodox, or belong to other established confessions. One consequence is that minority churches have increased in numbers in many countries, such as Orthodox churches in France, Catholic and Orthodox churches in Sweden, Protestant churches in Italy and Ireland, and Pentecostal and independent churches across the continent. In this way, Christian migrants have contributed to a more diverse Christian presence in Europe. Migrant churches and foreign-language congregations of various denominations are found today in most European cities of a certain size.[102]

We shall now take Norway as a case. With the exception of its Sami population, it has traditionally been a relatively homogenous land, ethnically, linguistically, and religiously. In 2017, the Christian daily newspaper *Dagen* had a story about a Brazilian married couple, a doctor and a dentist, who had moved to Bergen, Norway's second-largest city, as missionaries.[103] According to the article, it was a strong personal missionary vocation from God that led the Brazilians to sell their apartment, their car, and their firm

99. Mandes and Rogaczewska, "I Don't Reject the Catholic Church," 267.

100. Coleman, "Christianity in Western Europe," 497.

101. Allen, "Migrant Churches."

102. Jackson and Passarelli, *Mapping Migration*.

103. Algrøy. "Norge—Brasil."

in their native land, to say farewell to family and friends, and to set out for the little land far in the north. They spent more than eighteen months as missionaries in Norway, in association with others from Nepal, Japan, Uganda, and the USA. A hundred years ago, Norway was a missionary "great power," in the sense that it had sent out more missionaries per head of population than any other European country.[104] Today, there are probably more missionaries from foreign countries in Norway than Norwegian missionaries abroad.

A survey in 2015 found more than 250 migrant Christian communities in Norway, most of which had been established in the previous twenty years.[105] Worship is conducted in a total of over forty different languages in these communities. Especially in the largest cities, there is a large variety of worship on offer, with communities and Christianity from every corner of the world. The development accords with what can be seen elsewhere in Europe.

Migrant Christian communities in Norway are very varied. They are usually founded by immigrants or persons with a minority background, or else they have been established as a specific linguistic fellowship within an existing Norwegian denomination. Apart from this, they have little in common. They are made up of Christian immigrants from different parts of the world and represent a huge theological and institutional spectrum, from German Lutherans to Filipino, Polish, or Chilean Catholics, Nigerian Pentecostals, Oriental Orthodox from Ethiopia, or Eastern Orthodox from Bulgaria. Some communities have close ties to mother churches in their homeland, or are branches of other migrant Christian communities in Europe. Others again are independent, with no link to other churches or communities. And some have formed close links to existing Norwegian churches and parishes, either as a special linguistic group that is fully integrated into the parish or through a looser and more pragmatic cooperation. Some communities are registered as denominations, while others are unregistered and have a more temporary character. Some consist mostly of asylum seekers or immigrants present illegally in Norway; others can consist of prosperous oil workers or international businesspeople. Some have priests or pastors who came to Norway as refugees, students, employees, or missionaries, while others use the services of clergy from Norwegian churches or have their own.

There are several reasons why Christian immigrants organize themselves in specific communities. Several studies show that continuity in ethnic or national identity is decisive. For others, a common language is the

104. Nielssen, "Til jordens ender."
105. Desta, "National Report."

most important factor, while for others again, the emphasis seems to lie on a spirituality and identity of their own on a supranational and more regional level, such as Latin American or African charismatic Christianity.[106] Migrant communities also play an important social role. They are important meeting places where immigrants can feel at home and be included in relatively close fellowships.[107] The communities are important because they create spaces where immigrants can be something more than just immigrants. Many of them also offer social, financial, or practical aid to persons who have newly arrived.[108] If you are looking for an apartment to rent or for a job, the community can help you.

A desire for continuity with the culture, language, and spirituality of a person's homeland does not, however, necessarily mean that immigrants reproduce the religiosity from their countries of origin. Migration also leads to changes in religiosity. Some migrants become more religious, others less; and some change their confession. The Christianity that is found in the migrant communities is also shaped by the societal conditions in the host land and by their own concrete life situation.[109] In this way, while new forms of Christianity are imported from the world to the European host land, at the same time completely new forms of Christianity are created there too.

OUTLOOK

In this chapter, we have seen how Christianity in various ways continues to shape Europe, and how it is changing. The charismatic movement that is strong and vigorous in other regions of the world has also left its traces on Europe. Since 1980, the Vatican has encouraged the foundation of new Catholic orders with the goal of spreading the faith. Many of these are inspired by the charismatic movement, and their presence is particularly visible in Italy and France. In the Anglican church in England, an Evangelical, charismatic wing has long been a central element of the ecclesiastical leadership, and it is strongly present in the parishes. As in other parts of the world, charismatic movements have led to a renewal in the established churches, while at the same time new churches have been established. In this chapter, the emphasis has been on the established churches; but in Europe, as elsewhere, there is a great variation in the ecclesial landscape.

106. Synnes, "Kristne migrantmenigheter"

107. Synnes, "Kristne migrantmenigheter," 67–68.

108. Synnes, "Kristne migrantmenigheter," 77–78.

109. Nordin, "Religiösitet bland migranter," 270–71; Synnes, "Kristne migrantmenigheter," 66–68.

For historical reasons, the established churches in Europe still possess great financial and political weight globally. This weight is used, for example, in questions about women's equality and new family values. The churches in Europe are split in the positions they take on these topics. But it is also here that we find some of the most remarkable champions of women's rights, especially in the Protestant churches in northern Europe. Via ecumenical commissions, contact between churches in different countries, development aid, and active participation in international institutions such as the UN and the EU, these churches work together with partners in other countries to promote women's rights both in the churches and in society in general.

The UN has spoken in favor of a stronger inclusion of religious actors in the global work for development. This is happening at the same time as a conservative alliance of religious organizations (mostly Christian) has become a more active lobbying group at the UN. Their agenda includes the strengthening of a conservative view of the family, gender roles, and reproductive health.[110]

The alliances do not follow geographical boundaries. They bear witness to a global Christianity with various transnational networks, fighting passionately for contradictory goals.

110. Vik et al., *Lobbying for Faith and Family*, 15.

10

The Globalization of Christianity

Tradition and Change

IN THE PAST, IT took more time to communicate over great distances. In September 1946, the thirty-year-old Indian pastor M. M. Thomas received a letter from the World Student Christian Federation in Geneva, inviting him to become the general secretary of this international Christian student movement. Thomas had worked for the organization in India, and he accepted the invitation. In January 1947, he sailed from his home in Kerala to Bombay (now Mumbai) and took a ship from there to Europe. Just before he went on board the SS Strathmore, he received a telegram that his wife Pennamamma had given birth to a son, three weeks before the child was due. He replied in a warm telegram of congratulations and sailed for England. The journey continued with a train to Paris, and then on to Geneva, where he arrived on February 20. In January of the following year, he was back in India for his first visit. India had become independent, and his son was one year old. In the next decades, M.M. Thomas became one of the most influential theologians in the ecumenical movement, a builder of bridges between traditional European theology and the theology that was developed in the global South.[1]

It is hard to exaggerate the enormous changes that have taken place in the world in the last two or three generations. European empires have been

---

1. Thomas, *My Ecumenical Journey*, 1–4.

disbanded and countries in the South and East have gained autonomy, while technology has revolutionized communication across national borders. Seven decades ago, Thomas's exchange of letters with Geneva took months. Today, text and images, ideas and points of view are exchanged in minutes and seconds. In January 1964, Paul VI was the first pope in history to travel by air. One year later, this made it possible for him, as the first pope, to set his feet on American soil, four hundred and fifty years after the Catholic missionaries had first arrived on the continent.[2] Unlike popes in the past, who by and large remained in Rome, the popes in recent decades have had a busy program of travel to every corner of the world. The pope's traditional office is now closely linked to modern means of communication, and in 2012, the pope got an account on Twitter.

The changes have given space for more democracy and openness. Many countries in Latin America, Africa, and Asia that once were dictatorships are now democracies. An easier access to information has meant that more people can make their voices heard and can influence political developments. But the possibilities of communication have also created a concentration of power and homogenization. A few—often western—cultural expressions are allowed to dominate, at the expense of local variation. A limited number of global companies, mostly from the USA, control a large proportion of the world's resources.

Like everything else, Christianity in our time is affected by these huge global changes. In this book, we have pointed to changed relationships between the state and the churches in countries with large Christian populations. In China and Russia, state oppression has been replaced by forms of regulation that have given Christians a much greater freedom. In Mexico, the state has watered down earlier restrictions and has given the Catholic church a greater freedom of action than in the past.[3] In Latin America and Africa, the democratization of states and the liberalization of the economy have proven a good soil for the emergence of new religious actors, especially Pentecostal revivals, which exemplify the new plurality within Christianity that are putting established churches under pressure. Global Christianity is more pluralistic than before. At the same time, there also exist homogenizing tendencies. There are many similarities between Pentecostal revivals in Africa, Asia, and Latin America. And when the Brazilian Pentecostal church IURD establishes itself in southern Africa, it does so with rather obvious

---

2. Allen, "Fun Facts."

3. The developments in Russia and Mexico are regarded as among the most important changes globally in the relationship between state and religion in the period between 1990 and 2008. See Fox, *Political Secularism*, 223.

copies of the church's rituals, sermons, and marketing in Brazil.[4] The fact that such standardized forms of Christianity are spread more quickly than in the past also leads to uniformity.

Despite the great variety in Christianity that is presented in the chapters of this book, we wish to emphasize especially two main characteristics of Christianity in the twenty-first century: the shift of the center of gravity from the global North to the global South, and the strong growth of charismatic Christianity—in both Protestant and Catholic forms.

Although every exercise of religion takes place in one particular place and cannot be made placeless and abstract, there are some aspects of Christianity in our time that have such a world-encompassing character or intention that they cannot be presented within the framework of a chapter with a regional orientation. Christianity takes place not only locally, but also globally. This is first and foremost a question of how the churches and Christian organizations collaborate on a global level, whether through the ecumenical movement or through the construction of other alliances across traditional lines of division. In this chapter, we shall first look at the two main tendencies, before we present Christianity's global network. We shall close by asking whether we are also justified in speaking of a third main tendency, that is to say, secularization.

FROM NORTH TO SOUTH

The center of gravity of the world's Christians is moving away from Europe and North America. It can now be found in Africa, Latin America, and to some extent in Asia. In the light of Christianity's long history, this is a new development, and the attention paid to it is even newer. There is still a strong tendency for textbooks on Christianity to make European and North American Christianity the norm, and the books that hold the dominant position in theological faculties take Europe and North America as the primary framework of understanding. But the average churchgoer today is not to be found either in Germany, Protestantism's core country, or in Italy, Catholicism's historical center; one will find her or him in one of the big cities in Africa and Latin America, on a Catholic church bench or on a plastic chair in a Pentecostal church. And for the first time in almost 1,300 years, the most powerful Christian leader in the world is not from Europe. Today's Pope is the first non-European on the chair of Peter since the Syrian Pope Gregory III died in 741.

4. One example is the church's South African homepage: https://www.uckg.org/.

An often-used calculation of the numbers of Christians in the world says that in 1900, more than 80 percent of the world's Christian population lived in Europe or North America. In Europe alone, there were about 380 million of the world's estimated 558 million Christians. One hundred and ten years later, this had changed radically. Europe was indeed still the largest Christian continent, with 588 million Christians, but there had been a much greater growth on all the other continents. Europe and North America had less than 40 percent of the world's Christians, and Europe on its own only a quarter. The relative weakening of traditional European Christianity is even greater than these figures suggest, because a growing proportion of Christians in Europe have brought their Christianity with them from Africa, Asia, or Latin America as migrants to Europe. The same calculation also includes prognoses for the future and suggests that in 2050, the proportion of Christians in Europe and North America will have declined to 27 percent. According to these predictions, Christianity's share of the entire world population will remain fairly stable at roughly one-third, as it is today.[5]

The causes of these changes are complex, but two are particularly important. The first is Christian mission from the North to the South, which became possible *inter alia* thanks to colonization and to the gradual establishing of western dominance. Although Africa and Asia have ethnic groups that were Christian long before Europe became the dominant Christian continent, the growth in the number of Christians happened principally within Christian traditions that were brought to these continents from Europe and North America. The second cause is population growth. While population figures in Europe are more or less static, Latin America, Africa, Asia, and the Middle East all experience an enormous growth in population. It is not only as a proportion of Christians that Europe's importance is strongly reduced, but also as a proportion of the world population. This also means that the growth in the number of religious believers outstrips the growth in the number of those who say that they have no religious adherence. It seems that the world as a whole is becoming more religious.

The great plurality that has always existed in Christianity becomes more visible in a globalized world. The chapters with a regional orientation have shown the variety in Christianity's expressions in different parts of the world. We have said that Christianity *occurs* in various ways, in order to underline that Christianity is precisely the practices and the words that are *de facto* expressed and that occur, rather than an eternal and static idea. The chapters have also brought up a number of topics that are both global and local. We have discussed questions that concern Christians everywhere in

5. Jenkins, *Next Christendom*, 3.

the world, but that are given different—and sometimes contradictory—answers from place to place and from church to church. This applies (for example) to the relationship between church and state, the role of the churches in political life, nation-building, war and conflict, the economy, gender and sexuality, the climate, welfare, and migration.

Is it meaningful to speak of "Christianity," or must we rather talk of different "Christianities"? Are the woman who took the altar for "the Holy Death" out onto the street in Mexico City, and the Patriarch of Moscow who has the ear of the Russian President in great questions of foreign policy, both representatives of "Christianity," or are they rather representatives of different "Christianities"? The answer must be: yes, they are *both* of these. The local and historically conditioned aspects of Christianity in differing contexts make the content of faith, the practices, organization, and societal role so different that these two persons would scarcely recognize each other's Christianity. But even if we put this noun in the plural, without a definite article—"Christianities"—we have not removed every presupposition that something is held in common here. When individuals or fellowships define their religious faith, their identity, or their praxis as Christian, they are making themselves a part of the entire field that can be called global Christianity, and that encompasses more than two billion persons.

THE GROWTH OF THE
PENTECOSTAL CHURCHES

The other major tendency among the world's Christians today is the growth in charismatic forms of Christianity. The onward march of the Protestant Pentecostal movement over almost the entire globe is particularly important. The term "Pentecostal" embraces such a wide spectrum that one can find it natural to use the plural, "Pentecostal movements," in order to make the differences clear. These movements consist of churches that are spread throughout the world, but share "family likenesses." Some churches that resemble each other establish formal and informal global fellowships, and can be recognized by (for example) having basically the same theology and similar forms of worship. Some of the larger global Pentecostal churches like the Assemblies of God (USA) or the Redeemed Christian Church of God (Nigeria) have strong formal global structures, while independent megachurches everywhere in the world meet their "family members" via less binding networks. There is not one single common structure that brings all the world's various Pentecostals together—the differences are too great for that.

The Pentecostal movements have grown primarily by attracting members from the established churches, both Catholic and Protestant. The most dramatic growth has occurred in Africa and Latin America in a period that coincided with democratization, the deregulation of the economy, and the development of new technology. Pentecostals made effective use of the new sphere for action opened up by these changes. They built churches with their own television and radio stations, and employed the public sphere to communicate messages about conversion and new possibilities, in a completely different way than the established churches. With new instruments and a strong missionary zeal, Pentecostals have built churches and elaborated a theology that appeals to both poor and rich in an age marked by great upheavals.

One striking aspect of the Protestant Pentecostal movement in many places is its complex interplay with another form of religiosity: the so-called popular religiosity or belief in spirits. Wherever European Christianity has encountered new contexts, there has been a conflict with religious ideas that were widespread locally. Different ecclesiastical traditions have dealt with this in different ways. The Catholic tradition has often gone further than the traditional Protestant churches in embracing popular religiosity. At the same time, the Catholic church has integrated local religious forms into its own frameworks, so that (for example) belief in spirits and in many gods were transformed into the cult of the saints, with altars at the roadside or in people's homes. The established Protestant churches have often rejected more categorically such forms of popular religiosity, and some missionaries in the past were strongly influenced by the ideas of the Enlightenment. A paradox in the Pentecostal charismatic churches is that they frequently and very clearly reject and condemn popular religiosity—but the rejection is at the same time a confirmation. It is presupposed that the spirits have genuine power: they represent evil, and one must fight against Satan himself. This does not fundamentally challenge the worldview in which spirits and the veneration of ancestors have their place, and the experiences with spirits that are generated by this worldview are not rejected. Instead, they acquire a meaning in the Pentecostal revival's new cosmological drama. Despite the expectation of a radical conversion and of being "born anew," the change can in practice be less than is demanded by other forms of Christianity.

The Pentecostals' paradoxical embrace of traditional cosmology is attractive because it is at the same time adapted to modern lifestyles. It is the big cities that are by far the most important location for the Pentecostal churches, and the big cities in Latin America, Africa, and Asia are growing at a tremendous pace. While Europeans and North Americans are most concerned about the migration from the South to the North, the largest movement of people is taking place in the global South, from rural areas to the cities. Urbanization is breaking up the traditional fellowships and strengthening the modern emphasis on the individual rather than on the collective. The Pentecostal churches have a twofold message for this situation: salvation concerns precisely *you* as an individual person; you yourself are responsible vis-à-vis God. It is *you* who must convert, you who are "born anew." It is *your* choice. At the same time, conversion brings the individual into a new fellowship that can be experienced as just as strong as the fellowship in the traditional societies. In the best case, it is equally supportive, while it is also experienced as something personally chosen. In one sense, the market of churches and preachers is a market where the individual can make her or his own choices. This is why the Pentecostal movement grows most where the states attempt only to a small degree to regulate this religious market by means of restrictions on the establishing of new religious bodies or by giving privileges to one particular form of religion. There seems to be a link between authoritarian states, as in the Middle East or in Russia, and the absence of competition between religious groups. Apart from in Western Europe, charismatic Christianity flourishes in countries with a strong degree of religious freedom.

Stronger individualism is probably a central presupposition for the growth of the Pentecostal churches. They also confirm and consolidate the attention to the individual rather than to the collective. Systems and structures move into the background, and it is assumed that the individual to some extent chooses one's own fate and is responsible for it.

There is another potential consequence of the orientation to the individual. Another ambivalence in Pentecostal Christianity is its relationship to authorities. On the one hand, the new Protestant churches often have a strongly hierarchical structure centering on strong leaders who are exposed to very little systematic control and who acquire great power over many persons. On the other hand, traditional structures of authority are rejected, both those in the general culture and those in the established churches. In theory, everyone can become a leader, independently of background and education. Moreover, those who belong to the churches have, in principle, some measure of control over the leaders, because they can choose to leave that church and go somewhere else. Not even the largest Pentecostal churches have the monopoly situation that the traditional churches have had in many places, at any rate in times past. There may be a democratizing impulse in this situation. When we add that women often have greater access to formal positions than they have had in the traditional churches, and not least when we take into account the formal and informal instruction in organizational work that is a consequence of getting involved in the church, the Pentecostal churches can be places that enable people to influence developments in society.

In the previous chapters, we have seen the advance of Pentecostal churches on most continents. This means that their forms of Christianity influence Christians throughout the world. But we have also noted another very important phenomenon: in many places, the established churches are beginning to resemble the Pentecostal churches more strongly, for example, by making use of charismatic hymns and prayers for healing, and by emphasizing experience at the expense of doctrinal content. It is perhaps not surprising that traditional Baptist churches in India resemble the new Pentecostal churches, since the two ecclesial traditions are closely related, and the influence goes in both directions. But we have also seen that Catholic parishes in Latin America renew themselves by adopting many of the forms of the Pentecostal churches. Corresponding tendencies can be found in Catholic parishes everywhere in the world; this is what we have called the Catholic charismatic revival. The wind of charismatic revival has also blown strongly in the traditional Protestant churches, among Lutherans, Reformed, Methodists, and Anglicans. We can therefore speak of a growth in charismatic forms of Christianity that goes far beyond the Pentecostal churches, although these have led the way and must be seen as the origin of the charismatic movement.

Unlike many of the traditional churches, the Pentecostal churches are not a group with clear boundaries. If we include all the churches that have free forms of worship, that do not practice infant baptism, and that do not belong within any of the other great ecclesial traditions, we are confronted with a variety that may be larger than any other ecclesial current. Nevertheless, we can speak of clear common traits in the basic understanding of what it is to be a Christian. Christianity is to be genuine, sincerely felt, and self-chosen. Rituals are important in practice, but reflection on them is based on the premise that the central matter is one's personal conviction, and perhaps individual morality. The origin of this understanding of Christianity, or indeed of religion as a whole, can be found in the Protestantism of the past, but they come to full flowering in the growth of the Pentecostal churches, from which they are then adopted by other churches.

This trait led the French scholar Olivier Roy to speak of a "Protestantization" of Christianity and of religion as a whole.[6] He describes a situation in which "religion and culture part ways." The process is propelled above all by migration. Migrants who leave one cultural context and put down roots in another find it necessary to draw a distinction between religion

6. Roy, *Holy Ignorance*, 195.

and culture in a completely different way from what occurs in more homogeneous societies. This is true whether one crosses national borders or moves into the big city. And those who themselves do not move, but who experience a growing variety in their own milieu, need to clarify what belongs to culture and what belongs to religion. This in turn can help to standardize religion and to lead to skepticism about what does not fit into the forms, about what is untidy and hybrid. And this can lead in the direction of fundamentalism and suspicion across the religious boundaries, when one desires to highlight the specific character of one's own religion and to make it clear that is different from what is "only culture."

THE GLOBAL NETWORK OF CATHOLICISM

Roughly one half of the world's Christians belong to the Catholic church. "Catholic" means "universal," and the visible structure and hierarchy of the church appear in some ways to be clear and tidy. The church has one official doctrine and uniform rules for practices based on religion, covering everything from the celebration of the eucharist to abortion.

But although unity across geography and culture is one important aspect of the Catholic self-understanding, the church's leaders also emphasize that the church must adapt to various cultures and living conditions. This is why it contains a vast variety, and if we are to describe the Catholic church today, a description of the varied Catholic life in Latin America gives a more representative picture than a presentation of life within the walls of the Vatican. Nevertheless, Catholic Christianity is exercised and formed to an essential degree through the church's power structures and network. The power structure is not identical with the Vatican, but it is closely linked to the church-state in the heart of Rome and to the central bureaucracy, the *Curia*, that is localized there.

The election of the Latin American Pope Francis in 2013 was a fruit of the global shift of gravity in the Catholic church, and it has consequences for the church's ability to exercise influence in what is the largest Catholic continent. The Vatican's power over Latin American Catholicism was also clear some decades earlier, when the church's leaders sidelined the leading figures of liberation theology. This took place both by forbidding them directly to speak and to teach, and by relocating and marginalizing those who (in the Vatican's eyes) deviated too far from the defined "correct doctrine." We also see the importance of the Vatican in China, where the conflict between the Catholic church and the authorities concerns precisely the formal bond and the necessary loyalty of Chinese Catholicism to the global church fellowship, represented by the pope's right to appoint bishops. But as a global reality, the Catholic church does not only exercise influence over internal organizational matters such as the nomination of bishops. It has other global interests too.

The Catholic church's institutional headquarters is a state of its own, in principle like other states, At the same time, this church-state differs essentially from other states by having Catholicism's highest leader, the pope, as its head of state. The Vatican City is not an ordinary member of the United Nations, but the Holy See has observer status at the organization's centers in New York and Geneva. It is also a member of a number of special organizations in the UN, which gives it both influence and obligations. The Holy See gets power, but it can also be exposed to criticism: in 2014, for example, the UN Committee on the Rights of the Child criticized the Holy See for its handling of cases of abuse in the church.[7]

The recent history of the Vatican is an example of a collaboration between globalization and Christianity. The diplomatic presence of the Holy See throughout the world has been considerably strengthened. The greatest increase in state-to-state accords came under Pope John Paul II. From his election as pope in 1978 until his death in 2005, the countries with diplomatic links to the Holy See increased from eighty-five to 174. This diplomatic corps is used from everything from ensuring economic transfers to the church, to mediating in situations of conflict. When the Holy See's diplomacy contributed to a peaceful accord that ended a territorial dispute between Chile and Argentina in 1983, international observers took note.[8] In the fall of 2016, the parties in the political crisis in Venezuela declared that they were willing to negotiate only if the Holy See was the mediator. Although the mediation broke off after a few weeks and the conflict remained unresolved, this shows that the Holy See's diplomacy can play an important role in certain highly tense situations.

When one attempts to understand Christianity and other religions, the visibility and unity of the Catholic church with regard to structure and praxis can function as an unconscious ideal for how religion "ought" to find expression. But if one looks for a corresponding tidiness in other religions and churches, one overlooks thereby the fact that it is the Catholic church, with its global organizational structure, that is the exception. Other churches too have nevertheless taken large steps over the past one hundred and fifty years in the direction of greater unity and concord among themselves. This applies especially to the traditional Protestant churches, which have

7. See "Vatican 'Must Immediately Remove' Child Abusers."
8. Lindsley, "Beagle Channel Settlement."

formed global structures for each ecclesial family, in addition to the World
Council of Churches and the World Evangelical Alliance.

GLOBAL CHURCH ALLIANCES

"At last! We are brothers!" exclaimed Pope Francis when he embraced Patriarch Kirill at the airport in Havana on February 12, 2016. After many years
of preparation, a pope and the head of the Russian Orthodox church met
for the first time. In the declaration from their meeting, they highlight their
common interests: support for the Christian minorities in the Middle East,
defense of heterosexual marriage, and the fight against secularization. The
meeting on Cuba was the result of several decades of ecumenical endeavors—that is to say, work for understanding and cooperation across the traditional church boundaries. At the same time, it illustrated the emergence of a
new form of alliance-building in defense of what the Russian church leader
calls "traditional values." From about the turn of the millennium, there have
arisen new, often fairly loose, forms of cooperation that in some cases are in
contrast to, and pose a challenge to, the ecumenical collaboration in which
the established Protestant churches have led the way.

In the second half of the nineteenth century, new global organizational
structures for several of the traditional Protestant churches, such as Methodists, Reformed, and Anglicans, came into existence. The Lutherans and others followed from the first half of the twentieth century onward, and all the
large Protestant traditions have global structures of this kind today. These
world communions are forums for collaboration and coordination between
closely related churches. In many cases, they also function as meeting places
where churches that were established as a result of mission from Europe and
North America can meet their "mother churches" on a more equal footing.
By means of the global organizations, representatives of the various ecclesial
families discuss what it means (for example) to be Lutherans, Anglicans, or
Methodists, but the global structures usually have no direct power to take
decisions that affect individual member churches.

From the beginning of the present century, several of the global church
organizations have experienced strong internal tensions as a consequence of
differing views on LGBTQ rights and same-sex marriage. The main tendency has been for European and North American Protestant churches to have
a more liberal praxis, while churches in Africa, Asia, and Latin America
have taken a restrictive view and seen the development in Europe and North
America as a breach with traditional Christian doctrine. This means that
the lines of conflict to some extent also follow the distinction between the

old churches and the younger mission churches, and tensions linked to historical oppression and to the marginalization of African, Asian, and Latin American cultural expressions come to the surface. The conflict has been particularly severe in the Anglican Communion, where the church in Nigeria was one of those that broke contact with the English "mother church." But the picture of a conservative "South" against a more liberal "North" is more complex than is sometimes said.[9] Some Protestant churches in Latin America, for example, have taken more liberal standpoints. The same is true of many of the churches in South Africa, which enjoy great respect throughout the world because of the fight against the apartheid regime in the 1970s and 1980s.

Although the global structures of the various church families are important, the ecumenical movement is an even more important meeting place for global Christianity. This applies in particular to the most prominent organizational expression of this movement, the World Council of Churches, which has roughly 350 member churches from the whole world, mostly Protestant and Orthodox. According to the organization itself, these churches have altogether a total of more than five hundred million members. The Catholic church is not a member of the Council; nor are most of the world's Pentecostal churches.

The World Council of Churches also has roots going back to the end of the nineteenth century, and its history is interwoven with the missionary zeal of the European Protestant churches at the beginning of the twentieth century. For a long time, a number of the big missionary organizations kept their distance from ecumenical work, which they saw as excessively open to theological plurality, and too little oriented to the conversion of new persons to the Christian faith. The World Council of Churches as we know it today was founded in 1948, and brought together two related ecclesial impulses. One was the need for the churches to study the theological differences between them, in order to create a more clearly visible unity; the other was oriented to practical collaboration, not least in connection with an involvement in society that was based on the Christian faith. These two main currents still shape the work that has its origin in the World Council of Churches, both through its member churches and through the international secretariat in Geneva.

It is not by chance that it came into existence precisely in the first years after the Second World War and in parallel to the Universal Declaration of Human Rights, the foundation of the UN, and the beginning of the dismantling of European colonialism. Something of the same impulses lie in the

9. Hasset, *Anglican Communion in Crisis.*

background: the desire for a committed global cooperation and a growing recognition that such a cooperation presupposes a form of equality across cultural dividing lines. This is why the ecumenical movement is also a modern movement propelled by the belief that Christians can unite on some fundamental Christian truths that support the values presupposed by the UN and by human rights.

The World Council of Churches and the ecumenical movement have lost something of their importance over the last decades. There may be several reasons for this. One reason is linked to the modern impulse that has indeed celebrated variety, but has nevertheless had unity and concord as its basis and its goal. The growing Pentecostal churches have mostly not wanted to be a part of the World Council of Churches. At the same time, the Council's member churches have often looked skeptically at this new movement, both because the traditional churches disapprove of preaching about material prosperity and miracles, and because the new churches have wooed and won members from the established Protestant churches. The Orthodox member churches in the World Council have begun to demand a greater influence on the Council's work. They have also expressed skepticism about endeavors to attain theological unity and about some aspects of church involvement in society. It has become more and more difficult for the organization to balance ecclesial plurality and unity.

While the World Council of Churches faces challenges, the organization itself is also to some extent a victim of its own success, or at any rate, a victim of the success of some its fundamental ideas. A few generations ago, the differences between Reformed, Baptists, Methodists, and Anglicans—to say nothing of Orthodox Christians—were experienced as so great that it was difficult to collaborate. Many were not convinced that they shared the same—true—Christian faith. Ecumenical endeavors were pioneer work. Today, many Christians see the disputes between Christians in the past as incomprehensible, or at any rate as irrelevant. Churches from various traditions cooperate closely, and in some places they have even united with each other. This lessens the need and the commitment to resolve the theological questions that divide the churches.

The challenges to the ecumenical movement do not, however, have solely theological and ideological causes. Money is also an important explanation. Over a very short period, a shortage of money reduced the secretariat of the World Council of Churches in Geneva by half. The Council is financed by the member churches. The weaker financing may be caused by the fact that the churches find the Council less relevant, but it is also connected to other important aspects of the development of global Christianity. An increasing number of member churches are at home in the global South, and have fewer resources to set aside for international cooperation. Traditionally, the activity has been paid for by the big churches and missionary organizations in North America and Europe, but these are going through hard times with regard both to membership numbers and to their financial resources. In particular, the COVID-19 pandemic has had relatively large economic consequences for several of the big Protestant mainline churches in the USA, and this in turn will influence their ability to sponsor international ecumenical work. The shift in gravity in global Christianity from the North to the South also has material consequences for the possibility of the established churches to engage in global collaboration.

In many countries in the global South, national church councils have been important channels of aid money from ecclesiastical actors in Europe and North America. Organizations such as Bread for the World in Germany and Christian Aid in Great Britain can stand as representatives for a huge family of international aid organizations linked to the Protestant churches, known as "Action by Churches Together" (ACT). These too are a part of the ecumenical movement in a wide sense. In their homelands, churches and Christian organizations form the primary anchor, and in the countries where they carry out development aid and emergency relief aid, projects directed by churches and Christian organizations are among the most important partners. The goal of the financial transfers is development, and since the organizations often administer large sums of state aid, they emphasize explicitly that the aid money will not go to missionary work or to build up the churches' position in the recipient countries. It is nevertheless indubitable that the church actors who transmit aid help to bind churches and Christians together across continents and cultures, in the same way as other aid organizations forge ties between the continents in other societal spheres, such trades unions or cultural life. There are also global church aid and development organizations such as Caritas Internationalis, World Vision International, Lutheran World Relief, and International Orthodox Christian Charities. These are important actors in international aid.

The World Council of Churches and the ecumenical movement have only to a small extent embraced Pentecostal churches and other Evangelical churches with a strong commitment to traditional mission. These groups have organized themselves in other global networks. The so-called "Lausanne Movement" has brought together since 1974 Christian leaders whose main concern is global evangelization. One of those who took the initiative for its foundation was the prominent American evangelist Billy Graham.

The World Evangelical Alliance is a central actor in the Lausanne Movement. It too has roots going back to the nineteenth century, but it was in the 1950s that it became a significant international movement. It focuses on bringing together both regional and national "Evangelical alliances" of churches and organizations that put the emphasis on missionary work. Many of the churches that are associated with this movement are Pentecostal. Some churches are members in both the World Council of Churches and the World Evangelical Alliance, but there are clear differences between the two global church networks in their membership and the form of their work.

As many of the chapters in this book have shown, one source of conflict has been the mission by charismatic and Evangelical Christians that has targeted members of traditional churches. It was therefore a sensation when the World Council of Churches, the World Evangelical Alliance, and the Catholic church published a common declaration about mission in 2011.[10] This was the first time in history that these three organizations, to which more than 95 percent of the world's Christians belong, had launched a common document. The declaration affirmed that mission must take place in an ethically defensible manner, and not violate people's integrity. One interpretation of this agreement saw it as an attempt to reduce the level of conflict between Evangelical groups and traditional churches, and to prepare the ground for increased trust and cooperation among them.

While the World Council of Churches has worked to promote theological understanding and church cooperation in the areas of peace, development, and human rights, the Evangelical organizations have had a more conservative political agenda and have been content with bringing together churches with their historical roots in the Protestant churches. In the present century, however, we have observed a new tendency in connection with international church cooperation. Churches and Christian organizations that have been very distant from each other both historically and theologically are increasingly coming together in alliances linked to specific political questions. This cooperation is particularly visible in the intersection between religion and politics, for example, when planned legislation would regulate questions in which the churches are strongly involved. This applies especially to what are often called "traditional family values" and to the defense of Christian privileges in countries where Christianity has historically had a strong position. One example is the alliances the Russian Orthodox church has formed with Catholics and with Evangelical Christians—as well as with Muslims—to get the concept of "traditional values" included in resolutions by the United Nations Human Rights Council.[11] Another example was the mobilization that took place in the same groups to support Italy when the European Court of Human Rights took up the

10. WCC, "Christian Witness."
11. Horsfjord, "Negotiating Traditional Values."

Lautsi case (about whether it was discriminatory to place crucifixes on the walls in Italian classrooms).[12] The Christian actors understand these issues as a sharp conflict between "Christianity"—or "religion"—on the one hand and "secularism" on the other. The novelty is that very different Christian groups now collaborate in the encounter with this "common enemy." One can get the impression that ethical and political questions of this kind have such a high priority for these groups that they lay aside the mutual suspicion that has been connected throughout history to their differing theological understandings of baptism, the eucharist, and forms of worship.

SECULARIZATION?

In the 1960s and 1970s, scholars put forward theories about an accelerating and irreversible secularization, but the tone changed completely at the turn of the millennium. Many held that the revolution in Iran in 1979 and the aftermath of the fall of the Berlin Wall in 1989 showed that "God was back." This view seemed to be confirmed when fear of violent Islamism made its way onto the political agenda throughout the world in the present century. The two main tendencies that we have identified in global Christianity, the shift in gravity from North to South and the growth of Pentecostal charismatic Christianity, were discovered in full earnest in the same period, and helped further to convince many people that the secularization theory had a more limited validity that had earlier been supposed. Many held that this theory applied best to Europe.

One weakness in much of the early discussion of secularization was the disagreement about what "secularization" actually meant. A threefold understanding of the concept has been employed by many people from the 1990s onward. First, "secularization" can refer to a process in which religion as a phenomenon and an area of society is separated more clearly from other parts of society: in other words, one envisages a "religious sphere" as distinct from a "political sphere" or an "economic sphere." It is assumed that this kind of differentiation is a necessary part of a modern society, not only in regard to religion, but in regard to many parts of society. Secondly, "secularization" can indicate that religion is privatized and takes on a less central role in society. Thirdly, "secularization" can describe a situation in which religion plays a constantly diminishing role in the lives of more and more persons, where personal faith and religious praxis are declining, and where fewer people identify with religious fellowships.[13]

12. Annicchino, "Winning the Battle."

13. Casanova, *Public Relations in the Modern World.*

The picture of global Christianity that emerges in the present book indicates that secularization in the sense of marginalization or decline for the churches is not an unambiguous global trend. There is no reason to draw swift conclusions from the European context—for example, from the decline in the traditional majority churches in Europe—about general developmental traits that are valid across the globe. The reminder that the great majority of the world's Christians live outside Europe, and belong to vital church fellowships, challenges European stereotypes about a dying Christianity. The growth of Pentecostalism demonstrates that the world is not facing a linear development from religion to non-religion.

Some have held that the best answer to the question of how far the world is becoming more secularized is to point out that religion is not disappearing: it is merely changing its character. It is hard to disagree that religion is continually changing and that new forms of religion are replacing other forms. It is highly unlikely that the great majority of the world's population will become convinced atheists in the foreseeable future. But the question is whether religion and religiosity can change so much that it nevertheless remains meaningful to speak of secularization.

There are, at one and the same time, tendencies indicating that the world is becoming more secularized and other tendencies indicating the opposite. On the one hand, we see that new forms of Christianity are growing. The charismatic movement can be said to have revitalized the established churches both by opening the doors to new religious expressions and by giving laypersons a larger place in new ecclesial structures. Through social media, television screens, and a very flexible church structure, the Pentecostal churches have made Christianity even more accessible than it was in the past. Democratization and economic liberalization in Eastern Europe, Latin America, Africa, and parts of Asia have given Christian actors and institutions new possibilities, as owners of media outlets, as suppliers of welfare services, or in a close collaboration with political elites. Despite their declining numbers, the churches in Europe remain important suppliers of welfare services, and Christian identity politics has taken on a new relevance in a context of increasing pluralism.

On the other hand, the preceding chapters have also pointed to a number of aspects that can *support* the idea of a gradual secularization—as a global tendency too. One of the main challenges in understanding secularization has been to understand the differences between North America and Europe. Those who wrote about secularization in the 1960s and 1970s assumed that Europe was the pioneer and that the rest of the world would follow after modernization came. The USA was an exception, but it would follow in the long term. When Christianity appeared to be growing in the

USA in the 1980s and 1990s, it gradually came to seem obvious that the earlier analysis was mistaken: it was Europe that was the exception, and the rest of the world, including the USA, represented the norm. Religion was strong. But recent years have challenged this understanding too. The major churches in the USA, both Catholics and traditional Protestants, are experiencing a decline in the number of members. Immigrants compensate for this, but the tendency is nonetheless clear. Surveys from 2007 onwards indicate that few countries in the world have gone through such a rapid secularization as the United States.[14] What is more, Evangelical and Pentecostal churches are finding it hard to reproduce themselves. New generations do not necessarily feel at home in churches built on the premise that the individual is "converted" or "born again."

There are signs in Latin America that may indicate a development in the same direction. It is particularly on the Southern Cone in the region that we see the tendency for people to leave the churches, first and foremost the Catholic church. Chile is an illustrative example in this regard. Here, only half of the population consider themselves Catholic after a drop of adherents to the church from 74 percent in 1995 to 51 percent in 2020.[15] The majority of those who leave the Catholic church in Chile state that they no longer have a religion, and the same development is observable in Argentina. Many within this group consider themselves agnostics or atheists.[16] The Catholic church may indeed be losing members at high speed to the Pentecostal churches, but we should not forget that the Pentecostal churches also have two doors, an entrance and an exit. Although many join these churches, there is also a considerable number who leave them. Some go back to other churches, but others settle down outside church fellowships. A similar movement has not yet been documented in other parts of the world, but we are justified in asking whether it nevertheless will happen. When religion and culture part company, as the Pentecostal churches presuppose; when the emphasis on the individual's free choice means that you experience yourself as in charge of your own life; and when you experience having a greater influence on the world around you—then it can perhaps be easier to envisage a life without the church. And when preachers and pastors fail over time, indeed over generations, to fulfill promises of healing and economic prosperity, it is not unreasonable to think that many will head for the exit door.

14. Inglehart, *Religion's Sudden Decline*, 1.

15. Corporación Latinobarometro, "Informe Latinobarometro," 39.

16. Esquivel et al., "Ateos."

We have heard from the Evangelical churches in India that their leaders are disturbed to see new generations adopting western customs, including a lessening in loyalty to the churches. We hear from China of a considerable surge of interest in Christianity on the part of academics and intellectuals, many of whom, however, seem to have no interest in getting involved in the churches. It is hard to imagine a Christianity without churches. The churches' growth in Eastern Europe is determined to a large extent by the collapse of Communism a generation ago. At present, many churches in this part of Europe look both large and influential, but the numbers who attend services have stagnated, and their political influence can decline if the political power relationships change again. It is perhaps the Middle East that differs most from the rest of the world. Here, religion, culture, and political power relationships interact in complex situations in authoritarian states, and it is hard to envisage a revitalization or strong growth any time soon, although there are continually new missionary endeavors targeted at Muslims, and some scholars report Christian revivals among Muslims in the Middle East and Asia.[17]

There are more than two billion Christians in the world. Those who want to understand society, politics, and the daily lives of ordinary people, almost anywhere in the world, are well advised to study the many and varied forms of expression of global Christianity and to try to grasp how it influences the different areas of society. But understanding also includes a critical look at both the descriptions that are given and the many prognoses that are presented.

17. Miller and Johnstone, "Believers in Christ."

Bibliography

Abreu, Maria José de. "The Fedex Saints: Patrons of Mobility and Speed in a Neoliberal City." In *Things: Religion and the Question of Materiality*, edited by Dick Houtman and Birgit Meyer, 321–38. New York: Fordham University Press, 2012.

Adefarasin, Paul. *Change Your World: The Call for a Performing Generation*. Lagos: Rock, 2006.

Adogame, Afeosemime U. *The African Christian Diaspora: New Currents and Emerging Trends in World Christianity*. London: Bloomsbury, 2013.

———. *Who Is Afraid of the Holy Ghost? Pentecostalism and Globalization in Africa and Beyond*. Trenton, NJ: Africa World, 2011.

Agadjanian, Alexander. "Tradition, Morality, and Community: Elaborating Orthodox Identity in Putin's Russia." *Religion, State and Society* 45 (2017) 39–60.

Akingbade, Akinkunmi. "Urbanisation in Africa: A Blessing or a Curse?" https://venturesafrica.com/urbanisation-africa/.

Akkara, Anto. *Kandhamal, a Blot on Indian Secularism*. Delhi: Media House, 2009.

"Alcohol Returns to Baghdad." *Independent*, October 23, 2011. http://www.independent.co.uk/news/world/middle-east/alcohol-returns-to-baghdad-862969.html.

Alencar, Gustavo de. "Grupos protestantes e engajamento social: Uma análise dos discursos e ações de coletivos evangélicos progressistas." *Religião & Sociedade* 39 (2019) 173–96.

Algrøy, Eivind. "Norge—Brasil: 1–0." *Dagen*, January 28, 2017.

Allen, Elise Ann. "Vatican and China Renew Debated Deal on Picking Bishops." *Crux*, October 22, 2020. https://cruxnow.com/vatican/2020/10/vatican-and-china-renew-debated-deal-on-picking-bishops/.

———. "Vatican, China Courtship a Classic Case of One-Step Forward, One-Step Back." *Crux*, November 26, 2020. https://cruxnow.com/church-in-asia/2020/11/vatican-china-courtship-a-classic-case-of-one-step-forward-one-step-back/.

Allen, John L., Jr. "Fun Facts and More about Life aboard the Papal Plane." https://cruxnow.com/papal-visit/2015/09/18/fun-facts-and-more-about-life-aboard-the-papal-plane/.

Allen, Julie K. "Migrant Churches as Integration Vectors in Danish Society." *Scandinavian-Canadian Studies* 25 (2018) 116–34.

269

Alves, Daniel, and Ari P. Oro. "Renovação Carismática Católica: Movimento de superação da oposição entre catolicismo e pentecostalismo?" *Religião & Sociedade* 33 (2013) 122–44.

Amnesty International. "Massehenging i syrisk fengsel." htpps://www.amnesty.no/aktuelt/massehenging-i-syrisk-fengsel.

Andersen, Morten S. "Det portugisiske imperiet: Handel, ideologi og misericórdias." *Internasjonal Politikk* 66 (2008) 133–42.

Anderson, Allan. *An Introduction to Pentecostalism.* Cambridge: Cambridge University Press, 2004.

———. *An Introduction to Pentecostalism: Global Charismatic Christianity.* Cambridge: Cambridge University Press, 2013.

———. *To the Ends of the Earth: Pentecostalism and the Transformation of World Christianity.* Oxford: Oxford University Press, 2013.

———. "Varieties, Taxonomies, and Definitions." In *Studying Global Pentecostalism: Theories and Methods,* edited by Allan Anderson et al., 13–29. Berkeley: University of California Press, 2010.

Andrés, Rafael Ruiz. "Los múltiples rostros de la secularización: el caso español (1960–2019)." PhD diss., Universidad Complutense de Madrid, 2019.

Annicchino, Pasquale. "Winning the Battle by Losing the War: The *Lautsi* Case and the Holy Alliance between American Conservative Evangelicals, the Russian Orthodox Church, and the Vatican to Reshape European Identity." *Religion and Human Rights* 6 (2011) 213–19.

Ariel, Yaakov. "Israel in Contemporary Evangelical Christian Millennial Thought." *Numen* 59 (2012) 456–85.

Arns, Paulo Evaristo. "Palavras de Dom Paulo Evaristo Arns." In *Teologia Afro-Americana: II Consulta ecumênica de teologia e culturas afro-americana e caribenha,* edited by Ecumenical Association of Third World Theologians, 13–16. São Paulo: Paulus, 1997.

ARRCC. "Who We Are." https://www.arrcc.org.au/who-we-are.

Asamoah-Gyadu, Kwabena J. "An Introduction into the Typology of African Christianity." In *Anthology of African Christianity,* edited by Isabel Apawo Phiri et al., 261–64. Oxford: Regnum, 2016.

Ascensio, Luis M. "La Iglesia ante la emancipación en la Nueva España." In *Historia general de la Iglesia en América Latina,* edited by Alfonso A. Alvarado. Salamanca: Ediciones Paulinas, 1984.

Austen, Denise A., and Paul W. Lewis. "Concluding Remarks." In *Asia Pacific Pentecostalism,* edited by Denise A. Austin et al., 400–406. Boston: Brill, 2019.

Austen, Denise A., and Shane Clifton. "Australian Pentecostalism: From Marginalised to Megachurches." In *Asia Pacific Pentecostalism,* edited by Denise A. Austen et al., 372–99. Boston: Brill, 2019.

Australian Bureau of Statistics. "Religion in Australia." https://www.abs.gov.au/ausstats/abs@.nsf/Lookup/by%20Subject/2071.0~2016~Main%20Features~Religion%20Data%20Summary~70.

Auweele, Bart V. "Den romersk-katolske kirke i Vesteuropa siden 1945." In *Fra modernitet til pluralisme: Nation, stat, folk, kirke i det 20: århundredes Europa,* edited by Jens Holger Schjørring and Jens Torkild Bak, 221–45. København: Anis, 2008.

Avvakumov, Yuri P. "Ukrainian Greek Catholics, Past and Present." In *Churches in the Ukrainian Crisis*, edited by Thomas Bremer and Andrii Krawchuk, 21–44. London: Palgrave Macmillan, 2016.

Bäckström, Anders, et al., eds. *Welfare and Religion in 21st Century Europe, Vol. 1: Configuring the Connections*. Farnham: Ashgate, 2010.

Bailey, Sarah Pulliam. "Some of the U.S.'s Most Important Catholic Leaders Are Condemning Trump's Travel Ban." *Washington Post*, January 30, 2017. https://www.washingtonpost.com/news/acts-of-faith/wp/2017/01/30/some-of-the-u-s-s-most-important-catholic-leaders-are-condemning-trumps-travel-ban/?utm_term=.12667334bf74.

Bandeira, Olívia, and Brenda Carranza. "Reactions to the Pandemic in Latin America and Brazil: Are Religions Essential Services?" *International Journal of Latin American Religions* 4 (2020) 170–93.

Bantjes, Adrian A. "Burning Saints, Molding Minds: Iconoclasm, Civic Ritual, and the Failed Cultural Revolution." In *Rituals of Rule, Rituals of Resistance: Public Celebrations and Popular Culture in Mexico*, edited by William H. Beezley et al., 261–84. Wilmington: SR, 1994.

Battle, Michael. *The Black Church in America: African American Christian Spirituality*. Malden, MA: Blackwell, 2006.

Bays, Daniel H. *A New History of Christianity in China*. Malden, MA: Wiley-Blackwell, 2011.

Beatty, Andrew. "The Pope in Mexico: Syncretism in Public Ritual." *American Anthropologist* 108 (2006) 324–35.

Beeson, Mark, and Matt McDonald, eds. "Special Issue: The Politics of Climate Change in Australia." *Australian Journal of Politics and History* 59 (2013) 331–500.

Behera, Marina Ngursangzeli. "Introduction." In *Interfaith Relations after One Hundred Years: Christian Mission among Other Faiths*, edited by Marina Ngursangzeli Behera, 1–10. Oxford: Regnum, 2011.

Bellah, Robert N. "Civil Religion in America." *Daedalus* 96 (1967) 1–21.

Bellin, Eva. "Faith in Politics: New Trends in the Study of Religion and Politics." *World Politics* 60 (2008) 315–47.

Bender, Courtney. *Religion on the Edge: De-Centering and Re-Centering the Sociology of Religion*. New York: Oxford University Press, 2013.

Berger, Peter L., et al. *Religiøse USA—sekulære Europa? Et tema og variationer*. Frederiksberg: Anis, 2010.

Berlinerblau, Jacques. *Thumpin' It: The Use and Abuse of the Bible in Today's Presidential Politics*. Louisville: Westminster John Knox, 2008.

———. "Why So Little Religious Politicking in This Presidential Election?" https://www.chronicle.com/blogs/brainstorm/why-so-little-religious-politicking-in-this-presidential-election.

Bevans, Stephen B. *Models of Contextual Theology*. Maryknoll: Orbis, 2002.

Beyer, Peter. *Religion and Globalization*. London: Sage, 1994.

———. *Religions in Global Society*. New York: Routledge, 2006.

Binns, John. *An Introduction to the Christian Orthodox Churches*. Cambridge: Cambridge University Press, 2002.

Birman, Patricia. "Conversion from Afro-Brazilian Religions to Neo-Pentecostalism." In *Conversion of a Continent: Contemporary Religious Change in Latin America*, edited by Timothy J. Steigenga and Edward L. Cleary, 115–32. New Brunswick, NJ: Rutgers University Press, 2007.

Blancarte, Roberto J. "The Changing Face of Religion in the Democratization of Mexico: The Case of Catholicism." In *Religious Pluralism, Democracy, and the Catholic Church in Latin America*, edited by Frances Hagopian, 225–56. Notre Dame: University of Notre Dame Press, 2009.

———. "Religion and Constitutional Change in Mexico, 1988–1992." *Social Compass* 40 (1993) 555–69.

Boadi, Adelaide M. A. "Engaging Patriarchy: Pentecostal Gender Ideology and Practices in Nigeria." In *Religion, History, and Politics in Nigeria*, edited by Chima J. Korieh and G. Ugo Nwokeji, 172–79. Lanham, MD: University Press of America, 2005.

Boer, Roland. *Political Myth: On the Use and Abuse of Biblical Themes*. Durham: Duke University Press, 2009.

Boff, Clodovis. "Carismáticos e libertadores na igreja." *Revista Eclesiástica Brasileira* 60 (2008) 36–53.

Bond, Chelsea J., et al. "Now We Say Black Lives Matter but . . . the Fact of the Matter Is, We Are Just Black Matter to Them." *The Medical Journal of Australia* 213 (2020) 248–50.

Boorstein, Michelle. "As Biden Is Sworn in, President of U.S. Bishops Assails Him over Abortion." *Washington Post*, January 21, 2021. https://www.washingtonpost.com/religion/2021/01/20/usccb-bishops-gomez-inauguration-statement-biden-abortion/.

Bowler, Kate. *Blessed: A History of the American Prosperity Gospel*. New York: Oxford University Press, 2013.

Boyd, Lydia. *Preaching Prevention: Born-Again Christianity and the Moral Politics of AIDS in Uganda*. Perspectives on Global Health. Athens: Ohio University Press, 2015.

Brekke, Torkel. *Faithonomics: Religion and the Free Market*. Oxford: Oxford University Press, 2016.

———. *Fundamentalism: Prophecy and Protest in an Age of Globalization*. Cambridge: Cambridge University Press, 2012.

Bremer, Thomas. "Religion in Ukraine: Historical Background and the Present Situation." In *Churches in the Ukrainian Crisis*, edited by Thomas Bremer and Andrii Krawchuk, 3–19. Sveits: Palgrave Macmillan, 2016.

———. "Shoulda, Coulda, Woulda—Missed Opportunities, Lost Chances, Bad Options for the Moscow Patriarchate." *Canadian Slavonic Papers* 62 (2020) 443–51.

Brendemoen, Bernt. "Kristne i Tyrkia—fra maktfaktor til marginal minoritet." In *De kristne i Midtøsten: Kampen for tilhørighet*, edited by Berit Thorbjørnsrud, 75–94. Oslo: Cappelen Damm Akademisk, 2015.

Briggs, Biobele Richards. "Taxation of Pentecostal Churches in Africa: Paradigm of Pentecostals in Uganda." *African Journal of Business Management* 2 (2008) 1–12.

Brubaker, Rogers. "Between Nationalism and Civilizationism: The European Populist Moment in Comparative Perspective." *Ethnic and Racial Studies* 40 (2017) 1191–226.

Bruce, Steve. *Secularization: In Defence of an Unfashionable Theory*. Oxford: Oxford University Press, 2011.

Brüning, Alfons. "Orthodox Autocephaly in Ukraine: The Historical Dimension." In *Churches in the Ukrainian Crisis*, edited by Thomas Bremer and Andrii Krawchuk, 79–101. London: Palgrave Macmillan, 2016.

Brusco, Elizabeth. "The Reformation of Machismo: Ascetism and Masculinity among Columbian Evangelicals." In *Rethinking Protestantism in Latin America*, edited by Virginia Garrard-Burnett and David Stoll, 143–58. Philadelphia: Temple University Press, 1993.

"Cameron Attends RCCG's Festival of Life in London." *The Guardian*, April 27, 2015. https://guardian.ng/news/cameron-attends-rccgs-festival-of-life-in-london/.

Carpenter, Ami C. "Changing Lenses: Conflict Analysis and Mexico's Drug War." *Latin American Politics and Society* 55 (2013) 139–60.

Carranza, Brenda. "Apresentação. Erosão das democracias Latino-Americanas—a ascensão política dos cristãos." *Ciências Sociais e Religião* 22 (2020) 1–17.

Carranza, Brenda, and Christina V. D. Cunha. "Conservative Religious Activism in the Brazilian Congress: Sexual Agendas in Focus." *Social Compass* 65 (2018) 486–502.

Casanova, José. "The Problem of Religion and the Anxieties of European Secular Democracy." In *Religion and Democracy in Contemporary Europe*, edited by Gabriel Motzkin and Yochi Fischer, 63–74. London: Alliance, 2008.

———. *Public Religions in the Modern World*. Chicago: University of Chicago Press, 1994.

———. "Public Religions Revisited." In *Religion: Beyond a Concept*, edited by Hent de Vries, 101–19. New York: Fordham University Press, 2008.

———. "Religion Challenging the Myth of Secular Democracy." In *Religion in the 21st Century: Challenges and Transformations*, edited by Lisbet Christoffersen et al., 19–36. Farnham: Ashgate, 2010.

Casci, Tanita. "Kansas Revives Evolution." *Nature Reviews Genetics* 2 (2001) 238.

Casper, Jayson. "They Will Know We Are Christians by Our Drinks." *Christianity Today*, March 17, 2017. https://www.christianitytoday.com/ct/2017/april/they-will-know-we-are-christians-by-alcohol-muslim-world.html.

"The Catholic Church in America: Earthly Concerns." *The Economist*, August 18, 2012. https://www.economist.com/briefing/2012/08/18/earthly-concerns.

CCME. "Areas of Work." https://ccme.eu/index.php/areas-of-work/.

Chaillot, Christine. "The Role of Pictures, the Veneration of Icons, and the Representation of Christ in Two Oriental Orthodox Churches of the Coptic and Ethiopian Traditions." *Studies of the Department of African Languages and Cultures* 50 (2016) 101–14.

Challand, Benoît. "From Hammer and Sickle to Star and Crescent: The Question of Religion for European Identity and a Political Europe." In *Religion, Politics, and Law in the European Union*, edited by Lucian N. Leustean and John T. S. Madeley, 65–80. New York: Routledge, 2010.

Chesnut, R. Andrew. *Competitive Spirits: Latin America's New Religious Economy*. New York: Oxford University Press, 2003.

———. "Conservative Christian Competitors: Pentecostals and Charismatic Catholics in Latin America's New Religious Economy." *The SAIS Review of International Affairs* 30 (2010) 91–103.

Chitando, Ezra. "Human Sexuality in African Christianity." In *Anthology of African Christianity*, edited by Isabel Apawo Phiri et al., 993–96. Oxford: Regnum, 2016.

"Chris Coons Says Joe Biden Is a Man of Faith." *Washington Post*, August 20, 2020. https://www.washingtonpost.com/video/politics/chris-coons-says-joe-biden-is-a-man-of-faith/2020/08/20/a62ebb60-9bce-4a0b-abdd-fbf3e1ee7d44_video.html.

CIA. "The World Factbook." https://www.cia.gov/the-world-factbook/.

Cimino, Richard. "'No God in Common': American Evangelical Discourse on Islam after 9/11." *Review of Religious Research* 47 (2005) 162–74.

Clarke, Peter. "'Pop-Star' Priests and the Catholic Response to the 'Explosion' of Evangelical Protestantism in Brazil: The Beginning of the End of the 'Walkout'?" *Journal of Contemporary Religion* 14 (1999) 203–16.

Clarke, Sathianathan. *Dalits and Christianity: Subaltern Religion and Liberation Theology in India.* Delhi: Oxford University Press, 1998.

Cleary, Edward L. "The Brazilian Catholic Church and Church-State Relations: Nation Building." *A Journal of Church and State* 39 (1997) 253–72.

———. "The Catholic Charismatic Renewal." In *Conversion of a Continent: Contemporary Religious Change in Latin America,* edited by Timothy J. Steigenga and Edward L. Cleary, 153–73. New Brunswick: Rutgers University Press, 2007.

———. *The Rise of Charismatic Catholicism in Latin America.* Gainesville: University Press of Florida, 2011.

Cohen, Raymond. *Saving the Holy Sepulchre: How Rival Christians Came Together to Rescue Their Holiest Shrine.* Oxford: Oxford University Press, 2008.

Coleman, Simon. "Christianity in Western Europe." In *The Wiley Blackwell Companion to World Christianity,* edited by Lamin Sanneh and Michael J. McClymond, 488–99. Hoboken, NJ: Wiley & Sons, 2016.

Conference of Catholic Bishops in India. "As an Organization." https://ccbi.in/as-an-organisation/.

Congregation for the Clergy. "The Priest, Pastor and Leader of the Parish Community: Instruction." https://www.vatican.va/roman_curia/congregations/cclergy/documents/rc_con_cclergy_doc_20020804_istruzione-presbitero_en.html.

Connor, Phillip. "6 Facts about South Korea's Growing Christian Population." *Pew Research Center,* August 12, 2014. https://www.pewresearch.org/facts-tank/2014/08/12/6-facts-about-christianity-in-south-korea/.

Conomos, Dimitri. "Mount Athos." In *The Encyclopedia of Eastern Orthodox Christianity,* edited by John A. McGuckin, 403–4. Malden, MA: Wiley-Blackwell, 2011.

Corporación Latinobarómetro. "Informe Latinobarómetro Chile 1995–2020." https://www.scribd.com/document/495544221/INFORME-LATINOBAROMETRO-CHILE-1995-2020.

Crocombe, R. G. *The South Pacific.* Suva: University of the South Pacific, 2001.

Cross, Samuel H., and Olgerd P. Sherbowitz-Wetzor, trans and eds. *The Russian Primary Chronicle: Laurentian Text.* Cambridge: Mediaeval Academy of America, 1953.

Crux Staff. "Church in Philippines Emerges as Strongest Opposition Party." *Crux,* August 20, 2017. https://cruxnow.com/global-church/2017/08/church-philippines-emerges-strongest-opposition-party/.

Cumoletti, Mattea, and Jeanne Batalova. "Middle Eastern and North African Immigrants in the United States." https://www.migrationpolicy.org/article/middle-eastern-and-north-african-immigrants-united-states-2016.

Curanovic, Alicja. *The Religious Factor in Russia's Foreign Policy.* London: Routledge, 2012.

Dalby, Douglas. "Catholic Church's Hold on Schools at Issue in Changing Ireland." *New York Times,* January 21, 2016. https://www.nytimes.com/2016/01/22/world/europe/ireland-catholic-baptism-school.html.

Daniel, Wallace L. *The Orthodox Church and Civil Society in Russia*. College Station: Texas A&M University Press, 2006.

Datafolha. "Intenção de voto para presidente da república—25/10/18." http://media.folha.uol.com.br/datafolha/2018/10/26/3416374d208f7def05d1476d05ede73e.pdf.

Daughrity, Dyron B. "The Indianness of Christianity: The Task of Re-Imagination." In *Re-Imagining South Asian Religions: Essays in Honour of Professors Harold G. Coward and Ronald W. Neufeldt*, edited by Pashaura Singh and Michael Hawley, 245–70. Leiden: Brill, 2013.

Daughrity, Dyron B., and Jesudas M. Athyal. *Understanding World Christianity: India*. Minneapolis: Fortress, 2016.

"David Cameron Says the UK Is a Christian Country." *BBC*, December 16, 2011.

Davie, Grace. *Europe, the Exceptional Case: Parameters of Faith in the Modern World*. London: Darton Longman & Todd, 2002.

———. "Europe: The Exception That Proves the Rule?" In *The Desecularization of the World: Resurgent Religion and World Politics*, edited by Peter L. Berger, 65–84. Grand Rapids: Eerdmans, 1999.

———. *Religion in Britain: A Persistent Paradox*. 2nd ed. Chichester: Wiley-Blackwell, 2015.

———. *Religion in Modern Europe: A Memory Mutates*. European Societies. Oxford: Oxford University Press, 2000.

———. "Welfare and Religion in Europe." *Theology* 118 (2015) 10–17.

De Mesa, José M. "Filipino Folk Catholicism, Philippines." In *A Dictionary of Asian Christianity*, edited by Scott W. Sunquist, 291. Cambridge: Eerdmans, 2001.

"Deadly Blast Outside Egypt Church." *Al Jazeera*, January 1, 2011. http://www.aljazeera.com/news/middleeast/2011/01/20111111533958901.html.

"Deaths Inside: Indigenous Australian Death in Custody 2021." *The Guardian*. https://www.theguardian.com/australia-news/ng-interactive/2018/aug/28/deaths-inside-indigenous-australian-deaths-in-custody.

Delgado-Molina, Cecilia. "Evangélicos Y Poder Político En México: Reconfigurando Alianzas Y Antagonismos." *Encartes* 3 (2020) 52–64.

Denysenko, Nicholas. "Explaining Ukrainian Autocephaly: Politics, History, Ecclesiology, and the Future." *Canadian Slavonic Papers* 62 (2020) 426–42.

———. *The Orthodox Church in Ukraine: A Century of Separation*. DeKalb, IL: Northern Illinois University Press, 2018.

———. "Reflections on Resolving Problems in the Ukrainian Church Crisis." *Canadian Slavonic Papers* 62 (2020) 508–15.

Desta, Lemma. "National Report on Migrant and Multicultural Churches in Norway." http://migrantmenigheter.no/national-report-on-migrant-and-multicultural-churches-in-norway/.

Dillon, Michele. "Trends in Catholic Commitment Stable over Time." *National Catholic Reporter*, October 24, 2011. https://www.ncronline.org/news/trends-catholic-commitment-stable-over-time.

Dinham, Adam, and Matthew Francis. *Religious Literacy in Policy and Practice*. Bristol: Policy, 2015.

DiSalvo, Daniel, and Jerome E. Copulsky. "Faith in the Primaries." *Perspectives on Political Science* 38 (2009) 99–106.

Djupe, Paul A., et al. "Are the Politics of the Christian Right Linked to State Rates of the Nonreligious? The Importance of Salient Controversy." *Political Research Quarterly* 71 (2018) 910–22.

Doniger, Wendy. "Foreword: The Vie from the Other Side: Postpostcolonialism, Religious Syncretism, and Class Conflict." In *Popular Christianity in India: Riting between the Lines*, edited by Selva J. Raj and Corinne G. Dempsey, xi–xix. Albany: State University of New York Press, 2002.

Donovan, Todd. "The Irrelevance and (New) Relevance of Religion in Australian Elections." *Australian Journal of Political Science* 49 (2014) 626–46.

Douglas, Steve. "Religious Environmentalism in the West. II: Impediments to the Praxis of Christian Environmentalism in Australia." *Religion Compass* 3 (2009) 717–37.

Dube, Peter. "South Africa to Tax 'Commercial' Churches." *Africa Review*, November 27, 2015.

"Egypt's Coptic Christians Flee Sinai after Killings." *Al Jazeera*, February 26, 2017. https://www.aljazeera.com/news/2017/2/26/egypts-coptic-christians-flee-sinai-after-killings.

Eisenstadt, Shmuel N. "Multiple Modernities." *Daedalus* 129 (2000) 1–30.

ELCJHL. *COCOP Report 2016: Palestinian Women in Church and Society*. Jerusalem: Evangelical Lutheran Church of Jordan and the Holy Land, 2016.

Ellis, Stephen, and Gerrie ter Haar. *Worlds of Power: Religious Thought and Political Practice in Africa*. Studies in Contemporary History and World Affairs 1. New York: Oxford University Press, 2004.

Elsässer, Sebastian. "The Coptic Divorce Struggle in Contemporary Egypt." *Social Compass* 66 (2019) 333–51.

Erasmus. "Diverse, Desperate Migrants Have Divided European Christians." *The Economist*, September 6, 2015. https://www.economist.com/erasmus/2015/09/06/diverse-desperate-migrants-have-divided-european-christians.

Ernst, Manfred. "Changing Christianity in Oceania: A Regional Overview." *Archives de Sciences Sociales des Religions* 57 (2012) 29–45.

Ernst, Manfred, and Anna Anisi. "The Historical Development of Christianity in Oceania." In *The Wiley Blackwell Companion to World Christianity*, edited by Lamin Sanneh and Michael J. McClymond, 588–604. Chichester: Wiley-Blackwell, 2016.

Eshete, Tibese. "Ethiopia, Eritrea, Somalia, and Djibouti." In *Christianity in Sub-Saharan Africa*, edited by Kenneth R. Ross et al., 144–56. Edinburgh: Edinburgh University Press, 2017.

Esquivel, Juan Cruz, et al. "Ateos, agnósticos y creyentes sin religión. Análisis cuantitativo de los sin filiación religiosa en la Argentina." *Sociedad y religión* 30 (2020) 1–24.

"Exit Poll Results and Analysis for the 2020 Presidential Election." *Washington Post*, December 14, 2020. https://www.washingtonpost.com/elections/interactive/2020/exit-polls/presidential-election-exit-polls/.

Fallaw, Ben. *Religion and State Formation in Postrevolutionary Mexico*. Durham: Duke University Press, 2013.

Feagin, Joe R. *The White Racial Frame: Centuries of Racial Framing and Counter-Framing*. New York: Routledge, 2013.

Fer, Yannick. "Religion, Pluralism, and Conflicts in the Pacific Islands." In *Blackwell Companion to Religion and Violence*, edited by A. Murphy, 461–72. Malden, MA: Wiley-Blackwell, 2011.

Ferguson, Adele. "God's Millionaires: Pentecostal Churches Are Not Waiting to Inherit the Earth. They Are Taking It Now, Tax-Free." *Business Review Weekly*, May 26, 2005. http://www.trinityfi.org/press/GodsMillionaires.html.

Ferrari, Silvio. "Law and Religion in Europe." In *Religion in the 21st Century: Challenges and Transformations*, edited by Lisbet Christoffersen et al., 149–62. Farnham: Ashgate, 2010.

———. "State Regulation of Religion in the European Democracies: The Decline of the Old Patterns." In *Religion and Democracy in Contemporary Europe*, edited by Gabriel Motzkin and Yochi Fischer, 103–13. London: Alliance, 2008.

Flam, Helena. "Sexual Abuse of Children by the Catholic Priests in the US: From a 'Charismatic Bureaucracy' to a Governance Regime." *Journal of Political Power* 8 (2015) 385–410.

Flint, Andrew R., and Joy Porter. "Jimmy Carter: The Re-emergence of Faith-Based Politics and the Abortion Rights Issue." *Presidential Studies Quarterly* 35 (2005) 28–51.

Fordham, Helen. "Curating a Nation's Past: The Role of the Public Intellectual in Australia's History Wars." *M/C Journal* 18 (2015). https://doi.org/10.5204/mcj.1007.

Forman, Charles W. *The Island Churches of the South Pacific: Emergence in the Twentieth Century*. Maryknoll, NY: Orbis, 1982.

Formicola, Jo Renee. "Catholic Moral Demands in American Politics: A New Paradigm." *Journal of Church and State* 51 (2009) 4.

———. "The Vatican, the American Bishops, and the Church-State Ramifications of Clerical Sexual Abuse." *Journal of Church and State* 46 (2004) 479–502.

Fox, Jonathan. *Political Secularism, Religion, and the State: A Time Series Analysis of Worldwide Data*. Cambridge: Cambridge University Press, 2015.

———. *A World Survey of Religion and the State*. Cambridge: Cambridge University Press, 2008.

Francis, Pope. *Evangelii Gaudium*. https://www.vatican.va/content/francesco/en/apost_exhortations/documents/papa-francesco_esortazione-ap_20131124_evangelii-gaudium.html.

Francis, Pope, and Ahmad Al-Tayyeb. "A Document on Human Fraternity for World Peace and Living Together." https://www.vatican.va/content/francesco/en/travels/2019/outside/documents/papa-francesco_20190204_documento-fratellanza-umana.html.

Francisco, José Mario C. "The Philippines." In *Christianities in Asia*, edited by Peter C. Phan, 98–127. Chichester: Wiley-Blackwell, 2011.

Fraser, Valerie. "Accommodating Religious Tourism: The Case of the Basilica of the Virgin of Guadalupe in Mexico." *Interiors* 6 (2015) 329–50.

Freeman, Dena. *Pentecostalism and Development: Churches, NGOs, and Social Change in Africa*. Basingstoke: Palgrave Macmillan, 2012.

French, Todd E. "Orthodoxy in the Ukraine." In *The Encyclopedia of Eastern Orthodox Christianity*, edited by John A. McGuckin, 604–6. Chichester: Wiley-Blackwell, 2011.

Freston, Paul. "Researching the Heartland of Pentecostalism: Latin Americans at Home and Abroad." *Fieldwork in Religion* 3 (2010) 122–44.

———. "The Universal Church of the Kingdom of God: A Brazilian Church Finds Success in Southern Africa." *Journal of Religion in Africa* 35 (2005) 33–65.

Frigerio, Alejandro. "Analyzing Conversion in Latin America." In *Conversion of a Continent: Contemporary Religious Change in Latin America*, edited by Timothy J. Steigenga and Edward L. Cleary, 33–51. New Brunswick: Rutgers University Press, 2007.

Frykenberg, Robert Eric. *Christianity in India: From Beginnings to the Present.* Oxford: Oxford University Press, 2008.

Gardiner-Garden, John. *The 1967 Referendum: History and Myths.* https://parlinfo.aph.gov.au/parlInfo/search/display/display.w3p;query=Id%3A%22library%2Fprspub%2FFJTZM6%22;src1=sm1.

Garret, John. *Footsteps in the Sea: Christianity in Oceania to World War II.* Suva: Institute of Pacific Studies, 1992.

Gastón, Espinosa. "Today We Act, Tomorrow We Vote: Latino Religions, Politics, and Activism in Contemporary U.S. Civil Society." *The Annals of the American Academy of Political and Social Science* 612 (2007) 152–71.

George, Him, and Kim Huynh. *The Culture Wars: Australian and American Politics in the 21st Century.* South Yarra: Palgrave Macmillan, 2009.

Gifford, Paul. *African Christianity: Its Public Role.* Bloomington: Indiana University Press, 1998.

———. *Ghana's New Christianity: Pentecostalism in a Globalising African Economy.* London: Hurst, 2004.

———. "Introduction: Democratisation and the Churches." In *The Christian Churches and the Democratisation of Africa*, edited by Paul Gifford, 1–14. Leiden: Brill, 1995.

Gill, Anthony. *Rendering unto Caesar: The Catholic Church and the State in Latin America.* Chicago: University of Chicago Press, 1998.

Gill, Lesley. *The School of the Americas: Military Training and Political Violence in the Americas.* Durham: Duke University Press, 2004.

Gluth, James L. "Religion and American Public Opinion: Foreign Policy Issues." In *Oxford Handbook of Religion and American Politics*, edited by Corwin E. Smidt et al., 243–65. Oxford: Oxford University Press, 2009.

Göçmen, İpek. "The Role of Faith-Based Organizations in Social Welfare Systems: A Comparison of France, Germany, Sweden, and the United Kingdom." *Nonprofit and Voluntary Sector Quarterly* 42 (2013) 495–516.

González, Ana Marta, et al., eds. *Frontiers of Globalization: Kinship and Family Structures in Africa.* Trenton, NJ: Africa World, 2011.

González, Ondina E., and Justo L. González. *Christianity in Latin America: A History.* Cambridge: Cambridge University Press, 2008.

Gooren, Henri. "Conversion Careers in Latin America." In *Conversion of a Continent: Contemporary Religious Change in Latin America*, edited by Timothy J. Steigenga and Edward L. Cleary, 52–71. New Brunswick, NJ: Rutgers University Press, 2007.

Grant, Peter. "Now for Sale in Chicago: Prime Catholic Church Real Estate." *Wall Street Journal*, May 18, 2016. https://www.wsj.com/articles/now-for-sale-in-chicago-prime-catholic-church-real-estate-1463506522.

Gross, Toomas. "Changing Faith: The Social Costs of Protestant Conversion in Rural Oaxaca." *Ethnos* 77 (2012) 344–71.

Grossi, Miriam Pillar, and Rodrigo Toniol. *Cientistas sociais e o coronavírus.* São Paulo: ANPOCS, 2020.

Grung, Anne Hege. "De kristne i Libanon: Et tegn på håp?" In *De kristne i Midtøsten: Kampen for tilhørighet*, edited by Berit Thorbjørnsrud, 157–72. Oslo: Cappelen Damm Akademisk, 2015.

Grzymała-Busse, Anna. *Nations under God: How Churches Use Moral Authority to Influence Policy*. Princeton: Princeton University Press, 2015.

———. "Poland Is a Catholic Country: So Why Are Mass Protests Targeting Churches?" *Washington Post*, October 28, 2020. https://www.washingtonpost.com/politics/2020/10/28/poland-is-catholic-country-so-why-are-mass-protests-targeting-churches/.

Gundelach, Peter. "The Impact of Economic Deprivation and Regional Differences on Individual Secularization in Western Europe." *Nordic Journal of Religion and Society* 27 (2014) 131–50.

Gunn, Joshua, and Mark Lawrence McPhail. "Coming Home to Roost: Jeremiah Wright, Barack Obama, and the (Re)Signing of (Post) Racial Rhetoric." *Rhetoric Society Quarterly* 45 (2015) 1–24.

Guth, Stephan. "Kristnes bidrag til islamsk kultur og arabisk identitet." In *De kristne i Midtøsten: Kampen for tilhørighet*, edited by Berit Thorbjørnsrud, 57–74. Oslo: Cappelen Damm Akademisk, 2015.

Haar, Gerrie ter, and Stephen Ellis. "The Role of Religion in Development: Towards a New Relationship between the European Union and Africa." *The European Journal of Development Research* 18 (2006) 351–67.

Hackett, Rosalind. "Discourses of the Demonization in Africa and Beyond." *Diogenes* 50 (2003) 61–75.

———. "Traditional, African, Religious, Freedom?" In *Politics of Religious Freedom*, edited by Winnifred Fallers Sullivan et al., 89–101. Chicago: Chicago University Press, 2015.

Hadaway, C. Kirk. "2008 Presidential Address: Congregationally-Based Religion: Boon or Bane for Faith in the West?" *Review of Religious Research* 52 (2009) 117–33.

Hadj-Abdou, Leila. "The 'Religious Conversion' of the Freedom Party." In *Saving the People: How Populists Hijack Religion*, edited by Nadia Marzouki et al., 29–45. London: Hurst, 2016.

Hagopian, Frances. "Introduction: The New Landscape." In *Religious Pluralism, Democracy, and the Catholic Church in Latin America*, edited by Frances Hagopian, 1–66. Notre Dame: University of Notre Dame Press, 2008.

———. "Social Justice, Moral Values, or Institutional Interests? Church Responses to the Democratic Challenge in Latin America." In *Religious Pluralism, Democracy, and the Catholic Church in Latin America*, edited by Frances Hagopian, 257–334. Notre Dame: University of Notre Dame Press, 2009.

Harding, Susan F. "American Protestant Moralism and the Secular Imagination: From Temperance to the Moral Majority." *Social Research* 76 (2009) 1277–306.

Hartch, Todd. *The Rebirth of Latin American Christianity*. Oxford: Oxford University Press, 2014.

Harvey, Paul, and Philip Goff. *The Columbia Documentary History of Religion in America since 1945*. New York: Columbia University Press, 2005.

Hasset, Miranda K. *Anglican Communion in Crisis: How Episcopal Dissidents and Their African Allies Are Reshaping Anglicanism*. Princeton: Princeton University Press, 2007.

Hasson, Nir. "New Details Emerge on Greek Orthodox Church's Massive Asset Sell-Off in Israel—And the Mystery Only Deepens." *Haaretz*, October 20, 2017. https://www.haaretz.com/israel-news/new-details-emerge-on-greek-orthodox-churchs-fire-sale-in-israel-1.5460636.

Hatuqa, Dalia. "Holy Land for Sale." https://foreignpolicy.com/2019/01/07/holy-land-for-sale/.

Hazran, Yusri. "Emigration of Christians from the Arab Middle East: A New Reading." *The Journal of the Middle East and Africa* 10 (2019) 189–210.

Heelas, Paul, and Linda Woodhead. *The Spiritual Revolution: Why Religion Is Giving Way to Spirituality*. Malden, MA: Blackwell, 2005.

Hellestveit, Cecilie. *Syria: En stor krig i en liten verden*. Oslo: Pax, 2017.

Henderson, Barney. "Jacob Zuma Blames Christianity for South Africa's Problems." *The Telegraph*, December 21, 2011. https://www.telegraph.co.uk/news/world news/8971472/Jacob-Zuma-blames-Christianity-for-South-Africas-problems. html.

Heneghan, Tom. "Merkel Urges Germans: Stand Up for Christian Values." *Reuters*, November 15, 2010. https://www.reuters.com/article/us-germany-cdu-christianity/merkel-urges-germans-stand-up-for-christian-values-idINTRE6AE3K520101115.

Hervieu-Léger, Danièle. *Religion as a Chain of Memory*. New Brunswick, NJ: Rutgers University Press, 2000.

Heuser, Andreas. "Encoding Caesar's Realm—Variants of Spiritual Warfare Politics." In *Pentecostalism in Africa: Presence and Impact of Pneumatic Christianity in Postcolonial Societies*, edited by Martin Lindhardt, 270–90. Leiden: Brill, 2014.

Hewitt, W. E. "Popular Movements, Resource Demobilization, and the Legacy of Vatican Restructuring in the Archdiocese of São Paulo." *Canadian Journal of Latin American and Caribbean Studies* 18 (1993) 1–24.

Hien, Josef. "From Private to Religious Patriarchy: Gendered Consequences of Faith-Based Welfare Provision in Germany." *Politics and Religion* 10 (2017) 515–42.

———. "The Return of Religion? The Paradox of Faith-Based Welfare Provision in a Secular Age." MPIfG Discussion Paper 14/9, Max Planck Institute for the Study of Societies, 2014. https://www.econstor.eu/bitstream/10419/97179/1/785290907.pdf.

"Hillary Rodham Clinton: By the Book." *New York Times*, June 11, 2014. https://www.nytimes.com/2014/06/15/books/review/hillary-rodham-clinton-by-the-book.html?mtrref=www.google.com&gwh=81A979641DN8F92FD0A84ADD649A70 2E&gwt=pay.

"HIV and AIDS in East and Southern Africa Regional Overview." http://www.avert.org/professionals/hiv-around-world/sub-saharan-africa/overview.

Hogan, Tom. "Bush Political Philosopher." *YouTube*, February 23, 2013. https://www.youtube.com/watch?v=xMiP9zfqlTI.

Hooper, John. "Pope Attacks 'Globalisation of Indifference' in Lampedusa Visit." *The Guardian*, July 8, 2013. https://www.theguardian.com/world/2013/jul/08/pope-globalisation-of-indifference-lampedusa.

Hoornaert, Eduardo, et al. *História da igreja no Brasil: Ensaio de interpretação a partir do povo*. Petrópolis: Editora Vozes, 1977.

Horsfjord, Vebjørn L. "Negotiating Traditional Values: The Russian Orthodox Church at the United Nations Human Rights Council (UNHRC)." In *Religion, State, and the United Nations*, edited by Anne Stensvold, 62–78. London: Routledge, 2017.

———. "Religionspolitikk i Europa." *Teologisk tidsskrift* 2 (2013) 337–59.

Htun, Mala. "Life, Liberty, and Family Values." In *Religious Pluralism, Democracy, and the Catholic Church in Latin America*, edited by Frances Hagopian, 335–64. Notre Dame: University of Notre Dame Press, 2009.

Hughes, Jennifer Scheper. "Contemporary Popular Catholicism in Latin America." In *The Cambridge History of Religions in Latin America*, edited by Virginia Garrard-Burnett et al., 480–90. New York: Cambridge University Press, 2016.

Human Rights Watch. "Unequal and Unprotected: Women's Rights under Lebanese Personal Status Laws." https://www.hrw.org/report/2015/01/19/unequal-and-unprotected/womens-rights-uner-lebanese-personal-status-laws.

Hunt, Stephen. "Introduction." In *Handbook of Global Contemporary Christianity: Themes and Developments in Culture, Politics, and Society*, edited by Stephen Hunt, 1–28. Leiden: Brill, 2015.

Huntington, Samuel P. *The Clash of Civilizations and the Remaking of World Order*. New York: Simon & Schuster, 1996.

———. "The Clash of Civilizations?" *Foreign Affairs* 72 (1993) 22–49.

Hurd, Elizabeth Shakman. "Religious Freedom, American-Style." *Quaderni di Diritto e Politica Ecclesiastica* 1 (2014) 231–42.

Imo, Cyril. "Evangelicals, Muslims, and Democracy." In *Evangelical Christianity and Democracy in Africa*, edited by Terence Ranger, 37–67. Oxford: Oxford University Press, 2008.

Inglehart, Ronald. *Religion's Sudden Decline: What's Causing It, and What Comes Next?* New York: Oxford University Press, 2021.

Institutio Brasileiro de Geografia e Estatística. *Censo demográfico 2010*. https://biblioteca.ibge.gov.br/visualizacao/periodicos/94/cd_2010_religiao_deficiencia.pdf

"Islam and Alcohol: Tipsy Taboo." *The Economist*, August 18, 2012. https://www.economist.com/international/2012/08/18/tipsy-taboo?fsrc=scn%2Frd_ec%2Ftipsy_taboo.

Jackson, Darrel, and Alessia Passarelli. *Mapping Migration: Mapping Churches' Responses in Europe*. Brussels: Churches' Commission for Migrants in Europe and World Council of Churches, 2016.

Jeffrey, Terence P. "Obama: Sermon on Mount Justifies Same-Sex Unions." https://cnsnews.com/news/article/obama-sermon-mount-justifies-same-sex-unions.

Jenkins, Philip. "Godless Europe?" *International Bulletin of Missionary Research* 31 (2007) 115–20.

———. *The Next Christendom: The Coming of Global Christianity*. 3rd ed. New York: Oxford University Press, 2011.

Johnson, Ian. "Decapitated Churches in China's Christians Heartland." *New York Times*, May 21, 2016. https://www.nytimes.com/2016/05/22/world/asia/china-christians-zhejiang.html.

Johnson, Jenna. "Donald Trump Likes That Proverbs Verse That Might Not Exist." *Washington Post*, September 16, 2015. https://www.washingtonpost.com/news/post-politics/wp/2015/09/16/donald-trump-likes-that-proverbs-verse-that-might-not-exist/?noredirect=on&utm_term=.6ac2bd3bc23.

Johnson, Marilynn. "The Quiet Revival New Immigrants and the Transformation of Christianity in Greater Boston." *Religion and American Culture: A Journal of Interpretation* 24 (2014) 231–58.

Johnston, Douglas M. "American Evangelical Islamophobia: A History of Continuity with a Hope for Change." *Journal of Ecumenical Studies* 51 (2016) 165–73.

Jokhadar, Carmen. "Residents of Historic Syrian Town Remain Resilient in Face of War." http://www.al-monitor.com/pulse/culture/2014/02/syria-christians-saidnaya -resilient-war.html#.

Joseph, John. *The Modern Assyrians of the Middle East: Encounters with Western Christian Missions, Archaeologists, and Colonial Power.* Leiden: Brill, 2000.

Kalman, Matthew. "A Palestinian Brewery Grows in the West Bank." *Time*, October 8, 2009.

Kalu, Ogbu. *African Pentecostalism: An Introduction.* Oxford: Oxford University Press, 2008.

Kaoma, Kapya John. *Colonizing African Values: How the U.S. Christian Right is Transforming Sexual Politics in Africa.* Somerville, MA: Political Research Associates, 2012.

Karlsson, Bengt G. "Entering into the Christian Charma: Contemporary 'Tribal' Conversions in India." In *Christians, Cultural Interactions, and India's Religious Traditions*, edited by Judith M. Brown and Robert Eric Frykenberg, 133–53. London: RoutledgeCurzon, 2002.

Kårtveit, Bård H. "'In Fifteen Years There'll Be None of Us Left!': Dilemmas of Attachment, Resilience, and Migration among the Christians of Bethlehem." PhD diss., University of Bergen, 2010.

———. "Tilhørighet og utvandring blant kristne palestinere." In *De kristne i Midtøsten: Kampen for tilhørighet*, edited by Berit Thorbjørnsrud, 95–114. Oslo: Cappelen Damm Akademisk, 2015.

Katz, Itmar, and Ruth Kark. "The Church and Landed Property: The Greek Orthodox Patriarchate of Jerusalem." *Middle Eastern Studies* 43 (2007) 383–408.

Khalel, Sheren, and Matthew Vickery. "Syria's Christians Fight Back." https://foreignpolicy. com/2015/02/24/syrias-christians-fight-back-assyrian-militias/.

Khatib, Line. *Islamic Revivalism in Syria: The Rise and Fall of Ba'thist Secularism.* London: Routledge, 2011.

Khoury, Fouad I. *Imams and Emirs: State, Religion, and Sects in Islam.* London: Saqi, 1990.

Kilpatrick, Hilary. "Monasteries through Muslim Eyes: The Diyarat Books." In *Christians at the Heart of Islamic Rule: Church Life and Scholarship in 'Abbasid Iraq*, edited by David Thomas, 19–37. Leiden: Brill, 2003.

Kim, Sebastian C. H., and Kersteen Kim. *Christianity as a World Religion: An Introduction.* 2nd ed. London: Bloomsbury, 2016.

Kloster, Sven Thore. "Norske persepsjoner av kristne i Midtøsten: Fremmede, fiender, forfulgte eller følgesvenner?" In *De kristne i Midtøsten: Kampen for tilhørighet*, edited by Berit Thorbjørnsrud, 237–58. Oslo: Cappelen Damm Akademisk, 2015.

———. "Om forfulgte kristne—den vanskelige diskursen." *Kirke og kultur* 118 (2013) 12–26.

Knox, Zoe. *Russian Society and the Orthodox Church: Religion in Russia after Communism.* London: RoutledgeCurzon, 2005.

Knutsen, Torbjørn L., and Jennifer L. Bailey. "Protestantismens arv og liberalismens politikk: Et blikk på USAs religiøse liv." *Internasjonal Politikk* 66 (1998) 319–48.

Kochan, Natalia. "Shaping Ukrainian Identity: The Churches in the Socio-Political Crisis." In *Churches in the Ukrainian Crisis*, edited by Thomas Bremer and Andrii Krawchuk, 105–21. London: Palgrave Macmillan, 2016.

Koepping, Elizabeth. "India, Pakistan, Bangladesh, Burma/Myanmar." In *Christianities in Asia*, edited by Peter C. Phan, 9–42. Chichester: Wiley-Blackwell, 2011.

Kollman, Paul. "Classifying African Christianities: Past, Present, and Future: Part One." *Journal of Religion in Africa* 40 (2010) 3–32.

Krawchuk, Andrii. "The Orthodox Church of Ukraine on the Inter-Orthodox Agenda at Amman: The Dynamics of Ecclesiastical Recognition." *Canadian Slavonic Papers* 62 (2020) 463–76.

———. "Redefining Orthodox Identity in Ukraine after the Euromaidan." In *Churches in the Ukrainian Crisis*, edited by Thomas Bremer and Andrii Krawchuk, 175–202. London: Palgrave Macmillan, 2016.

Kristensen, Regnar A. "La Santa Muerte in Mexico City: The Cult and Its Ambiguities." *Journal of Latin American Studies* 47 (2015) 543–66.

Krogstad, Jens M., and Jynnah Radford. "Key Facts about Refugees to the U.S." *Pew Research Center*, October 17, 2019. http://www.pewresearch.org/fact-tank/2017/01/30/key-facts-about-refugees-to-the-u-s/.

Kverme, Kai. "Patriarken, generalen og doktoren: ulike visjoner for Libanons fremtid." In *De kristne i Midtøsten: Kampen for tilhørighet*, edited by Berit Thorbjørnsrud, 173–92. Oslo: Cappelen Damm Akademisk, 2015.

Laborde, Antonia. ""La gente te mira raro cuando dices que te casas por la Iglesia."" *El País*, January 10, 2017. https://elpais.com/politica/2016/12/19/actualidad/1482162082_252517.html?rel=buscador_noticias.

Lange, Raeburn. *Island Ministers: Indigenous Leadership in Nineteenth Century Pacific Islands Christianity*. Canberra: Pandanus, 2005.

Langston, Scott M. *Exodus through the Centuries*. Malden, MA: Blackwell, 2006.

Larraquy, Marcelo. *Código Francisco*. Buenos Aires: Penguin Random House, 2016.

Larsen, Fredrik. "Australia besto en gang av 500 'nasjoner': Så kom katastrofen som ødela alt." *Aftenposten Historie*, January 24, 2021. https://www.aftenposten.no/historie/i/jBLkan/australia-besto-en-gang-av-500-nasjoner-saa-kom-katastronfen-som-end.

Lazo de la Vega, Sandra, and Timothy J. Steigenga. "Indigenous Peoples: Religious Change and Political Awakening." In *The Cambridge History of Religions in Latin America*, edited by Virginia Garrard-Burnett et al., 559–90. New York: Cambridge University Press, 2016.

"Lebanon Net Migration Rate 1950–2021." https://www.macrotrends.net/countries/LBN/lebanon/net-migration.

Leis-Peters, Anette. "The German Dilemma: Protestant Agents of Welfare in Reutlingen." In *Welfare and Religion in 21st Century Europe, Vol. 1: Configuring the Connections*, edited by Anders Bäckström et al., 95–112. Farnham: Ashgate, 2010.

Lende, Gina. "City of Gods and Goods: Exploring Religious Pluralism in the Neoliberal City." In *Routledge International Handbook of Religion in Global Society*, edited by Jayeel Cornelio et al., 374–85. London: Routledge, 2020.

———. "The Rise of Pentecostal Power: Exploring the Politics of Pentecostal Growth in Nigeria and Guatemala." PhD diss., MF Norwegian School of Theology, 2015.

Leustean, Lucian N., and John T. S. Madeley. *Religion, Politics, and Law in the European Union*. London: Routledge 2010.

Levine, Daniel H. "The Future of Christianity in Latin America." *Journal of Latin American Studies* 41 (2009) 121–45.

Levitsky, Steven, and Kenneth M. Roberts. *The Resurgence of the Latin American Left*. Baltimore: Johns Hopkins University Press, 2011.

Lia, Brynjar. "Korsfarernes medløpere eller lydige undersåtter? Jihadistbevegelsens syn på kristne minoriteter i Midtøsten." In *De kristne i Midtøsten: Kampen for tilhørighet*, edited by Berit Thorbjørnsrud, 193–214. Oslo: Cappelen Damm Akademisk, 2015.

Lincoln, Bruce. *Holy Terrors: Thinking about Religion after September 11*. Chicago: University of Chicago Press, 2009.

Lindsley, Lisa. "The Beagle Channel Settlement: Vatican Mediation Resolves a Century-Old Dispute." *Journal of Church and State* 29 (1987) 435–55.

Lipka, Michael. "Key Findings about American Catholics." *Pew Research Center*, September 2, 2015. https://www.pewresearch.org/fact-tank/2015/09/02/key-find ings-about-american-catholics/.

Livingston, Jonathan N., et al. "Feeling No Ways Tired: A Resurgence of Activism in the African American Community." *Journal of Black Studies* 48 (2017) 279–304.

Lodwick, Kathleen L. *How Christianity Came to China: A Brief History*. Minneapolis: Fortress, 2016.

Løland, Ole Jakob. "Hugo Chávez's Appropriation of the Liberationist Legacy in Latin America." *Relegere: Studies in Religion and Reception* 6 (2016) 123–60.

———. *Lidio: En uvanlig historie*. Oslo: Spartacus, 2009.

———. "Obamas effektive bibel." *Kirke og Kultur* 119 (2014) 113–26.

———. "Om gjenfødelsen i Latin-Amerika." *Teologisk Tidsskrift* 5 (2016) 400–19.

———. "The Political Conditions and Theological Foundations of the New Christian Right in Brazil." *Iberoamericana: Nordic Journal of Latin American and Caribbean Studies* 49 (2020) 63–73.

———. "The Position of the Biblical Canon in Brazil: From Catholic Rediscovery to Neo-Pentecostal Marginalisation." *Studies in World Christianity* 21 (2015) 98–118.

Lomnitz, Claudio. "Secularism and the Mexican Revolution." In *Beyond the Secular West*, edited by Akeel Bilgrami, 97–116. New York: Columbia University Press, 2016.

Longest, Kyle C., and Christian Smith. "Conflicting or Compatible: Beliefs about Religion and Science among Emerging Adults in the United States." *Sociological Forum* 26 (2011) 846–69.

Loos, Noel, "The Australian Board of Missions, the Anglican Church, and the Aborigines, 1850–1900." *Journal of Religious History* 17 (1992) 194–209.

Louth, Andrew. "The Patristic Revival and Its Protagonists." *The Cambridge Companion to Orthodox Christian Theology*, edited by Mary B. Cunningham and Elizabeth Theokritoff, 188–202. Cambridge: Cambridge University Press, 2008.

Lubaale, Nicta. "Independents." In *Christianity in Sub-Saharan Africa*, edited by Kenneth R. Ross et al., 252–63. Edinburgh: Edinburgh University Press, 2017.

Maddox, Marion. *God under Howard: The Rise of the Religious Right in Australian Politics*. Crows Nest: Allen & Unwin, 2005.

———. "Right-Wing Christian Intervention in a Naive Polity: The Australian Christian Lobby." *Australian Journal of Political Science* 49 (2014) 132–50.

Magowan, Fiona, and Carolyn Schwartz. "Introduction: Spiritual Renewal and beyond in the Australia-Pacific Region." In *Christianity, Conflict, and Renewal in Australia and the Pacific*, edited by Fiona Magowan and Carolyn Schwartz, 1–19. Leiden: Brill, 2006.

Mahmood, Saba. "Religious Freedom, the Minority Question, and Geopolitics in the Middle East." *Comparative Studies in Society and History* 54 (2012) 418–46.

Mallimaci, Fortunato, et al. "Religiones y creencias en Argentina (2008–2019): Resultados de la segunda encuesta nacional de creencias y actitudes religiosas en Argentina." *Sociedad y Religión* 30 (2020) 1–31.

Manchin, Robert. "Religion in Europe: Trust Not Filling the Pews." *Gallup*, September 21, 2004. http://news.gallup.com/poll/13117/religion-europe-trust-filling-pews.aspx.

Mandes, Sławomir, and Maria Rogaczewska. "'I Don't Reject the Catholic Church—The Catholic Church Rejects Me': How Twenty- and Thirty-Somethings in Poland Re-evaluate Their Religion." *Journal of Contemporary Religion* 28 (2013) 259–76.

Marshall, Ruth. *Political Spiritualities: The Pentecostal Revolution in Nigeria*. Chicago: University of Chicago Press, 2009.

Marzouki, Nadia, et al. eds. *Saving the People: How Populists Hijack Religion*. London: Hurst & Company, 2016.

Matovina, Timothy M. *Latino Catholicism: Transformation in America's Largest Church*. Princeton: Princeton University Press, 2012.

Matthee, Rudi. "Alcohol in the Islamic Middle East: Ambivalence and Ambiguity." *Past & Present* 222 (2014) 100–25.

McCauley, John F. "Africa's New Big Man Rule? Pentecostalism and Patronage in Ghana." *African Affairs* 112 (2012) 1–21.

McConnell, M. W. "Establishment and Disestablishment at the Founding, Part I: Establishment of Religion." *William and Mary Law Review* 44 (2003) 2105–208.

McDermott, Dan. "Shaping the Church, Shaping the City." *NIMEP Insights* 2 (2006) 44–54.

McDougall, Debra. "Saving States, Saving Souls: Australian Interventions in Solomon Islands." In *Christianity, Conflict, and Renewal in Australia and the Pacific*, edited by Fiona Magowan and Carolyn Schwartz, 255–77. Leiden: Brill, 2016.

McElwee, Joshua J. "Archbishop Warns of 'Balkanization' in US Church." *National Catholic Reporter*, June 2, 2014. https://www.ncronline.org/news/politics/archbishop-warns-balkanization-us-church.

———. "Francis Appoints Indianapolis' Tobin as Archbishop of Newark, First Cardinal in Archdiocese's History." *National Catholic Reporter*, November 7, 2016. https://www.ncronline.org/news/vatican/francis-appoints-new-cardinal-tobin-archbishop-newark.

McGuckin, John A. "Patriarchate of Constantinople." In *The Encyclopedia of Eastern Orthodox Christianity*, edited by John A. McGuckin, 135–42. Chichester: Wiley-Blackwell, 2011.

Melanchthon, Monica J. "The Servant in the Book of Judith: Interpreting Her Silence, Telling Her Story." In *Dalit Theology in the Twenty-First Century: Discordant Voices, Discerning Pathways*, edited by Sathianathan Clarke et al., 231–51. New Dehli: Oxford University Press, 2010.

Melo, Sydnei. "Deus, a Bíblia e os evangélicos na constituinte (1987–1988)." *Caminhando* 23 (2018) 81–105.

Merz, Johannes. "Mediating Transcendence: Popular Film, Visuality, and Religious Experience in West Africa." In *New Media and Religious Transformations in Africa*, edited by Rosalind Hackett and Benjamin Soares, 99–115. Bloomington: Indiana University Press, 2015.

Meyer, Birgit. "Christianity in Africa: From African Independent to Pentecostal-Charismatic Churches." *Annual Review of Anthropology* 33 (2004) 447–74.

———. "Pentecostalism and Globalization." In *Studying Global Pentecostalism: Theories and Methods*, edited by Michael Bergunder et al., 113–32. Berkeley: University of California Press, 2010.

Mickens, Robert. "The Vocations Shortage Has Become an Acute Crisis." *National Catholic Reporter*, July 6, 2015. https://www.ncronline.org/blogs/roman-observer/vocations-shortage-has-become-acute-crisis.

Micklethwait, John, and Adrian Wooldridge. *God Is Back: How the Global Revival of Faith Is Changing the World*. New York: Penguin, 2009.

Mikaelsson, Lisbeth. "Gjenfødsel på caminoen til Santiago de Compostela." *DIN—Tidsskrift for religion og kultur* (2011) 94–108.

Miller, Duane A., and Patrick Johnstone. "Believers in Christ from a Muslim Background: A Global Census." *Interdisciplinary Journal of Research on Religion* 11 (2015) 1–19.

Miller, Robert J., et al. *Discovering Indigenous Lands: The Doctrine of Discovery in the English Colonies*. Oxford: Oxford University Press, 2012.

Minority Rights Group International. "World Directory of Minorities and Indigenous Peoples: Jordan–Christians." http://minorityrights.org/minorities/christians-2/.

Moffett, Samuel H. *A History of Christianity in Asia*. Vol. 1. Maryknoll, NY: Orbis, 1998.

"A Moment of Truth: A Word of Faith, Hope, and Love from the Heart of Palestinian Suffering." http://kairospalestine.ps/index.php/about-us/kairos-palestine-document.

Montefiore, Simon S. *Jerusalem: The Biography*. New York: Knopf, 2011.

Morales Cano, Lucero, and Avis Mysyk. "Cultural Tourism, the State, and Day of the Dead." *Annals of Tourism Research* 31 (2004) 879–98.

Morán Faúndes, José Manuel, et al. "Strategies of Self-Proclaimed Pro-life Groups in Argentina: Effect of New Religious Actors on Sexual Policies." *Latin American Perspectives* 43 (2016) 144–62.

Mordechai, Nisan. *Minorities in the Middle East: A History of Struggle and Self-Expression*. 2nd ed. Jefferson, NC: McFarland & Co., 2002.

Morello, Gustavo. "Transformations in Argentinean Catholicism, from the Second Half of the Twentieth Century to Pope Francis." In *Secularisms in a Postsecular Age? Religiosities and Subjectivities in Comparative Perspective*, edited by José Mapril et al., 231–51. Cham: Springer International, 2017.

Morgan, Kimberly J. "The Religious Foundations of Work-Family Policies in Western Europe." In *Religion, Class Coalitions, and Welfare States*, edited by Kees van Kersbergen and Philip Manow, 56–90. New York: Cambridge University Press 2009.

Mourão, Paulo R. "Determinants of the Number of Catholic Priests to Catholics in Europe—An Economic Explanation." *Review of Religious Research* 52 (2011) 427–38.

Moyn, Samuel. "Religious Freedom and the Fate of Secularism." In *Religion, Secularism, & Constitutional Democracy*, edited by Jean L. Cohen and Cécile Laborde, 27–46. New York: Columbia University Press, 2016.

Muketha, Dorcas K. "Ameru Women's Spirituality: Negotiation of Spiritual Practices among Methodist and Pentecostal Church Christian Women in Igembe Constituency." PhD diss., MF Norwegian School of Theology, 2016.

Müller, Jan. "The End of Christian Democracy: What the Movement's Decline Means for Europe." https://www.foreignaffairs.com/articles/western-europe/2014-07-15/end-christian-democracy.

Napolitano, Valentina. "The Virgin of Guadalupe: A Nexus of Affect." *The Journal of the Royal Anthropological Institute* 15 (2009) 96–112.

Natarajan, Swaminathan. "Indian Dalits Find No Refuge from Caste in Christianity." *BBC*, September 14, 2010. https://www.bbc.com/news/world-south-asia-11229170.

Navarro, Carlos G. "Religious Change in Mexico: Perspectives from Recent Data." *Social Sciences and Missions* 24 (2011) 75–100.

NCLS Research. "Australian Church Attenders on Overseas Mission Trips 2015–2016." https://shop.ncls.org.au/media/1173/ncls-fact-sheet-17010-attenders-on-mission-trips-in-2016.pdf.

———. "Most Churchgoers Say Climate Change Is Happening and Steps Should Be Taken to Respond." http://www.ncls.org.au/news/views-on-climate-change.

Nelavala, Surekha. "Visibility of Her Sins: Reading the 'Sinful Woman' in Luke 7:36–50 from a Dalit Feminist Perspective." In *Dalit Theology in the Twenty-First Century: Discordant Voices, Discerning Pathways*, edited by Sathianathan Clarke et al., 252–65. New Dehli: Oxford University Press, 2010.

Nesbit, Jeff. "Donald Trump Vowed to Close the Gap between Church and State." *Time*, August 15, 2016. http://time.com/4452309/trumps-evangelical-voters/. retrieved December 20, 2016.

Newland, Lynda. "Miracle-Workers and Nationhood: Reinhard Bonnke and Benny Hinn in Fiji." *The Contemporary Pacific* 22 (2010) 74–99.

"Nicholas II and Family Canonized for 'Passion.'" *New York Times*, August 15, 2000. https://www.nytimes.com/2000/08/15/world/nicholas-ii-and-family-canonized-for-passion.html.

Nielssen, Hilde. "Til jordens ender. Om hvordan verden ble brakt til Norge og omvendt på etnografiske utstillinger i misjonsregi." *Norsk antropologisk tidsskrift* 18 (2007) 196–215.

Nordin, Magdalena. "Religiositet bland migranter - Sverige-Chilenares förhållande till religion ock samfund." PhD diss., Lund University, 2004.

Norget, Kristin. *Days of Death, Days of Life: Ritual in the Popular Culture of Oaxaca.* New York: Columbia University Press, 2006.

Norris, Pippa, and Ronald Inglehart. *Sacred and Secular Religion and Politics Worldwide.* 2nd ed. Cambridge: Cambridge University Press, 2011.

Norwegian Church Aid, and the World Council of Churches. "The Protection Needs of Minorities from Syria and Iraq." https://www.oikoumene.org/sites/default/files/Document/MinorityReport_SyriaIraq_2016.pdf.

O'Mahony, Conor. "Religious Education in Ireland." In *Routledge International Handbook of Religious Education*, edited by D. Davis and E. M. Miroshnikova, 156–58. Milton Park: Routledge, 2013.

Obadare, Ebenezer. "Pentecostal Presidency? The Lagos-Ibadan 'Theocratic Class' & the Muslim 'Other.'" *Review of African Political Economy* 33 (2006) 665–78.

Obama, Barack. *The Audacity of Hope: Thoughts on Reclaiming the American Dream.* Edinburgh: Canongate, 2007.

———. *Dreams from My Father: A Story of Race and Inheritance.* Edinburgh: Canongate, 2008.

———. "Remarks at the Selma Voting Rights March Commemoration in Selma, Alabama." http://.www.presidency.ucsb.edu/ws/index.php?pid=77042.

Oduro, Thomas. "Independent Churches in Africa." In *Anthology of African Christianity*, edited by Isabel Apawo Phiri et al., 431–41. Oxford: Regnum, 2016.

Ojo, Matthews, and Adewale Adelakun. "Christianity and Sexuality in Africa." In *Routledge Companion to Christianity in Africa*, edited by E. Bongmba, 473–86. New York: Routledge, 2016.

Olson, Laura R. "The Religious Left in Contemporary American Politics." *Politics, Religion & Ideology* 12 (2011) 271–94.

Olupona, Jacob K. *African Religions: A Very Short Introduction*. Oxford: Oxford University Press, 2014.

Oren, Michael. "Israel and the Plight of Mideast Christians." *Wall Street Journal*, March 9, 2012. https://www.wsj.com/articles/SB10001424052970203960804577239923033348982.

Orta, Andrew. "Inculturation Theology and the 'New Evangelization.'" In *The Cambridge History of Religions in Latin America*, edited by Virginia Garrard-Burnett et al., 591–602. New York: Cambridge University Press, 2016.

Østbø, Jardar. "The New Third Rome: Readings of a Russian Nationalist Myth." PhD diss., University of Bergen, 2011.

Østebø, Terje, et al. "Religion and the 'Secular Shadow': Responses to COVID-19 in Ethiopia." *Religion* (2021). https://doi.org/10.1080/0048721X.2021.1943769.

Palestinian Center for Policy and Survey Research. "Migration of Palestinian Christians: Drivers and Means of Combating it." http://pcpsr.org/en/node/806.

Parry, Susan. "African Christianity, Public Health, and Epidemics." In *Anthology of African Christianity*, edited by Isabel Apawo Phiri et al., 1154–59. Oxford: Regnum, 2016.

Pasura, Dominic, and Marta B. Erdal, eds. *Migration, Transnationalism, and Catholicism*. London: Palgrave Macmillian, 2017.

Patterson, Amy Stephenson. *The Church and AIDS in Africa: The Politics of Ambiguity*. London: FirstForum, 2011.

Paul VI, Pope. *Apostolicam actuositatem*. https://www.vatican.va/archive/hist_councils/ii_vatican_council/documents/vat-ii_decree_19651118_apostolicam-actuositatem_en.html.

Pelikan, Jaroslav. *The Spirit of Eastern Christendom (600–1700)*. Chicago: University of Chicago Press, 1974.

Pelz, Mikael L., and Corwin E. Smidt. "Generational Conversion? The Role of Religiosity in the Politics of Evangelicals." *Journal for the Scientific Study of Religion* 54 (2015) 380–401.

Pepper, Miriam, and Jason John. "Ecological Engagement." In *An Informed Faith: The Uniting Church at the Beginning of the 21st Century*, edited by William W. Emilsen, 189–213. Preston: Mosaic, 2014.

Pepper, Miriam, and Rosemary Leonard. "Climate Change, Politics, and Religion: Australian Churchgoers' Beliefs about Climate Change." *Religions* 7 (2016) 47.

Pérez-Agote, Alfonso. *Cambio religioso en España: Los avatares de secularización*. Madrid: Centro de Investigaciones Sociologicas, 2012.

Pew Research Center. "America's Changing Religious Landscape." http://www.pewforum.org/2015/05/12/americas-changing-religious-landscape/.

———. "During Benedicts Papacy Religious Observance among Catholics in Europe Remained Low but Stable." http://www.pewforum.org/2013/03/05/during-benedicts-papacy-religious-observance-among-catholics-in-europe-remained-low-but-stable.

————. "Eastern and Western Europeans Differ on Importance of Religion, Views of Minorities, and Key Social Issues." https://www.pewforum.org/2018/10/29/eastern-and-western-europeans-differ-on-importance-of-religion-views-of-minorities-and-key-social-issues/.

————. "Global Christianity: A Report on the Size and Distribution of the World's Christian Population." http://www.pewforum.org/2011/12/19/global-christianity-exec/.

————. "Global Survey of Evangelical Protestant Leaders." http://www.pewforum.org/2011/06/22/global-survey-of-evangelical-protestant-leaders/.

————. "Global Views on Morality." http://pewglobal.org/2014/04/15/global-morality/.

————. "How Many Christians Are There in Egypt?" http://www.pewresearch.org/2011/02/16/how-many-christians-are-there-in-egypt/.

————. "Many Evangelicals Favor Trump because He Is Not Clinton." http://www.pewresearch.org/fact-tank/2016/09/23/many-evangelicals-favor-trump-because-he-is-not-clinton/.

————. "Middle East's Christian Population in Flux as Pope Francis Visits Holy Land." http://www.pewresearch.org/fact-tank/2014/05/19/middle-easts-christian-population-in-flux-as-pope-francis-visits-holy-land/.

————. "Philippines." http://www.globalreligiousfutures.org/countries/philippines#/?affiliations_religion_id=0&affiliations_year=2010&region_name=All%20Countries&restrictions_year=2016.

————. "Religion in Latin America: Widespread Change in a Historically Catholic Region." http://www.pewforum.org/2014/11/13/religion-in-latin-america/.

————. "Religious Belief and National Belonging in Central and Eastern Europe." http://www.pewforum.org/2017/05/10/religious-belief-and-national-belonging-in-central-and-eastern-europe/.

————. "Spirit and Power: A 10-Country Survey of Pentecostals." http://www.pewforum.org/2006/10/05/spirit-and-power/.

————. "Table: Christian Population in Numbers by Country." http://www.pewforum.org/2011/12/19/table-christian-population-in-numbers-by-country/.

————. "Table: Religious Composition by Country, in Numbers." http://www.pewforum.org/2012/12/18/table-religious-composition-by-country-in-numbers/.

————. "The Tea Party and Religion." http://www.pewforum.org/2011/02/23/tea-party-and-religion/.

————. "Traditional African Religious Beliefs and Practices." http://www.pewforum.org/2010/04/15/traditional-african-religious-beliefs-and-practices-islam-and-christianity-in-sub-saharan-africa/.

Pfrimer, Matheus H., and Ricardo Barbosa. "Brazil's War on COVID-19: Crisis, Not Conflict—Doctors, Not Generals." *Dialogues in Human Geography* 10 (2020) 137–40.

Phan, Peter C. "Vietnam, Cambodia, Laos, Thailand." In *Christianities*, edited by Peter C. Phan, 129–48. Chichester: Wiley-Blackwell, 2011.

Philippine Statistics Authority. *2015 Philippine Statistical Yearbook*. Queson City: Philippines Statistics Authority, 2015.

Phillips, Michael. "Aboriginal Reconciliation as Religious Politics: Secularisation in Australia." *Australian Journal of Political Science* 40 (2005) 111–24.

Phiri, Isabel A., and Chammah J. Kaunda. "Gender." In *Christianity in Sub-Saharan Africa*, edited by Kenneth R. Ross et al., 386–96. Edinburgh: Edinburgh University Press, 2017.

Phiri, Isabel. "The Circle of Concerned African Women Theologians." *The Ecumenical Review* 57 (2005) 34–41.

Piggin, Stuart, and Peter Lineham. "Christianity in Australia and Oceania (ca. 1800–2000)." In *The Wiley Blackwell Companion to World Christianity*, edited by Lamin Sanneh and Michael J. McClymond, 575–87. 1st ed. Chichester: Wiley-Blackwell, 2016.

Pindani, Mercy, et al. "Perception of People Living with HIV and AIDS regarding Home Based Care in Malawi." *Journal of AIDS and Clinical Research* 4 (2013). http://dx.doi.org/10.4172/2155-6113.1000201.

Plekon, Michael. "The Russian Religious Revival and Its Theological Legacy." In *The Cambridge Companion to Orthodox Christian Theology*, edited by Mary B. Cunningham and Elizabeth Theokritoff, 203–17. Cambridge: Cambridge University Press, 2008.

"Pope Francis in Manila: Pope Departs Philippines after Record-Breaking Mass." *BBC*, January 19, 2015. https://www.bbc.com/news/world-asia-30875645.

Prior, John. "Indonesia." In *Christianities in Asia*, edited by Peter C. Phan, 61–76. Chichester: Wiley-Blackwell, 2011.

Putnam, Robert D., and David E. Campbell. *American Grace: How Religion Divides and Unites Us*. New York: Simon & Schuster, 2010.

Ranche, Apolonio. "Iglesia Filipina Independiente." In *A Dictionary of Asian Christianity*, edited by Scott W. Sunquist, 359–60. Grand Rapids: Eerdmans, 2001.

Ranger, Terence O. *Evangelical Christianity and Democracy in Africa*. New York: Oxford University Press, 2008.

RCCG. "Mission and Vision." http://rccg.org/who-we-are/mission-and-vision/.

Reiss, Wolfram. *Erneuerung in der Koptisch-Orthodoxen Kirche: Die Geschichte der koptisch-orthodoxen Sonntagsschulbewegung*. Hamburg: Lit Verlag, 1998.

"Reorganisation of the Two Vicariates in the Arabian Peninsula." http://www.catholic-church.org/kuwait/bishop_speaks19.htm.

Resende, Madalena M., and Anja Hennig. "Polish Catholic Bishops, Nationalism, and Liberal Democracy." *Religions* 12 (2021). https://doi.org/10.3390/rel12020094.

Reuters. "Pope Calls on Every European Parish to Host One Migrant Family Each." *Jerusalem Post*, September 6, 2015. https://www.jpost.com/Breaking-News/Pope-calls-on-every-European-parish-to-host-one-migrant-family-each-415380.

Reuters Staff. "Millions of Devotees in Philippines Join Black Nazarene Procession." *Reuters*, January 9, 2017. https://www.reuters.com/article/us-religion-philippines-black-nazarene/millions-of-devotees-in-philippines-join-black-nazarene-procession-idUSKBN14T0O0.

Richters, Katja. *The Post-Soviet Russian Orthodox Church: Politics, Culture, and Greater Russia*. London: Routledge, 2013.

Riedl, Rachel B. "Transforming Politics, Dynamic Religion: Religion's Political Impact in Contemporary Africa." *African Conflict & Peacebuilding Review* 2 (2012) 29–50.

Robbins, Joel. "Comments to Part 3: Christian Renewal and Change in Regional Development." In *Christianity, Conflict, and Renewal in Australia and the Pacific*, edited by Fiona Magowan and Carolyn Schwartz, 207–14. Leiden: Brill, 2016.

————. "Whatever Became of Revival? From Charismatic Movement to Charismatic Church in a Papua New Guinea Society." *Ritual Studies* 15 (2001) 79–90.

Robinson, Carin. "From Every Tribe and Nation? Blacks and the Christian Right." *Social Science Quarterly* 87 (2006) 591–601.

Roof, Wade C. *Spiritual Marketplace: Baby Boomers and the Remaking of American Religion.* Princeton: Princeton University Press, 1999.

Rotberg, Robert I. *When States Fail: Causes and Consequences.* Princeton: Princeton University Press, 2010.

Roy, Olivier. "Beyond Populism: The Conservative Right, the Courts, the Churches and the Concept of a Christian Europe." In *Saving the People: How Populists Hijack Religion,* edited by Nadia Marzouki et al., 185–202. London: Hurst & Company, 2016.

————. *Holy Ignorance: When Religion and Culture Part Ways.* London: Hurst, 2010.

Runions, Erin. "Biblical Provocations to Biocapital in the U.S. Culture Wars." *The Bible and Critical Theory* 12 (2016) 1–23.

"Russia's Patrick Kirill in Furore over Luxury Watch." *BBC,* April 5, 2012. https://www.bbc.com/news/world-europe-17622820.

Sabella, Bernard. "Palestinian Christians: Historical Demographic Developments, Current Politics, and Attitudes towards Church, Society, and Human Rights: The Sabeel Survey on Palestinian Christians in the West Bank and Israel—Summer 2006." https://www.fosna.org/files/fosna/events/SabeelSurveyPalestinianChristians.pdf.

Salden, Von Simone. "Shrinking Catholic Church Imports Priests." https://www.spiegel.de/international/germany/priest-shortage-forces-catholic-church-to-import-preachers-to-germany-a-934804.html.

Sat-7. "We Are Sat-7." www.sat7.rg.

Schlamelcher, Jens. "The Decline of the Parishes and the Rise of the City Churches." In *Religion in the Neoliberal Age: Political Economy and Modes of Governance,* edited by Tuomas Martikainen and François Gauthier, 53–68. Farnham: Ashgate, 2013.

Schwartz, Carolyn, and Françoise Dussart. "Christianity in Aboriginal Australia Revisited." *The Australian Journal of Anthropology* 21 (2010) 1–13.

Sherinian, Zoe C. "Dalit Theology in Tamil Christian Folk Music: A Transformative Liturgy by James Theophilus Appavoo." In *Popular Christianity in India: Riting between the Lines,* edited by Selva J. Raj and Corinne G. Dempsey, 233–53. Albany: State University of New York Press, 2002.

Siker, Jeffrey. "President Obama, the Bible, and Political Rhetoric." *Political Theology: The Journal of Christian Socialism* 13 (2012) 586–609.

Singh, Jerome A., and Salim S. Abdool Karim. "Trump's Global Gag Rule: Implications for Human Rights and Global Health." *The Lancet Global Health* 5 (2017) 387–89.

Sinitiere, Phillip L. *Salvation with a Smile: Joel Osteen, Lakewood Church, and American Christianity.* New York: New York University Press, 2015.

Sitoy, T. Valentino. "Filipinization Controversy." In *A Dictionary of Asian Christianity,* edited by Scott W. Sunquist, 289–91. Grand Rapids: Eerdmans, 2001.

————. "Philippines." In *A Dictionary of Asian Christianity,* edited by Scott W. Sunquist, 654–57. Grand Rapids: Eerdmans, 2001.

Smidt, Corwin E. *American Evangelicals Today.* Lanham, MD: Rowman & Littlefield, 2013.

Smith, Amy Erica. *Religion and Brazilian Democracy: Mobilizing the People of God.* Cambridge: Cambridge University Press, 2019.

Smith, Helena. "Greece in Revolt as Scandals Sweep the Orthodox Church." *The Guardian*, March 20, 2005.

Smith, James H. "Religious Dimensions of Conflict and Peace in Neoliberal Africa: An Introduction." In *Displacing the State: Religion and Conflict in Neoliberal Africa*, edited by James Howard Smith and Rosalind I. J. Hackett, 1–26. Notre Dame: University of Notre Dame Press, 2012.

Smith, Jonathan Z. *Relating Religion: Essays in the Study of Religion*. Chicago: University of Chicago Press, 2004.

Soothill, Jane. "Gender and Pentecostalism in Africa." In *Pentecostalism in Africa: Presence and Impact of Pneumatic Christianity in Postcolonial Societies*, edited by Martin Lindhardt, 191–219. Leiden: Brill, 2015.

Souza, André Ricardo de. "Igreja Católica e mercados: A ambivalência entre a solidariedade e a competição." *Religião & Sociedade* 27 (2007) 156–74.

Spector, Stephen. "This Year in Jerusalem: Prophecy, Politics, and the U.S. Embassy in Israel." *A Journal of Church and State* 61 (2019) 551–71.

Stålsett, Sturla J. "Liberation Theology: Religious Resistance to Globalisation? The Chiapas Uprising as a Case." In *The Power of Faiths in Global Politics*, edited by Sturla J. Stålsett et al., 143–54. Oslo: Novus, 2004.

Stark, Rodney, and Buster G. Smith. "Pluralism and the Churching of Latin America." *Latin American Politics and Society* 54 (2012) 35–50.

Steen-Johnsen, Tale. *State and Politics in Religious Peacebuilding*. Basingstoke: Springer, 2016.

Stene, Nora. "Mobilisering og motstand: den koptiske søndagsskolen." In *De kristne i Midtøsten: Kampen for tilhørighet*, edited by Berit Thorbjørnsrud, 135–56. Oslo: Cappelen Damm Akademisk, 2015.

Stoeckl, Kristina. *The Russian Orthodox Church and Human Rights*. London: Routledge, 2014.

———. "The Russian Orthodox Church as Moral Norm Entrepreneur." *Religion, State, and Society* 44 (2016) 132–51.

Sweeney Brigid. "Catholic Church's Financial Woes, Consolidations Aren't New." https://www.chicagobusiness.com/article/20160408/NEWS07/160409846/catholic-parish-closures-have-hit-chicago-boston-new-york.

Synnes, Ronald M. "Kristne migrantmenigheter i Oslo." https://www.kifo.no/wp-content/uploads/2016/09/Migrantmenigheter-i-Oslo_-KIFO-Rapport-2012_2.pdf.

Tadros, Mariz. "Copts of Egypt: Pope Francis, Al-Azhar, and the Reality of Sectarianism on the Ground." *Open Democracy*, April 26, 2017. https://www.opendemocracy.net/en/5050/copts-egypt-pope-al-azhar-sectarianism/.

Tank, Pinar. "Er Tyrkia USAs nye modell i Midtøsten?" *Babylon Nordisk tidsskrift for Midtøstenstudier* 3 (2005) 50–55.

Thavis, John. *The Vatican Diaries*. New York: Penguin, 2014.

Thomas, M. M. *My Ecumenical Journey*. Trivandrum: India Ecumenical, 1990.

Thorbjørnsrud, Berit. "De kristne i Midtøsten: en innføring." In *De kristne i Midtøsten: Kampen for tilhørighet*, edited by Berit Thorbjørnsrud, 15–36. Oslo: Cappelen Damm Akademisk, 2015.

———. "De kristne i Midtøsten: kun på museum?" In *Midtøsten etter den arabiske våren*, edited by Peter Normann Waage, 15–55. Oslo: Arneberg, 2012.

———. "Den arabiske halvøy: der kristendommen blomstrer?" In *De kristne i Midtøsten: Kampen for tilhørighet*, edited by Berit Thorbjørnsrud, 215–36. Oslo: Cappelen Damm Akademisk, 2015.

———. "Mellom by og ørken: kirkebygging på Den arabiske halvøy." *Kirke og kultur* 124 (2019) 242–64.

———. "Pave Frans i Emiratene—et historisk viktig besøk?" *Kirke og kultur* 124 (2019) 338–54.

Thorsen, Jakob E. "The Catholic Charismatic Renewal and the Incipient Pentecostalization of Latin American Catholicism." In *The Cambridge History of Religions in Latin America*, edited by Virginia Garrard-Burnett et al., 462–79. New York: Cambridge University Press, 2016.

———. *Charismatic Practice and Catholic Parish Life: The Incipient Pentecostalization of the Church in Guatemala and Latin America.* Leiden: Brill, 2015.

Thuesen, Nils Petter, "Oseania." https://snl.no/Oseania.

"Timeline: The Heated Battle between the Vatican and American Nuns." *Huffington Post*, April 17, 2015. https://www.huffpost.com/entry/vatican-american-nun-timeline_n_7087260.

Titeca, Kristof. "The Spiritual Side of LRA." In *Lord's Resistance Army: Myth and Reality*, edited by Tim Allen and Koen Vlassenroot, 59–73. London: Zed, 2010.

Toft, Monica Duffy, et al. *God's Century Resurgent Religion and Global Politics.* New York: Norton, 2011.

Tomlinson, Matt, and Debra McDougall, eds. *Christian Politics in Oceania.* New York: Berghahn, 2013.

Tonkinson, Robert. "Spiritual Prescription, Social Reality: Reflections on Religious Dynamism." *Anthropological Forum* 14 (2004) 183–201.

Trompf, Garry W. "New Religious Movements in Oceania." *Nova Religio: The Journal of Alternative and Emerging Religions* 18 (2015) 5–15.

Ukah, Azonseh. "African Christianities: Features, Promises, and Problems." *Working Paper* 79 (2007) 1–20.

UNESCO. "Baptism Site 'Bethany Beyond the Jordan' (Al-Maghtas)." http://whc.unesco.org/en/list/1446.

Van Klinken, Adriaan S. "African Christianity: Developments and Trends." In *Handbook of Global Contemporary Christianity: Themes and Developments in Culture, Politics, and Society,* edited by Stephen Hunt, 131–51. Leiden: Brill, 2015.

———. *Transforming Masculinities in African Christianity: Gender Controversies in Times of AIDS.* Farnham: Ashgate, 2013.

Vasquez, Manuel A., and Anna L. Peterson. "Oscar Romero and the Politics of Sainthood." *Postscripts: The Journal of Sacred Texts and Contemporary Worlds* 5 (2011) 265–91.

"Vatican 'Must Immediately Remove' Child Abusers—UN." *BBC*, February 5, 2014. https://www.bbc.com/news/world-europe-26044852.

Vik, Ingrid, et al. *Lobbying for Faith and Family: A Study of Religious NGOs at the United Nations.* Oslo: Norad, 2013.

Voas, David, and Alasdair Crockett. "Religion in Britain: Neither Believing nor Belonging." *Sociology* 39 (2005) 11–28.

Vogt, Kari. "Den arabiske våren." In *Midtøsten etter den arabiske våren*, edited by Peter Normann Waage, 9–13. Oslo: Arneberg, 2012.

———. "Lederskap, motstand og reform: Den koptisk-ortodokse kirke etter den arabiske våren." In *De kristne i Midtøsten: Kampen for tilhørighet*, edited by Berit Thorbjørnsrud, 115–34. Oslo: Cappelen Damm Akademisk, 2015.

Waddy, Charis. *Women in Muslim History*. London: Longman, 1980.

Waghorne, Joanne P. "Chariots of the God/s: Riding the Line between Hindu and Christian." In *Popular Christianity in India: Riting between the Lines*, edited by Selva J. Raj and Corinne G. Dempsey, 11–37. Albany: State University of New York, 2002.

Walker, Shaun. "Russia Orthodox Church Sacks Ultra-Conservative Senior Priest." *The Guardian*, December 25, 2015. https://www.theguardian.com/world/2015/dec/25/russian-orthodox-church-sacks-father-vsevolod-chaplin.

WCC. "Christian Witness in a Multi-religious World." https://www.oikoumene.org/sites/default/files/Document/ChristianWitness_recommendations.pdf.

———. "EHAIA Consultation." https://archived.oikoumene.org/en/resources/documents/other-ecumenical-bodies/church-statements-on-hivaids/2001-ehaia-consultation.

———. "Kairos Palestine Document." https://www.oikoumene.org/resources/documents/kairos-palestine-document.

———. "Who Is the World Council of Churches?" https://www.oikoumene.org/about-the-wcc.

WEA. "Who We Are." https://worldea.org/who-we-are/.

Wickeri, Philip. "China Christian Council." In *A Dictionary of Asian Christianity*, edited by Scott W. Sunquist, 146. Grand Rapids: Eerdmans, 2001.

———. "Three-Self Patriotic Movement." In *A Dictionary of Asian Christianity*, edited by Scott W. Sunquist, 846. Grand Rapids: Eerdmans, 2001.

Wilkinson, Michael. "The Emergence, Development, and Pluralisation of Global Pentecostalism." In *Handbook of Global Contemporary Christianity: Themes and Developments in Culture, Politics, and Society*, edited by Stephen Hunt, 93–112. Leiden: Brill, 2015.

Wollschleger, Jason, and Jeremy R. Porter. "A 'Walmartization' of Religion? The Ecological Impact of Megachurches on the Local and Extra-Local Religious Economy." *Review of Religious Research* 53 (2011) 279–99.

Wolton, Dominique. *A Future of Faith: The Path of Change in Politics and Society*. New York: St. Martin's Essentials, 2018.

Wood, Richard. "The Catholic Bishops in the U.S. Public Arena: Changing Prospects under Pope Francis." *Religions* 7 (2016). https://doi.org/10.3390/rel7020014.

Wood, Thomas. "Racism Motivated Trump Voters More Than Authoritarianism." *Washington Post*, April 17, 2017. https://www.washingtonpost.com/news/monkey-cage/wp/2017/04/17/racism-motivated-trump-voters-more-than-authoritarianism-or-income-inequality/.

Woodhead, Linda. "The Rise of 'No Religion' in Britain: The Emergence of a New Cultural Majority." *Journal of the British Academy* 4 (2016) 245–61.

———. "The Rise of 'No Religion': Towards an Explanation." *Sociology of Religion: A Quarterly Review* 78 (2017) 247–62.

World Bank. "Brazil." https://data.worldbank.org/country/brazil?view=chart.

———. "Mexico." https://data.worldbank.org/country/mexico?view=chart.

———. "Population, Total – Russian Federation." https://data.worldbank.org/indicator/SP.POP.TOTL?locations=RU.

―――. "World Development Indicators: Energy Dependency, Efficiency and Carbon Dioxide Emissions." http://wdi.worldbank.org/table/3.8.

World Weather Attribution. "Attribution of the Australian Bushfire Risk to Anthropogenic Climate Change." https://www.worldweatherattribution.org/bushfires-in-australia-2019-2020/.

Ying, Fuk-tsang. "Mainland China." In *Christianities in Asia*, edited by Peter C. Phan, 149–70. Chichester: Wiley-Blackwell, 2011.

Zaimov, Stoyan. "Iraqi Christians Risk Being Killed by Isis as Church Leaders Debate Whether to Stay or Flee." *The Christian Post*, June 22, 2016. http://www.christianpost.com/news/iraqi-christians-risk-killed-isis-genocide-church-leaders-debate-stay-flee-refugees-166864/.

Zinn, Howard. *USA: Folkets historie*. Translated by Morten Hansen. Oslo: Oktober, 2006.

Zocca, Franco. "New Caledonia." In *Globalization and the Re-shaping of Christianity in the Pacific Islands*, edited by Manfred Ernst, 265–316. Suva: Pacific Theological College, 2006.

―――. "'Winds of Change' Also in PNG?" *Catalyst* 25 (1995) 174–87.

Zuckerman, Phil. "Why Are Danes and Swedes So Irreligious?" *Nordic Journal of Religion and Society* 22 (2009) 55–69.

Zurlo, Gina. "A Demographic Profile of Christiantiy in Sub-Saharan Africa." In *Christianity in Sub-Saharan Africa*, edited by Kenneth R. Ross et al., 3–18. Edinburgh: Edinburgh University Press, 2017.

Zylstra, Sarah Eekhoff. "Pope Francis Quiet on Catholic Persecution of Protestants in Mexico." *Christianity Today*, February 18, 2016. http://www.christianitytoday.com/gleanings/2016/february/pope-francis-catholic-persecution-protestant-mexico-chiapas.html.

Index

Made in the USA
Coppell, TX
18 January 2024

27856225R00174